THE STRUGGLE FOR THE SOUL OF THE FRENCH NOVEL

Also by Malcolm Scott

MAURIAC: THE POLITICS OF A NOVELIST

The Struggle for the Soul of the French Novel

French Catholic and Realist Novelists, 1850–1970

Malcolm Scott
Senior Lecturer in French
University of St Andrews

MACMILLAN

First published 1989

Published by
THE MACMILLAN PRESS LTD
Houndmills, Basingstoke, Hampshire RG21 2XS
and London
Companies and representatives
throughout the world

Printed and bound in Great Britain at
The Camelot Press Ltd, Southampton

British Library Cataloguing in Publication Data
Scott, Malcolm, *1939–*
The struggle for the soul of the French novel:
French Catholic and Realist novelists, 1850–1970.
1. Fiction in French, 1850–1970. Special subjects.
Religion. Critical studies
I. Title
843′ .009′382
ISBN 0–333–49149–1

For Isabelle

Acknowledgements

My thanks are due to the British Academy and to the University of St Andrews for their financial support of the research on which this book is founded, and to colleagues in the St Andrews University French department for their advice and encouragement. I am grateful also to the Department of French in the University of Hull for inviting me to give the lecture which clarified for me the relationship of Catholic novelist to Realist, and to the editorial board of *Forum for Modern Language Studies* for allowing me to reproduce in amended form material on Barbey d'Aurevilly and Zola which first appeared in an article in that journal.

Abbreviations

To avoid the tedium of copious notes, abbreviated details of volume and page numbers accompany quotations and source references in the text wherever possible. These abbreviated forms are indicated in a note on the first reference to any particular text.

Contents

Introduction

That the decline of Christian belief and the rise of the novel are parallel symptoms of the same radical change in western culture over the last two centuries is not a new idea. What T. S. Eliot called the 'gradual secularization of literature'[1] has been seen as particularly manifest in the development of narrative forms. Lines have been traced from sacred myth to epic and then to 'secular narrative', each stage corresponding to a different epoch in Man's changing conception of the world.[2] These changes are seen by some as healthy indicators of the demise of superstition and ignorance; the novel has sometimes been regarded as a kind of literary thermometer, a chart of increasing health and strength. Lukács called it 'the epic of a world abandoned by God', but that he welcomed this abandonment as a sign of the world's advancement is shown by his alternative definition: 'the art-form of virile maturity, in contrast to the normative childlikeness of the epic'.[3] The novel's history has often been presented as that of a literary form germinating in the 'man-centred culture'[4] of the Renaissance, nourished in the rich soil of the Enlightenment, and coming to its nineteenth-century flowering as the characteristic art of an age of science. Its estrangement from traditional values, especially Christianity, is implicit in many of these accounts.

On the other hand, it has often been argued that Christianity's gift to western literature of a source of moral drama and psychological depth has especially enriched the novel.[5] Historians point to the seminal role of Saint Augustine in creating 'psychology' in narrative, and of the Bible as a 'great storehouse of plots'.[6] The novel's graduation as a serious genre, according to nineteenth-century writers like Nodier and Madame de Staël, was dependent on its having a moral purpose, which meant in practice a purpose compatible with Christian morality.[7] The seeds of conflict, however, lay buried within this claim: seriousness implied respect for truth, and notions of what was true, as the century wore on, were increasingly at loggerheads with traditional moral concepts. The old classical partners, the *vrai* and the *bien*, could no longer be relied upon to share the same bed in comfort.

What was at stake can perhaps be explained with the help of Lukács' notion of 'totality'. Writing of Greek myth as a system of perceiving and interpreting the universe as an integrated whole, Lukács comments that Christianity also offered such a 'totality', a structure within which all that exists can find a meaningful place. 'In Giotto and Dante, Wolfram von Eschenbach and Pisano, St Thomas and St Francis, the world became round once more, a totality capable of being taken in at a glance' (op. cit., 37). The idea that a literary genre can lay claim to the explanatory and expressive functions that have previously been the prerogative of world religions may seem a strange one, but something of this sort lies behind the novel's pre-eminence in modern times. It was when the novel emerged as a literary form capable of serving as the vehicle for just such a total world-view, a structure in which every element of the culture could be housed – when, in Balzac's words, it achieved 'la valeur philosophique de l'histoire',[8] when it became 'the entertainment, the history, the sociology and the psychology of the west',[9] and could 'control the field of present social and psychological reality'[10] – that its challenge to the former great totality, Christianity, became necessary, both for its internal process of self-identification and its external campaign of self-assertion. It was no longer a fiction grafted on to a historical setting, as in the time of *La Princesse de Clèves*, but a genre purporting to reflect and explain history or even, in the Goncourts' phrase, become in itself 'L'Histoire morale contemporaine'.[11] The novel, to use Balzac's terminology again, 'competed' with reality (1, 52), while overlapping with it in order to achieve the illusion of authenticity. What the nineteenth-century novel shares with reality as a result of this overlap is a code of probabilities of what might happen or be expected to happen, based on the evidence of the senses, and especially of the eyes. Its totality is coextensive with the seen world. The tension between this reliance on the seen and the unseen dimension on which revealed religion depends is one of the principal themes of this book. It will argue that the very notion of an invisible, spiritual order was a threat to the novel's claim to represent totality, and that the novel adopted a defensive scepticism, a refutation of Christian supernaturalism necessary to its pursuit of a sense-based realism.

This tension was certainly much more strongly felt in France than in Britain, and the reader who views literary history from the perspective of the English novel might well find the above analysis over-dramatic. Are not Richardson and Fielding, Jane Austen and Dickens the equals of their French counterparts in their evocation of the social scene and its concomitant psychological patterns, and do they not combine this evocation, without obvious strain, with a sense of Christian morality and an acknowledgement of the existence of divine Providence, guiding the outcome of human affairs? The differing climates of the English and French novels, on which Taine and Brunetière commented many decades ago, is a subject beyond the bounds of this book, but one hypothesis might be proffered which is of direct relevance to the present study. It springs from the thesis of Auerbach's great work, which is that the separation of styles in literary cultures dominated by classical theory produced a rift between the sublime subject-matter of Christianity and the low mimetic discourse of genres like the Realist novel – a rift which is non-existent in early Christian narrative or in its Mediaeval revival, for 'the story of Christ, with its ruthless mixture of everyday reality and the highest and most sublime tragedy [. . .] had conquered the classical rule of styles'.[12] Applying this idea to English literature, one can see it as having escaped the consequences of this rift because of a Protestant familiarity with the Bible stories, the characters of which range from great kings to poor fishermen, in all of whose lives the divine intervenes; a harmonious coexistence of Christian belief and naturalistic portraiture extends in an unbroken line from Mediaeval mystery via Bunyan to the Victorians. In France, religious strife and especially Catholic reaction to Protestant accusations of graven image making had interfered with what could be shown in drama or described in fiction; later, the Mediaeval Christian heritage was overlaid by the rarefied classical tradition of which Auerbach speaks, which meant that Realism, when it came, had to be imposed from without, its revolutionary spirit merging with other forms of revolution, especially the positivistic, anti-miraculous currents of the Enlightenment. While English novelists, preoccupied with questions of behaviour, on the whole took for granted broader questions of the nature of reality, the French had to create ontological ground rules for a genre that was nothing short of a fictional form of natural philosophy.

The evidence for the above view of Realism will be presented in the first chapter of this book, which deals with the mainstream French novelists of the half-century that separated Balzac from Proust – namely the Goncourt brothers, Flaubert, Maupassant and Zola – and in the third chapter which centres on Zola. To refer to these novelists collectively as 'Realists', and to substitute the term 'Naturalism' when discussing the more intense and systematic realism of Zola, is a standard convention, adopted here for ease of reference. Nobody will suspect me of wishing to suggest that these novelists formed a concerted movement or 'school', and my discussion of them will be the best indicator of my ability to tell them apart. One of my aims, however, is to show how their work is linked through their attitudes to Christianity. I do not imply that they see the challenge to Christianity as their prime motive for writing, or even as a conscious motive at all, separate from others. They were more often conscious of building Realism on the ruins of fantasy, of the Romantic imagination that was increasingly discredited after 1848. In that Christian belief could be seen as an established form of fantasy, a system of wish-fulfilment, a deluding myth with a metaphorical rather than empirical relationship to history, the deflation of Christianity was part of the deflation of Romanticism. As far as the ensuing development of our cultural identity is concerned, it was the most important part, although none of the many books on French Realism has focused clearly enough on it.

A fresh look at the Realists is only one of the book's aims, and indeed only its starting-point, for more space will be given to a second group of novelists. What to call this second group poses labelling problems of a more difficult sort than for the Realists. The term 'Catholic novelist', which is the only one I can think of to embrace Barbey d'Aurevilly, Bloy, the later Huysmans, Mauriac, Bernanos and Julien Green, has been blighted by unhelpful preassumptions that it must refer to a novelist who puts his art to the service of the orthodox views of the Catholic Church and faith. To define a 'Catholic novel', according to a professor at the Institut Catholique, is to 'déterminer les conditions auxquelles devrait répondre un roman, pour que l'auteur ne fût pas en opposition avec l'enseignement traditionnel, avec la morale catholique'.[13] Such views, not so much prescriptive as proscriptive, arise from a fundamentally non-literary approach to literature which has bedevilled much Catholic criticism of both Catholic and non-Catholic authors. This approach announces its presence in the frowning question marks of such titles as *Mauriac, romancier catholique*? or 'Barbey, romancier catholique?'[14] and in numerous volumes by writers who make no secret of their distaste for the ambivalent world of fiction. No serious novelist could emerge unscathed from such scrutiny, and it is for reasons of self-protection that most of the major Catholic writers, despite the profundity of their faith, rebelled against the application of a label which smacked of conscription to a nonliterary cause. Their well-known preference for phrases like

'Catholic who writes novels' or 'novelist and Catholic' is understandable. Cecil Jenkins endorses this preference, arguing that terms like 'the Catholic novel' are misleading because 'the novel, in that it persuades essentially from the particularity of individual experience, can never adequately be viewed as the expression of a collective orthodoxy'.[15] The assertion that novelists write from within their own experience is a truism; but their writing would scarcely be intelligible if that experience were not in part a shared one, an individual's view of what it is like to live within a group. One such group is the Christian or Catholic community, and to blur a writer's independent stance within it by artificially prising apart the intimately interrelated passions that drive him to write – a passionate religious conviction and a passionate urge to write – is something of a semantic red herring. As long as one does not presuppose that the two passions always pull in the same direction, as long as one recognises the frequent tensions between 'Catholic' and 'novelist' that lend to their combination the taut and explosive character of oxymoron, then one can and should use the term 'Catholic novelist' as meaning something essentially different from its diluted substitutes. In using it from now on in this book, dispensing with the tedium of inverted commas, I am encouraged by Albert Sonnenfeld's confident assertion: 'There *is* something called the Catholic Novel', and by his definition of what that something is, which is as good a single-sentence definition as I have seen:

> It is a novel written by a Catholic, using Catholicism as his informing mythopoeic structure or generative symbolic system, and where the principal and decisive issue is the salvation or damnation of the hero or heroine.[16]

This book, however, seeks to define the Catholic novel from a different angle, in terms of its relationship to other possibilities within the genre. It sets out to show how Realism and the Catholic novel, hitherto discussed as two separate subjects, attracting different sorts of reader and critic, are in fact the two sides of one single, even broader subject: the struggle between two opposed visions of the real, expressed in and through the novel form. This struggle, since the representation of the real is the substance of the novel, involved the whole ethos of the genre and especially the question of whether it is fundamentally inimical to Christian conceptions of the world or whether its forms can be adapted to express them. The

Catholic novel will be explored and defined here as a particular response to Realism; and to explain why it had to be that, Realism itself will be presented as a particular response to traditional Christian views of the real, for which Catholicism, in France, is the established majority voice. Religious differences will not be discussed for their own sake and certainly not with any religious *parti pris*. My interests are literary ones, as were those of the writers I shall discuss. They will include a number of major figures from each of the two groups. Of my chosen Catholic novelists, three, those from Mauriac onwards, are twentieth-century writers, and my concern here is to show that the Catholic novel in more recent times can be read with deeper understanding in the light of its original quarrel with Realism. The starting-point of the study is the period after 1850, after the death of the writer who called the novel 'la création moderne la plus immense' (*Illusions perdues*, III, 513) and in whose work lay the seeds of both rival growths. No study of the options available to novelists after 1850 can omit mention of Balzac, and this is especially true of the attempt to explore the impact on the novel of philosophical and religious schism, for Balzac, often seen as a new beginning and even as 'the first modern novelist', was also the last novelist to seek to reconcile the warring ideologies of the post-revolutionary era. Brief discussion of the implications of his role for my subject is a necessary part of this introduction.

* * *

In the laying of the philosophical base of the *Comédie Humaine*, no source of intellectual energy was denied. Elements were fused together which in less universal minds would remain irreconcilable opposites: the enquiring and revolutionary outlook of the Enlightenment, the stability of traditional Catholicism, the novelty of the new sciences or crypto-sciences, the poetic dreams of the mystics and illuminists. There is no better model of Balzac's eclectic genius than the 'cénacle' of thinkers and writers in *Illusion perdues*, in which every shade of political and philosophical opinion coexists in mutual respect for its opposite. His refusal to contemplate closed frontiers was manifest, firstly, within his view of religion, in his denial of any essential difference between Christianity and Swedenborgian mysticism. In Swedenborg's angels, those creatures into whom all men are destined to be transformed when they outlive their earthly phase, Balzac saw the image of the Christian and Catholic truth that

Man is not 'une créature finie' but rather an incomplete being on the road to perfection (*Avant-propos*, I, 54). The mysticism of the Christian Buddha, as Balzac called Swedenborg, and that of his much-admired 'philosophe inconnu' Claude Saint-Martin, did not challenge Christianity, but liberated it from an over-narrow perspective, revealing its links with Indian, Egyptian and Asian religions. 'Le Mysticisme,' said Balzac, 'est précisément le christianisme à l'état pur' (*Le Livre mystique*; VII, 607). It exists in his work in juxtaposition to those elements that would identify him more obviously with Christian views: his well-known claim to write in the light of two great truths, Religion and Monarchy, his defence of Catholicism as a bulwark of social order, and statements such as: 'Tout homme qui pense doit marcher sous la bannière du Christ' (*La Peau de chagrin*; VI, 450) and 'Croire, c'est vivre. Il faut défendre l'Église' (*Jésus-Christ en Flandre*; VI, 528). More broadly still, Balzac refused to recognise any conflict between religion, in his expanded sense of that term, and modern science. The concept of a unity of composition at the heart of creation, the evolutionary theory that gave him the conceptual framework of the *Comédie Humaine*, was, he argued, not a scientific innovation, but an idea anticipated in the writings of the mystics (I, 51). Evolution was compatible with the Fall (*La Peau de chagrin*; VI, 437); science was the inheritor of Moses' rod (*Le Curé de village*, VII, 286); scientific knowledge and spiritualist intuition led to the same conclusions (*Louis Lambert*, VII, 296).

Whether such intellectual ecumenism informs the actual fictional world of Balzac's novels as opposed to its abstract justification is another matter. 'Unity of composition' is a fine advertisement for a novelist as well as a seductive theory of life-forms, and to achieve it promised to make him superior to Walter Scott (I, 52). For such a prize, cloaking divisions in the edifice was a small price to pay. Although the structure of the *Comédie Humaine* disguises the fact, with its sectionalisation into two apparently central *Études* (*Études de mœurs* and *Études philosophiques*), the mystical works which largely constitute the latter lie in the extremities of Balzac's world, detached in various ways from its centre. They are often remote in time (*Les Proscrits*) or space (*Séraphîta*) or both (*Jésus-Christ en Flandre*), or are set apart by atypical narrative voices, like that of the curiously diffident and ill-informed (and thus quite unbalzacian) narrator of *Louis Lambert*.The polarity of Paris and the provinces is also important here. Paris, that focal point of the social reality which Balzac set out to chronicle, is, in his novels, a world of mystery, certainly; but the mystery is resolvable given a close scrutiny of physical appearances and knowledge of the economic facts.

Mysteries of a supernatural sort are alien to the modern city, 'temps et lieu où la magie devait être impossible' (*La Peau de chagrin*; VII, 439). The uncertainty suggested by this 'devait' is due to the context: Balzac is about to unfold the story of Raphaël's fatal encounter with the magical wild ass's skin. *La Peau de chagrin*, that bridge between the two *Études*, admits the fantastic, and belongs to a different ontological universe from that of the other novels of the city. The conflict, in its final part, between the scientists who try to comprehend the phenomenon of the skin and the opacity of its talismanic power raises questions of the nature of reality which are remote from the concerns of *Le Père Goriot* or *Illusions perdues*. What is true of illuminist fantasy is also true of orthodox religion, given Balzac's identification of the two. Divine assistance for Lucien de Rubempré in his struggle against the journalists would be as aesthetically destructive to Lucien's fictional credibility as if he were to borrow Raphael's magic skin for the afternoon. The *idea* of God is a comfort to Lucien's mistress Coralie on her death-bed, but her prayers cannot be answered by unambiguous divine intervention, unless our perception of the novel's anatomy is to be radically changed. It may be true that Balzac's moral assumptions are based on the Ten Commandments,[17] and that 'he raises at least two of the great New Testament questions: What must I do to gain the world? and, by implication, its opposite: What must I do to save my soul?'[18] These questions, however, are raised and answered on a terrestrial plane. Balzac's tempters are human demons, not Satan incarnate. Vautrin, seducing Rastignac in the garden or Lucien by the road-side, is a devil of a man rather than the Devil in Man. Balzac may borrow the character of Melmoth from Mathurin's gothic rewriting of the Faust legend, but he treats his material in a comic and ultimately dismissive way, the satanic pact in *Melmoth Réconcilié* reducing itself in the end to the question of passing on syphilis. His Parisian women too, although he argues in the *avant-propos* that the Catholic writer has more sublime archetypes at his disposal than his Protestant counterpart, are creatures of flesh. The polarity of Virgin and Magdalene leaves them stranded in the domestic or erotic middle ground, existing only for their men-folk. 'Lucien!' mingles with 'Dieu!' in Coralie's death-cry. Esther Gobseck is 'saved': saved for Lucien.

Balzac's most edifying novel, *L'Envers de l'histoire contemporaine*, written at the end of his life under the influence of the devout Madame Hanska, is set in the corrupt city, and relates the efforts of a charitable Christian group to undo its evil. But what might be called his 'religious' novels are more typically set in remote rural surroundings, where, as in *Le Curé de village,* the rehabilitation of a community can serve as a metaphor for the doctrine of expiation. A key provincial novel is *Le Lys dans la vallée,* but even this text reveals the distance between Christian ideas and Balzac's imagination. The central theme is that of many a later Catholic novel: the conflict between love of God and love for a person. Madame de Mortsauf's attraction to Félix de Vandenesse is controlled by her sense of maternal and wifely duty, as well as by Christian beliefs made no less intense by her reading of Saint-Martin and Swedenborg, although her death-bed regrets at her lost happiness subvert the novel's conventional piety. At a deeper level Balzac's imagery separates eros from agape. Félix makes a tragic error in associating Madame de Mortsauf with the image of the flower as a symbol of nature and emotional freedom, for the 'lily' which she offers him in response is her immaculate purity. Her literalness divides her from him too: when she aspires to 'le glorieux amour des anges' or talks of achieving 'la spiritualité de l'ange qui est en nous' (VI, 371), these Swedenborgian references are no mere metaphors. By contrast, Félix's evocation of the 'divine child' to which their stars have led them like modern Magi is an unintentionally blasphemous allusion to their adulterous love. In his desire to be by her side, he yearns to possess the wings of seraphs, and similar celestial imagery allows him to contrast his 'divine' love for her with his 'animal' love for Lady Dudley. In his purely metaphorical use of mystical terminology, Félix reveals Balzac's awareness of the gap between the language of faith and faith itself. Félix's grief at his loved one's death inspires in Balzac an image which is sublimely Christian as a verbal structure but, being applicable to all life's experiences, is not specifically religious in substance: 'Nous avons tous dans la vie un Golgotha où nous laissons nos trente-trois premières années en recevant un coup de lance au cœur' (VI, 387). There are many examples in Balzac's writings of such de-christianised 'Christian' formulae, among them his celebrated reference to Goriot as 'ce Christ de la paternité', where the comparison is one of degree and not of kind.

The final lesson that Félix draws from his experiences is the typical Realist one: the folly of great expectations. 'Voilà la vie! la vie telle qu'elle est: de grandes prétentions, de petites réalités' (VI, 388). It draws no religious conclusion, however, and Bertault's view that 'Balzac mit le réalisme au service de l'idée catholique' (op cit., 144) is truer as a description of his declared intentions than of his achievement. Balzac was acutely aware of the discontinuity between the empirical and mystical faces of his work. He expressed in the preface to his *Livre mystique* his unease at having 'mis les pieds de Séraphîta dans la boue du globe', and he adds: 'Si les savants admettent un univers spirituel et divin, ils reconnaîtront que les sciences de l'univers matériel n'y sont d'aucune utilité' (VII, 608).

Balzac's two universes are the principal sources of the two currents that this book will chart. The connections were quite direct, but there has been little discussion of them since Verhaeren's remark that the Alexandrian provinces of the *Comédie Humaine* were divided after his death into two territories, one occupied by the Realists, the other by Barbey d'Aurevilly.[19] Balzac wrote in *Illusions perdues* that glory and fortune awaited a new Catholic writer. He himelf cannot, unambiguously, be said to be that writer, but the religious elements in his work were substantial enough for Barbey to confer the title upon him. 'Le Catholicisme,' said Barbey, 'n'a besoin de personne, mais le catholicisme, nous osons le prévoir, réclamera un jour Balzac comme un de ses écrivains les plus dévoués car, en toute thèse, il conclut comme le catholicisme conclurait.'[20] None of which prevented Émile Zola from embracing Balzac as the immediate precursor of experimental Naturalism. These divergent views of Balzac were only possible because the *Comédie Humaine* is not a monolith. Its creator had not given the genre a definitive form, but only alternative forms, each of which would be championed by others as the potentially definitive direction which the novel should take. Balzac had established its importance as a total model of the real, which is why, to Realist and Catholic alike, it was vital, in the post-Balzac era, to command the philosophical heights of the great modern genre.

1

The Sceptical Mode

Baudelaire and Sainte-Beuve, meeting by not improbable chance on the steps of a brothel, decide to seek alternative entertainment in conversation, and wander off in protracted discussion of the immortality of the soul. Jules de Goncourt, while having his teeth polished, finds himself a captive if willing listener to a dentist's monologue on God, Christ and the Church. These anecdotes come from that inexhaustible source of information on the intellectual preoccupations of men of letters in nineteenth-century France, the diaries of the Goncourt brothers.[1] They are merely two of many such stories related by Jules and Edmond suggesting the extraordinary durability, for an age of scientific fervour, of religion as talking-point and focus of debate. 'Dîner chez Uchard,' note the brothers, and add: 'Grande conversation sur la religion' (II, 201). The hosts and the venues change, the topic is invariable. Flaubert's Sunday gatherings feature 'des causeries qui sautent de sommet en sommet, montent aux origines du paganisme, aux sources des dieux, fouillent les religions' (V, 108). In a report of an evening with the artist Gavarni, only two interrelated subjects of conversation are recorded: religion, miracles (II, 150). At the celebrated dinners at Magny's restaurant, where all the above mentioned celebrities were wont to carouse with Taine, Renan, Turgenev and others, only sex rivalled religion for frequency and intensity of treatment. 'Une grande discussion sur la religion, sur Dieu,' writes Jules one morning after, 'la discussion qui ne manque jamais, entre gens intelligents, de se faire jour au café et de monter sur la table avec les gaz et la digestion' (VI, 43); and he leaves us an exemplary image of the polemical indefatigability of Hippolyte Taine, his beard still dripping after vomiting out of Magny's window, returning to the fray with an impassioned argument on the God of Protestantism (VI, 163).

The tone of these rumbustious encounters was to say the least irreverent, especially when the fiercely anti-clerical Gavarni was present, and religion was often exploited by the Goncourts as the source of some of their best jokes. But for the aesthete brothers humour shades into seriousness as they contemplate the works of

God alongside those of Man, and find the latter the superior artist. 'L'homme a créé plus que Dieu,' they write. 'La pensée humaine est plus vaste que l'infini divin' (VIII, 183). Such *bons mots*, however, even in their cruder versions – 'Dieu a fait le coït, l'homme a fait l'amour' (I, 193) – cannot disguise the centrality of religious issues to the most serious discussions of the Goncourts and their companions. The impression they give is that of an intellectual class no longer believing in God but finding the *possibility* of his existence an insurmountable obstacle in the path of free thought. Thus every statement on God or the soul required its bracketed 'if': 'Dieu (s'il y a un Dieu),' wrote Flaubert to Louise Colet, 'lit dans ma conscience (si j'ai une conscience)';[2] every speculation had to be couched in interrogative form:

> L'immortalité de l'âme est-elle? [write the Goncourts] Et qu'est-elle? Une immortalité personnelle? ou collective? [. . .] Pourquoi sur cette terre? Pourquoi la mort? Et puis, après la mort? C'est la grande pensée. . . (III, 132).

The Goncourts' doubts ranged widely, from the philosophical to the social and ethical planes. Influenced by the charismatic Gavarni, with his faith in mathematics as the sole truth (I, 170) and his denial of an immaterial order (I, 110), they were drawn at times to embrace science, that 'révolte de l'ignorance humaine' (II, 32), and to see all metaphysical speculation as vain (II, 117). Mysticism and martyrdom embarrassed them, smacking of mental unbalance, 'd'une maison de fous et d'un hôpital d'âmes' (II, 160). Yet if religion's claim to truth was diminished by superstition and supernaturalism, it was nevertheless as dependent on them, they wrote, as wine on the grape (V, 141). They were half-persuaded by Gavarni's scornful diatribes on the wealth and pomp of the Catholic Church (I, 152), and worried, as members of a privileged class, by the thought that Christianity was 'peuple par essence' (IV, 201). The Church's hold on immature minds depressed them and the killjoy prudishness of a priest overheard telling a little girl not to sing the Mirliton or look at nude statues struck them as typical of its gloomy and guilt-ridden outlook (V, 71).

The brothers also regarded the Christian glorification of suffering as neurotic. 'La Névrose,' they quip, 'vient du Golgotha' (VIII, 109). Suffering, especially in terminal illness, was the greatest stumbling-block to their belief in a merciful God. The slow death of Rose

Malingre, the servant woman whom they took as the model for Germinie Lacerteux, inspired anguished accusations of divine cruelty: 'Il y a des moments où de Sade semble expliquer Dieu' (V, 143). They ascribe the death, at the age of thirty-one, of a brilliant and newly married doctor friend to the mercilessness of 'le Méchant dans le ciel' (VI, 192). 'Un Dieu de bonté, là-haut, au-dessus de cela,' they cry mockingly, 'allons donc! et comment ferait-il pour être plus méchant?' (VIII, 166).

Nevertheless, the thought that there might yet be a God up there, whatever his nature, was not totally rejected by the Goncourts. When their mother died, Jules expressed his envy of those who know the consolation of believing in eternal life, and he defined his position as one of oscillation between materialist and spiritualist conceptions of reality (III, 69). The brothers' anguished objections to Christianity never lapse into blasphemy, for which Jules expressed their common disgust (VII, 85): they saw blasphemy as the product not of a reasoned atheism but of a desperate desire for a liberating unbelief, and they describe their friend Villedeuil as 'blasphémant pour secouer l'idée de Dieu' (I, 129). The frenzied espousal of an atheist or materialist viewpoint was alien to their characteristically even-handed attitude, which led them to understand some men's need for God. 'Un Dieu lui manque,' they say of their comrade Saint-Victor (V, 145). Ultimately, they saw faith and reason as two unconnected psychic phenomena, the one irrelevant to the other (II, 15). How can science demolish faith? they ask. Can one analyse God or prove to a Catholic that the host he swallows at Mass is not the body of the risen Christ? (IV, 232) The Goncourts, in a word, were truer intellectual agnostics than any of their more self-consciously God-defying friends. Despite their affection for Gavarni, they dismissed as a *lapalissade* his oft-repeated statement that science had killed the notion of God (VIII, 116). They rejected the dogmatism they so often encountered in the Magny circle, especially that of Sainte-Beuve, whom they saw, in his professions of atheism, as a fickle and superficial time-server (VII, 25). 'Il faut avoir une âme de prêtre,' they conclude, 'pour écrire contre la religion' (VI, 220).

Flaubert, although his attitudes are less voluminously documented than the Goncourts', makes enough references to religion in his correspondence to show that for him too there were few more vital questions. 'On ne vit pas sans religion,' he tells Louise in response to her account of a visit from a depressed Musset. 'Ces gens-là n'en ont aucune, pas de boussole, pas de but' (FC II, 116). What Flaubert meant by 'religion' on this occasion is not clear, but that he believed in the psychological benefit of faith in some extra-material goal is illustrated in another letter to his mistress:

> Nous ne valons quelque chose que parce que Dieu souffle en nous. C'est là ce qui fait même les médiocres forts, ce qui rend les peuples si beaux aux jours de fièvre, ce qui embellit les laids, ce qui purifie les infâmes: la Foi, l'Amour. 'Si vous avez la foi, vous remuerez les montagnes.' Celui qui a dit cela a changé le monde, parce qu'il n'a pas douté. (FC II, 250–1)

Despite fleeting temptations to transform himself into a Brahmin (FC I, 282), Flaubert's well-known views on the 'bêtise' of ever reaching a conclusion were always likely to come between him and religious commitment. His malicious humour was a handicap too, leading him to make such tongue-in-cheek assertions as 'Moi, je déteste la Vie. Je suis catholique' (FC II, 478). Writing from Jerusalem to Louis Bouilhet, however, he expressed his willingness to be moved by religion, his sense of what might be 'si c'était possible' (FC I, 667). Appalled by the commercialisation of Christianity in the Holy City, Flaubert even took refuge in Matthew's Gospel – but only, in the end, to recognise his unbelief with no sense of regret. 'Je n'ai été là,' he records, 'ni voltairien, ni méphistophélique, ni sadiste. J'étais au contraire très simple. J'y allais de bonne foi, et mon imagination même n'a pas été remuée' (ibid.). Unable to embrace Christianity for himself, but respectful of its potential as a rejuvenating force in the lives of others, Flaubert recognised, in his olympian scorn for all entrenched viewpoints, the partiality, overstatement and extremism that characterised both sides in the ideological battles of the day. The 'materialists', he judged, reduced Man to the level of a pig just as wrong-headedly as the 'spiritualists' gave him the wings of an angel (FC II, 378).

Something of Flaubert's attitude filtered into the following generation of writers and was embodied in the man whom he himself described as his disciple: Maupassant. It was in a letter to Flaubert that Maupassant confided:

> La religion m'attire beaucoup. Car, parmi les . . . . [*sic*] de l'humanité, celle-là me semble capitale, c'est la plus large, la plus multiple et la plus profonde.[3]

Compared with the encyclopaedic knowledge of world religions acquired by Flaubert for the writing of *La Tentation de Saint-Antoine*, Maupassant's approach to the subject was relatively lacking in intellectual depth.[4] But he had learned from Flaubert to mistrust fixed ideological positions. The narrator of his story 'Mon oncle Sosthène' declares that one can be a free-thinker for the same reason that one can be a religious man – 'par bêtise'; and he goes on: 'Je n'ai pas de colère contre les temples, qu'ils soient catholiques, apostoliques, romains, protestants, russes, grecs, bouddhistes, juifs, musulmans.'[5] Maupassant's anarchic spirit sometimes leads him to anticipate with glee any sally against established authority – 'à commencer,' he tells his cousin Le Poitevin, 'par le nommé Dieu, dont l'autorité d'ailleurs ne me paraît pas indiscutable'.[6] Yet nowhere in his correspondence is there evidence of any philosophical conviction of the rightness or wrongness of religious belief.

While Maupassant's aloofness from religious quarrels might be ascribed to instinctive independence of character or to downright intellectual shallowness, or both, Émile Zola's professions of impartiality were underpinned by careful reference to the most progressive philosophies of the day. The challenge of Zola's work to Catholicism was such a major one, the evolution of his thought and art so relevant to this study, that a separate chapter will be necessary to discuss them. It is enough to note at this stage his declaration that Naturalism, the philosophy of art which pushed Realism to its most intense form, did not necessarily deny the existence of God. 'L'écrivain naturaliste,' wrote Zola, 'estime qu'il n'a pas à se prononcer sur la question d'un Dieu.'[7] On ne nie pas Dieu,' he explained, 'on tâche de remonter à lui, en reprenant l'analyse du monde. S'il est au bout, nous le verrons bien. La science nous le dira. Pour le moment, nous le mettons à part' (X, 1219). Zola owed this determination to be an exemplary philosophical positivist, never prejudging issues and remaining within the bounds of current evidence, to his admiration for Émile Littré, as he showed by echoing the words just quoted in an obituary tribute to the latter: 'Pour lui, l'inconnu doit être réservé; Dieu n'est pas nié, mais mis à part' (XIV, 611). Such scrupulous postponement of the hasty conclusion is easier for the philosopher, however, than for the novelist, who cannot delay drafting the philosophical ground rules of his book until next year's sequel; as Zola himself remarked: 'Littré [. . .] n'était pas un créateur' (ibid.). To turn from the diaries and letters of the novelists to their fictional writings is to be struck by a much sharper challenge to Christian beliefs, practices and institutions. Why this should be so is a fundamental question about the nature of the Realist novel.

* * *

An aim common to most novelists during the second half of the nineteenth century was to depict as fully as possible the physical appearance and social structures of the modern world. Thus churches as buildings and the Church as institution were necessary ingredients of their novels on a purely documentary level. The grander the scale of the social panorama, the truer this was, and it is in the novels of Zola that churches and church ceremonial, as an important aspect of life at all social levels, are the most fully and frequently depicted. Some of Zola's most memorable set-piece descriptions are of church interiors, like that of Notre-Dame-des-Grâces in Passy, decked with flowers for the *mois de Marie (Une page d'amour)* or Saint-Roch with its sculpted Christ flanked by Virgin and Magdalene (*Pot-Bouille*). It would be an inhibiting theory of literature that would deny the value of these descriptions for their own sake, providing as they do a concrete link between reality and fiction, between Zola's age and ours. Similarly, the accounts of baptism, first communion, weddings and funerals, as they appeared to nineteenth-century writers, are essential parts of their achievement as social historians, which is how they often defined themselves. The same function is fulfilled by the depiction of the Church's social role, or of popular attitudes towards it, and in such material the novels of Zola are uniquely rich.

The documentary aspect of fiction, although an important one, is not sustained for long in a state of innocence. Zola's famous definition of art reminds us that these particular 'corners of creation' are always seen 'through a temperament' (XII, 810). The novelist's angle of vision asserts itself, satirical intention meets rhetorical device. Underfunded country churches falling on the heads of priests already tortured enough by the attentions of misnamed 'filles de la Vierge', working-class folk turning to the Church only on the occasion of their daughter's wedding – such details, in *La Terre* or *L'Assommoir*, reveal as much of the author's viewpoint as they do of historical realities. Maupassant's cameo of the blessing of the boats ceremony in *Une vie* moves swiftly from *reportage* to unflattering portraits of provincial clerics:

> Les trois vieux chantres, crasseux dans leur blanche vêture, le menton poileux, l'air grave, l'œil sur le livre de plain-chant, détonnaient à pleine gueule dans la claire matinée. [. . .] Le prêtre, d'une voix empâteé, gloussa quelques mots latins dont on ne distinguait que les terminaisons sonores.[8]

Such mild irreverence, but escalating from dirty cassocks to incomprehensible and socially irrelevant Latin chants, is typical of Maupassant's presentation of the clergy. His short stories are full of insalubrious priests, or negligent ones, arriving late for their duties or hurrying quickly through them in half-swallowed utterances for which his favourite term, like Flaubert's for the same thing, was 'un marmottement'.

The satire is light and superficial here, but the irony cuts more deeply when religious practice is given a more developed social setting. The Goncourts explore the relationship between the wealthy middle-class world of Renée Mauperin and a certain type of clergy through the character of the abbé Blampoix, 'le prêtre du monde, du beau monde et du grand monde',[9] self-appointed saviour of the faubourgs Saint-Germain and Saint-Honoré, and especially prized in such circles for his talent as marriage-broker. The type is alive nearly two decades later in the form of Zola's abbé Mauduit, who has graced every death-bed in the quartier Saint-Roch and has mastered the art of closing his eyes to the moral bankruptcy of the bourgeoisie (*Pot-Bouille*). That religion existed merely for the convenience and protection of the middle class is an idea expressed with increasing acerbity from the mocking sketches of Monnier's *La Religion des Imbéciles* (1846) to the harsher denunciations of Maupassant and Zola, in whose work religious attitudes are often the banners of class warfare. The *bien-pensants* who accompany Boule-de-Suif on the coach from Rouen to Le Havre and who persuade her to sleep with a Prussian officer in order to ensure their swift passage boast of possessing 'de la Religion et des Principes' (1, 90). The same façade cloaks middle-class turpitude in Zola's novels, whereas the poor regard religion as an irrelevance in the daily struggle for bread. 'Est-ce que vous avez besoin d'un bon Dieu et de son paradis pour être heureux?' Étienne Lantier asks his fellow miners in *Germinal* (V, 146). Empty churches, to Count Muffat's father-in-law in *Nana* signify imminent revolution; he would have readily agreed with the Goncourts' Monsieur Bourjot that 'il faudrait que toutes ces canailles allassent à la messe' (RM, 212). The brothers, whose interest in the working class was a notoriously dilettante one and who could never have been suspected of harbouring any sympathies for the political left, nevertheless expose through Bourjot the complicity between Catholicism and reaction: 'Il se précipitait vers les doctrines d'ordre, il se retournait vers l'Église comme vers une gendarmerie, vers le droit divin comme vers l'absolu de l'autorité et la garantie providentielle de ses valeurs' (112). The same alliance is evoked by Maupassant's fanatical abbé Tolbiac, who tells the young châtelaine: 'Il faut que nous soyons unis pour être puissants et respectés. L'église et le château se donnant la main, la chaumière nous craindra et nous obéira' (*Une vie*, 262). One of the most powerful images of the exploitation of religion in the interests of repressive authority appears in *La Fille Élisa*, written by Edmond de Goncourt after Jules' death. In the prison cell where the former prostitute Élisa serves her sentence for the killing of her lover, a crucifix hangs above a sign saying DIEU ME VOIT – 'et au-dessous de l'œil divin [. . .] il y avait, au trou imperceptible fait par un clou dans la porte, l'œil d'un inspecteur en tournée dans les corridors.'[10] The eye of God and the eye of the law become indistinguishable from each other, and the nail used to drill the spy-hole seems a mocking image of the nails of the Crucifixion.

In *Madame Bovary* too there are reflections of the same contract between Church and political regime. One of the newest buildings in Yonville is the church, renovated under Charles X, a symbol of the clericalism of the Restoration period. Above its altar hangs a painting of the Holy Family, a gift from the Minister of the Interior; in exchange, the *tricolore* flies from the steeple. Flaubert's eye for such detail was matched by Zola's, and it is in the Rougon-Macquart cycle that the Church is most provocatively identified as the accomplice of state power. In the first novel of the series, *La Fortune des Rougon*, it is the clergy which plots and leads the insurrection in Plassans and wins power for Louis-Napoleon Bonaparte. In *La Conquête de Plassans*, the abbé Faujas' usurpation of power in the Mouret household represents in miniature the rape of France by the Emperor; but under the surface, a more fundamental takeover is in process, embodied in the gradual expulsion of the Mourets and the priest from their bourgeois home by Faujas' working-class sister and her husband. Thus does Zola express his view of the Church as a sinister force but, like the regime it supports, an ultimately doomed one.

* * *

In the forefront of Realism's presentation of the Catholic Church is a character type of which all the leading novelists create memorable individual examples: the priest; and the manner in which he is depicted is crucial for the interpretation of many a text. Not all Realist priests are negative figures. One can cite to the contrary Maupassant's abbé Picot, 'gai, vrai prêtre campagnard, tolérant, bavard et brave homme' (*Une vie*, 35), and Zola's well-meaning pro-worker priest Ranvier in *Germinal*. But the majority of them are shallow and incompetent, figures of fun at best, callous and sinister at their worst. One of the best known examples of clerical *bêtise* is Flaubert's Bournisien, whose failure to recognise Emma Bovary's problems aggravates her self-induced despair. Maupassant's priests, in their altogether different encounters with the fair sex, rejoin the traditions of the *fabliaux*, as in the tale of the cleric who visits his supposedly chaste nephew and inadvertently climbs into bed along-side the young man's girlfriend – this in a tale appropriately entitled 'Une Surprise'. The confrontation of religion with sexuality, treated here as farce, has more serious overtones in other Maupassant stories. In 'Clair de lune' (one of two *contes* bearing this title) the abbé Marignan is shaken to learn that his niece, whom he had hoped to see become a nun, has a lover, but the sight of the couple walking happily in the moonlight causes the priest to question his former mistrust of human love. Perhaps God, he reflects, has made the night specially as a setting for lovers; perhaps love is legitimised, even sanctified. The abbé feels an obscure shame, 'comme s'il eût pénétré dans un temple où il n'avait pas le droit d'entrer' (I, 599), a shame that recalls that of Adam and Eve though the story implies that human love is a greater paradise than the biblical one. The abbé stops on the brink of denying God and tries instead to reconcile his discovery with his faith in Providence, but the experience has changed for ever his notion of life's priorities. The story is typical of Realist and Naturalist concern with the man beneath the priest's vestments and with the sexual urges which these writers see, much more than religious aspirations, as constituting the prime nature of human beings. Another Maupassant priest, in 'Le Baptême' (again, two stories share this title), holds in his arms a newly baptised infant and sobs in unspoken frustration at his own eternal separation from the joys of paternity. Yet another, in 'Le Champ des oliviers', is so overcome to find that he has a son that he murders the latter and then kills himself: the roles of priest and father are tragically incompatible. A similar fascination with the priest's encounter with sex is shown by Paul Alexis in his story 'Après la bataille', which he contributed to the Naturalist volume *Les Soirées de Médan*. Here a priest, wounded by the invading Prussians, is picked up by a young widow travelling home with her husband's corpse, and through the mutual comfort they offer each other he recognises his true nature as a sexual being.

The central text on this theme is Zola's novel *La Faute de l'abbé Mouret*, in which a priest has a love affair with a girl, only to reject her and their unborn child on resuming his priestly function. Although this novel predated the stories by Maupassant and Alexis described above, Zola did not invent the character of the *prêtre amoureux*, of which there is no shortage of examples in Romantic literature. Lamartine's narrative poem *Jocelyn*, especially, invites comparison, for it too relates the abandonment of a girl by a priest who has been her lover. *Jocelyn* is an obvious source of *Mouret*, but what Zola adds to the original melodrama is a sharpness of anti-clerical satire, a questioning of the nature of the man within the priest, a probing of the neuroses common to both sexual and religious experience. No text in the whole of the Rougon-Macquart cycle challenges Christian attitudes and values more radically than this one, although this has not always been recognised. F. W. J. Hemmings sees a neutral Zola at work here, on the grounds that his preparatory notes for the novel reveal no ironical intention, and he supports his judgement by referring to a review by Zola of Ernest Daudet's *Le Missionnaire* (a novel on a similar theme) in which he objects to the use of novels as weapons for or against Catholicism.[11] Other reviews, however, give different impressions. Writing of Lavalley's novel *Aurélien* Zola, as was his custom in incidental writing, pleads his freedom from *parti pris*, but supports nonetheless the author's opposition to priestly celibacy. The priest, he goes on, is rightly less venerated than of old, acceptable as a human brother but not as the spokesman of the divine. His pretension to chastity denies nature in a way that Zola finds 'repugnant' (X, 317). This review prefigures very accurately Zola's ironical stance towards the central character of his novel. Serge Mouret is sexually neutered by his priestly calling, and this offence against nature is temporarily righted by his making love to Albine in the overgrown park called Le Paradou, after which 'il se sentait complet' (III 176).

Despite the absolute clarity of what the novel conveys here, its coherence has been questioned. Hemmings objects that because Serge is suffering from amnesia, 'he must be exonerated at least from the fault of consciously rejecting the demands of the religious life he had embraced' (ibid.), and he implies that this is a flaw in the novel's logic. But this is to take the 'faute' of the title in its conventional moral sense, or even in its special Catholic sense: that is, a sin. The priest's loss of memory, far from being an error on Zola's part, is a deliberate narrative device, used to obliterate Serge's sense of sin and to invalidate Christian interpretation from the outset. A further comparison with *Jocelyn* is useful here. Lamartine's priest does not set out to seduce the girl Laurence; his love is not premeditated. He believes her to be a boy, left in his care by a dying father, and the relationship that develops only gradually reveals itself as a sexual one. Jocelyn cannot be blamed for his love, but only for abandoning the girl who needs him. Exactly the same is true of Zola's priest. Whereas Hemmings seems to identify Mouret's fault as loving Albine, for Zola, in ironical reversal of Christian morality, it is in not loving her enough. It is in his betrayal of her, in his rejection of life in favour of what is specifically identified as a religion of death.

The novel's challenge to Catholic values is thus undeniable, even though the forces that constitute the other side of the conflict – nature and sex – are not depicted in glorified and unproblematic terms. What Valerie Minogue calls Zola's 'characteristic ambivalence'[12] towards sex is certainly evident in the lovers' post-coital shame; and if nature is supposed to be Man's guiding light, then the fact that only Serge's half-witted sister Désirée relates easily to it (in her relationship with animals) creates an immediate difficulty. Zola here reveals, not confusion, but rather artistic integrity. To depict the discovery of sex as the path to eternal happiness, to pretend that human beings have no difficulty in accepting their condition and earthly environment would have been obvious distortions of the truth he sought to portray. If Le Paradou is the site of conflict between the two lovers, if it is wild and disturbing and tainted with the memories of the tragic love of its former owners, it is because Zola did not want to create a paradise on earth. There are no earthly paradises. Yet earth and life constitute for Zola the only sure reality, and his hope is founded on their eventual improvement. That is why the fault of the abbé Mouret is a crime against life.

Zola also implies that sex, far from belonging to a world remote from religious experience, is part and parcel of it. Serge's special devotion to the Holy Virgin contains unmistakable sexual elements, and Frère Archangias, the lay brother who embodies Catholic misogyny at its fiercest, is not wrong in suspecting this. Serge hides pictures of the Virgin under his pillow. Alternately erotic symbol and mother figure (replacing his own mother, burned alive in her Plassans home), the Virgin is a compound of all that he seeks from the female sex. He imagines himself 'buvant le lait d'amour infini qui tombait goutte à goutte de ce sein virginal' (III, 80). As he recites his countless *Aves* he is voicing a declaration of love, 'cette parole sans cesse la même qui revenait, pareille au "Je t'aime" des amants' (III, 82). His eyes fix on her bodice, on her heart pierced by a sword, and he feels the urge to kiss her breast. As he recites the litany, each appelation is a step towards obscure sexual union, and the end of his prayer leaves Serge 'les genoux cassés, la tête vide, comme après une grande chute' (III, 84), in anticipation of the pleasurable fatigue he will discover with Albine. Zola's pre-Freudian conviction of the sexual element within Man's spiritual aspirations produces a parody of the cult of the Virgin, which was so strong in Second Empire France.

La Faute de l'abbé Mouret directly influenced Maupassant's treatment of the priest figure, especially in his attitudes to sex and procreation. Frère Archangias' terror at the spectacle of farmyard reproduction, and his killing of a nestful of baby birds, are echoed in the story 'Le Saut du berger' and also in *Une vie*. In both texts, a priest destroys a litter of puppies, whose birth has been innocently attended by a group of peasant children. The abbé Tolbiac in *Une vie* is given an ideological opponent in the shape of Baron le Perthuis, father of the heroine Jeanne and direct fictional descendant of Albine's father, the old libertarian Jeanbernat. Seeing nothing but beauty in sex and procreation, he rejects Catholic prudery as an exacerbation of middle-class taste; and of priests he declares:'Il faut combattre ces hommes-là, c'est notre droit et notre devoir. Ils ne sont pas humains' (*Une vie*, 267–8). Less rigorous a thinker than Zola, less reluctant to pronounce a naïve faith in life-giving sex (which ironically, was to kill him, through syphilis), Maupassant's talents were those, not of a creator of philosophies, but of a denouncer of hypocrisy and falsehood. Through the mouth of the Baron, he produces a sort of Realist's Ecce Homo: 'Le voilà, le voilà, l'homme en soutane! L'as-tu vu maintenant?' (ibid., 274). This is not just the voice of one character, a cranky and profligate anti-clerical. The entire narrative structure of *Une vie* maroons the abbé Tolbiac at its negative pole. Increasingly fanatical, he delights in assuring Jeanne that all her troubles have been sent as deserved punishment from God, and refuses to consecrate her father's burial. He is the prime embodiment of an anti-life viewpoint, a foil for the text's humanitarian affirmations. The novel is not quite anti-religious, for the conflicts at its heart are not between religious belief and unbelief, but between a wide-ranging liberal religion and a perverted clerical fanaticism. But there can be no mistaking the view of the Catholic Church which it projects. Jeanne's young son, misunderstanding his great aunt's inarticulate reply to his question: 'Where is God?', tells his grandfather: 'Le bon Dieu, il est partout, mais il n'est pas dans l'Église' (292). The child's naïve comment carries more than a grain of Maupassant's truth.

* * *

It is implied in *La Faute de l'abbé Mouret* that priestly devotion and even, by extension, all Christian faith betray essentially feminine aspects of character. Albine's view of her former lover in his priestly vestments makes this clear: 'Toute sa virilité séchait sous cette robe de femme qui le laissait sans sexe' (III, 220). The association between religion and femininity is one of the constants of Realist characterisation, and religious experience one of the principal channels by which it explores female psychology. Misogynism and sexism combine with religious scepticism to produce some of the most markedly ironic portraits of character in the Realist corpus. La religion,' quip the Goncourts, 'est une partie du sexe de la femme' (II, 94), and they add to their own *bon mot* one of Gavarni's: 'Savez-vous de quoi me fait l'effet une femme qui n'a pas de religion? D'une sorte d'hermaphrodite' (III, 242). The diary is full of comments on the dubious sensuality of women's religion. Convent girls are described as having their heads stuffed with 'tout ce vaporeux mystique', which will make them ill suited as wives of brutish husbands (II, 151). Religion is seen as 'cette grande machine de la femme', church-going as a chance to show off new dresses; to a woman, 'Dieu lui semble *chic*' (V, 129). The sanctification of Marie Alacoque, foundress of the cult of the Sacred Heart, is regarded by the brothers as no less than the glorification of 'le paganisme féminin' (VII, 8). Such views abound in their novels too. The attitude of middle-class ladies to religion is summed up simply: 'Les femmes en raffolaient' (RM, 67). The Goncourts are echoed nearly two decades later by Maupassant, whose heroine Jeanne 'était toute de sentiment; elle avait cette foi rêveuse que garde toujours une femme' (*Une vie*, 262). She shares with another of his female characters, Madame Walter, 'ces idées superstitieuses qui sont souvent toute la raison des femmes'.[13]

The unavowed sexuality of Serge Mouret's love of the Virgin has its counterpart in women's attachment to the masculinity of Christ. 'Les femmes,' says Flaubert's Hilarion as part of his subtle undermining of the hapless Saint-Antoine, 'sont toujours pour Jésus, même les idolâtres' (I, 61). Passion for the person of Christ, expressed in the language of human love – Jesus as 'l'Époux de son âme, le Roi de son amour, le Bien-aimé de son coeur' – underlies the vocation of the Goncourts' sœur Philomène.[14] Sexual and religious awakening, the second as the by-product of the first, are explored in the account of her adolescence; without heavy irony, and indeed with compassion for their character, the Goncourts nevertheless suggest that religious yearnings are the product of imminent puberty. The account of Philomène's first communion, the moment of 'receiving God', is expressed in a blend of the diffuse – 'un ineffable sentiment de défaillance' – and of the more suggestively precise – 'ravissement', 'évanouissement' – that hints at sexual initiation, sharply and intimately felt but indescribably unfamiliar (SP, 44). However mildly and undogmatically, the text contrasts that which is undeniably real – the emotion and its unspoken physiological causes – with what is fondly imagined: the encounter with the divine. The former exists not only in Philomène's flesh but also in the authoritative testimony of the narrator; the latter is a strand in the imagination of a simple girl.

Of all the examples of the type to which Philomène belongs, the convent girl unable to disentangle spiritual and amorous impulses, the best known is Emma Bovary. Like Philomène, 'les comparaisons de fiancé, d'époux, d'amant céleste et de mariage éternel qui reviennent dans les sermons lui soulevaient au fond de l'âme des douceurs inattendues'.[15] 'La religion' and 'les délicatesses de cœur' are interlaced in her imagination through the figure of Mademoiselle de la Vallière, royal mistress turned Carmelite, to whose legend her thirteen-year-old eyes are opened by illustrations on dinner plates in the inn next door to the convent. Menacing reality intrudes in the shape of the 'égragnitures' left by past diners' knives, but Emma is sublimely oblivious to reality, preferring instead distorted romantic images which are often the product of religious reverie. Religion itself is not the prime target of Flaubert's irony, but it provides another level on which the portrait of the muddled, self-deceiving woman can be sharpened. It merges with the broader theme of romantic delusion when Emma reads *Le Génie du christianisme* and when her brain swims with Lamartinian clichés of falling leaves, dying swans and the voice of the Eternal 'discourant dans les vallons' (I, 326). Emma's direct descendant is Angélique in Zola's *Le Rêve*, to whom the saints and martyrs of Voragine's Golden Legend are more real than the flesh and blood people around her, and whose adolescent fantasies of handsome young lovers are interchangeable with her longing for Christ. Another Zola heroine, Hélène in *Une page d'amour*, recognises more clearly that even prayer, far from being a refuge from the temptations of adulterous love, can be a sublimation of erotic yearnings, 'toujours la même passion, traduite par le même mot ou le même signe' (III, 1068).

To less innocent women, churches, in the words of Bel-Ami, 'sont bonnes à tous les usages [. . .] Il leur semble tout simple de filer l'amour au pied des autels' (398). Fewer places are more convenient as sites for amorous rendezvous, away from prying eyes, or more stimulating, the senses quickening as candles flicker in incense-laden darkness. The church of the Trinity is the haunt of Bel-Ami and Madame Walter, he pretending to pray while muttering words of seduction into her ear, she hypocritically imploring heaven's protection from his charms. For Emma and Léon, Rouen cathedral is the preferred meeting-place, and it is here, in the 'boudoir gigantesque' of the church, that takes place the final apotheosis of Emma as perfume-laden sex-object, her face resplendent in the reflections of stained glass (I, 510).

Often the object of the female's pursuit need not be imported, but is already inside the church: namely, the priest himself. The Goncourts' Germinie Lacerteux falls in love with her young confessor, follows him from confessional to vestry and back. When prudently diverted to a less seductive minister of God, she simply stops going to church, and when asked what the priests have done to her to cool her ardour, she answers: 'Rien'.[16] This is clearly meant as a complaint.

Germinie's working-class sisters in Zola's *Le Ventre de Paris* have more success with priests, at least in the eyes of the malicious gossips who see the *charcutière* Lisa Quenu going to church with suspicious regularity: 'La grosse donne dans le curés, maintenant. Ça la calmera, cette femme, de se tremper le derrière dans l'eau bénite' (II, 739). The eroticism of confession is suggested as Lisa, awaiting her turn, sees, under the door of the confessional, the hem of a blue dress lying suggestively at the feet of the priest; the chapel of the Virgin is 'toute moite de silence et d'obscurité'; women recline 'pâmées sur des chaises retournées, abîmées dans cette volupté noire'; stained glass images burn 'comme des flammes d'amour mystique'; Lisa feels 'une indécence dans cette ombre, un jour et un souffle d'alcôve' (II, 740). The wife of her cousin Mouret, in *La Conquête de Plassans*, knows no such inhibitions. Confessing to the priest whom she loves is an undisguised sexual experience; it is 'extase', 'évanouissement', marked by attraction to the very odour of the priestly garb, rising to the crisis of 'sanglots nerveux' and climaxing in overwhelming fatigue (II, 919).

Another female character whose slide into religious belief is a preordained hazard of her sex is Madame Gervaisais, the eponymous heroine of the Goncourts' last joint novel. A reader of philosophical works which have led her to reject the supernatural and an aesthete subscribing to 'une religion du Beau, du Vrai, du Bien',[17] Madame Gervaisais stands aloof from Christian belief when she arrives in Rome with her mentally retarded son Pierre-Charles. What she seeks in visiting churches is not 'l'approche de Dieu dans sa maison' (113), but simply peace. She possesses nevertheless 'un respect de femme pour la personne du Christ' (97), and gradually comes to regard him as '[le] patron de son sexe' (148). When her son falls ill, her identification with the Virgin as the archetype of the suffering mother further erodes her scepticism, and fosters the growth of the religious sensibility which is 'caché [. . .] au fond de la femme' (172). This process is represented as one of decline, as the regression of a sharply intelligent woman to the banality of female religiosity. Under the influence of the atmosphere of Rome, or what the narrator calls '[la] contagion sainte' (183), and believing her prayers to be responsible for her son's recovery, she becomes a fanatical convert, abandoning friends and artistic pursuits for the company of her austere confessor. Her vision darkens, she sees sin all around, and her devotion takes on the sinisterly sexual overtones of so many other women in the Realist corpus, her thoughts full of lurid images of penetration by God and by Christ. Her son, whose illness had led her to religion in the first place, is now seen as the rival to her divine consort, an obstacle to union with him. In their description of the 'haine sainte' (252) directed by mother against son, of 'cette monstrueuse victoire dénaturée sur le sang, la dernière et suprême victoire de la religion' (ibid.), the Goncourts express more overtly than in any other of their novels their dismay at the effects of Christian belief on human behaviour. Like Zola and Maupassant they espouse the cause of nature in its eternal struggle with grace: 'La Grâce finissait d'assassiner la Nature. En elle, la femme, l'être terrestre, n'existait plus. [. . .] L'humanité s'en était allée d'elle' (255–6).

Like Zola too, they identify this life-denying Catholicism as a religion of death. Madame Gervaisais, in her final phase, is 'amoureuse de la mort' (256), obsessively visiting the Catacombs to stare at the skulls and skeletons, 'prête à dire, avec Job, à la pourriture: "Vous êtes ma mère!", à dire aux vers: "Vous êtes mes frères et mes sœurs!" ' (259). Though the novel has its formal ending in Madame Gervaisais' death as she awaits an audience at the door of the Pope, these scenes of horror constitute its real conclusion. It is to this corruption that religious conversion has led the woman, the chosen bride of Christ.

* * *

In the portraits of priests and penitents which abound in Realist novels, religious belief is used as a means to artistic ends. Such all-consuming emotions, such fiercely held convictions, are effective delineators of personality, producing psychological types that, with particular colouring and different sets of circumstances, can be turned into sharply etched individual characters. With the added pathos of self-delusion, the vulnerability of the credulous pilgrim embarked on a false track, the novelist has the ingredients of a rich emotional mix as well as a source of powerful irony. Flaubert exploits these possibilities as well as anyone in his account of Emma Bovary's reading. Depicting Emma as she contemplates a pile of pious works supplied by Bournisien, the narrator tells us: 'Madame Bovary n'avait pas encore l'intelligence assez nette pour s'appliquer sérieusement à n'importe quoi . . .' He is caught here in a rare moment of overt judgement of Emma, for this can only be *his* opinion; it is certainly not hers, and no other witness to her thoughts is present. But despite what he has just said, Emma seems after all to apply a critical sense to this material, seeing it as betraying ignorance of the world. Then comes a further switch: she reads the books despite her low evaluation of them: 'Elle persista pourtant, et, lorsque le volume lui tombait des mains, elle se croyait prise par la plus fine mélancolie catholique qu'une âme éthérée pût concevoir' (I, 487). Shafts of irony fly in all directions here: against Emma and against the religious literature which she scorns but nevertheless reads, and which she turns into a means of reaching the lofty heights of romantic melancholia where her ego can flourish. It is a strange passage, with apparent contradictions: Emma is unintelligent, yet has critical judgement; she is unable to apply herself seriously to anything, yet she persists in her reading. Such contradictions are deliberate, designed to create a series of disconnected views of this fickle and inconsistent character, unable to make use of what meagre intellectual strength she might possess. A central aspect of Emma's character is illuminated here, and the religious element in her nature has supplied the necessary lighting.

Religion does not emerge unscathed from its role as an ironic reflector of character. The cumulative effect of novel after novel in which religion is disguised sexuality, or a prop to establishment values, or a sentimental stimulus, undermines not just the integrity of the character concerned, but the status of religion itself. It appears a purely subjective phenomenon with no external referent. The very concentration of novelists on what is happening within their characters detaches religious emotion from the transcendental world to which it is supposed to relate. The contrast between the imagined world of a character who believes in God and the enveloping world of the novel itself, in which God does not and cannot appear, is a further source of ironic distance between protagonist and narrator which the best of the Realists exploit to great advantage. It is instructive to compare at this point Maupassant's novel *Fort comme la mort* with the much earlier, pioneering Realist text of Duranty, *Le Malheur d'Henriette Gérard*. Duranty's universe is ontologically and metaphysically neutral. He describes the surface of social life with no reference to a spiritual dimension. A mildly acerbic anti-clericalism is conveyed through priest characters whose significance is wholly social, involved as they are in the marital schemes of the Gérard family. But on the truth or falsehood of the spiritual beliefs that these priests represent, the text implies no particular view. In Maupassant's novel, however, through a series of apparently trivial references, the philosophical ground rules for the interpretation of the fictional universe are firmly established. The Baron de Corbelle, seeking to justify his taste in social companions, 'le fit avec des arguments inconsistants et irréfutables, de ces arguments qui fondent devant la raison comme la neige au feu, et qu'on ne peut saisir, des arguments absurdes et triomphants de curé de campagne qui démontre Dieu'.[18] In other words, the baselessness of believing in God is taken here as proverbial, as a yardstick of the absurd and the unprovable, not by a character, but by the narrator himself, and it conditions what may or may not happen in the text. Thus, when the reader sees the comtesse de Guilleroy pray for the soul of her dead mother, he knows he has been forewarned of the narrator's detachment from such impulses. When the countess calls for divine intervention, implores 'un secours surnaturel contre les dangers prochains' (214), he knows that such aid is not only logically but aesthetically impossible in a tale told by this particular teller. Our mode of reading, our strategies for interpreting the text, are thus effectively manipulated.

There are Realist novels in which prayers *are* answered, in which miracles happen and God manifests his presence in the most visible and audible ways. When this happens, we know that the novelist is displaying his conjuring tricks, enjoying his own ironic devices. At the end of *Bel-Ami*, for example, Christ arrives in person at the wedding of the caddish hero to the wealthy Suzanne Walter. This is given as a piece of straight narrative: 'L'encens répandait une odeur finie de benjoin, et sur l'autel le sacrifice divin s'accomplissait; l'Homme-Dieu, à l'appel de son prêtre, descendait sur la terre pour consacrer le triomphe du baron Georges Du Roy' (571). Even more spectacularly, in *La Faute de l'abbé Mouret*, Jesus converses in familiar fashion with Serge in the young priest's moment of decision:

> L'abbé Mouret disait tout à Jésus, comme à un Dieu venu dans l'intimité de sa tendresse et qui peut tout entendre. [. . .] Et Jésus répondait que cela ne devait pas l'étonner. [. . .] Jésus se montrait tolérant; il expliquait que la faiblesse de l'homme est la continuelle occupation de Dieu. [. . .] Là, Jésus avait un léger rire de bienveillance (III, 229).

Jesus' laugh probably had nothing on Zola's while these words were being written. Neither this passage nor Maupassant's needs much comment, so obviously do both novelists' tongues protrude into their cheeks. The ironic adoption of the character's false standpoint – triumphant in the case of Bel-Ami and his cohorts, hallucinatory in the case of Serge – is kept at a distance by the use of the imperfect tense, placing the 'events' outside the current chronological sequences of the novel, and outside the ontological assumptions on which the narrator bases his story. There are narratives written wholly from within a perspective alien to the novelist. Flaubert's *Légende de Saint-Julien l'Hospitalier* is one. In it the supernatural events are presented straightforwardly, as the tale requires. Reader and author share the same suspension of disbelief. Of Julien's mother, the narrator simply tells us: 'A force de prier Dieu, il lui vint un fils' (II, 624), but in a story in which stags speak and old men appear out of moonbeams to predict Julien's saintly future, this can hardly be taken as a Flaubertian conversion to belief in Providence. In any event, the final sentence of the text gives the whole work its necessary frame and isolates it from contemporary modes of judgement: 'Et voilà l'histoire de saint Julien l'Hospitalier, telle à peu près qu'on la trouve, sur un vitrail d'église, dans mon pays' (II, 648). Here – in mediaeval stained glass – are such miraculous events possible. Modern novels have different conventions, but it is a delightful paradox that no Christian novelist would dare depict the intervention of the divine into human lives as freely and as cheerfully as do Maupassant, Zola and Flaubert!

In most Realist texts, God, when he is invoked, suffers from acute deafness. In a famous scene in *L'Assommoir*, Gervaise, having prayed for fine weather, is submerged in a snow storm. There are more serious examples than this. Emma Bovary on her death-bed suddenly seems better following the last rites – 'comme si le sacrement l'eût guérie' (I, 591). Charles' hopes of a miraculous recovery are raised . . . and dashed, for this calm is merely the prelude to a horrific death agony. This cruel failure of the miracle in its moment of promise is echoed in Angélique's death scene at the end of *Le Rêve*. She too has just received extreme unction, and has lapsed into the appearance of death, which moves the bishop to kiss her on the lips. At once she comes to life: has God's mercy restored the girl who has devoted her life to him? No, for this is a temporary reprieve; Angélique dies shortly after. Complaints of God's cruelty abound in these texts, ironic or grave according to the circumstances. 'Il y a un bon Dieu contre moi!' cries Anatole in the Goncourts' *Manette Salomon*,[19] seeking a scapegoat for his failure as a painter. Emma too 'exécrait l'injustice de Dieu' (I, 352) as a way of cloaking from herself her own inadequacies. Charles' reaction to Bournisien when Emma dies – 'Je l'exécre, votre Dieu!' (I, 591) – is more profoundly moving, except that, because the reader knows that God has played no part in Emma's banal demise, it falls short of the tragic. Flaubert's denial of tragic status to his heroine, his creation of an ironic and anti-tragic novel, depends on the relegation of the metaphysical to the role of just one more delusion in the mind of a hapless character. The Goncourts, by contrast, seeking to raise the lowly to tragic level, allow Germinie to see the lucklessness of her life as a modern equivalent of fate, in which Christian notions of providence are cleverly manipulated:

> Elle se sentait dans le courant de quelque chose allant toujours, qu'il était inutile, *presque impie*, de vouloir arrêter. Cette grande force du monde qui fait souffrir, la puissance mauvaise qui porte le nom d'un dieu sur le marbre des tragédies antiques, et qui s'appelle Pas-de-chance sur le front tatoué des bagnes, la Fatalité l'écrasait, et Germinie baissait le tête sous son pied. [. . .] Cette file de douleurs qui avait suivi ses années et grandi avec elles, tout ce qui s'était succédé dans son existence comme une rencontre et un arrangement de misère, sans que jamais elle y eût vu apparaître la main de cette Providence dont on lui avait tant parlé, elle se disait qu'elle était une de ces malheureuses vouées en naissant à une éternité de misères. . . (GL, 181)

Though Germinie invests the adverse currents of life with a religious aura – that is, she feels a sense of impiety because she resents them – it is clear that, whereas Greek tragedy depends on the malice of the gods, nineteenth-century Realist tragedy, as conceived by the Goncourts, depends on God's absence: there is no trace of Providence. The brothers' masterly *trompe-l'œil* has it both ways: fate, always a useful *literary* device, exists, but God, traditional source of solace, remains invisible. Germinie is dwarfed by a force larger than herself, raising her plight to a grander plane, but the force is without spiritual substance, thus protecting the Goncourts' philosophical position.

God's failure to protect men from suffering is a common theme in Realist fiction. It is expressed through the mouth of the young doctor Barnier, who falls in love with sœur Philomène and who spends his days combating disease and pain. 'Vous trouvez,' he asks the nun, 'un père à remercier au bout de tout cela?' (SP, 151). Barnier is a sceptic, whose question is a rhetorical device in his argument with Philomène. In Zola's *Thérèse Raquin*, it is, on the contrary, a life-long believer who rejects God for his non-intervention on behalf of the victims of violence. Madame Raquin, Thérèse's mother-in-law, learns from the mouth of Thérèse that she and Laurent have conspired to drown Thérèse's first husband, the old woman's son Camille; but mute and paralysed, her only recourse is to implore God which she does in vain. What is revealed to her is not God's mercy but the inescapable brutality of human beings, which her faith in heaven's redemptive powers had cloaked from her all through life. Only one conclusion is possible: 'Dieu était mauvais; il aurait dû lui dire la vérité plus tôt, ou la laisser s'en aller avec ses innocences et son aveuglement. Maintenant, il ne lui restait qu'à mourir en niant l'amitié, en niant le dévouement. Rien n'existait que le meurtre et la luxure' (I, 635–6). Zola uses here the misguided optimism of a blissful Christian view of life as the revealed untruth on which to found his portrayal of human bestiality. Edmond de Goncourt employs a similar strategy in *La Fille Élisa*, but adds a further factor. The young soldier who forces his brutal sexual attentions on Élisa, leading her to the act of killing which in turn causes her imprisonment, is a Christian, through whom the text weaves a series of associations between religious ecstasy, eroticism and violence. The fact that the soldier had been, in civilian life, a shepherd, is also significant, allowing the image of the Good Shepherd himself to emerge in sinister light, while Élisa is left echoing the words of the crucified Christ: why has God abandoned her?

The accusation of God's wickedness is expressed most forcefully of all by Maupassant. His tale 'Moiron' is about a child murderer whose career of killing has been triggered by the deaths of his own children. God, he reasons, could have saved his children; for him murder is simply protest by emulation. 'Je compris que Dieu est méchant,' Moiron tells the narrator. 'Pourquoi avait-il tué mes enfants? J'ouvris les yeux, et je vis qu'il aime tuer. Il n'aime que ça, monsieur. Il ne fait vivre que pour détruire! Dieu, monsieur, c'est un massacreur' (II, 989). Maupassant's last work, a literary testament which was barely begun before his final decline into madness and death, was designed as an elaboration of this theme of divine cruelty. It was to be called *L'Angélus*. Although only fragments of it were written,[20] Maupassant's verbal testimony to the poet Auguste Dorchain shows that his aim was to create a bitter parody of the Nativity, the story of a crippled boy born in a stable to a life of unrelenting pain. The first extant fragment introduces the pregnant comtesse de Brémontal, who has prayed to the Virgin Mary, patroness of mothers, for the birth of a daughter. Prussian officers arrive at the house (for Maupassant has returned to the period of his first great success *Boule de suif*) and eject the young countess into the night. . . . A second brief fragment introduces a young doctor, Paturel; the third is a dialogue between him and a priest, the abbé

Marvaux. In this fragment, Paturel says that all gods are monsters, that his experience as a doctor has given him evidence of the crimes of so-called Providence that he could write up in a legal 'dossier de Dieu'. The priest replies that the concept of God is hard to grasp, but that Christ, whom he adores, makes God accessible. But to this exemplary Christian thought he adds that Christ too was a victim of God, that his love of mankind was a reflection of his human, not his divine, self; and that this is why Christ had to be punished more severely than any man has ever been. The fourth and final fragment is a speech by this same troubled priest, and, echoing the words of the killer Moiron, it is perhaps the most ferocious onslaught on the Christian God in the whole of the Realist canon. God is presented as an unrelenting sadist, giving life merely to extinguish it, inventing cholera and typhus as instruments of torture, creating animals whose beauty and vitality cloak with cruel mockery the physical corruption into which they are doomed to fall. This was the final passage Maupasssant was ever to write, his message to posterity. The career that had begun with satire of religious bigotry ends in an explosion of fury against God himself.

* * *

The spectacle of nature, and especially of animals, links Maupassant's first novel *Une vie* to this last unfinished text. In both, the opposition of innocent nature to divine cruelty reverses the Christian message of grace redeeming a fallen physical universe. Horses running free in meadows, birds singing in their nests, all unaware of their inevitable fate at the hands of the great destroyer that men call God, are manifestations of life's flawed beauty; despite their inherent pathos, they occupy the positive pole in Maupassant's view of the world, against the stern and life-denying dictates of so-called Providence. Other Realist novelists use animals, especially birds, as emblems of innocent freshness and vitality and as representatives of an eternal natural order, in contrast to which the Christian church appears a mere fleeting expression of one cultural phase in the earth's long history. In the Rome visited by Madame Gervaisais, the lesson of the transience of all civilisations, embodied in the monuments of antiquity and extending by implication to the Church of Rome itself, is underpinned by the encroachment of nature into the ruins, and by the flight of birds around the crumbling stones. 'Des oiseaux volaient familièrement dans le monstrueux nid de pierre,' runs the text; '[. . .] La ruine revenait à la nature [. . .] – toutes les revendications et toutes les reprises de la nature éternelle sur la Ville éternelle' (MG, 83). In the authors' earlier novel *Renée Mauperin*, a description of a country church visited by the dying heroine includes the same contrast between nature's animation and dead ecclesiastical stone:

> L'église avait comme un murmure de voix éteintes, l'azur jouait dans les vitraux. Des envolées de pigeons partaient à tout instant et couraient se nicher dans le creux des sculptures et les trous des vieilles pierres. La rivière qu'on voyait bruissait; un poulain blanc courait à l'eau fou et tout bondissant. (RM, 278–9)

Was Zola thinking of this passage when describing Serge Mouret's dilapidated church? The elements of the picture are the same, but as usual it is Zola who hones them into the most intense degree of polemical sharpness. As Serge says mass, a veritable invasion is taking place, nature forcing its way into the church, interrupting, deriding, challenging the supremacy of the priest's religion. The sun does not simply play on the stained glass windows as in the Goncourt text; it bursts in, illuminates the previous bleakness of the nave, seems to bring a smile to the face of the plaster Virgin, but leaves in shade the corner where 'le grand christ [. . .] mettait la mort'. Birds enter the church via the broken windows, their songs drowning the voice of the priest and the ringing of the bells of the mass; at the supreme moment when 'le corps et le sang d'un Dieu allaient descendre sur l'autel', Mouret's housekeeper is chasing sparrows from the altar. As Christ comes to redeem 'la nature damnée', damned nature asserts itself, healthy, free and joyful, needing no redemption. Serge's sister Désirée arrives with a bevy of chicks. The sun beams more brightly, the gold of the holy vessels paling in its rays. 'L'astre demeura seul maître de l'église,' writes Zola; 'les murailles badigeonnées, la grande vierge, le grand christ lui-même, prenaient un frisson de sève, comme si la mort était vaincue par l'éternelle jeunesse de la terre' (III, 25–8). Seldom can an allegedly objective Naturalist have written so ambiguously partial an opening scene. When we follow Serge Mouret out of his church, see it from outside, the same testimony to nature's force goes on. The exterior walls are eaten by vegetation. The implacable opposition of nature and church is even expressed in the hostile contact between thistles and the hem of Frère Archangias' robes as he walks across the fields. The natural world has declared war on the usurping Christian deity; and when the priest, lying with Albine in the shade of the Tree of Life, finally follows nature's laws, this is identified as the triumph for which the opening scene of the book was the preparation: 'Et c'était une victoire pour les bêtes, les plantes, les choses, qui avaient voulu l'entrée de ces deux enfants dans l'éternité de la vie. Le parc applaudissait formidablement' (III, 175). Animals, plants, *things*. It is matter itself, 'les atomes de la matière', the substance of the physical world, in opposition to the spiritual, that has won the day.

* * *

So far Realism's challenge to Christianity has been discussed in the context of themes and characters. Zola's identification of *things* as the accomplices of nature in its opposition to a false spiritualisation of life suggests a new area of study: things, concrete objects, as Realist discourse presents them. The representation of the physical world is a dominant concern of nineteenth-century literature, one which had been gathering momentum in the previous century but held back by the ossifying traditions of French classicism, with its preference for the refined and the abstract. When the breakthrough came, one feature of it was increasingly numerous descriptions of the objects with which men and women surround themselves: their clothes, their houses, their furniture and possessions, those companions of our daily lives the presence of which, in a work of fiction, enhances the illusion of the real. The Goncourts' Charles Demailly already has the makings of a novelist in his sensitivity to objects: whether furniture, a wineglass or wallpaper, 'les choses [. . .] étaient pour lui parlantes et frappantes comme les personnes'.[21] Objects, to the Goncourts, need not even be specified in order to give an impression of solidity and totality, and work as reflectors of character: Renée Mauperin looks at 'les objets au mur, les choses sur la cheminée' and concludes: 'Il y a de ma vie ici. C'est un peu moi, tout ça!' (RM, 152–3).

As this last example shows, and as Vivienne Mylne reminds us in her book on the eighteenth-century novel, 'concrete objects are introduced for purposes other than the grotesque and sordid effects which chiefly characterise the *roman réaliste* of the seventeenth century'.[22] However, novelists were often accused of just such trivialisation. Georges May records the distaste expressed by the abbé Desfontaines for 'la bassesse [des] objets' in Marivaux's *Vie de Marianne*, especially the details of the furnishings of the miserable bedroom where the heroine is abandoned following the death of her guardian (op. cit., 174). Similar objections were voiced by Chateaubriand, who criticised in a preface to *Atala* the effects of too great a concern with reproducing 'nature': 'De là les détails fastidieux de mille romans où l'on décrit jusqu'au bonnet de nuit, et à la robe de chambre'.[23] Although his own fictional writings show that he did not eschew completely what was becoming the characteristic discourse of novels – *Atala* itself contains a description of père Aubry's grotto, with its papyrus mat, its water bottles, vases and spade – this criticism, from the author of *Le Génie du christianisme*, is an interesting echo of that of the cleric Desfontaines. Did Catholic opinion already sense, by the turn of the nineteenth century, that this explosion of concrete objects was going to challenge not just the language of classicism but also the invisible spiritual dimension in which the Christian puts his faith? By Balzac's time, such an opposition between spiritual and concrete was consciously sensed. In the latter's *Jésus-Christ en Flandre*, in which Christ appears to save from a shipwreck all those passengers and crew who follow him, the conflicting advantages of trusting the Holy Virgin and trusting a bailer (*écope*) are sharply juxtaposed, the boat's impenitent skipper crying 'Sainte Écope!' and not 'Sainte Vierge!' (VI, 525).

The same opposition reappears in Zola. It is not quite present in his first novel *La Confession de Claude*, although it is certainly foreshadowed there. Zola had not yet rejected all vestige of belief in 'le Dieu que le Christ nous révéla',[24] and the focus of his satire falls less specifically on Claude's religiosity than, more generally, on his poetic nature, at odds with the harshness of urban life. To dramatise this struggle, he uses conventional poetic images in the opening sentences – 'manteau de brouillard', 'soirées intimes', 'printemps éternel' – to exemplify Claude's romantic way of describing the world, and concrete nouns, objects, to represent reality through the narrator's eyes – fourteen of them in the second paragraph alone. Objects are employed not as descriptive devices but as agents of the real, their physicality clashing with the abstract vocabulary to create a stylistic conflict which exactly parallels the central thematic one. Neither conflict directly involves religious values, but as Zola's religious scepticism hardens, this stylistic feature of his work is given a vital role in expressing it. In *Thérèse Raquin*, the utter amoral physicality of the characters – 'des personnages souverainement dominés par leurs nerfs', in whom 'l'âme est parfaitement absente' (I, 519–20) – is underlined by the way in which they emerge from amidst a mass of objects. The opening description of Madame Raquin's shop moves from paving-stones to walls to windows, then to gaslights and cheap jewellery and bonnets, and to the face of Thérèse, peering motionlessly and impassively through the shop-window.

It is *La Faute de l'abbé Mouret* which illustrates this feature of Zola's writing best. Conversely, the sense of this phrase, in that novel, 'une victoire pour les bêtes, les plantes, *les choses*', is clarified by what has just been said. Nature's invasion of Mouret's church is only part of a larger-scale invasion of the spiritual by the physical, with concrete objects in the vanguard of the attack. The opening paragraph is a polemical text in miniature. Serge's housekeeper La Teuse props her broom and feather duster against the altar, crosses the church to ring the Angelus, bumping into pews as she goes, grips the knotted bell-rope in her fists and hangs on it, skirts rolling, bonnet askew, blood rushing to her broad face. For a novel about the moral dilemmas of priestly celibacy, the opening is startlingly and aggressively pitched at the level of the low mimetic. Ordinary life has occupied the sanctum. The altar, meeting place between Man and Christ, becomes, through the juxtaposition of La Teuse's humble accessories, just another object. So do the sacred vessels, which La Teuse sweeps unceremoniously into her zinc bucket: they are objects to be scrubbed clean like any other. As for the priest's vestment, kept in 'un ancien buffet de cuisine' (III, 20), they are going the way of all matter, reaching the point of no repair. Even holy objects are of this world, whatever may be their supposed representation of the next.

There are many such ironic juxtapositions in the Rougon-Macquart novels. Muffat, in his despair at Nana's irresistible hold on him, 'pensa à Dieu', goes into a church, tries to pray; but 'rien ne répondait': the only reality is that of the sound of clogs echoing down the aisle (IV, 182). At the end of '*L'Œuvre*, the priest's prayers at Claude Lantier's grave have to compete with the roar of a passing railway engine, and its presence draws the text away from elegiac piety to geometric lines of telegraph wires; the physical reality of the modern industrial world, which Claude the painter had ignored to the detriment of his art, manifests itself more forcefully than religious ritual. In *La Terre*, the threat to the Church's role in rural societies is embodied in the encroaching rain and patches of mould cutting in two the face of God in a mouldering fresco (V, 797). Religious objects, *objets de culte*, are often demystified by the proximity of humbler objects, reminding us that all is matter: in the disorder of the Campardou family's apartment in *Pot-Bouille*, 'des cartons s'écroulaient parmi des vêtements à Gasparine, la vierge au cœur saignant gisait contre le mur, calée par une cuvette neuve' (IV, 510).

Zola is not alone among Realist or Naturalist novelists in exploiting such effects, for similar examples abound in both Flaubert's and Maupassant's work. The room where the old servant Félicité, in the first of the *Trois Contes*, keeps her parrot Loulou 'avait l'air à la fois d'une chapelle et d'un bazar tant il contenait d'objets religieux et de choses hétéroclites'. On a table are a water-jug, two combs, a cube of blue soap in a chipped dish; hanging on the walls, rosaries, medallions, a collection of Holy Virgins, a coconut holy-water bowl – all of them equally arbitrary and without significance (I, 617). In *Fort comme la mort*, the scene switches abruptly from the great oak Christ, in front of which the countess is praying, to the face-powders, creams and hairbrushes which the lady wields 'avec une tension de pensée aussi ardente que pour la prière' (316). The crucifix, a present from her lover and fraught with associations other than pious, is reduced to the status of a talismanic object, an emblem of just one of the countess's cults.

Realist novelists' indefatigable attraction to religious objects can even be seen in *Les Bourgeois de Molinchart*, that humdrum account of provincial life by the earnest Champfleury. In this novel, the old spinster Ursule Creton harbours in her home a curious museum of bones and other alleged relics of saints, together with two wax Christ-children in cotton wigs and, most prized possession of all, a three-dimensional representation of the Crucifixion, with tiny nails, hammer, sponge and vinegar-flask, the whole thing placed in a bottle like a model sailing-ship, and animated when vigorously shaken. At the other end of Realism's broad literary scale, Jacques Arnoux, in Flaubert's *L'Éducation sentimentale*, sells grotesque objects like these in the last phase of his slide into the world of commercial art. The narrator compares Arnoux's public show of religious zeal with the erratic behaviour of someone who has suffered a stroke, but Arnoux has not lost his senses altogether: it is 'pour faire son salut et sa fortune' that he turns to this latest business venture – a well timed one, for, following 1848, a new pro-clerical era has dawned. Such personal and political sarcasm, important though it is, hardly accounts, however, for the length and detail of Flaubert's description of the sanctimonious bric-à-brac cluttering Arnoux's shop window:

> Aux deux coins de la vitrine s'élevaient deux statues en bois, bariolées d'or, de cinabre et d'azur; un saint Jean-Baptiste avec sa peau de mouton, et une sainte Geneviève, des roses dans son tablier et une quenouille sous son bras; puis des groupes en plâtre: une bonne sœur instruisant une petite fille, une mère à genoux près d'une couchette, trois collégiens devant la sainte table. Le plus joli était une manière de chalet figurant l'intérieur de la crèche, avec l'âne, le bœuf et l'Enfant Jésus sur de la paille, de la vraie paille. Du haut en bas des étagères, on voyait des médailles à la douzaine, des chapelets de toute espèce, des bénitiers en forme de coquille et les portraits des gloires ecclésiastiques, parmi lesquelles Monseigneur Affre et notre Saint-Père, tous deux souriant. (II,425)

Something more profound than topical satire and mild irreverence to the Pope and to the archbishop of Paris, Monseigneur Affre, is going on in passages like this. Their recurrent theme is the way in which the most sacred of concepts, beliefs and personages are translated into the most banal concrete form. When Emma Bovary's ecstatic dreams of '[les] envahissements de la grâce [. . .], des félicités plus grandes, un autre amour flottant au-dessus de la terre' devolve into the materiality of rosaries and amulets and the desire for emerald-studded reliquaries on which to press her lips (I, 486–7), she is simply readapting to the norms of the human condition: to life in a world of objects. The contrast is striking between the vagueness of the mystical aspirations expressed through Flaubert's choice clichés and the specificity of the objects that come to represent them. These objects, for all their tawdriness, have a reality – a manger 'avec *de la vraie paille*' – grounded in common experience. Sœur Philomène's silk-collared Virgin and wax Jesus (193) exude a physicality which challenges the substance of their referent. Belief in a spiritual and supernatural domain, on which the Christian concept of reality has been founded for two thousand years, is dependent on the physical for intelligible expression, and in this dependence lies its vulnerability. Religion emerges, in Realist novels, as the product of our responses to material images, beyond which lie, literally, nothing. Marcel, the man-servant of Bouvard and Pécuchet, is seen dusting his masters' wax Baptist and star-crowned Virgin, and 'n'imaginant rien au paradis de plus beau' (II, 924); as usual, Flaubert's irony hits the nail on the head. There is nothing in paradise, more beautiful or otherwise.

In questioning the very existence of the dimension to which religious objects allegedly refer, these novelists are paradoxically reversing a process which contributes to the richness of Realist discourse. Objects in the nineteenth-century novel, as well as reflecting character and situation and providing a solidity that underpins the authenticity of the fiction, are often accorded a symbolical function. Charles Bovary's famous hat, or the bouquet from his first wedding, are objects which contain layers of implied meaning. In the case of the still in *L'Assommoir* or the mine in *Germinal*, the symbolic significance so out-distances the initiating object as to create a mythical level of meaning. Yet religious objects, which outside the context of Realism have traditional symbolic associations, are deliberately emptied of such significance, refused enlargement into myth. They are subjected to a levelling process: they are objects like other objects, no more and no less. Flaubert, attending the christening of his niece a decade before writing *Madame Bovary*, and observing the baptismal water and flickering candles, unconsciously anticipated what he and other novelists were to make of such phenomena: 'En contemplant tous ces symboles insignifiants pour nous', he writes, 'je me faisais l'effet d'assister à quelque cérémonie d'une religion lointaine exhumée de sa poussière'; and he goes on to describe the greater substantiality of real objects, unpretentiously juxtaposed with the alleged message-bearing paraphernalia of the Church: 'Ce qu'il y avait de plus intelligent à coup sûr, c'était les pierres qui avaient autrefois compris tout cela et qui peut-être en avaient retenu quelque chose' (FC I, 262). In *Madame Bovary*, when symbolic significance is restored to sacred objects, it is on a purely temporary basis and for strictly deflationary purposes. As Emma lies dying, Bournisien 'essaya de lui mettre dans la main un cierge bénit, symbole des gloires célestes dont elle allait tout à l'heure être environnée. Emma, trop faible, ne put fermer les doigts, et le cierge, sans Monsieur Bournisien, serait tombé à terre' (I, 588). Even blessed candles are subject to Newton's laws, need the support of flesh-and-blood hands and are sometimes saved from contact with the earth by priests who appear, like *Monsieur* Bournisien, to lose their elevating titles in the process.

A special role is given to religious statues and pictorial representations. Emma, so moved in her convent days by pious vignettes, finds on arrival at Yonville a statue of the Virgin to test even her low aesthetic threshold, and which is described in terms that suggest its crudely idolatrous function: 'tout empourprée aux pommettes comme une idole des îles Sandwich' (I, 356). The Saint Peter owned by Bouvard and Pécuchet has 'les joues fardées, de gros yeux ronds, la bouche béante, le nez de travers et en trompette' (II, 799). Sometimes, strings of references to such statues form structural patterns in texts. The Virgin to whom Philomène prays 'comme on prie l'espérance' (50), is succeeded by the bronze Christ which the anti-religious doctor Barnier sees as an appropriate image of a deaf and implacable deity (51), and Philomène herself, in the final scene of the novel, becomes a metaphorical statue, an image of religion's lifelessness: 'Elle s'agenouilla et elle pria comme prient les statues d'église agenouillées dans le marbre: sa robe ne bougeait pas plus sur elle que le drap ne remuait sur le mort' (245). The pattern is repeated in *Madame Gervaisais*, as pagan statues and gaudy Christs give way to an image of the Pope as a statue, while the 'rocaille luxurieuse' (175) of religious statuary is ironically mocked many pages later by the echoing 'hideuse rocaille' (259) of the ossuary in the Catacombs.

Zola, for his part, did not like statues, seeing sculpture as the outmoded art of a theological age – in a word, as sheer fetishism. The news that a halo of gaslights was to be constructed around the head of Joan of Arc's statue at Orléans was seized by him as, so to speak, a heaven-sent opportunity to mock the clerical party, and he responded with equal glee to the installation of an electric organ in Saint-Augustin (XIII, 231). What next? he asked. An electric burning bush? The joke reappears in Maupassant's *Bel-Ami*, when the Jewish financier Walter invites his Catholic business associates to view his newly acquired painting of Christ walking on the waters, 'éclairée à la lumière électrique' (479), while Zola uses a wooden Virgin in *Le Docteur Pascal* as a foil for the vitality of Clotilde, and in *Pot-Bouille* allows a statue of the same holy personage to be transported across the church by two workmen, 'comme une grande fille blanche, tombée raide d'une attaque nerveuse' (IV, 516).

It would be easy to list many more examples of this sort in Realist fiction.Their sheer frequency points to a seriousness beneath the humour. The question of how men represent God is a preoccupation of the Goncourts. They imagine him in various physical guises: as a white-haired old man, 'ainsi que les membres de l'Institut le peignent dans les coupoles des églises' (I, 41), as an official with a rainbow draped around his waist like the belt of a police commissioner (I, 120), or as a 'Bartholo céleste' with a handful of keys, winding up the heavenly bodies before retiring at night (II, 133). But the fondest images are those of their friends at Magny's:

> Les formules pleuvent. Contre nous, plastiques, qui ne le concevons, s'il existe, que comme une personnalité, comme un être figuré, un bon Dieu à la Michel-Ange avec une barbe, Taine et Renan et Berthelot jettent des définitions hégéliennes, le montrent dans une diffusion immense et vague dont les mondes ne seraient que des globules, des morpions. [. . .] Renan arrive à comparer Dieu, son Dieu à lui, le plus religieusement et le plus sérieusement du monde, à une huître! (VII, 213)

The very need to 'see' God, the impulse towards visualisation, significantly stronger for the brothers, endowed with the 'plastic' imagination of art critics and novelists, than for philosophers more at home (oysters apart) in abstraction, throws further light on the emerging gulf between Christianity and literary Realism. In a moment of fantasy, Jules and Edmond picture themselves summoned before the Almighty on Judgement Day and asked to account, not just for what they have *done*, but also for what they have *seen* (I, 41). Seeing is postulated as a prime factor in human experience, as Man's principal mode of cognisance and the starting-point for his interpretation of his environment. 'Je suis un homme pour qui le monde visible existe,' the Goncourts approvingly quote the novelist Villemessant as saying (II, 103). What we see, we take to exist – which renders religion instantly problematic, based, as the brothers say, on devotion 'pour un dieu qu'on ne voit pas' (IV, 132). God's invisibility drives men to rely on plastic representations of him. These are often aesthetically crass, and produce a repugnance in men like Flaubert, who writes from Jerusalem to Louis Bouilhet of 'un Christ taillé en bas-relief, grandeur naturelle et épouvantable avec ses côtes peintes en rouge' (FC I, 666), or generate scepticism as to the truth of what they purport to represent: 'tout cela ment,' Flaubert adds in the same letter, 'tout cela ment'.

The Goncourts express in medical and ocular imagery the centrality of the visible in nineteenth-century culture in general and in its novels in particular. 'Le dix-neuvième siècle,' they write, 'a opéré l'humanité de la cataracte' (VII, 240). Previous literature they designate as 'une littérature de presbyte, c'est-à-dire, d'ensemble', compared with the 'littérature de myope, c'est-à-dire, de détails' (VI, 75) to which they themselves were leading contributors. The very type of modern literature, to them, was *Madame Bovary*, in which objects were as much alive as characters, milieux as important as passions: 'C'est une œuvre qui peint aux yeux, bien plus qu'elle ne parle à l'âme. La partie la plus noble et la plus forte de l'œuvre tient beaucoup plus de la peinture que de la littérature. C'est le stéréoscope poussé à sa dernière illusion' (IV, 124). Such evaluation was not without ambivalence. For a pair so proud of being of one mind (their diary, they promised, would be the work of 'un seul *moi* [. . .] et un seul *je'* [I, 29]), the brothers were, this time, in two. While conceding that Flaubert's novel was 'le dernier mot du vrai dans le roman', they deemed it to lack the imaginative wealth of the less true *Paul et Virginie* (IV, 124). And, having identified Flaubert's art as akin to that of the painter, they developed the idea in conflicting directions, arguing at times that painting is inferior to literature because its domain is the purely material (V, 51), and at other moments describing painting as a noble art, addressing itself to the soul, while literature, because '[elle] peut et doit descendre jusqu'au peuple, au laid et à l'horrible', connives at shocking the eyes (VI, 199). But despite these contradictions, their discussion draws attention to certain close associations in Realist novels between writing and painting. Several novelists create characters who act as spokesmen for their own artistic credo (or else as ironic figures, voicing 'wrong' views of art). These characters are often writers – the Goncourts' Demailly, Zola's Sandoz, Huysmans' Durtal; but they are, at least as frequently, painters: the Goncourts' Coriolis, Huysmans' Cyprien Tibaille, Maupassant's Bertin, Zola's Claude Lantier. 'Ah! tout voir et tout peindre!' exclaims the last-named of these, embracing in his painter's eye the cosmos that Zola was committed to capturing in words (V, 467). The identification is a key one in the analysis of Realist writing. The latter depends on a whole range of sense impressions, including Zola's celebrated olfactory sensibilities; but visual effects, and visual techniques, dominate. The character's-eye-view is paramount; narrative angles are sought from which to survey the seen world and merge optical impression with psychological reflection. Octave Mouret's habitual stance on the stairs of his department store – 'en haut de l'escalier de l'entresol, contre la rampe' (IV, 799) – not only represents his authority over the sales staff, but also provides the text with a vantage point from which the reader's gaze can be directed down into the body of the shop and prepared for the multiplicity of visual images on which the evocation of Zola's world rests. The opening scenes of both *Germinal* and *L'Œuvre*, in which the illusion of the physical setting is created through the eyes of the newly arrived outsider acting as surrogate reader, or the first chapter of the Goncourts' *Manette Salomon*, in which the eye follows Anatole, the guide in the Jardin des Plantes, up the slope to the Labyrinth from where a panoramic view is presented of the whole physical milieu of the novel – these are further examples amongst the many that could be listed. And even when no characters are invoked to serve as our eyes, when only narrator and reader are present at the outset of a descriptive passage, an opening 'on *voyait* . . .' is a staple element of Zola's technique.

The world of the Realist novelist is the world of the seen, and its discourse is geared to the recording of the visible. The Goncourts, describing midnight mass in the village church of Champigny, render what is visible, including the inevitable gaudy statue of the Virgin as well as 'l'haleine visible, blanche et lumineuse' of the priest (VII, 36). Their language makes no attempt to penetrate beyond these surfaces, for that is not its domain. Likewise, that of Zola can only show the images of Serge Mouret's faith, his words feeding on visible artefacts. Flaubert, describing the Holy Land, can use the language of the seen – 'J'ai regardé la ville sainte, tout étonné de la voir. [. . .] Puis j'ai pensé au Christ que j'avais vu monter sur le mont des Oliviers, Il avait une robe bleue, et la sueur perlait sur ses tempes'; but then he reveals to his correspondent that the source of this vision is not miraculous, but aesthetic: he is recreating in his mind's eye a fresco seen in a church on the eve of his departure (FC I, 664). Seeing miracles is possible only in art, not in reality. There is a Realist novelist lurking in Flaubert's Antipas, for when Jacob exclaims: 'Jésus fait des miracles!', the narrator adds: 'Antipas désirait en voir' (II, 670). Pécuchet whispers to Bouvard when they stumble across Marcel fervently praying to his blue plaster Virgin: 'Il assiste peut-être à des choses que tu lui jalouserais, si tu pouvais les voir' (II, 953). The religious quest of Flaubert's indefatigable searchers, in his final and unfinished novel, stops at the boundaries of the seen, for the genre and its language can take them no further.

The aesthetic of Realism is closely associated with the notion that seeing is believing, and if ever it required a patron saint, the choice could only fall on Thomas. Readers are often placed in the role of doubters towards characters' visual deceptions and optical delusions, have sinister and even frightening aspects, as in the case of Élisa's pathetic lover in Edmond de Goncourt's novel, whose superstitious 'visions' lead to obsessions with hellfire and fear of demons disguised as white wolves. More usually the delusion is used simply to underline the gullibility of the victim, like Renée Mauperin, who swears she has seen her Virgin nod her head approvingly to her. Renée admits that it was probably an effect of the light, and the same rational explanation is offered of the visions of Satan that trouble Flaubert's Saint-Antoine: 'C'est la torche, sans doute, qui faisait un jeu de lumière' (I, 35). Emma Bovary's hallucinations, however, are left uncorrected, except by subtle modulations of narrative voice:

> Alors elle laissa retomber sa tête, croyant entendre dans les espaces le chant des harpes séraphiques et apercevoir en un ciel d'azur, sur un trône d'or, au milieu des saints tenant des palmes vertes, Dieu le Père éclatant de majesté, et qui d'un signe faisait descendre vers la terre des anges aux ailes de flamme pour l'emporter dans leurs bras. (I, 486)

The most perfect model in Flaubert's work, and perhaps in the whole Realist corpus, of how the religious imagination is shaped by, and reshapes in turn, visual perceptions of reality is to be found in *Un cœur simple*. There is a passage in the third chapter of the tale which describes the old servant Félicité trying, as she listens to a sermon in church, to assimilate religious concepts to the experience of her eyes. It moves through fine gradations from what she can actually see to what she can visually imagine, then to the less easily visualisable and finally to areas of abstraction where her mind cannot take her because the eyes cannot lead the way. The starting-point, significantly, is a pictorial representation, in stained glass, of the Holy Ghost surveying the Virgin and Christ-child, flanked by a victorious Saint Michael. Her eyes thus stimulated, Félicité, as the sermon unfolds, 'croyait voir le paradis, le déluge, la tour de Babel'; inner pictures of the Passion drive her to tears, lead her by association to images of Christ's humility, his birth in the stable, his life amidst creatures and objects made sacred by his presence. Lambs are sanctified by the Lamb, doves by the symbolic Dove of the Holy Ghost. Christ himself she finds hard to visualise, thinks of him as fire or wind; and as for dogma, 'elle n'y comprenait rien' (II, 601).

The basis has thus been laid for Félicité's confusion of the demarcations between the visible and the supernatural, a confusion that Flaubert treats with a combination of sympathy and irony, the one tone nourished by the other. 'Pour de pareilles âmes,' the narrator comments respectfully after describing how the old woman, kissing the dead body of her mistress' daughter, half expects to see her come to life, 'le surnaturel est tout simple' (II, 609). More particularly, having established the association in Félicité's head between bird and Holy Ghost, the former image can now be linked to her stuffed parrot, Loulou, which she ends up by seeing as the Third Person of the Trinity. The crucial step comes by pure chance: as Félicité, in distress at life's material difficulties, implores the Holy Ghost's help, she happens to be looking at Loulou, and this haphazard use of the parrot as a kind of visual aid for the abstract concept hardens into habit, helped in turn by reflections of light rebounding from the bird's glass eye and producing 'un grand rayon lumineux qui la mettait en extase' (II, 619). On the day of the old woman's death, the association is completed. The verb '*croire* voir', used in the passage quoted above to describe the start of her confusion, reappears at the end to confirm it, and to frame the whole of her religious experience between two optical misreadings: 'Quand elle exhala son dernier souffle, elle crut voir, dans les cieux entr'ouverts, un perroquet gigantesque, planant au-dessus de sa tête' (II, 622). Flaubert's compassion for his character at this point in the text is total, but through his choice of a stuffed parrot as the object of her devotion, he engineers the collapse of supernatural belief into unambivalent delusion.

* * *

'Religion' exists for the Realists, but is always grounded in the tangible and the human. Germinie Lacerteux loves her mistress 'religieusement, [. . .] avec l'ardeur d'une expiation, la contrition d'une prière, l'élancement d'un culte' (GL, 73). Love, even sexual love, is recognised as a religious instinct by Clotilde in *Le Docteur Pascal*. For the painter Coriolis in *Manette Salomon*, nature is the focus of religious emotion, and art the true miracle. Ideals such as utopian socialism can be described as religions, and indeed are in both *Germinal* and *La Débâcle*. To Zola, religion was any enthusiasm characterised by quasi-mystical fervour; it was defined by its intensity as an inner state rather than by the truth of its referent. This intensity could be experienced as fear, and thus the capitalist system, mercilessly crushing the working class, becomes a menacing god, its temples, as in *Germinal*, described in the language of church architecture. Commerce too is a religion, a profitable diverting of woman's religious nature to the veneration of fashion, a new cult of which the altar is built in Mouret's department store, 'la cathédrale du commerce moderne' (IV, 889), 'cette chapelle élevée au culte des grâces de la femme' (IV, 711). Even vice can be the focus of religious awe, a drink-shop transformed into a cathedral (III, 919); and so can lust – the same image is used to describe the female sex organs in *La Terre* (V, 954). In Realist and Naturalist writing, especially in Zola's, Diderot's exhortation 'Élargissez Dieu!' is obeyed with unprecedented energy, and its effect is to dilute the unique status of the God of Christianity.

The very enterprise of Realism, its conquering of new horizons, was accompanied by a sense of missionary zeal. The Goncourts express this in a characteristically mocking way in *Charles Demailly*, when the critic Couturat echoes both Genesis and New Testament in his playful deflation of the avant-garde novelist Pommageot, who has just produced what sounds from its title – *Les Amours d'un donneur d'eau bénite* – like a classic of the Realist genre:

> Vive Pommageot! le réalisme était en Pommageot, et Pommageot était en réalisme! A bas les phrases! Brûlons un poète! Vive Pommageot! Pommageot, fils de la Vérité! Des lampions! des lampions! Enfoncé Balzac! Monsieur est ton ami? Ça se voit! Messieurs! Pommageot et son ami, Dieu et son peuple, c'est comme cela que commence la Bible! (CD, 34–5)

Whatever weight one gives to Pommageot, or to Couturat, the Goncourts' own commitment to describing the world in a wholly secular context is beyond doubt. Edmond's heroine Élisa, stumbling on a *cabinet de lecture*, reads novels inspired by the religious revival of the Restoration, in which the theme of pilgrimage mingles with pious legend, pirate stories and tales of platonic love, and religion becomes romance. The Goncourts' failed painter Anatole, who lacks the authors' passion for 'l'étude d'après nature', for 'la vie qui pose là devant le regard', for 'la lutte acharnée, passionnée, de la main de l'artiste contre la réalité visible' (MS, 103–4), is a slave to a lifeless and academic style of painting typified by dull religious subjects, like his own canvas 'Le Christ humanitaire'. Ironically, Anatole lives close to the very nature which, artistically, he spurns, through his job as a guide in the Jardin des Plantes. In the same novel, another painter, Crescent, is at least a *paysagiste*, but he too allows an outmoded religiosity to produce conventionally pantheistic representations of nature. A third painter, the central male character of *Manette Salomon*, Coriolis, shows the way with his 'modern' paintings. The first, 'Un conseil de révision', is a naturalistic depiction of officials and civil servants. The second, 'Un mariage à l'église', illustrates once more how religious subjects and settings serve as foils for Realism: the picture shows an apparently conventional church interior, but divested of piety. The interest centres on the ordinary couple who are being married and on their families. Priests are present, naturally, and are drawn with deflating frivolity but humanised by everyday objective details: 'deux spirituelles silhouettes de prêtres, en surplis, dont l'un se chatouillait les lèvres avec le pompon de sa barrette', while the figure of an old woman at prayer is transformed from pious image into social comment by her 'bonnet sale et troué' (322). Coriolis' next canvas, a painting of the beach at Trouville, is also interesting for its simultaneous inclusion and reduction of an element that occupies an increasingly small place in the contemporary imagination, and seen as if through the wrong end of a telescope: 'Et tout au bout de la plage, au bord de l'écume de la première vague, tout seul, un vieux petit curé s'apercevait tout en noir, lisant son bréviaire en longeant l'immensité' (332). Finally, adding his arguments to Coriolis' examples, another painter, Chassagnol, described by Ricatte as the Goncourts' *porte-parole*,[25] defines the aims of the new 'école de l'Ironie' as 'une création contre la Création, une reconstruction de l'univers par l'homme, le remplacement de l'œuvre divine par quelque chose de plus humain, de plus conforme au *moi fini*, une bataille contre Dieu!' (420–1).

The equation of Christianity with the outmoded in art, expressed by the Goncourts through their painters, is applied to the domain of architecture by another painter, Zola's Claude Lantier. All the arts, Claude tells his friend Dubuche in *L'Œuvre*, are subject to evolutionary pressures. Along with literature, painting and music, architecture must mirror its age, in which Christianity is as philosophically redundant as Greek myth: 'Par terre, les temples grecs qui n'avaient plus leurs raisons d'être sous notre ciel, au milieu de notre société! par terre, les cathédrales gothiques puisque la foi aux légendes était morte!' (V, 546). In his enthusiasm for the 'siècle neuf' and the 'nouveau peuple' that it will spawn, Claude echoes the slogan 'À peuple nouveau, art nouveau!' with which Hugo had welcomed another revolution, that of Romanticism. The same source and the same fictional character combine in an earlier novel to express the same idea even more graphically. In *Le Ventre de Paris*, Claude and the escaped convict Florent walk together under the covered galleries of the Halles, 'où leurs pas sonnaient comme sous la voûte d'une église', and from this metaphorical church their gaze falls upon a real one, the old edifice of Saint-Eustache, its side door framed within the wrought iron girders of the market buildings. Claude, on Zola's behalf, 'voulait y trouver un symbole', and an (unacknowledged) borrowing from Hugo helps him find it: 'Ceci tuera cela' (II, 732). The phrase is, of course, the title of a chapter in *Notre-Dame de Paris*, in which Hugo meditates on the supplanting of the symbolic mediaeval language of architecture by the printed word. Zola uses it to signify the conquest of industrial iron over ecclesiastical stone, in which he sees a paradigm of the defeat of the ancient by the modern: 'Voyez-vous, il y a tout un manifeste,' says Claude; 'c'est l'art moderne, le réalisme, le naturalisme, comme vous voudrez l'appeler, qui a grandi en face de l'art ancien' (ibid.). Realism or Naturalism – Zola uses these words interchangeably – is thus not a mere aesthetic code. It is the spirit of the modern, the inevitable coming of which signals change at the heart of the entire culture. The defeat of the Church in its architectural forms is the symptom of its demise as institution, God's masons are dead, says Claude, and nobody really believes that God lives in the dwellings they built for him. The levelling process by which sacred objects revert to the status of matter is at work on churches as well as on rosaries or crucifixes; modern churches, says Claude, are indistinguishable from libraries, observatories or barracks. Zola surreptitiously aids the process by conferring on his mines, shops and markets the status of cathedrals. They are the churches of the new religion of modernity for which Realism is a synonym. Zola's erection of this new cult on the ruins of the old will be the subject of a separate chapter, but he is already writing its liturgy in the third volume of the Rougon-Macquart.

* * *

The evidence accumulated in this chapter of Realism's challenge to Christianity has been drawn from a wide spectrum of major texts by Realism's principal authors, written over a period of virtually half a century but revealing, for the most part, an astonishing conformity of attitude. It establishes that any definition of Realism which does not allocate a central role to this challenge is seriously incomplete and even misleading. Far from being a peripheral aspect of Realism, it was an element which united otherwise divergent talents, and which affords an angle from which one can legitimately speak of Realism as a coherent intellectual phenomenon. Because of its focus on tangible and visible reality, Realism was bound to challenge Christianity's belief in a supernatural and spiritual order in its very nature as a literary mode. A Realist novel, despite what Stendhal said, is not a mirror held up to life, with all the chaotic formlessness which that would imply. More subtly, it seeks to create the illusion of life by a correspondence between what is accepted as plausible in fiction and what, on the evidence of observation and experience, is perceived as possible in life. It eschews the exceptional and rationalises the miraculous. It is the typical literary mode of the ironic or sceptical age, the age in which Nietzsche declared God to be dead (as did Zola in *Germinal* (V, 146)), the age in which it is hard to sustain beliefs that are not rooted in demonstrable fact. The subversion of Christianity, however, was not Realism's prime aim; indeed, the respect in which, in their private capacities, most of the practitioners of Realism held Christianity, was demonstrated at the beginning of this chapter. But this subversion was nevertheless necessary as part of Realism's justification of itself, of its areas of exploration and its techniques of description and narration. There was no room in the Realist aesthetic for the supernatural dimension on which revealed religion depends; and if there is no room for the supernatural *within* a Realist novel, neither can there be a place for it *outside*, for the novel, *tel qu'en lui-même enfin le réalisme le change*, has no 'outside'. It purports to be a total model of the possible. What it cannot contain aesthetically cannot exist philosophically. Artistic exclusion implies material annihilation. Even when the Realist novelist is not consciously writing in an anti-Christian or anticlerical vein, the very secularity and materiality of his assumptions force off the page all possibility of an extra-material order of things.

It is possible to speak of the gravitational pull between a literary genre and its conceptual content. Realism certainly exercised such a pull. The Goncourts felt it when they contemplated, with a surprise akin to that of first-time fathers, their newly delivered *Madame Gervaisais*. Where had it come from? How could they, the Goncourts – 'dont les sympathies de race et de peau penchent pour le pape' – have produced 'un livre méchant à l'Église'? By what 'force irrésistible qui est dans l'air'? 'Toujours la fatalité du livre,' they inadequately conclude, and add: 'Eh, que sait-on du pourquoi de ce qu'on écrit?' (VIII, 109–10). One could enlist this bewildered realisation of the gulf between the philosophical tolerance of citizens Jules and Edmond de Goncourt and the finished product of their literary labours in support of the tired old theory called the 'intentional fallacy', but its value in that context would only extend so far. One would search in vain for a committed Catholic writing despite himself a book like *La Faute de l'abbé Mouret*, or for an atheist unwittingly producing a *Journal d'un curé de campagne*. The act of writing does not transform beyond recognition the private convictions of the writer, or produce from nothing standpoints to which he would normally be opposed. But it magnifies existing and unconscious potentialities within him. The Goncourts had doubts, which their distaste for dogmatism prevented from hardening into out-and-out opposition to Christianity. But within the fictional world inhabited by Madame Gervaisais, the weight of the visible and the attraction of a life-affirming philosophy combine to create a novel inimical to Catholic orthodoxy.

Realism was the dominant, almost the official, mode of the novel throughout the second half of the nineteenth century, but its influence and significance extended far beyond that period. 'It may well be,' comments Cecil Jenkins, 'that Realism *was* the novel.'[26] Even after the polemically self-conscious period of Realism, and despite Proust and Gide and all the twentieth-century metamorphoses of the genre, the basically mimetic aesthetic of Realism, its dependence on the seen or on what can be imagined on the basis of the seen, remained the dominant mode of the novel, thus posing problems for the novelist who is also a Christian and who seeks a fictional mode of expression for his very different conception of reality. This, though, is to anticipate the later chapters of this book. It is time instead to discuss the work of a writer who, in the nineteenth-century heyday of Realism, already challenged its monopoly of the genre.

2

The Limping Devil of Barbey d'Aurevilly

The quasi-religious fervour with which the Realist novelist undertook the literary expression of his world is embodied in the pioneering writer Pommageot in the Goncourts' first novel *Charles Demailly*. In the same text, another character, a journalist haranguing his fellow writers in a crowded restaurant, espouses a more traditional kind of religious outlook. He attacks the current passion for the modern, mocks the fashionable 'physiological' explanation of traditional moral and religious concepts, and argues that original sin is the most significant fact in our lives. The Goncourts call this man Franchemont, but it is obvious, both from his external portrait – a flamboyant and merciless polemicist, an intransigent authoritarian, with blazing eyes and of exalted language – and from his own speech, sprinkled with references to historical or literary figures like Lauzun, Richelieu and Don Juan and with aphorisms enlivened by sexual paradox ('Une femme de génie est un homme'), that this is a thinly veiled caricature of the novelist and critic Jules-Amédée Barbey d'Aurevilly.[1] Barbey was an easy target for satire, with his overripe persona and outspoken defence of reactionary views, and with a personal reputation that jarred with his public support of Christian morality. But he was also the only novelist of any stature, between Balzac's death and the emergence of Huysmans and Bloy, to challenge the genre's seemingly inexorable anti-Christian trend.

As the Goncourts imply, Barbey's detestation of the intellectual climate of his age was the starting-point of his every attitude. The man-centred philosophy of modern times, he declares in the preface to *Les Prophètes du passé*, is, like all philosophies which do not place God at their heart, simply unintelligible; and he lays the blame squarely at the feet of Descartes, whose separation of philosophy from theology, he argues, created a schism more fundamental than the one perpetrated by Luther. The Cartesian Cogito, exploited and distorted by later thinkers, had led directly to the arrogant rationalism of the nineteenth century, to the new orthodoxy founded on Man's self-judgement. Thus did Barbey's imagination, fertilised by the counter-revolutionary notions of De Maistre and Bonald, create a new version of original sin by which Descartes' descendants are tainted. Of the Hegelian philosopher Charma, Barbey commented to his friend Trebutien: 'Ce n'est pas *sa* philosophie que je méprise, c'est la philosophie elle-même ainsi que Descartes nous l'a faite.'[2] He was particularly scathing of the Cartesians' traditional division of Man into body and soul, and stood nearer to Joseph de Maistre's view of the moral origin of sensation than to the physiological explanations of behaviour popular among the Realists. 'La soif morale,' he wrote, 'produit chez moi la soif du corps, tant il est vrai que l'on ne sait guères comment l'âme se distingue du corps dans cette fusion d'argile et d'éther qu'est l'homme!'[3] To him, human beings were 'pauvres machines [. . .] dont le mécanisme nous est inconnu' (II, 752), and his rejection of the intellectual optimism of his age, of its perception of the world as no more than ultimately decipherable matter, lay at the heart of his sense of spiritual exile.

Barbey was not always a Catholic, but even the free-thinking Barbey of the 1830s and 40s placed his trust less in reason than in imagination, and saw the crucial link between the latter and a sense of the divine. 'L'imagination,' he wrote in his early story *Léa*, 'est la seule faculté qui ne trouve pas sur son chemin la borne de l'incomprehensible. N'y a-t-il pas pour elle un Dieu?' (I, 30). Though imagination could deceive in this respect as in others – the same text evokes the suggestive purity of a starry night-sky 'qui parle d'un monde à venir et qui ment peut-être' (I, 42) – Barbey preferred its perilous liberty to the inhibiting safety of logic. The vehicle for the imagination's flights of fancy, however, was still, for the young Barbey as for the Realists, the world revealed by the eyes, by 'ces yeux du corps que rien ne remplace' (CG II, 195). 'Votre lettre,' he wrote to a friend travelling in Switzerland, 'm'a fait voir par les yeux de l'esprit – tristes yeux! – ce que vous voyez par les yeux du corps, que j'estime bien davantage. Vous savez que je suis un matérialiste grossier!' (CG II, 43). There is an element of jest here; there is none in a letter of the same period in which Barbey expresses to Trebutien his anguish at the gulf between himself and his brother Léon, who has just entered holy orders: 'Mon cœur bat pour les choses visibles; lui les tient en pitié' (CG I, 230).

Barbey's espousal of Catholicism strengthened his artistic estrangement from his age. From his announcement to Trebutien: 'J'ai fait mes Pâques, samedi dernier, cinq de mai [1855], au maître-autel de Saint-Sulpice' (CG IV, 212), his criticism of contemporary culture focused on its anti-Christian aspects. The Great Exhibition of the same year signified for him 'l'adoration du Très-Saint-Sacrement de la Matière, les Quarante-heures de tous les Cochons de volupté ou de bien-être qui s'appelle le XIXe siècle. Une pareille fête date ère de la fin de toute pensée, de toute âme, de toute forte spiritualité' (CG IV, 222). He had already forged, as this example shows, the vituperative polemical style of which the most frequent targets were fellow novelists, from Stendhal, whose 'matérialisme' he found 'presque crapuleux',[4] to the Goncourts – dubbed by him, after a celebrated contemporary grave-robber, 'ces Sergeant-Bertrand de la littérature'[5] – and above all Zola, the arch-enemy, whose novels he greeted with a succession of destructive reviews. Zola, he wrote, 'a voulu travailler exclusivement dans le Dégoûtant'; he was '[un] Hercule souillé qui remue le fumier d'Augias et qui y ajoute', 'un Michel-Ange de la crotte' (OH XVIII, 223–31).

Barbey's literary criticism, collected in the twenty-six volumes of *Les Œuvres et les hommes*, reveals a finer critical sense than such personalised abuse might suggest. These two faces of his writing were in truth interdependent, his sharper perceptions honed by the same passion as provoked the explosive outbursts. His approach was not a crudely moralising one, but was based on taste, enriched by his ability to reach beyond technical considerations to their philosophical base. He might have said, before Sartre, that a novelist's technique reflects his metaphysics, for his critical method is founded on precisely this conviction. He argues in an essay on Duranty that the latter's recourse to banal phenomena as key elements of plot – he quotes the shower of rain at the end of *Les Malheurs d'Henriette Gérard* which makes the heroine change her entire life's plan – is a symptom not just of lack of imagination but of the general rejection of the sublime that lies at the root of Realism (OH IV, 282–5). He identified in the discourse of many nineteenth-century novels a challenge to a Christian sense of life. The author of *Madame Bovary*, he remarked, 'n'a point de spiritualité. Il doit être un matérialiste de doctrine comme il l'est de style, car une telle nature ne saurait être inconséquente' (OH IV, 61). He reiterated, in a review of *L'Éducation sentimentale*, the same view of a Flaubertian vision of life embodied less tellingly in thematic content than in sheer style and form (OH XVIII, 91).

This critical instinct led him to identify the subversive nature of both *Madame Gervaisais* and *La Faute de l'abbé Mouret*. In the former, he argued, the Goncourts' analyses of a purely physical dimension of life were more like those of entomologists than novelists: they had stripped away the sublimity of religious conversion and planted a knife deeply between the shoulder-blades of Catholicism (OH XVIII, 41). In the latter, beneath Zola's alleged scientific impartiality, there lay, he said, a deliberate polemical aim. In defining this, Barbey identified Zola's Naturalism, more starkly than other conservative critics of the day who were content to revile Zola's so-called coarseness and obscenity, as a conscious counter to Christian idealism. 'C'est le naturalisme de la bête,' he wrote, 'mis, sans honte et sans vergogne, au-dessus du noble spiritualisme chrétien!' He seized on the final scene of the book as the epitome of this ideology, seeing the announcement of the simple-minded Désirée that her cow has given birth to a calf as 'la clé du monstrueux physiologisme' of the novel. Albine, he reminds us, has just died at her own hands, abandoned by the priest who has made her pregnant, and in consolation for the loss of an immortal soul Zola offers us the birth of an animal. Between this Naturalism and Christianity, Barbey goes on, there is more than a question of literary taste; there is a fundamental divergence of values.

The critical reviews of Barbey often echo, or are echoed by, his own fictional writings, and the latter often assume the same polemical role. One example is 'A un dîner d'athées', one of the six stories in *Les Diaboliques*. The framework of the tale – the regular Friday dinners of a group of hard-bitten ex-soldiers, anti-clerical doctors, lapsed monks and married priests, timed to begin at the same hour as the Pope's dinner in Rome – probably has its historical source, as Jacques Petit suggests (II, 1324) in a dinner given by Sainte-Beuve on Good Friday 1868, but it also has obvious parallels with Barbey's review of *Madame Gervaisais*, in which he imputes the irreligious irony of the novel to the influence of the authors' fellow diners at Magny's, and broadens his attack into a diatribe against all such 'dîners contre Dieu' (OH XVIII, 43). His analysis of the Goncourts' surreptitious anti-Catholicism, which he contrasts scornfully with the frank incredulity of the eighteenth century, is amplified in the story by a further series of contrasts. The fictional diners have lived through the fire of the Revolution. Unlike the erudite cynics of a more scientific age, their atheism is built on the experience of implacable horror. One of them, the well-named abbé Reniant, is the embodiment of the destructive spirit of the Revolution, and the story he tells of the feeding of communion hosts to pigs lets loose a flood of impiety on the part of his approving listeners. According to Petit (loc. cit.), Barbey shows his admiration for the excesses of this brand of atheism. It certainly provides the pretext for the violence so crucial to his style, but the weight of the narrative pulls rather in the contrary direction, with the central figure of Mesnilgrand taking to a church the heart of the dead child whose story is related in the horrific final sequence. This softening of the impious Mesnilgrand casts a correspondingly negative light on his unrepentant colleagues, whose atheism, it is implied, is the mere outward sign of religion's tenacious hold on their consciences at a deeper level. Like another of their number, Rançonnet, they all have 'l'idée de Dieu dans l'esprit, comme une mouche dans le nez' (II, 192).

The theme of unrepentance recurs in another story in the same volume, 'Le Bonheur dans le crime', in which two lovers live in blissful remorselessness despite having conspired to kill the man's wife. Similarities between this tale and Zola's *Thérèse Raquin*[6] have been dismissed as coincidental by Petit, who sees its origin in an anecdote related by Barbey's friend Yvarn-Freissinet and sketched by Barbey in a letter to Trebutien as early as 1854, more than a decade before Zola's novel was written (II, 1281–2). However, the possibility remains that at the time of preparing the story for its publication in 1874, Barbey was aware of its potential as an ironic reply to Zola. Just a year earlier, in a review of *Le Ventre de Paris*, he referred to the forthcoming stage version of *Thérèse Raquin* in terms that suggested a recent re-reading of the novel. The latter, he said, was less depraved than the most recent offering of its progressively degenerate author. Unlike the catalogue of *charcuterie* that was *Le Ventre de Paris*, it dealt at least with a human subject, with 'les épouvantables remords des natures physiques' (OH XVIII, 202). This is a direct echo of Zola's description of Thérèse's lover Laurent: 'Ses remords étaient purement physiques'.[7] But what Barbey then says about the remorse of Zola's protagonists – that it is 'plus fort que leur abrutissement' – shows him differentiating, as Zola refused to do, between physical and psychological categories. Barbey reopens here an old dispute about how far Zola succeeded in creating a purely physiological form of guilt. Try as he might to ascribe Laurent's hallucinatory visions of the murdered Camille to sheer physical fear – to 'ses nerfs irrités et sa chair tremblante'; insist though he will that 'le misérable n'éprouvait pas un repentir; la passion de Thérèse lui avait communiqué un mal effroyable, et c'était tout', Zola did not convince every reader that he was not forcibly transposing familiar psychological categories to a physiological domain by sheer vehemence of language. Sainte-Beuve, for one, had argued this very point.[8] Read from this angle, Barbey's story functions as an ironic commentary on Zola's novel. Opening in that recurring site of Naturalist explanations of Man, the Jardin des Plantes (where Zola's Laurent obsessively observes the behaviour of animals), it is presented from the viewpoint of a doctor, a scientific observer of the type so common in Zola. He is hardly a neutral observer, however, being a declared opponent of Catholicism, and proudly announcing on which side of the ideological fence he stands. 'Le Médecin,' he tells the narrator, 'est le confesseur des temps modernes. [. . .] Il a remplacé le prêtre, Monsieur, et il est obligé au secret de la confession comme le prêtre' (II, 89). The key to deciphering such secrets lies for him in medical analysis, and the meaning of Barbey's text turns on the puncturing of this intellectual confidence. The doctor's microscopic examination of the implacable happiness of the murderous couple founders in the face of their absolute, diabolic refusal of moral guilt. Whereas the 'materialist' Zola creates characters in whom guilt should, logically, not exist but, dramatically, has to, the Catholic Barbey, more consistently, presents guiltlessness as the result of the free expulsion of God from the hearts of the criminal lovers. Barbey often expressed his desire to write 'en repoussoir de la cochonnerie zolaïenne'.[9] Whether or not he was doing so consciously in 'Le Bonheur dans le crime', reading the story alongside *Thérèse Raquin* provides a telling illustration of their diametrically opposed conceptions of the nature of Man.

The paradox of Barbey's critical stance, distinguishing his reviews from more typical products of the Catholic press, lay in his commitment to imaginative literature and to the novel, whose potential greatness he saw in its very freedom from the limitations which the Realists were imposing upon it. The preoccupation with techniques of 'showing', argued Barbey, led to impoverishment. 'A ses yeux,' he says of the modern novelist, '(et c'est bien à ses yeux qu'il faut dire), le fond importe peu' (OH III, 149). He was aware that he was opposing the entire orientation of fiction since the eighteenth century, as he showed by attacking Lesage, a purveyor of 'lanternes magiques sans magie' (OH XIX, 309), a writer who 'ne jeta sur rien des regards profonds' (OH XIX, 314). Thus Barbey repudiated the heritage of one of the great pioneers of the novel, in whom Dickens recognised as the provider, in *Le Diable boiteux*, of an image of the narrative artist's relationship with his public. 'The historian,' writes Dickens, 'takes the friendly reader by the hand, and springing with him into the air, and cleaving the same at a greater rate than ever Don Cleophas Leandro Perez Zambullo and his familiar travelled through that pleasant region in company, alights with him upon the pavement . . .'[10] Don Cleophas is of course the reluctant tourist to whom the intimate domestic scenes of life in Madrid are revealed by the limping devil Asmodée through the latter's disconcerting ability to lift the roofs off houses and peer in. Not only Dickens, but Mauriac too – who borrowed the name of Asmodée as the title of his first play – saw this as a metaphor for the revelatory process, the unrobing and exploration of reality, which was the *raison d'être* of the novel. That Lesage should entrust the role to a pagan devil – Asmodée, whose alternative name is that of the lust-demon Cupid – betrays again the novelist's awareness of the provocative and subversive nature of his mission, his assumption of his art as the vehicle of the secular conscience, his acceptance not only of the inevitability of conflict with the traditional religious view of life, but of its necessity. Lesage's limping devil is modern narrative art itself, caught in the exercise of its first halting steps and, in Barbey's judgement, already impelled in a false direction by 'ce pauvre diable de Lesage' (OH XIX, 117).

For every devil a redeeming angel. In Barbey's literary gospel the saviour of the novel was Balzac. One of the greatest achievements of 'cette Majesté intellectuelle' (ibid., 40) lay in the divorce he had decreed between novel-writing and the necessity of religious scepticism. 'Le sentiment chrétien pénètre cette généreuse nature,' Barbey wrote (ibid., 51). Though Catholicism needed no champion, it would one day regard Balzac as one of its faithful.[11] How this view of Balzac could coexist alongside the persuasion on the part of Realists and Naturalists that Balzac was *their* precursor was suggested in the Introduction. Barbey had visited another wing of the Balzacian edifice, and his opinion rested primarily on two novels, *Le Médecin de campagne* and *Le Curé du village*. The belief these texts instilled in him, that the century's greatest novelist was also a great Christian thinker, could only reinforce the conviction that the territory of fiction need not be colonised exclusively by irreligious writers. He told Trebutien: 'Je trouve très impertinent pour nous autres, catholiques, que les Drôles de l'incrédulité aient la prétention d'être les seuls qui puissent écrire des livres d'imagination et de sentiment'; Catholic writers 'ont à prouver qu'ils peuvent tout faire de ce que peuvent faire les ennemis; être spirituels, intéressants, pathétiques, forts sur la passion humaine, et catholiques toujours, par-dessus le marché!' (CG III, 112).

Although Barbey did not use here, or for that matter anywhere, the term 'Catholic novel', his typical combination of protest and enthusiasm had brought him to the verge of precisely that notion: the need for a type of novel which would express a Christian and Catholic view of life in direct polemical riposte to the scepticism of mainstream novelists. His pursuit of a theory on which to build such a novel and his attempt, in the actual writing of his novels, to create a 'Catholic novel', were to be unfocused, spasmodic and tentative, always coexisting with other literary aims, sometimes even conflicting with them.[12] Yet it is in his work, more than in any other writer's, that the Catholic novel has its tentative beginnings. The middle of the nineteenth century was hardly a propitious time for such a development. Socially and morally conservative and clerical but intellectually iconoclastic and positivistic, the climate of the early years of the Second Empire presented the literary vanguard to the Realists almost as a gift. The Catholic writer would have to strive hard to look anything other than dull and old-fashioned, and to make matters worse he had the Catholic press peering over his shoulder, even more ready to condemn him for supposed moral laxity than the overt reprobate of whom no better could be expected. The Catholic novel was bound, in these circumstances, to raise moral problems before literary ones. Barbey had his own watchdog in the shape of the pious Trebutien, whose misgivings about his friend's work opened a phase in their correspondence, in the years 1850–1, in which Barbey developed his thoughts on the moral stance of the Catholic fiction-writer. Here was the start of a debate into which no Catholic novelist for the next hundred years could avoid being drawn.

The text which alarmed Trebutien was the short story 'Le Dessous de cartes d'une partie de whist', another of the stories eventually comprising *Les Diaboliques*, and which, like the two already discussed, dwells on the absoluteness of evil: the discovery of a dead baby in a flower-stand in an aristocratic salon creates an unresolved mystery, a crime to which no character is penitent enough to provide the solution. Barbey, in his response to Trebutien, could see nothing in his tale to offend Catholicism, a creed which does not forbid knowledge of vice or crime. False prudery, calling vice virtue and falsifying reality, he argued, leads to the sophistry of a Rousseau or a George

Sand. Describing sin truthfully is consistent with the aims of both art and religion, for 'Vérité ne peut jamais être péché ou crime'. If a reader is corrupted by a work, this is not the fault of the writer provided he has not made vice attractive (CG II, 167).

The weakness of this argument – though this did not prevent its becoming the classic moral defence of the Catholic novelist, reiterated in its essentials by writers up to and including Mauriac – lies in its total dependence on a flatly mimetic view of art as an impassive reflector of a pre-existing reality. The writer's imaginative reconstruction of the world and his responsibility for the angle, weight and tone of his presentation are simply discounted. Self-defence had prompted Barbey to a theoretical formulation inadequate as an account of literary processes. He was echoing Stendhal's aphorism of the novel as a mirror carried along a high road, but expressing it with a literality that would have been rejected not just by Stendhal but by Zola too, who replaced the metaphor of the faithful mirror by that of an inevitably and necessarily distorting screen. The less sophisticated Trebutien applauded Barbey's notion, and Barbey was encouraged to develop and refine it. Catholicism, he says in a later letter, is 'la science du bien et du mal'; it looks unflinchingly into the cesspit of the soul. The writer who does likewise reconciles art and religion, assumes a role analogous to that of the confessor, whom nothing offends and whose contemplation of evil is inoffensive. Censorship of the novelist's freedom to depict truth would be an emasculation not just of art but of Catholicism. 'Soyons mâles,' Barbey urges, 'larges, élevés, opulents comme la Vérité Éternelle!' (CG III, 51). The alternative to telling the truth, he adds in a further letter to Trebutien, is silence, the abandonment of art, the death of the genre. 'Voulez-vous tuer le Roman?' he asks. 'Oui ou non? C'est de cela qu'il retourne' (CG III, 53).

So satisfied was Barbey with this statement of his position that when his brother, the priest Léon, objected to his novel *Une vieille maîtresse* he referred him contentedly to the first of this series of letters, and that same letter, with small amendments and borrowings from the one immediately following, was reproduced as the central section of the preface to a new edition of the novel. Barbey thought he had written 'une bonne théorie de l'art catholique dans le roman' (CG III, 51). It was in fact not an aesthetic theory at all, but it was a crucially important manifesto of independence from conservative Catholic opinion. For driving this wedge between his art and the expectations of a society in which his political and religious sympathies might otherwise have won him an honoured place, Barbey was eventually to pay the price of the obscenity charges levelled against *Les Diaboliques* and of the legal proceedings to which they led. His refusal of the role of pious spokesman was nevertheless vital for the health of his own art and for the future development of the Catholic novel, protecting the genre at its outset from absorption into the literature of the parish magazine.

It remains a disappointment that Barbey made no more sophisticated exploration of the relationship of faith and fiction. To Louis Veuillot's perception of a conflict between the two – 'le chrétien sent le besoin d'épaissir et de multiplier les voiles, l'artiste de les déchirer', said Veuillot in response to Barbey's new preface (I, 1300) – he had no answer. His status as theorist is certainly inferior to that of Chateaubriand, whose ideas he admired but did not exploit. *Le Génie du christianisme* – 'ce livre,' in Barbey's words, 'qui fut une révolution après une autre' (OH XVI, 140) – had stressed half a century earlier the literary potential of a Christian form of narrative. Christianity, Chateaubriand argued, was a source of dramatic themes (the clash of divine and human loves), of new types of character (the priest), of imagery, of atmosphere, of *merveilleux* and mystery; above all, it fostered a sense of Man's dual nature, which the literary psychologist could turn to good advantage. Had Barbey chosen to adopt and develop these notions, they could have enriched the conceptual foundations of the new fiction for which he erratically strove. On the other hand, theories are less likely to spawn new genres than major exemplary works are, and there were no such works, in the literature of French Romanticism, which Barbey could recognise as a model or guide for the writing of a Catholic novel.

Chateaubriand himself had been less interested in the novel, still awaiting recognition as a major genre at the turn of the century, than in the epic. *Les Natchez* attempts a christianisation of Homer in its evocation of ancient saints, as well as of Christ and the Virgin, who converse on the affairs of men in the manner of gods from Olympus. With Milton as his inspiration, Chateaubriand introduces the character of Satan, traversing the forests of the New World and inciting the Indians to violence against the white man, until, halfway through the book, Satan disappears, to be replaced by psychological motivation stemming from within the characters. In the words of the author, caught in the act of realising for which century he is writing, 'le roman remplace le poème'.[13] There was hardly a model there for Barbey. As for Hugo, through whom religious sentiment had been given a central place in Romantic literature, Barbey had little but scorn for his 'grand jeu des extases, des ravissements et des visions en Dieu' (OH XXIV, 191). The successive instalments of *Les Misérables* were met with a series of broadsides from Barbey which, as usual, had their positive as well as their destructive element. In rejecting Hugo's priest Monseigneur Bienvenu as a creature shorn of spirituality, reduced to a sentimentalised 'morale évangélico-niaise' and revealing Hugo's ignorance of the priesthood,[14] Barbey anticipated an important area of characterisation in his own and later Catholic novelists' work.

Paradoxically, whilst the great Romantic writers of fiction seemed inadequate to Barbey as religious writers, established religious writers appeared to stray too far into the province of fiction. Such was his view of Lacordaire, whose pulpit oratory was a major element in the Catholic Revival of the July Monarchy, but whose book *Sainte Marie-Madeleine* he criticised for allegedly turning the story of Christ's friendship with the Magdalene into a Richardsonian novel in which the Saviour played Grandison. The Jesus of Lacordaire, he admitted, was an adorable man, but too much of a man, too much the friend of Lazarus' family, the convivial supper guest. No doubt the historical Jesus, the carpenter's son, was in reality all of these things, but in stressing Christ's earthly self, in a naturalistic rather than mystical light, Lacordaire had fallen prey to 'ce prosaïsme du temps qui doit tuer les religions comme la poésie, car il tue les âmes!' (OH I, 251). Unconsciously, Barbey reveals here the distance between Catholic and Protestant traditions. The Anglo-Saxon reader of the King James Bible has little difficulty in reconciling the man Jesus, in the midst of his humble companions, with the divinely sent Messiah. In retelling the tale, Lacordaire had reverted to the Gospel texts (dangerous in the age of Strauss and Renan) and reworked them with the tools of the psychologist. To Barbey the Christian mysteries were best left as such, protected from enquiry by the rites and traditions of the Church.

His reaction to Lacordaire's book is a reminder that beneath his unfocused search for a Christian narrative form lay the needs of a particular religious temperament. Ultimately the question: what sort of Catholic discourse? resolves itself into the broader question: what sort of Catholicism? Barbey's religion had undergone a series of transformations from intellectual acceptance to emotional commitment. Embraced first as a bulwark of moral and social order, as 'la monarchie de Dieu' (CG II, 105), providing divine corroboration of the terrestrial monarchy to which went Barbey's political allegiance, and later as 'la seule philosophie sérieuse' (CG IV, 68), the Catholic religion had eventually imposed itself upon Barbey at a profounder, non-rational level. 'Sa vérité surnaturelle ne m'était pas entrée dans le cœur, comme une Épée de feu, jusqu'à la garde,' he admitted to Trebutien. 'Elle y est maintenant et elle y restera' (CG IV, 255). Henceforth, total acceptance of a supernatural order lay at the heart of his religion. Without the supernatural, there could be no Catholicism, he declared in a letter to the editor of *Le Gaulois* in 1869; there would be merely a social institution, a 'majestueuse Haute Police', but no truth and no faith.[15] Thus Barbey rejected his own former reasons for being a Catholic and declared his opposition to that annexation of the Church to purely political ends which, beyond the bounds of his own lifetime, was to be the strategy of men of the Right up to Maurras and the Action Française. Above all he rejected all attempts to depict religious experience as a phenomenon generated wholly within Man, with no external and supernatural referent. Of Renan, for example, he wrote: 'C'est l'ennemi du *surnaturel*; c'est le critique qui montre comment *cela* pousse dans l'humanité, mais n'est jamais la vérité en soi, indéfectible, absolue, comme nous y croyons, nous' (OH I, 126–7).

Belief in a supernatural dimension, in an invisible world impenetrable by rationalism, drew Barbey's religion towards the traditions of popular Christianity, less dependent on doctrine than on unquestioning acceptance of the divine and of its negative counterpart the demonic. Within such a conception of the world, superstition was a form of intelligence, 'la compréhension plus vive des mystères de la vie humaine' (II, 555), and the miraculous tales of folklore could be given credence without any sense of heresy. Jean Canu describes the child Barbey peering for hours through his window in the hope of glimpsing the skirts of the mysterious peasant-woman who, his governess assured him, plucked her geese up in the sky.[16] Such confident scrutiny of the heavens had its equivalent in Barbey's adult religion. His literary preferences are again the best source of information on this, for Barbey left no direct religious testament. Most works of piety he dismissed as being 'sans saveur' – a phrase he applied equally to his own brother's volume of verse *Rosa mystica* (II, 1046) and to the *Imitation of Jesus Christ* (II, 790), which he once described as a book for monks (OH I, 449). His praise was unstinting, however, for the woman writer who, he told Trebutien, had humanised the *Imitation* (CG IV, 88): Eugénie de Guérin, whose writing, along with that of her brother, the poet and Barbey's dearest friend Maurice, provided, he said, a relief from 'l'état actuel d'une littérature qui s'en va vers le *trivial* sous prétexte de *Réalisme*' (CG IV, 282–3).

Eugénie's letters and diaries scarcely appeal to modern taste; before the end of the century, Huysmans was already expressing his disdain for their banality of both content and style.[17] Eugénie offers a stream of pious aphorisms: that moral beauty is superior to physical beauty, that all seasons of the year are good because all are sent by God, that the countryside under snow or the sight of newborn lambs are reasons for praise, that humble tasks are glorified if done in God's name. Her days are organised around prayer and the winning of souls for God. A sceptic, or perhaps a Realist novelist, would notice how much her piety depends on tangible objects and on her craving for visual corroboration. To an image of Saint Theresa that hangs by her bed, she prays: 'Faites-moi passer votre regard pour chercher Dieu'.[18] She almost envies her dead brother Maurice because he can *see* heaven (288); Saint Paul too has seen 'ce que l'œil n'a point vu' (267). From Barbey's point of view, what is interesting in Eugénie's writing is her simple and unquestioning belief in the miraculous, in the intrusion of the supernatural into the everyday world. To an imagination prone to turn the flickering fires in the domestic grate into visions of angels and horned demons (17), there was no bar to accepting the marvellous tales that circulated in Eugénie's rural environment. A woman awaking from a coma claimed to have had what would nowadays be called an 'out-of-body' experience; 'qui sait,' asked the credulous Eugénie, 'tout ce que voit une âme moribonde?' (18). To her delight, a gypsy sang her a lament about a girl who, having removed the Host from the local church and placed it beneath a rose bush, thinking that God would be happier in the open air, was burned at the stake but forgiven by an angelic messenger as she died (59–60). Such tales enchanted Eugénie and overflowed without a break into her own life. She had her own extraordinary stories to tell. An image of Calvary by her bed unfailingly consoled her and granted her favours, even making a stain disappear from a soiled dress (38). There were less mundane miracles: she was utterly convinced by seemingly miraculous cures from illness. In the absence of medical remedies for the cholera that devastated the region and took the lives of close relatives, 'ayons recours,' said Eugénie, 'au miraculeux' (88). 'Je crois de tout mon cœur,' she declared on hearing that a blind girl had been restored to sight because of her exemplary faith (138). But as well as God's grace sinister forces populated Eugénie's world. Hinting at temptations that she dare not commit to paper, she wrote: 'Il y a des esprits malins répandus dans l'air' (112). Sometimes her meditations have a flavour of the occult, and suggest a taste for the kind of reading to which Balzac too was prone. A comment on the secret relationships between the eagle and a blade of grass, between angels and men (200), has a Swedenborgian ring. Her description of a funeral, of the bier thumping into the grave (171), the lugubrious sound of Man's departure, suggests the presence of literary as well as natural stimuli to her gothic imagination. She had an unerring instinct for the ominous: a letter from Barbey telling her that her sick brother was on the mend bore a stamp that had been smudged in transit, and into this black stain Eugénie read – *correctly* – the message of Maurice's impending death (173). Through all of this, she was just occasionally aware that she erred close to the limits of orthodox Catholicism. She wondered whether it was right to pray for the health of her dog Bijou (219). She knew that belief in the efficacy of medallions could raise suspicions of idolatry, but decided in the end that there was no harm in the products of a pure heart (88). More doctrinally minded souls than Eugénie might wonder if the admixture of romanticism and superstition in her religion might not weaken her status as a representative of the Catholic faith. The same objections have been raised about Barbey, and the question of his status as a Catholic novelist diverted into the more intractable question of his religious orthodoxy.[19] But such objections impose too rigid a judgement on a faith that is integrated into a personal view of the world and given meaning in the process. To argue that Eugénie and Barbey were not true Catholics would be to deny membership of the Church to the millions of their contemporaries who manifested their faith in regular practice but who did not plot the demarcation lines between beliefs that proved perfectly compatible for the purposes of interpreting their lives. The Catholicism that Barbey's novels express is not a body of dogma, but the popular Catholicism of the provinces. The comparison with Eugénie is an instructive one, for she represents in her unsophisticated way the type of religion of which he provides the literary reflection.

To the folk-tales of Eugénie's Gascony correspond those of Barbey's native Normandy. There is no direct evidence that he was familiar with any particular examples, but a twentieth-century collection of Norman tales[20] contains stories which his fiction often seems to echo. 'La Messe du revenant' relates a legend associated with the church of St-Martin-des-Champs near Condé-sur-Noireau, and which seems a likely source of the ending of Barbey's novel *L'Ensorcelée*: the beadle finds the church lit at midnight and sees a ghostly priest celebrating mass in penance for untold sins. 'La Vision de Gauchelin' recalls the same novel in its evocation of wandering shepherd-bandits devoted to the devil. Old women possessed of prophetic powers, like La Malgaigne in *Un prêtre marié*, appear in several of the stories. Others evoke the haunted moorlands of Barbey's novels or the lakes and rivers into which, as in *Un prêtre marié* again, devilish hands seek to pull the sinner. The character of Rollon, Norman folk-hero, to whom Barbey gave a modern form and a new function as the narrator of *Un prêtre marié*, appears in a number of tales. Whether any of these stories, or variants of them, were specifically known to Barbey must be a matter of conjecture, but the general influence on him of local folklore, probably in oral form, can hardly be doubted. Fairy tales were not what Barbey wanted to write, but the broad literary genre to which they belong – the fantastic – provided an escape from the sceptical perspectives of Realism. From the alliance between Barbey's particular brand of Catholicism and the literary devices of the fantastic spring, not only Barbey's Catholic novels, but the very genre of the Catholic novel itself, for all of the other Catholic novelists to be studied in this book were to follow his example, in different ways and to different degrees, in exploiting techniques that have their origins in fantastic literature.

Barbey's interest in the fantastic drew him to the gothic novel and tale of terror of the late eighteenth and early nineteenth centuries, in which he recognised modes of fiction that had been created as necessary alternatives to mainstream narrative. 'Au Nord comme au Midi,' he wrote, 'l'Europe, dégoûtée de matérialisme et de littérature *positive*, avait soif de surnaturel, la vraie poésie' (OH XII, 186).[21] In France Cazotte, with *Le Diable amoureux,* and in England Ann Radcliffe – 'une femme de génie' in Barbey's estimation (CG III, 112) – had been among the pioneers of the new wave, and other exemplars of the genre known to Barbey included Lewis, Mathurin, Hoffmann and Poe. He recognised in all these writers kindred spirits, sharing his fascination with a dark world beneath the surface of things, probing the underside of experience with imagination, not reason, as their guiding light. Between this mode of writing and the expression of a Christian and Catholic vision, Barbey was nevertheless lucid enough to see the difference. The use made of religious material in fantastic fiction – angelic visions, demonic temptations, biblical and liturgical elements – was invariably motivated by the desire to achieve spectacular literary effect rather than to persuade of a particular philosophical conception of reality, and a true 'foi au surnaturel', to use Barbey's phrase (OH XII, 190), was lacking. What Barbey called 'le fantastique' depended on the existence of this faith – not necessarily a faith identifiable as Christian, but a belief in the existence of an invisible, extra-material order. The mere pretence of such belief, designed to create fashionable shudders without troubling the reader's perceptions of the world one jot, he called 'fantaisie': it was perfected in 'cette comédie de terreur qu'Anne Radcliffe nous a jouée en maître' (OH XII, 191). Hoffmann, he thought, fell somewhere between the two and created a false 'fantastique' (ibid). Poe, whose importance Barbey realised before Baudelaire's translations began to appear,[22] and on whom he wrote four long and deeply reflective essays during a thirty-year period from 1853, began from a genuine religious experience – a sense of damnation and divine reproach – but his American heritage had impeded the deepening of true spirituality (OH XII, 357). Barbey appears to have seen the proof of a genuine 'foi au surnaturel' in an author's willingness to sustain to the end of his text the mysteries on which its challenge to reason is based, and to withhold a final rational explanation. His arguments anticipate those of Todorov, for whom the existence of the fantastic lies in sustained uncertainty, in the perpetuation of what he calls 'le surnaturel accepté'.[23] Ann Radcliffe, notoriously, offers natural explanations of phenomena that are only apparently supernatural: a ghost turns out to have been an innocent servant, the entry of an intruder into a room despite a locked door turns out to have been possible because of a secret panel in the wainscoting. Barbey declared his impatience with such concessions to rationality. In an analysis of *The Gold Bug,* he traces Poe's decision to explain the apparently miraculous properties of the scarab to his incorrigible Protestantism. 'Cet esprit,' he writes, 'fait [. . .] ce que le protestantisme a toujours fait à propos de tout: au lieu de se *confier*, il se *défie*, et il en appelle, de l'Imagination qui croit, à la Raison qui glose et qui explique' (OH XII, 357–8). Barbey associates here true imagination with true Catholicism – *his* Catholicism, impervious to reason.

Nowhere in these critical articles does Barbey grasp the essential problem of how to reconcile a 'foi au surnaturel', which could embrace any variety of occult or spiritualist belief or practice, and a recognisably Christian creed, although the distinction he makes in a letter to Baudelaire between his *literary* admiration for Poe and his *moral* condemnation of the same writer (CG VI, 91) shows his awareness of the gulf between the two planes, as does his exhortation to Trebutien: 'Si nous avons la foi, prions. Pas de batelage! Ne soyons pas des *chrétiens littéraires*' (CG V, 158). How successful Barbey himself would be in bridging this gulf will be one of the main concerns of the remainder of this chapter. What has been established so far is that he sensed a role for himself in the creation of a Catholic literature of the fantastic, with 'des saveurs plus pénétrantes' than Cazotte (OH XII, 183) and an insistence on the 'surhumaine réalité' lacking in Hoffmann and Poe (ibid., 184). The fantastic tradition had provided Barbey with a starting-point for the Catholic novel that was unavailable elsewhere in contemporary literature.

* * *

The horror element of gothic fiction had been a feature of Barbey's writing since his first published story *Le Cachet d'onyx* (1831) and the genre had also influenced *Léa* (1832), with its echoes of the vampire legend. The text in which the fantastic assumed major importance, however, was *Une vieille maîtresse* (1851), from the moment in that novel when the protagonists, the reformed rake Ryno de Marigny and his newly wedded bride Hermangarde, leave the sophisticated society of the Paris salon to live on the Normandy coast, where they are pursued by Ryno's former mistress, the tenacious Vellini. This change of scene corresponds to a radical switch in Barbey's career, for the Norman setting of his childhood, entering his fictional work for the first time, provides the backcloth to every one of his subsequent novels. Barbey's aim to be for Normandy what Scott and Burns were for Scotland[24] and his admiration for Shakespeare[25] also combine to bring into his work increased elements of the fantastic mode which he admired in these writers: Vellini is described as 'comme une des sorcières de Macbeth'.[26] But more than literary models, it is the Norman background itself, the atmosphere of 'cette côte d'où le merveilleux ne s'est pas envolé encore' (542), that contributes most to the infusion of these new elements. They are introduced through the characters of the fisherfolk who relate the legend of 'la blanche Caroline', the disputed mistress of two violent lovers, whose ghost walks the beach at night, and that of 'le

Criard', a sinister figure whose cries herald disaster. In this setting, the criteria of rationality break down. When Vellini appears on the scene, her hold on Ryno, sealed in their drinking of each other's blood in a cave known as 'Le Tombeau du Diable', seems of diabolic origin; and there is a scene in which she miraculously scrutinises Ryno's movements from afar with the aid of a 'magic mirror' that comes straight from the pages of Lewis' *The Monk*.

Barbey's handling of these elements, after what has been said above, comes as something of a surprise. Despite his criticism of Poe for leaving the door ajar to rational explanations of the fantastic, Barbey does precisely the same thing in several instances. When the wail of the Criard is heard, Hermangarde's instinct tells her that it is not a supernatural sound at all, but rather 'une voix humaine, [. . .] le cri d'une femme' (414) – the implication (scarcely less incredible) being that it is Vellini, announcing her arrival. When 'la blanche Caroline' is seen walking, the reader knows it is actually Hermangarde, searching for her straying husband. Vellini's belief in the magical potency of the blood pact is also refuted by the narrator in favour of a psychological explanation. The force of their past relationship, the influence of a 'mémoire du cœur' (514) with its echoes of Constant, the memory of the 'auld songs' (Burns again) of their 'longue intimité' (515): these are enough to drive Ryno back into his mistress's arms. Even the peasants' discussion of Vellini at the end of the novel introduces a problematic note: is she after all 'une favorite de Satan' or not? (542). Barbey deliberately withdraws here from the brink of out-and-out fantasy, in a way that is to become typical of him and important for the interpretation of this and later novels. Has he remembered, in spite of his declared scorn for the mid-nineteenth-century reading public, that he is nevertheless writing for it? In the novel's final pages, the vicomte de Prosny, in Paris, ponders the possibility that supernatural powers are at work in the Ryno-Vellini affair, only to ask how one can subscribe to such ideas 'au dix-neuvième siècle (551). This may, of course, carry ironical weight, challenging the reader to reject the facile rationalism of the unimaginative and unattractive Prosny, and throwing the book's ending back to where Barbey wants it: into the realm of the uncertain and ambivalent.

The transition is already under way from the 'foi au surnaturel' to the generation of Christian meaning. The creation of an alternative psychological plane introduces a dimension that the fantastic elements, unsupported, cannot create: the moral dimension necessary to the Christian writer. In this the oppositions between Hermangarde and Vellini are vital, and the terms in which they are expressed are derived directly from Balzac. Hermangarde is 'le lys' (508) to Vellini's 'torpille' (509) – in other words, as Madame de Mortsauf to Esther Gobseck. The conflicts of good/evil, spirituality/animality, angel/devil, and the contrasts between the religious devotion of one woman and the occult practices of the other establish the novel's moral poles. Vellini's love for Ryno is also specifically seen as a challenge to the Almighty: it is 'une passion surhumaine, forte comme Dieu même' (329). The moral implications of the action are principally stressed, however, in the self-analysis of the characters, often through the device of confession. The confessional motif is first introduced through Hermangarde who, in pious memory of 'sa mère dans le ciel', writes to 'sa mère sur la terre' (498), her grandmother Madame de Flers, expressing the need for a confident on whose breast to lay her head. Ryno likewise wishes to confide in Madame de Flers, and a specific reference is made to the sacrament of confession. 'J'ai agi avec vous,' writes Ryno, 'comme l'Église catholique – cette source de toute vérité – ordonne qu'on agisse avec Dieu [. . .] Je viens vous dire ainsi qu'à un confesseur . . . .' (524). His confessional urge, vestige of a Christian childhood, is described as being as irresistible as breathing. But in the course of his lengthy written confession, Ryno's conviction that he has been misunderstood and his instinct for self-justification clash with the religious aspects of confession, and what emerges is a self-ordained pardon in the style of the Romantic personal novel. The penitent's strategy is that of the Rousseau of the *Confessions*. He belittles his own sins by arguing their universality: do not all men behave thus? has the marquise not seen similiar cases? He insists he has been the powerless victim of fate, of the past, of memory, of instinct. He displays his noble sentiments by his refusal to blame Vellini. His intentions were always good. No one has helped him, not even God, whom he blames in the full flow of confession. His behaviour defies comprehension, and is thus exempt from judgement. His yielding to sexual temptation was his way of exorcising that devil for good – a sort of St Augustine's 'chaste but not yet!' Finally, the fact of confessing his sins is the ultimate proof of his goodness. He is honest but wretched. 'C'est moi le plus malheureux!' he claims. 'N'aurez-vous pas pitié de moi?' (509–23). Ryno, while ostensibly craving pardon, has forgiven himself on every count on the grounds of his own sense of his basic goodness. Is this usurpation of God's justice the sign of Barbey's intention that we should see and blame the anti-Christian nature of Ryno's confession? Or is Barbey discovering what many a novelist has discovered in the presence of his beloved creation: a complicity with his protagonist, or with the autobiographical elements within him, which overcomes moral censure? Does the meaning of the book turn on Mme de Flers' refusal of forgiveness to Ryno, or on Hermangarde's pathetic failure, as she reads her husband's letter, to understand 'ce labyrinthe du cœur de l'homme' – a heart created in the image of the earth 'dont une moitié plonge dans la lumière quand l'autre s'abîme dans la nuit' (528)? The novel is ambivalent here as it often is elsewhere. This need not lead us to stigmatise Barbey as an immoral or amoral writer, but it should identify him instead as a writer obeying the laws of his genre, creating a structure of moral viewpoints locked in necessary tension. *Une vieille maîtresse* is not Barbey's best novel, and in it he has not yet created a satisfying Catholic novel, for the other-worldliness of the fantasy and the real-world morality are in conflict throughout. But it already raises one of the main problems that Barbey's Catholic novels, and those of the other writers discussed below, will raise. The Catholic novelist, working in the genre which above all others mirrors the moral relativism of the age, is in a position of extreme difficulty: the clear victory of one point of view over another, which we seldom encounter in life, spells the death of his art, even when the victorious ideology is that for which, as a private individual outside the pages of his books, he would willingly give his life. Whatever the Catholic novel is, it is not propaganda.

* * *

Barbey's belief in the potential of the fantastic as a key element in Catholic fiction intensified as he worked on his next novel, *L'Ensorcelée* (1855). His new book, he announced, would be 'l'audacieuse tentative d'un fantastique nouveau, sinistrement et crânement surnaturel', producing a new kind of *frisson*. But, he added defensively, it would contain nothing to shock from a Catholic point of view. Dulac, of Veuillot's *L'Univers*, had even assured him that it could produce 'un effet catholique' (CG III, 112).

L'Ensorcelée is a historical novel set during the Chouan wars. Its central figure is a priest, the abbé Jehoel de la Croix-Jugan, who shows more military than spiritual zeal and who, despairing of a lost cause, tries to commit suicide by shooting himself in the face. He is saved by a peasant woman, but before fully recovering he is tortured by a group of revolutionary soldiers and left horribly disfigured. He later rejoins the church community, though his right to celebrate offices is suspended, and meets Jeanne le Hardouey, wife of a local farmer, who falls victim to a deep passion for him. This he exploits for political purposes, using Jeanne as a messenger and go-between for the Royalist cause which he still espouses. Jeanne's love for him produces deep guilt feelings in her, and a violent reaction on her husband's part when he is made aware of the attachment by a group of itinerant shepherds. Jeanne is found drowned – whether she has killed herself or has been murdered is never wholly clarified. The priest, eventually renouncing his political priorities in favour of his ineradicable priestly mission, is restored to authority by the Church, only to be shot dead by an unknown hand (presumably Jeanne's husband Thomas) while celebrating his first mass.

The framing of the story and the manner of its telling take Barbey further into the realm of the fantastic than he had previously gone. The tale is told to a first narrator by a second, the *herbager* Maître Louis Tainnebouy, with whom he sets out across the sinister Lande de Lessay. Tainnebouy relates the local legend of a ghostly priest – Croix-Jugan – who is said to celebrate mass in a deserted church on certain nights of the year, and the opportunity for its telling is the fact that Tainnebouy's mare goes lame in the middle of the moor, an event which Tainnebouy ascribes to the malificence of local shepherds who have cast a spell on her. This is the first element of magic in the book and the first sense of the title 'ensorcelée' (the bewitched mare), the main attribution of which is to Jeanne, 'spellbound' by her love for Croix-Jugan. The semantic linking of the main plot to the circumstances of its telling also conditions the alleged supernaturalism of the events. The magic arises out of the sinisterness of the moor, so that Barbey simultaneously creates an atmosphere of the uncanny and avoids guaranteeing the objective truth of the narrative. This structure is made even more elaborate by the quoting of yet further narrators, so that the fantastic events become even more remote and unreliably related. As in *Une vieille maîtresse* Barbey, like Radcliffe or Poe, once more holds back from total fantasy. He offers a running epistemological commentary on what might or might not be possible. If this were a novel, his main narrator playfully comments, he would have to avoid such irrational excesses (659). Knowing very well that he *is* writing a novel, and for a nineteenth-century readership on which he is dependent while scorning its values, Barbey recoils from the precipice of absolute supernaturalism while achieving in the narrative all the effects of the same. But in the final pages, with typical perversity, he loosens the hold of rationality by saying that he is ultimately inclined to believe all that Tainnebouy has told him (741), preferring the countryman's belief in the *merveilleux* to the arrogant claims of modern science to explain all human phenomena.

This alluring ambivalence is maintained in the apparently supernatural details of the text. Jeanne's passion for the priest is, on one level, the result of a spell cast on her by him; on another, brought about by a fatal, diabolic attraction symbolised in the fiery red glow on her face, the reflection both of hell-fire and of the fires that have burned Croix-Jugan. But there is no shortage of social and psychological reasons for Jeanne's emotions: the heritage of a fierce-tempered mother and her aristocratic resentment, as a Feuardent, of her humble status as farmer's wife, both incline her towards the militant but well-born priest. An ironic distance likewise separates the diabolical aspects of the latter's character from the testimony of the first narrator, for they are never witnessed directly but always through the eyes and minds of other characters. It is by others that he is described as 'un ministre de Lucifer' (648). The satanic features, the preternatural coldness of 'ce prêtre glacé' (642) are what others see and feel. In working his apparent spell over Jeanne, he is suspected by Tainnebouy of being the devil incarnate (663), while Jeanne's awareness of the spell exists within her and is not 'given' by the text: 'A ses propres yeux même, Jeanne-Madelaine dut [. . .] être ensorceléé' (659). Her terror of the 'l'esprit du mal' which possesses her can be read as guilt or superstition (667). The narrator allows these readings, then characteristically leans in the other direction by rejecting the doctor's medical explanation of Jeanne's state, 'cet état sans mon qui, comme toutes les maladies dont la racine est dans nos âmes, trompe l'œil de l'observation matérielle' (672).

The most totally fantastic characters, not only in this novel but in Barbey's entire work, are the wandering shepherds. Thomas meets a band of them on the moor, and in their 'magic' mirror he sees Croix-Jugan and Jeanne cooking his heart on a spit. Or does he? Is the sequence real of merely imagined by Thomas? Barbey litters his text with details that support either interpretation. As the scene opens Thomas is riding along, his head slumped low: is he already asleep and dreaming? Is he not, 'dans ces landages ouverts aux chimères et aux monstres de l'imagination populaire' (673), predisposed to weird imaginings? But when Thomas wakes – from sleep? from fainting at the horrific vision in the mirror? – he discovers the remains of a fire, serving perhaps to tip the balance towards belief in the reality of the encounter. This movement is reinforced further when he enters the priest's house and recognises the room seen in the mirror. These disorientating techniques, pitching the novel into nightmare, prepare the following scenes of horror and violence: Jeanne's body is found floating in the pool where the village women wash their clothes, and a shepherd drinks the blood-reddened water with overt delight.

There is nothing at all 'Christian' in scenes like these. Nevertheless even here Barbey is paving the way for later developments in the Catholic novel. The techniques of ambiguity that he employs in describing Thomas's meeting with the shepherds will be adopted by Bernanos in the scene in which his priest Donissan meets the satanic horse-dealer; while the disconcerting disappearance and reappearance of the shepherd at the edge of the pool, at one moment present and at the next gone, create the same nightmarish effect as in the Jambe-de-Laine sequences of *Monsieur Ouine*. In purely technical terms, the illusion is created in exactly the same way whether the supernatural element be an angel from heaven or a demon from hell. Even if Barbey does not quite bridge the gap here between fantasy and his religious beliefs, his techniques are adaptable by writers who can.

L'Ensorcelée embodies two strategies for persuading us that the fantastic elements are not only compatible with religion but provide support for a religious interpretation of the events. The strategy is the rhetoric of the first narrator: 'J'ai pour moi [. . .] l'irréfragable attestation de l'Église romaine, qui a condamné, en vingt endroits des actes de ses Conciles, la magie, la sorcellerie, les charmes, non comme vaines et pernicieusement fausses, mais comme choses RÉELLES, et que ses dogmes expliquaient très bien. Quant à l'intervention des puissances mauvaises dans les affaires de l'humanité, j'ai encore pour moi le témoignage de l'Église . . .' (584). Here is further evidence that for Barbey, in Jacques Petit's words, 'le fantastique n'est pas un but, mais un moyen' (1369, *n.*), and that the accusation that Barbey exploits Catholicism for gothic effect is unfair.[27] Second sight, premonitory dreams, mysterious diseases, miraculous cures, stigmata, physiological manifestations of states of soul – all these elements of the gothic have their attestation in some biblical or doctrinal source, and they are used by Barbey as effective shock tactics to force us out of our rational expectations of the universe: a process from which a religious interpretation of life can only benefit. Barbey creates the new Christian *merveilleux* which Chauteaubriand had anticipated.

The second bridge from fantasy to religion lies in the fictional rhetoric, in devices of character and plot. Croix-Jugan's failure to be a true priest is, in Christian terms, of great significance. More a soldier than a priest, he further sins by his attempted suicide, for which his hellish physical tortures can be read as punishment (639); and even when he resumes the priestly role, his diabolic pride and his consolation of others by appealing to *their* pride mark him again as a priest of Lucifer. Barbey creates an exemplary priest in the person of the abbé Caillemer, whose sole function in the novel is to serve as a contrast to him. The death of Jeanne also introduces a Christian theme, that of collective guilt, and it is the occasion for important religious scenes involving the two old peasant women La Clotte and Nônon Cocouan. In their Christian mourning for the dead woman, and especially in Nônon's conviction – part superstition, part piety – that Jeanne is watching her from beyond the grave, fantasy and religion combine effectively (699). The scene of Jeanne's funeral reintroduces the violence and horror so typical of Barbey: the crowd, seeking a scapegoat for Jeanne's death, attack and kill La Clotte. In Barbey's description of the satanic fury of the mob ('cette foule, cette légion, cet immense animal' (I, 708)), there are once more foreshadowings of Bernanos, this time of the lynching of Jambe-de-Laine in *Monsieur Ouine*.

The impact of La Clotte's death on Croix-Jugan is another factor in developing the Christian sense of the text. Although his first instinct is to seek revenge, the priest checks himself on seeing the emblem of the cross – both Chouan and Christian symbol – on the barrel of his pistols, and makes his choice between the two: to live as a priest again. He is killed before completing his first mass after reinstatement to priestly functions, and the reappearance of his ghost celebrating mass again reunites gothic and Christian themes. But the final passages pose a problem: is the renegade priest damned or not? The celebration of the mass might point in one direction: the priest is carrying out after death the functions of which the murder deprived him. But in fact the priest's ghost is eternally frustrated, unable to remember the words of the ceremony, condemned to an eternal hell of trying in vain to recapture the grace which he had voluntarily thrown away in his pursuit of a career of violence. The final Christian message is a sombre, admonitory one.

* * *

Barbey strives in *L'Ensorcelée* for the balance of fantasy and Christian meaning, but in the end the gothic elements outweigh the religious. The balance is more satisfactorily achieved in *Un prêtre marié* (1865), the central text for the study of Barbey as Catholic novelist. It is based on the historically true story of a married priest, Jean Lebon, who lived in Barbey's native area, near St-Sauveur-le-Vicomte.[28] In Barbey's version, the priest Jean Gourgues, known as Sombreval, who has lost his faith as a result of his scientific studies, and who has married and had a daughter, returns with the latter to Normandy to live in the castle called Le Quesnay. Their story is told by an invented narrator called Rollon Langrune in order to satisfy the curiosity of the first narrator about the portrait of a young girl contained in a locket, and fantastic elements are once again employed to heighten the fictional effect, to lift the action and characters to a surreal plane. Compared with the earlier novels, the *merveilleux* is more integral to the plot, which is built on the prophecies of the witch-like peasant woman La Malgaigne. She prophesies that Sombreval will become a priest, marry, return to his home area and meet his death by water. The novel opens as the third of these four predictions is being fulfilled. The prophecies also extend to Sombreval's daughter Calixte: she will die for her father's sin; and to the man who loves her, Néel de Néhou, whose death, says the old woman, Sombreval will also cause, and who she later predicts will die within three months of Sombreval and Calixte. These predictions come true, but what we have seen of Barbey's earlier novels warns that explanations other than supernatural ones might be possible. That Néel, for example, deliberately seeks his death in battle is made clear in the final two pages. 'Et Néel de Néhou?' (1222): the first narrator's sudden interrogative interrupts Rollon's story and restores the original narrative frame. Rollon's reply is couched in purely psychological terms: the inconsolable Néel, bored with the wife he has married at Calixte's request, seized with joy the opportunity of fulfilling the final prediction. Enlisting in the service of the Emperor, he 'se fit tuer dans une des plus célèbres batailles du temps, en poussant son cheval le poitrail sur une pièce de canon, qui coupa en quatre l'homme et le cheval' (1223). Néel chooses not only death but its moment and its means, the first to accord with the prophecy – 'C'était juste trois mois après la mort de Sombreval et de la Malgaigne' (1223), the second in emulation of the death on horseback of his friend Gustave, to which his own bravado had contributed. The dilution of fantasy continues in Rollon's casual playing-down of the importance of the locket, the enigma of which had been the pretext for the telling of the story in the first place: it becomes now just an object, 'probably' belonging to Sombreval, fished out of the pool and losing its colours through long immersion in water. The final paragraph restores Rollon's fantastical discourse: 'Quant à Sombreval, on n'en trouva pas un seul os pour le joindre au portrait – ce qui fit dire aux paysans de la contrée que le Diable, qui a le bras long, l'avait passé à travers les boues de l'étang, pour tirer jusqu'à lui, par les pieds, le PRÊTRE MARIÉ!' (1223). But this final flourish, coming after the rational account of Néel's self-determined death, is isolated as *Rollon*'s last word, underlining the partiality of his presentation. Néel's conscious decision to choose death[29] encourages similar psychological interpretations of the other characters' fates: that Sombreval perversely returns to Le Quesnay out of an unavowed fascination with his destiny; that Calixte dies of perfectly explicable causes, arising from her illness and from the shock of learning that her father's claim to have regained his faith is a lie. In the last resort fulfilled 'prophecy' in a fictional text is a synonym for the author's decisions on the fate of his characters, and the latter have to have a certain complicity in this process in order to maintain the necessary degree of psychological depth.

If the prophecies of La Malgaigne are problematic, so is Rollon's subjective narrative. Sombreval, at the end of the book, is damned only on Rollon's 'authority', coloured by his stern moral outlook. The rational recuperation of the text which the narrative invites places in an uncertain light the literality of the supernatural elements. Even Rollon is careful to present the more extreme beliefs about Sombreval (that he is in league with Satan, that he has an incestuous relationship with Calixte, that his negro servants are diabolic, that he drinks 'devil's brew' and eats 'la cuisine du diable' (913)) from the point of view of third parties, mainly superstitious and bigoted peasants. The 'mobilier de l'enfer' (ibid.) delivered to his house on a Friday 13th is described through their credulous eyes. Only maître Tizonnet, the lawyer responsible for the selling of the house to Sombreval, sees him as a client sent by the devil. The 'couronne de l'enfer' (1048) which the fires of Sombreval's forges project from the windows is described in such hellish terms only by the fathers of Néel and Bernardine, ready to believe any evil of him. Sombreval's devilish appearance as he emerges from the smoke and flames of his experiments is witnessed only by the abbé Méautis who has crossed 'l'antichambre de l'enfer' (1078) to meet him; even Rollon comments: 'L'abbé Méautis avait la vive imagination d'un poète' (1078). Barbey is quite prepared to let the reader be impressed by the 'diabolic' stature, the 'satanic' charm of Sombreval, and to exploit his memory, in the scene where priest meets scientist in the laboratory filled with its mysterious test-tubes and Voltaic piles, of a similar passage in Balzac's *La Recherche de l'Absolu*. The traditional mad alchemists of gothic fiction come to mind also: Sombreval even offers the abbé 'une chaise gothique' (1078). Le Quesnay has its literary antecedents as a kind of diabolic Otranto or Udolpho. Such intensity of colouring is the essence of Barbey's art, and devils pop up everywhere in his fiction, though they are usually of a metaphorical variety. The imagery of satanism plays a central role, mostly in Rollon's discourse. Sombreval is described by him as 'renversé de plus haut' (899), as 'un docteur plus qu'un apôtre' (899), with 'l'intelligence d'un Dieu' (890), but bitten by 'le serpent de la Science' (893). But to conclude that Sombreval is literally possessed or, at the end of the novel, reclaimed by Satan, even to talk unambiguously, as Petit does (1451, *n.*), of his satanism, seems to betray too simple a reading of the book's complexities.

There is a more rational level of the text on which Sombreval's researches represent one pole in the historic intellectual debate between science and religion. Rollon's stance means that this debate is not presented objectively. He talks of 'les sciences menteuses' (957), and his scorn for the scientists, both Sombreval and his father-in-law, is clear: 'matérialistes l'un et l'autre, expliquant tout par des combinaisons de gaz et de fluides, croyant tenir le secret de la création dans le creux de leurs fourneaux et de leur main' (893–4). For such intellectual pride, the metaphor of Satan is a traditional one and it draws attention to an important fact: namely, that Sombreval's sin is intellectual and spiritual, rather than the sexual one that the title of the novel might suggest. This does not reduce its enormity; on the contrary, sexual transgression in itself is less sinful than the substitution of the merely legal bond of marriage for the spiritual one ('legal', comments Rollon, is an atheist term (1082)). Sombreval's marriage seems motivated at least in part by its promise of closer proximity to his wife's father, the eminent scientist, and his original failing on the human plane was his apparent lack of concern for the woman he married, whose death leads him to assume a substitute role as mother, as well as father, of Calixte. These intellectual and emotional conflicts are set against the background of the nation's apostasy, that of the deicidal nineteenth century. The sins of this age are elevated to cosmic significance by the appearance of signs in the sky, of meteors that herald the Revolution. In all these ways Barbey makes possible a rational interpretation of the surface fantasy of his text, while using the gothic paraphernalia to create his typical literary effects. The meaning of the novel is to be found not in these effects but in the sense of other-worldliness which is generated through them, and in the kaleidoscopic constellation of moral viewpoints that cluster around the centre of the drama.

In translating the fantastic elements into Christian meaning three characters are vital: La Malgaigne, Calixte and the abbé Méautis. Although said to be 'hantée' and in league with 'ce monde qui pèse tant sur l'autre que nous étouffons sous son poids' (958), La Malgaigne's Catholic devoutness is legendary. She lives, as Rollon says, on the frontier of two worlds – and of the two, it is the invisible one which seems the more real to her. The familiar theme of sight reappears here: a sight which embraces and explores the real but plunges beneath its surface into a world of Christian supernature. The old woman's second sight is a paradigm of Barbey's Christian expansion of the visual processes of the novel genre. She is created to be the ideological adversary of Sombreval, 'cet observateur positif, ce savant qui n'admettait que la science' (965), and whose optics are those of the Realist novelist. Her predictions are imbued with religious meaning partly by their context. It is while standing with Sombreval under the porch of the village church that 'elle le voyait prêtre – puis marié – et puis possesseur du Quesnay' (907), a prediction seemingly endorsed by a thunderbolt from heaven which cuts the belfry in two.

Calixte's central role in bridging the space between fantasy and religion is prefigured by the red cross which marks her brow from birth: an emblem of her father's guilt and her own inherited blame, uniting the concept of sin with standard gothic imagery. An interesting comparison is possible with Hawthorne's *The Scarlet Letter*, which has never been mentioned as a possible source of Barbey's novel but offers several parallels to it, not only the 'physiological' sign of alleged guilt – in Hawthorne's novel, a red letter A – but also the themes of diabolic intervention and of the justice or injustice of the community's censure of the 'marked' woman. The cross and red head-band that Calixte wears to conceal it are familiar intensifying devices of Barbey's, symbols of wrong-doing or hidden passion like the scarlet curtain in the first of the *Diaboliques* or the crimson body of La Pudica later in the same volume, or else like the red flush on the face of Aimée de Spens in *Le Chevalier des Touches*. All of these images are associated with blood, through which Calixte is linked metonymically to Néel's bleeding head, suffered when Sombreval strikes him down, and later to the scar left on his brow after the mad chariot-ride performed to impress Calixte. Both young people are thus related to Sombreval by blood, the substance of material life. 'Je crois au sang,' affirms Sombreval; for him, it replaces what Christians call the soul (1061). Calixte, directly, and Néel by extension are members of Sombreval's doomed family; but Calixte's cross is also metaphorically transformed into a crown of thorns, symbol of her Christ-like assumption of her father's sin: 'Son front de crucifiée dilaté par la joie se gonflait sous le bandeau rouge qui l'encadrait comme une couronne d'épines ensanglantées [. . .] D'ange résigné passée Archange triomphant, elle montait d'un degré de plus dans l'éther de la vie at dans la hiérarchie du ciel' (1154). Where, one wonders, can such combinations of New Testament language and the romantic imagery of violence and blood be found in so intense coexistence, other than in the pages of Barbey? Through a welter of contrasting images, Calixte's 'pâleur surnaturelle' (921) opposes the alien stain on her forehead, expresses her lily-white purity, makes of her a virginal vision in divinely inspired antithesis to her father: he seeking to cure her through the sullied channels of science, she atoning for him by prayer and by a vicarious suffering that is both romantic and expiatory. She is a Christian beauty, an angel, a priestess – all these images are used, and another, biblical, image is grafted on to the fairy-tale fabric of her character: Calixte, in secret a Carmelite nun pledged to win back her father to the Church, is also Judith, and Sombreval Holophernes, whose head she seeks for God (996). Barbey had been anxious about the potential insipidity of Calixte's character, with previous examples of blushing heroines in his mind. 'Ferai-je avec Calixte,' he asked Trebutien, 'ce que Richardson a raté avec tout son génie? Intéresserai-je à une Perfection? Ferai-je du feu de cette lumière? et grâce au Catholicisme, aura-t-on enfin, dans l'art littéraire, ce que le Protestantisme n'a pu y mettre – un type de vertu intéressant comme s'il était passionné?' (CG IV, 301). There may be little originality in Barbey's ideas here, his notion of Catholic female types as potentially superior to Protestant ones deriving from Balzac's *avant-propos*, but in the event he lifts Calixte to a plane of lyricism not often equalled in his writings, a lyricism in which the romantic and the religious are successfully harmonised. But alongside these softer images of Calixte, she is also a vehicle for the straight gothic, as exemplified by her comatose sleep-walking, her access to superior knowledge while in a state of trance and her vision of a crucifix shedding blood.

The third character, the abbé Méautis, is one of Barbey's most original and influential creations, a prototype of the character who was to become such a feature of the Catholic novel: the young country priest, simple, ascetic and shabbily dressed (his 'realistic' aspect), but also a tragic and lonely figure faced by decisions of the utmost spiritual importance. Méautis' saintliness is founded on suffering: his sister has died in a fire, his mother driven mad by grief. 'Les saints,' he says, but without conscious reference to himself, 'sont peut-être au-dessus des anges parce qu'ils souffrent' (1052). In Méautis, Barbey has already created the heroic priest of Bernanos' novels, some sixty years in advance. He is also, more surprisingly, a curious prefiguration of Zola's priest Serge Mouret, whose personal tragedy – a mother killed in a fire, a mentally defective sister – offers an oddly inverted echo of Méautis', and who, for similar profoundly personal reasons, shares his adoration of the Holy Virgin above other aspects of his cult. Méautis represents the humane and orthodox voice of Christianity, and opposes, at least officially, the occult superstitions of La Malgaigne; privately, he is inclined to believe in the truth of her visions and voices, for all manifestations of the supernatural are potential allies of each other. His, and her, supernatural interpretation of Calixte's coma is opposed by that of the voice of medical science, Dr Ayre, who believes, with Littré and Zola, that even if science cannot yet explain all phenomena, it will one day. However, Ayre's hypothesis that Calixte might be in some superior state in which special knowledge is available to her seems to have less to do with science than with Barbey's reading of Poe's story *Mesmeric Revelation*, a literary source that Barbey integrates into the moral themes of his text. A new terror is sown in Méautis by the doctor's theory: that Calixte might discover the truth which he himself knows – that Sombreval's profession of regained faith is a lie, a means of alleviating his daughter's suffering. And a new dilemma is created: to forewarn her of the truth or not? The priest, now walking the knife-edge between potentially cataclysmic decisions, moves to the centre of the stage. We learn of his past, marked by extremes and excesses: his picking up a communion wafer vomited by a mortally ill man and swallowing it himself has made him 'un martyr de dégoût' (1127–8). Barbey calls him 'plus prêtre qu'homme' (1128), a phrase that suggests one of the sources of the character: Barbey's brother, the priest Léon. Writing of the latter to Trebutien, Barbey complains that the priest's tunic has devoured the human being; a jealous God has robbed his family of him for ever. The gulf between ordinary men, even devout Christians, and priests, Barbey goes on, is unbridgeable: they inhabit separate universes (CG I, 230–1). In this anguished personal awareness of the fissure between earthly and religious values lies the origin of Barbey's theme of the *honneur de Dieu*, the principle which motivates Méautis, his loyalty to a different domain of priority.

Two wholly different and ultimately incompatible moral authorities clash in Rollon's narrative: human sentiment or reason on the one hand (urging forgiveness for Sombreval and Calixte) and God on the other, unfathomable and implacable in his punishment of the renegade priest. The humanity of Méautis is represented by his own tragic past, and reinforced by unexpected sympathies between him and Sombreval: they form a complementary pair of characters, linked both by opposition (lapsed priest/true priest) and by similarity (natural father/spiritual father). While Sombreval lives for the physical salvation of Calixte, Méautis' priority is to work for the glory of God. 'Pour ce prêtre et pour ce mystique,' writes Barbey, 'il n'y avait en cause que Dieu dans le drame dont Calixte, Sombreval et Néel étaient les personnages' (1145). The priest's horror at Sombreval's pretence of regained faith is accompanied by a closer association with the views of La Malgaigne. Whereas earlier in the novel he had rejected her occult-based condemnation of Sombreval as a denial of God's mercy, he now sees, in her horror of Sombreval's second act of apostasy, the final substitution of the Christian for the visionary; he now accepts both the authenticity of her predictions and the rightness of her moral judgement. The conflict in Méautis leads him into another wave of condemnations of the 'diabolical' Sombreval, of his 'dessein sataniquement magnanime' carried out with 'l'obstination d'un Lucifer' (1149). As the narrator comments (1145), unless one understands the horror within Méautis at the injury to God's honour of which Sombreval is guilty, his role in revealing the truth of her father's apostasy to Calixte would be incomprehensible. Méautis' pity for Calixte makes him exclude her from blame and see her still as 'une fille innocente' (1149). In the struggle that takes place within him, 'l'Ange devait vaincre, mais l'Homme était presque égal en force avec l'Ange, dans cette âme de prêtre, où l'humanité débordait!' (1150). This balance or near-balance of moral forces in the priest is the fulcrum on which the entire novel sways. Pitched between two duties, Méautis confronts the tragic gap between human and divine measures of judgement. Zola, who blamed Méautis (X, 52), could or would not appreciate the intensity of his struggle, his religious and also aesthetic differences with Barbey closing his eyes to a thematic structure built not only on Christian notions of guilt but also on a sense of forces in deadlock, a sense reminiscent of classical and especially Cornelian tragedy. There are several echoes in this section of the book (Chapter XXIII) of seventeenth-century theatre: Sombreval is Tartuffe (1146), Méautis is Joad (1150) as well as Éliacin (1148) as Barbey strives for appropriate literary parallels to the conflicts within his novel. Méautis is the crucial figure in articulating these conflicts. In terms of the history of the Catholic novel he is a character of major, pioneering importance, the literary embodiment of the relationship between two planes of existence, and the seriousness with which he is depicted is a further and conclusive refutation of the old image of Barbey as a dilettante Catholic writer out for easy literary effect.

What makes *Un prêtre marié*, more than the earlier Barbey novels, a text justifying the use of the term 'Catholic novel' is the nature of the moral problem it poses. Whereas *Une vieille maîtresse* and *L'Ensorcelée* had centred on ethical questions of a type familiar to readers of secular novels (marital infidelity, political choice), *Un prêtre marié* has at its heart the question of offence to God – Sombreval's breaking of his priestly vows, compounded by his pretence of regained faith – an offence carrying a stain of guilt that extends beyond him to his daughter. The Catholic drama is not on the periphery of the novel, but at its centre, implicating the reading process on every level. The whole novel is structured in such a way as to create an ever-shifting network of moral viewpoints on the guilt or innocence of the central characters.

This structuring raises the question of narrative technique, an aspect of *Un prêtre marié* which has not received proper critical attention, but which is one of the keys to its interpretation. As has been described above, it shares with the two novels previously discussed a complex and multi-layered narrative presentation. A first narrator, who is assumed to be writing the text, and whom we can call 'Barbey', functions as a surrogate reader, priming our expectations from the start by his curiosity about the portrait in the locket, shown to him by his nameless hostess. This first narrator listens to, and records, the story of the girl in the portrait (Calixte) as told by a second narrator, Rollon Langrune, who draws in part from the indirect testimony of a third narrator, Jeanne Roussel. This use of multiple narrators not only confers a problematic status on the events of the story, but has profound implications for its meaning. Rollon is frequently taken as a mere self-portrait of Barbey – or as what Brian Rogers calls 'an [. . .] exaggerated self-idealisation'.[30] Roger Bésus argues in a similar vein: 'Il se trouve donc que ce roman de Barbey nous est donné comme le report par Barbey du récit fait par Barbey à Barbey!'[31] Barbey no doubt provided the justification for these easy parallels by the uses he was prone to make of the name of Rollon, that of the first duke of Normandy, which for him symbolised all things Norman. On his difference from writers who scorn the use of Norman *patois*, for example, he writes: 'Que le Diable m'emporte dans le côté d'enfer où cuit le vieux Rollon, si je vous comprends, mes amis, Normands infidèles, traîtres au pays et à son patois!' (CG III, 108). As for the name Langrune (a hamlet near Caen), he expressed to Trebutien his interest in its etymology (CG IV, 236). He often refers to Rollon as if he were a real-life writer, and seems to regard him, outside the context of this one novel, as an *alter ego* (CG IV, 300,321, etc.) even signing some of his letters 'Rollon'. Despite all of this, it would be wrong to identify as Barbey the Rollon who is the novel's principal narrator, and totally misleading to assume that he represents the definitive and authoritative moral viewpoint within it. The Rollon of the novel is a fictional character; he is introduced as such, and while his voice gives the book its acerbic tone and flamboyant colour, he is, from the moral point of view, merely an individual, the holder of a partial view, the exponent of one particular moral angle in the novel's constellation of moral angles. As has been seen, he holds the view, in opposition to the rational level of meaning, that diabolical forces are at play within Sombreval. His moral viewpoint is in accordance with this outlook, representing the harsh and intransigent side of the debate. He sees Sombreval's scientific pursuits, and all science, as a source of poisonous untruth; he supports the abbé Hugon's action of revealing the fact of Sombreval's atheism to his wife (just as later he supports

Méautis's decision to do the same to Calixte); he expresses agreement with the crowd's attack, not just on Sombreval but also on Calixte, and he sides with La Malgaigne against Néel. He represents one strand of opinion in the novel which perhaps reflects Barbey's reading of that stern and uncompromising philosopher of the Counter-Revolution, Joseph de Maistre. 'Ce grand esprit', 'ce mâle esprit', 'un admirable cerveau', '[un] merveilleux esprit' (II, 968, 997, 999) – Barbey's expressions of admiration are numerous, especially for the de Maistre of *Les Soirées de Saint-Pétersbourg*, in which are expressed two of the central ideas of Rollon's tale and of the morality that underlies it: namely, the notion of the moral origin and significance of illness (here, that of Calixte, as a sign of God's wrath against both her and her father), and secondly the idea of the transmission of moral blame from fathers to children. If Rollon can be described as professing a Maistrian morality, Barbey's admiration for which has ample external expression, it does not follow that the entire novel can be adequately resumed in such ideological terms. As Barbey says to Trebutien in words that are crucial for the understanding of this novel:

> Je crois que j'ai aussi mes *Soirées de Saint-Pétersbourg* dans la tête mais j'y ai aussi d'autres choses. Je n'ai pas que la tendance politique et philosophique. Dieu m'a pétri de je ne sais combien de limons! Peindre des sentiments, des passions et leurs luttes, les dramatiser en les peignant, c'est un besoin de mon esprit autant que de raisonner sur les choses et d'en interroger les principes. Je suis double et triple et multiple, mais tout ce faisceau de facultés, ce fagot, diraient mes ennemis (et peu importe, le fagot flambe!), tout cela, c'est moi. Faut-il casser son *moi* comme on casse un bouchon de cristal, et des dix mille facettes où se jouait la lumière n'en prendre qu'une?. (CG III, 111)

Too often Barbey has been seen as the exponent of one particular view, an orthodox or perhaps reactionary view; but he knew, and these words to Trebutien prove it, that novelists do not thrive on the expression of one view, that novels depend on conflict, and – in his words – the 'luttes' of sentiments and passions. If ever a novel has suffered from being regarded as the mere distillation of a reactionary morality, and needs to be seen afresh as a work of fiction structured on the interplay of contrasting moral viewpoints, it is *Un prêtre marié*. Rollon stands for only one of these viewpoints, and alternative value systems arise from the text, either through other characters, especially Néel, or else from what one could call a 'deep narrative' that tells a different story from Rollon's, and which is articulated through the combined resources of all the suggestive devices of the text. What expresses Barbey is not Rollon, but the entire novel.

Néel plays a major role in this process. He occupies the moral pole opposite to that of Rollon and La Malgaigne. In creating this dashingly heroic figure, Barbey is recalling to some extent the memory of his literary idol Byron. Néel's death-defying ride, to impress Calixte, is reminiscent of *Mazeppa*, and its physical result, for Néel, is a lifelong limp: another homage to Byron. It would be wrong to take the Byronic parallels much further, though; if there is a deeply Byronic figure in the text, representing the unbridled pride of the Byronic rebel, it is rather Sombreval than Néel.[32] Néel, more generally, is the handsome but doomed hero of romantic fiction, around whose sheer attractiveness an opposing set of values to those of Rollon and La Malgaigne is established, and whose love for Calixte is accompanied by a growing admiration for Sombreval's paternal qualities which radically alters the status of his personality. Néel, whose first encounter with Sombreval had seen him at the receiving end of the older man's fist, soon finds him 'presque beau' (935), to which Rollon at once interjects his scorn for Néel's judgement, blinded by love as he is. The same dissociation from Néel is expressed by Rollon in the following chapter – 'Pauvre Néel' (954) to be so deceived! So the novel shapes itself very early into a conflict between sympathy for the Sombreval–Calixte–Néel trio and the harsher judgement of them which is written into Rollon's narrative. A further element reinforces the attractiveness of Néel and his side of the conflict: the clash between him and his father, in which the *senex*, as comic tradition will have it, represents bigotry and austerity. The fathers of Néel and of Bernardine are both stern and prejudiced men, and Sombreval's father too, as recollected by his son, falls into the same typology: 'C'était un homme dur, absolu, avec un cœur de chêne plutôt qu'un cœur d'homme [. . .] je n'ai jamais cru aux pères qui maudissent' (1009). Such sentiments make Méautis recoil in horror, for the authority of the father is sacrosanct in his Christian code as well as Calixte's, who sees fathers as God's representatives on earth. The deep text, however, warns of the element of social convention and conditioning involved in such generalisations. The novel sways back and forth between these various sets of opposed judgements, sympathy being engendered now for one, now for another of the clashing viewpoints. Alliances of moral arguments coalesce, break down, reform in different configurations – Néel now against, now for Sombreval, Méautis now disagreeing, now agreeing with La Malgaigne, the human and religious scale of values constantly vying for supremacy. A symphony of constantly fluctuating moral centres of gravity is created; on great waves of sympathy and antipathy, the emotions of the implied reader are buffeted back and forth. And just as the Byronic element in the book is divided between Sombreval and Néel, so is the Maistrian element oddly divided between the two sides of the conflict. If Rollon's stern morality can in some respects be seen as Maistrian, de Maistre's elaborations on the doctrine of *réversibilité* lend something of their structure to the competing optimistic strand. The notion on which this doctrine is based, that of a chain of individuals interlinked through vicarious suffering, seems, as the novel progresses, to promise ultimate salvation for the unhappy trio: Sombreval's sin expiated by the suffering of Calixte, who in turn is redeemed romantically by the love of Néel. Barbey had announced his intention, to Trebutien, to base his novel on 'la grande idée chrétienne de l'Expiation' (CG IV, 269). The intention survives in the structure of the novel, though Rollon's narrative will have a less happy outcome than the optimistic pattern promises to yield.

The novel's ending has been the focus of much adverse critical comment, yet it is conditioned from the outset by the prophecies of La Malgaigne, which Barbey could scarcely have allowed to disappear from sight in the last chapter. Likewise, the retrospective nature of Rollon's narrative and the confidently inflexible morality written into it, is incompatible with a *dénouement* of forgiveness. Nevertheless, the ending poses problems to a reader who looks for a morality based on the apparent human merits of the characters. The strongest and most influential attack on *Un prêtre marié* from this point of view is that of Pierre Klossowski, who sees the novel as providing fodder for an anti-religious public in its separation of morality from religion. Sombreval, he argues, is honest and sincere, 'quitte à l'égard de sa conscience'; so 'que va-t-on lui chercher noise?'[33] Klossowski accuses Barbey, in refusing compassion for Sombreval's efforts as a father, of 'amoralisme absolu' (*vi*) and, following Zola (who anticipated his arguments in many respects), he links Barbey with Sade: 'Sade l'athée et Barbey le catholique sont moralement des nihilistes' (*vii*). But Klossowski commits the same error as many other critics in accepting Rollon's stance as the vantage point from which to read the novel. His argument becomes irrelevant if the text is approached as a problematic fictional structure incorporating not one view but several, and ending, not in vindication of Rollon, but in an ambivalence that is typical of Barbey and from which only very general conclusions can be drawn: namely, that in human actions the destiny of the immortal soul is inextricably involved, and that God's judgement is a matter of impenetrable mystery.

Further evidence that Barbey cannot be identified with the kind of stern moral strictures represented by Rollon is provided in his final novel *Une histoire sans nom* (1882). Its ingredients are by now familiar ones. A renegade Capuchin preacher, Riculf, seduces the girl Lasthénie while she is sleep-walking and makes her pregnant; she kills herself in horrific fashion, he pays the physical and symbolic price of having his hand severed at the wrist when attempting burglary. This violent action unfolds in Barbey's accustomed atmosphere of brimstone and sulphur. The setting, a small town in the Forez, is turned into a kind of natural hell through a series of images reminiscent of the *Inferno*: it lies in a deep hollow, an inverted cone, 'à diverse étages', with a circular road twisting like Dante's *bolge* through a series of 'balcons' (II, 267) or infernal ridges. Riculf, in tune with this setting, is obsessed by hell: it is the subject of his sermon in the local church, and the diabolical inspiration of his arrival in this place and his subsequent effect on Lasthénie is suspected by the old servant woman Agathe. The novel soon moves, as Barbey's novels always do, from the pungent atmosphere of the gothic to more serious moral issues, and the moral focus, as in *Un prêtre marié*, is on questions of guilt or innocence. The principal character in this respect, and the most interesting one in the book, is Lasthénie's mother, the austere Madame de Ferjol. At heart ardent and impulsive, she controls her instincts out of Christian principle. She is undemonstrative towards Lasthénie, mistrustful of all displays of affection, and fears the flesh so much that she has never even complimented her daughter on her beauty. Her puritanism is identified by the narrator as a heritage of Jansenism: it is '[une] piété venue de Port-Royal, et dont, à cette époque, la France des provinces portait encore l'empreinte' (II, 284). Even the crucifix with which she strikes herself, in self-reproach for not having protected Lasthénie, is a 'Jansenist' cross with arms raised high: to Madame de Ferjol, Christ is a figure of judgement and punishment, not of love, for all forms of love are to be feared. Even towards Lasthénie, she can show no love, and this, more than any agent from hell, is the reason for the 'vie infernale' which the two women share.

In drawing this portrait of the mother Barbey shows his awareness of the dangers of an unbending puritanism, closed to the possibility of God's forgiveness. 'La farouche janséniste,' he writes '[. . .] avait, hélas! plus de foi en la justice de Dieu qu'en sa miséricorde.' (II, 345) He attacks here the moral stance which Klossowski and others accuse him of defending in *Un prêtre marié*, which must make such accusations, to say the least, highly questionable. It is true that he is not without admiration for the force of Madame de Ferjol's character, for the 'probité, loyauté, religion, tous les atomes divins qui composaient cette noble femme' (II, 344), and for the final proud impenitence which prevents her from forgiving Riculf, just as he is susceptible to the extravagance of the egregious Rollon, but without having to agree with the moral code these fictional characters profess.

Barbey the novelist, in the last resort, never espouses one side in any conflict to the total annihilation of the other. There is an ambivalent pluralism in his work which makes him a more attractive novelist, to modern tastes, than has habitually been supposed. It makes *Un prêtre marié* a more accessible novel too, and at the same time no less a Catholic novel, but rather the very model of the genre in that it places the lives of its characters in a Christian perspective without sacrificing the tension proper to all great fiction. By his purely instinctive adaptations of the fantastic, at one moment using it to destroy the reader's comfortable expectations of a rationally coherent world, at the next diluting its absoluteness so as to allow moral concerns to occupy the centre of his stage, Barbey had laid down the essential base for the Catholic novel. The fashionable satanist had created his own limping devil.

3

Zola's New Testament

Barbey d'Aurevilly owes his image as a self-inflated, hypocritical and even sinister figure to the destructive portraiture of Émile Zola. The dandy in tight trousers and pleated tailcoat, the shrill Romantic, torturer of recalcitrant syntax and heir to the perverted Catholicism of the marquis de Sade – this was the persona created by Zola in his articles on Barbey,[1] in which he gave as good as he got for Barbey's onslaught on the Rougon-Macquart novels. Through the cannon-smoke of one of the nineteenth century's bloodier literary battlefields, the ideological positions of these two one-man batallions reveal their serious side. 'Il vient une heure,' says Zola, 'où l'on ne sait plus nettement où la réalité finit et où le rêve commence. Tel est depuis longtemps l'état de M. Barbey d'Aurevilly' (XII, 476). Barbey's preference for inhabiting a dream-world, in which, quips Zola, every street-walker is a *marquise* and a common mirror hanging on the wall a vast lake, placed him in the opposite literary camp to that occupied by the Realists. To this dweller within Baudelaire's 'chambre double', Zola was the importunate knocker at the door, reminding him of mundane reality. Barbey was an inevitable target of the campaign against romantic wishful-thinking, on the ruins of which Zola sought to build his own literary theories; but, more than this, he was the Catholic adversary who helped to channel Zola's broad scepticism in a specifically anti-Christian direction not foreseen or intended at the start of Zola's career. Their quarrel is a well-known minor fact of literary history, but how important it was for Zola's subsequent development has never been appreciated.

The initial encounter between the two occurred when Barbey reviewed *La Confession de Claude* in *Le Nain jaune* (30 December 1865), and dismissed it as 'trois cent vingt pages [de] ce que Cambronne plus concis jetait, en un seul mot, à la tête de l'ennemi'. Zola's swift reply was a review of the newly published *Un prêtre marié*, bearing the provocative title 'Le Catholique hystérique'.[2] Ignoring the book's complexities, Zola labelled it simply as a tract in defence of priestly celibacy, and drew from it a series of ideological prejudices which he attributed directly to Barbey: 'la science est maudite, savoir c'est ne plus croire, l'ignorance est aimée du Ciel; les bons paient pour les méchants; l'enfant expie les fautes du père; la fatalité nous gouverne, ce monde est un monde d'épouvante livré à la colère d'un Dieu et aux caprices d'un démon' (X, 49–50). Here Zola brought together for the first time the themes of science and religion, which he had hitherto discussed as separate issues. He had not yet renounced Christian belief, and had portrayed sympathetically the religious aspirations of Claude, the hero of his recent novel; and although his enthusiasm for science was already stirring, he still saw a place in a rational universe for 'le dieu infini et les lois immuables qui découlent de son être et régissent les mondes' (X, 313). Barbey's novel placed God's immutability in an altogether different perspective, and showed Zola the stark opposition between science and a traditional form of religion in which mingle superstition, occultism and the terror of a punishing deity.

Zola's response was specific and immediate: he wrote *Madeleine Férat*, the last of the pre-Rougon-Macquart novels, which parodies *Un prêtre marié* in a number of ways, including a new version of Sombreval's castle, complete with laboratory, from which hellish fires illuminate the surrounding countryside. Its occupant, M. de Viargues, has a past history which is borrowed from that of Néel de Néhou: both are noblemen, born in exile of mothers now buried in foreign soil. Like Sombreval, he pursues scientific researches. The most obvious echo of Barbey, however, is in the character of the old servant Geneviève, in whom the figure of La Malgaigne is instantly recognisable. In his review, Zola expressed a sneaking admiration for Barbey's characterisation of the old prophetess – as long, he said, as he was not expected to take her predictions seriously. His own character, Geneviève, utters similarly dire prophecies: that her master will make a pact with the devil, that Satan will visit him one night and strangle him. These prophecies, accompanied like La Malgaigne's by 'visions', 'come true' while remaining utterly false: the characters all meet their anticipated doom, but for unambiguously natural reasons. Zola has used his rewriting of Barbey to confirm his own belief in the intelligibility of universal laws.

Behind the main plot, based on Zola's odd theory of the permanent marking or 'impregnation' of the woman by her first lover, runs a second plot concerning the de Rieu couple, which is used by Zola to illustrate the kind of devilry in which he *did* believe: namely, that which resides in Man, a human 'cruauté diabolique', culminating in de Rieu's 'idée diabolique' (I, 873) of trapping his wife in a disastrous marriage with her lover after his own death. Here, to Zola, was the only form of menace from beyond the grave to which he could give credence. In his world, he was clearly stating, there is no room for the hell that possesses Barbey's imagination. As for devils, they were only to be found wearing laboratory smocks and brandishing Bunsen burners instead of their traditional toasting-forks. 'Le Lucifer moderne,' wrote Zola in this same period, 'cet ange révolté de la science, ne consent plus à effrayer les enfants, il veut instruire les hommes' (XIII, 121).

The effect of Zola's encounter with Barbey's novel was to harden his determination to combat superstition, and especially belief in the machinations of the devil. Whenever such beliefs are invoked in his novels, the spectre of Barbey is not far away. The rumours that spread through Plassans of the diabolic possession of François Mouret (*La Conquête de Plassans*) or that occult forces have helped Pierre Rougon rout the emperor's enemies (*La Fortune des Rougon*) are reminiscent of the mutterings of the Norman peasants about Sombreval, as are the legends of Croquemitaine attached to Florent by the butchers of Les Halles (*Le Ventre de Paris*) or the Montsou miners' fears of a subterranean devil (*Germinal*). In *Le Docteur Pascal*, local suspicion of Pascal's experiments is another echo of the same source, and when old Félicité Rougon describes her son's potions as 'sa cuisine du diable' (VI, 1167), she uses the self-same phrase by which Barbey's peasants allude to Sombreval's brew'.[3] In the same book, the itinerant Capuchin preacher who intones against the evils of science could have stepped from the pages of *Une histoire sans nom*.

His reading of Barbey led Zola to cling more fiercely to a rational and scientific interpretation of life, which in turn was eventually to erode any last vestiges of his adolescent religious yearnings. One can argue that it also played a part in forming his moral sense, and especially his indignation in the face of unjust suffering. The two young characters in *Madeleine Férat*, Madeleine and Guillaume, are condemned like Calixte and Néel by their rural community, but the narrator of Zola's novel, unlike Rollon Langrune, defends them against scandal: an assertion of Zola's humanitarian stance, found wanting in his Catholic adversary. The Rougon-Macquart novels are full of young people who suffer and die for their elders, not to placate an angry God but for very human reasons. Calixte's expiation of her father's apostasy has its dechristianised equivalent in the death of little Jeanne in *Une page d'amour* or in the martyrdom of Silvère Mouret in *La Fortune des Rougon*. The spurning of Silvère's girlfriend Miette by her fellow revolutionaries because she is the daughter of a criminal recalls the injustice inflicted on the equally innocent 'fille de prêtre' in the church at Le Quesnay.

Paradoxically, between these two ideological opponents, there were certain artistic similarities, a common liking for excess and violence, for images of blood and fire.[4] Even here, however, there is a major difference between them. In Barbey, horror translates perverse, satanic violence, an eruption from within the unfathomable depths of Man. In Zola, it is always subject to the overall priority of the scientific *enquête*. Only when François Mouret's madness has been established by careful 'observation' of its medical and environmental causes, and when Madame Faujas' blind love of her son has been similarly explained, does Zola permit himself scenes like the one which brings *La Conquête de Plassans* to a close: the fight of the two characters, sinking their fangs into each other like animals as the house blazes around them. Here, Zola would have said, he is working in the domain of the *connu*, charting the probable results of rationally observed psychological aberration; the world of Barbey, in contrast, is the world of the *inconnu*.

These opposed terms recur throughout Zola's writings, and indeed offer a path through them, from their first use in 1879 up to and beyond the end of the Rougon-Macquart cycle. Beginning as a near-synonym of 'ideal' or 'rêve', which represent the fanciful world of the lyrical dreamer against which rationalism, science and the novel – in a word, Naturalism – must struggle, 'l'inconnu' assumes increasingly specific philosophical connotations. The scientific method, wrote Zola, consists in 'marcher du connu à l'inconnu' (X, 1234) – that is, using verifiable phenomena as the basis for exploring new territories that will eventually surrender their mysteries to reason. He took this idea from the physiologist Charles Letourneau, who had written: 'Le mystérieux n'est que l'inconnu du présent, destiné le plus souvent à être connu dans l'avenir',[5] and applied it to the work of one of his idols, Claude Bernard. The latter's method, he wrote, was to 'traquer la vérité d'inconnu en inconnu' (X, 1218), and the 'experimental' novelist must emulate him, 'aller du connu à l'inconnu' in opposition to 'idealist' novelists who 'restent de parti pris dans l'inconnu, par toutes sortes de préjugés religieux et philosophiques, sous la prétention stupéfiante que l'inconnu est plus noble et plus beau que le connu' (X, 1189). Here the 'inconnu', rather than being a temporary vacuum to be filled by science, becomes an entity with its own philosophical and religious values.

Significantly, this semantic change is confirmed in one of Zola's essays on Barbey, where the old enemy emerges as the embodiment of all his negative principles, at once romantic, idealist, fantast – and Catholic. Barbey's novels, said Zola, show utter disrespect for truth and a preference for its adversary, belief in the supernatural. In him, the complicity between Catholicism and the 'inconnu' is finally made clear. Not just Barbey, but all Catholics, indeed all believers in God, are henceforth seen by Zola as standing in the way of the modern world's inexorable progress towards truth:

> Les catholiques et même les simples déistes, qu'ils soient romantiques ou doctrinaires, ont la prétention d'être les seuls grands, les seuls vertueux, les seuls charitables, parce qu'ils laissent l'inconnu à l'homme. Nous croyons, nous, que tous nos maux viennent de l'inconnu, et que l'unique besogne honorable est de diminuer cet inconnu, chacun dans la mesure de sa force. (XII, 507).

The ignorance which the Naturalist novelist must combat is identified here as that which Catholicism perpetuates in its own interests, the outmoded belief in a supernatural dimension which obstructs the triumph of the scientific method. The example of Barbey had helped Zola to complete the vital bridge between the *critique* of Romanticism and the rejection of Christianity, and to define Naturalism, in the same essay, in specifically anti-Christian terms:

> Nous ne sommes pas les ouvriers de la foi, mais les ouvriers de la méthode, je veux dire que nous nous en tenons aux faits prouvés, sans nous embarrasser des dogmes d'une religion sur le bien et le mal. (XII, 505)

In time, Zola saw Naturalism as much more than a prescription for the writing of novels. He skilfully publicised it as a universal method, based on observation, analysis and experimentation, and applicable to social and political as well as literary structures. Just as, in his own words, it was sufficient to replace the term 'médecin' by the term 'romancier' to convert Bernard's experimental physiology into a literary doctrine (X, 1175), so is the language of Naturalist theory made up of movable and interchangeable parts: 'Le théâtre/la République/la Russie [*sic*] sera naturaliste ou il/elle ne sera pas'

(X, 1235; X, 1380; XIV, 569). Naturalism, identified as the emancipating doctrine towards which the whole world was inexorably advancing, was an all-embracing recipe for tomorrow, and the metaphysical speculation of traditional religion belonged to yesterday: 'L'homme métaphysique est mort, tout notre terrain se transforme avec l'homme physiologique' (X, 1203). 'Bossuet man' must yield to 'Darwinian man' (XIV, 568–9), aware of his condition in a world ruled by the laws of science.

* * *

Catholicism's reaction to these direct challenges from Zola is attested by countless press reviews and comic-strip caricatures, but none of these express Catholic resentment of his annexation of fiction as directly as an extraordinary text by Roger de Fourniels, which was no less than a rewriting of *Germinal*. Fourniels, the author of a number of insipid children's books and a life of Jean-Baptiste Laroudie, the 'worker saint' of Limoges, published his *Floréal* the year after Zola's novel, borrowing his title from the same source as the original – the revolutionary calendar. It is a tale of life in a mining village, where bosses are benevolent distributors of five-franc pieces, and where the only disharmony comes from socialists like the eponymous hero, '[qui] avait des mots à vous donner la chair de poule',[6] and whose companions are not above blowing up the cross in the village square. Most of the main elements of Zola's novel have their would-be satirical equivalents: disputes over safety props (in which managers are in the right), pursuits up and down pit-ladders, strikes and political agitation. All ends happily when Floréal, in remembrance of his mother, sees the error of his ways and betrays his friends to the authorities. Utterly insignificant as literature, *Floréal* deserves rescue from its present oblivion as a document on the status of Zola as the Catholic community's principal bogey-man. The price Zola had to pay for killing Old Nick was to assume, himself, the role of the new one.

The time came, however, when forces much greater than prejudice and bigotry created a new challenge for Zola. By the late 1880s, the intellectual climate in France had changed. The decline of scientific optimism and, following Caro's introduction of Schopenhauer to France, of optimism *tout court*, combined with a kind of mystical backlash in the form a new idealist and spiritualist current exemplified by de Vogüé, Brunetière and Bourget,[7] forced Zola to take fresh stock of his position. The idea that science had failed to live up to the heady predictions that had been made for it – not so much by scientists themselves as by publicists like Zola – was reflected in both *L'Œuvre* and *La Joie de vivre*. His response, and his characteristic move from self-defence to counter-attack, came in five novels – *Le Rêve*, *Le Docteur Pascal* and the three books of the *Trois Villes* series, *Lourdes*, *Rome* and *Paris*. In these texts, relatively neglected by critics compared with the great novels of the Rougon-Macquart series, the theme of religious belief occupies the central role. From now on, the challenge to Christianity was a more conscious motive in Zola's writing than before.

Le Rêve came as a surprise, and its irony has often proved invisible to Catholic readers. Less provocatively offensive than its predecessors, it has sometimes been regarded as a glorious exception amidst Zola's work in its supposed sympathy to religious sentiment. Henri Guillemin, alert to any glimmer of a less irreligious Zola, takes at face value his statement in the *ébauche* that he wished to reflect the new idealist spirit, and to introduce into *Le Rêve* elements of 'l'inconnu, l'inconnaissable'.[8] In the novel itself, however, these familiar terms carry their accustomed ironic weight. 'Désespérément,' says the narrator, describing the vain death-bed pleas of the young Angélique for God's mercy, 'elle appelait l'inconnu, elle prêtait l'oreille à l'invisible' (V, 1289). Although he displays great compassion for the girl and understanding of her spiritual needs, he distances himself from her religious longings, presents them quite specifically as illusory. The invisible world, peopled by angels and saints, 's'élargissait de tout ce qu'elle ignorait, s'évoquait de l'inconnu qui était en elle et dans les choses. Tout venait d'elle pour retourner à elle, l'homme créait Dieu pour sauver l'homme, il n'y avait que le rêve' (V, 1214). Zola's adhesion to the materialist position was thus quite unambivalent. 'Dans ma série,' he wrote in his notes for the novel, 'je ne puis admettre l'au-delà, l'inconnu que comme un effet de forces qui sont en nous dans la matière et que nous ne connaissons pas, simplement' (V, 1320).

The yearning for an immaterial basis for hope becomes part of a dialectical process in *Le Docteur Pascal*, its opposition to faith in science dramatised in the relationship between Pascal Rougon and his niece Clotilde. Pascal's grudging admission that religious belief is a useful psychological prop to those lucky enough to be able to accept it does not satisfy her; she looks beyond the psychological utility of religion to its inherent truth. The ineradicable obstacle for

Pascal, as she says, is his relegation of the supernatural to the status of a provisionally unexplained mystery, the elucidation of which is the task of 'la conquête sans fin sur l'inconnu' (VI, 1221). The familiar term, once more, is at the centre of the novel's thematic structure and of the conflict of uncle and niece. A negative quality to him because irreconcilable with his factualism, the unknown represents to her the very hope which science has eradicated while putting nothing in its place.

Clotilde expresses a change of emphasis in Zola's attitude towards science. His disappointment at the slowness of scientific advance is evident. 'Encore,' says old Félicité scornfully of her son, 'avec sa science, s'il pouvait tout savoir!' (VI, 1173). Even Pascal admits that there are things that will possibly never be known to Man. Science is not rejected: it must go on searching. But Zola now allows a new element to play its part in scientific discovery: imagination, that old suspect quality of the lyric poet. 'Ces sciences où l'hypothèse balbutie et où l'imagination reste maîtresse,' he writes, 'elles sont le domaine des poètes autant que des savants! Les poètes vont en pionniers, à l'avant-garde, et souvent ils découvrent les pays vierges, indiquent les solutions prochaines' (VI, 1234).

Just as, years earlier, Zola had begun by mistrusting the fruits of imagination, and had identified them later with religion, so does his rehabilitation of imagination precede the next step in the evolution of his thought: to seek a new role for religion. This was to be the primary aim of the two novel cycles that followed *Les Rougon-Macquart*, but *Le Docteur* Pascal, last of the Rougon-Macquart novels, is also, in this respect, the prelude to them. In it, Zola begins to define his own religion, which is the religion of life. 'La vie,' muses Pascal, 'était l'unique manifestation divine. La vie, c'était Dieu' (VI, 1186). 'Je crois à la vie,' he tells his mother, '[. . .] qui marche quand même à la santé, au renouvellement continu, parmi les impuretés et la mort' (VI, 1227). His confirmation in this creed comes through the mutual love between himself and Clotilde, in which their intellectual differences are reconciled. There is a certain smudging of the edges between Zola's grand concepts, however. The relationship between Life, Love and Science is a poetic rather than logical one, based on thematic juxtaposition rather than clarity of idea. The love of the characters is realised, declared and consummated following the revelation by Pascal to Clotilde of his life's labours: the tracing of the genetic patterns in the Rougon-Macquart family. Pascal, says Clotilde, has now shown her 'la vérité': the true *inconnu* is the future to which the life force is taking Man, and of which science studies the mechanisms – the force in which she and Pascal participate through the sexual love that generates life. This love is divine: 'Et c'était la divinité en effet, l'entière possession, l'acte d'amour et de vie' (VI, 1278). After a night together, they open the window 'pour que le printemps entrât': 'Le soleil fécondant d'avril se levait dans un ciel immense, d'une pureté sans tache, et la terre, soulevée par le frisson des germes, chantait gaiement les noces' (ibid.). Here is the positive, long-postponed sequel to the scene in *Mouret* when sun and nature have to invade the church through the windows. Now they are invited in, for a ritual celebration of the religion of life. Pascal and Clotilde, in placing love above Christianity, fulfil the love that the latter creed, in the case of Serge and Albine, had frustrated. They redeem the real 'fault' of the abbé Mouret, his sin against life and love. The allusion is specific: 'Elle [Clotilde] était Albine, l'éternelle amoureuse' (VI, 1292). She is also, in a sustained biblical image, Abisaig the Sunamite, and Pascal the ageing King David, while the Rougon-Macquart family tree is compared to the genealogy of the Hebrew race (VI, 1290). Having thus annexed the Old Testament, Zola would soon go on to write his new one. It begins with the birth of Pascal's and Clotilde's child – 'le rédempteur peut-être', 'le messie attendu' (VI, 1400). The exaltation with which Zola declared his new religion is measured by the force of these potent images from the old.

Le Docteur Pascal also looks back. It is a celebration of Zola's literary achievement. Pascal's research into his family's genealogy is a metaphor for the composition of the Rougon-Macquart novels. Just as heredity is the instrument by which the life force assures continuity, so is the fictitious family tree of the Rougon-Macquart Zola's form of permanence. The ambitions of scientist and novelist coalesce, but the nature of their enterprise differs. Zola, who controls his world as its creator, as 'God', has *done* what Pascal can only dream of doing: he has 'captured' heredity, made the world 'à son gré'. The roles of scientist and novelist as seen by Zola earlier are now reversed: the former was the doer, through active experimentation, the latter the mere observer. Now the novelist Zola emerges as the doer, the creator; Pascal observes. This is a specific theme: early in the novel, Pascal still believes in intervention, defining his aim as a doctor as to contribute to 'la cité future de perfection et de félicité' (VI, 1186). He expounds his scientific Credo, his belief in the advancement of Man through scientific knowledge. But if Life is a force with its inexorable processes, what becomes of science's interventionist role? Recognising this dilemma, Pascal withdraws to a passive stance, trusting in evolution to accomplish its task, and abandoning his medical practice to devote himself to pure study. In redefining the scientist's role as that of an observer rather than an experimenter, Zola equalises the relative roles of scientist and writer, the latter no longer the poor cousin of the former.

Now that he was forced to dilute his claims for what science could do, Zola's theory of art had lost a prop, had become more exposed and more vulnerable. It is significant that *Le Docteur Pascal* begins, not with debate on the opposing claims of religion and science, but with a scene in which Clotilde paints pictures of the hollyhocks used in Pascal's genetic experiments. Pascal comments disparagingly on the contrast between the naturalistic techniques his niece previously employed in her painting – 'une minutie, une exactitude de dessin et de couleur extraordinaire' (VI, 1164), which he prefers – and what she now paints: 'toute une grappe de fleurs imaginaires, des fleurs de rêve' (ibid.), which signal to Pascal her departure into 'l'inconnu'. The opposition between the central characters is initially an aesthetic one. 'Peut-on perdre son temps à de telles imaginations?' asks Pascal scornfully. 'Il n'y a ni santé ni même beauté possible, en dehors de la réalité' (VI, 1217). He voices here Zola's mistrust of imaginative transpositions of reality. Clotilde's paintings represent another way of seeing, closely related to her spiritual outlook. Her original hard-headed realism had impressed Pascal, and the double contamination of her 'bonne petite caboche ronde et solide' – the phrase is used twice, in both aesthetic and religious contexts (VI, 1164–5) – perturbs him. The 'bonne petite caboche' typifies both the Naturalist aesthetic and religious scepticism. Although Zola, in recognition of the changed intellectual climate, was at this stage more tolerant of the need for an 'au-delà', and ready to create his own forms of religion, the challenge of these changes to the theories on which his life's work had been built was bound to concern him. When Clotilde tells Pascal that acceptance of an invisible dimension would interfere with his researches, this is truer still of the effect which such an acceptance would have on Zola's Naturalism. His comment in the *ébauche* of *Le Rêve*, quoted earlier, now becomes clearer: he could not admit the existence of 'l'au-delà or of 'l'inconnu', except as elements grounded in physical reality. He could not do so, not only for philosophical or religious reasons, but for aesthetic ones also. The ground rules of Realism were again at work, on Zola as they had been on the Goncourts. Their defence and justification were a necessary first step before Zola could go on to elaborate his religion of life.

* * *

The *Trois Villes* trilogy centres on the character of Pierre Froment, a priest who has lost his faith and who seeks first to regain and later to reform it as he travels to Lourdes, to Rome and back to Paris. Zola's own visits to Lourdes in 1891 and 1892 gave caricaturists an opportunity not to be missed. Cartoon portraits of the old reprobate in priestly garb or diluting the liquor of the *assommoir* with Lourdes water; of the father of the Rougons and the Macquarts being pursued as a traitor by an angry crowd of his progeny or, less solemnly, going to Lourdes a healthy man and returning on crutches: these images delighted readers of the bourgeois and popular press alike (VII, 480–3).[9] Zola's motives, however, were not those of a would-be convert or even of a mildly penitent anti-clerical. Nor was he just making his habitual preparatory *enquête* before starting to write a new novel. The true reason for the journeys is suggested in the novel itself. Zola went to Lourdes to carry out a reconnaissance of the enemy position, to assess the strength of the new wave of religious fervour that was sweeping France towards the end of the century. The visions of Bernadette were the most spectacular of a series of 'appearances' of the Virgin in nineteenth-century France. They had begun with her revelation to Catherine Labouré in the rue du Bac in 1830, followed by her apocalyptic warnings to the peasant children Maximin and Mélanie et La Salette in 1846. After the eighteen manifestations at Lourdes, she had reappeared at Pontmain in 1871. A sceptic might dismiss such phenomena with hardly a second thought, but a realist novelist was bound to take them more seriously. The stories could scarcely be true! But if credence were given to them, if public opinion were to warm to a conception of the world in which visits from heaven were as regular as shooting stars, his own philosophy, and with it his own aesthetic, was in imminent danger of redundancy.

Naturalism was already under threat. 1891 was the year of Jules Huret's investigation into current literary trends, the year in which, in response to Huret's questions, Anatole France, Édouard Rod and Huysmans all declared Naturalism to be in terminal decline, while Lemaître and Mallarmé both estimated that it would not outlive

Zola. The campaign of self-defence was on, beginning with Alexis' famous telegram to Huret: 'Naturalisme pas mort. Lettre suit.' Zola, identifying Naturalism as 'la forme de l'esprit qui, fatalement, le pousse à l'enquête universelle', could not see how it could ever die.[10] But doubt was in the air, and the best means of self-defence, for Zola, was to counter-attack the ideology which he saw as the greatest threat to the foundations of his work: the belief in an 'idéal', synonymous for him with the supernaturalism of Christianity.

It is against this background that *Lourdes* can best be understood. The entire novel is seen from the viewpoint of Pierre Froment. Corresponding intellectually and emotionally to Zola's own position, it is a careful balance of sympathy for the credulous pilgrims and rational doubt as to the validity of their belief. Pierre's own religious belief and priestly vocation have been destroyed by his scientific studies. His intellectual dilemma is complicated by his love for an invalid girl: Marie de Guersaint, paralysed following a riding accident, with whom he travels to Lourdes and for whose sake he is even prepared to pretend to have regained his faith – there are obvious parallels with Sombreval in these plot details. Like Serge Mouret, Pierre has accepted 'la chair morte' (39); he is the only male allowed into the women's treatment room at night, on the grounds that a priest is not really a man. The main thrust of the novel, however, is in Pierre's intellectual doubts and his 'torturant besoin de la vérité' (37).

Lourdes functions on the documentary level as a study of religious belief in a modern context. The faith which Zola had long since regarded as a mediaeval relic insinuates itself into the contemporary world through that recurring Zolian image of modernity, the railway engine. The train, especially the white train which transports the gravely ill and severely handicapped, is the means of transport towards the hoped-for miraculous cure in the waters of Lourdes. Echoing with the prayers and hymns of the pilgrims, the train is transformed into a symbol of religious hope: '[un] train de souffrance et de foi, [un] train gémissant et chantant' (102). Inside, tales of miracles proliferate, each more spectacular than the last, all persuading the sick and suffering that there is hope for them, that miracles will rain down from the invisible hands of the Virgin.

The stories are told of Sophie Couteau, cured of a deformed foot; of Pierre de Rudder, whose fractured leg was healed by one drink of Lourdes water; of Louis Bourriette, his sight restored by washing his blind eyes in water from the holy spring; of Célestine Dubois, relieved of the agony of a needle embedded deeply in her hand for seven years and which came out miraculously during her pilgrimage to Lourdes. The reader's options in the face of these accounts are outlined in the contrasting reactions of Monsieur de Guersaint, with his natural love of the miraculous, and of Pierre, unable to credit any of them but unwilling to shatter such comforting illusions. Zola's rhetorical vocabulary determines the meaning of the text, as do Pierre's inner thoughts: his conviction that the cures of Lourdes depend on wrong medical diagnoses.

Despite Zola's impatience with the speed of scientific progress, its laws, sadly for the desperate pilgrims of Lourdes, still rule the universe. Science is represented by Dr Ferrand, whose rejection of religion is all the more poignant because of his love for the nun, sœur Hyacinthe (an echo of the Goncourts' Barnier and Philomène). Doctor and novelist share the same vested interest, the same need to exclude non-natural laws from Man's understanding of the world: 'Ses idées de jeune médecin étaient bouleversées devant cette [. . .] certitude que, si le Ciel le voulait, la guérison se produirait avec l'éclat d'un démenti aux lois mêmes de la nature' (114). Another doctor, Chassaigne, has revolted on the contrary against the scientific explanation of life – but because of grief at the deaths of his wife and daughter. When he confronts Pierre, the doctor/priest oppositions of *Une page d'amour* and other novels are ironically and consciously reversed: the priest has lost his faith, the doctor is a convert to Christianity. Dr Chassaigne becomes a key figure in the novel's intellectual network, with his scorn for a medical science that was unable to save his loved ones. He rejects the argument that more proof is needed of the miracles at Lourdes: as so many phenomena defy explanation, and as doctors disagree amongst themselves, the supernatural explanation of the cures at Lourdes is as good as any. Pierre, like Zola, leans to the theory of temporarily unexplained natural forces. He echoes the words of *Le Roman expérimental*: 'Notre éternel espoir doit être d'expliquer un jour l'inexpliqué; et nous ne saurions avoir sainement un idéal, en dehors de cette marche à l'inconnu pour le connaître, de cette victoire lente de la raison, au travers des misères de notre corps et de notre intelligence' (152).

Marie's paralysis is the focus of this debate. Pierre's cousin, Dr Beauclair, though not believing in the alleged supernatural agency of Lourdes, has urged Marie to go there, seeing her condition as psychological in nature and capable of being cured by the natural effect of a further emotional shock. Beauclair's description of the effects he is predicting – even Marie's sensation of spitting out 'un mauvais poids diabolique' (47) – will prove accurate; from the outset Zola is engineering the denouement of his novel. He is also reiterating his conviction of the physiological origin of emotion. Like earlier Zola heroines (Catherine in *Germinal*, Françoise in *La Terre*, Pauline in *La Joie de vivre*), Marie's menstruation is retarded, and the 'spitting out of the devil' is a metaphor for the physical release, the expulsion of the menstrual blood which is the symbol of fecundity and the entry into adult life. Marie is 'cured', exactly as predicted. As so often, the device of prediction is used ironically by Zola, for this cure, despite what the Catholic medical officers at Lourdes say, is clearly due to wholly natural phenomena.

Yet Man's thirst for the miraculous remains unquenchable. It is spectacularly illustrated when one of the priests at Lourdes, incited by the crowd, tries to bring to life a man who has died during the journey. The scene is presented as one of collective hysteria, the crowd dissolving into one single will. Mass religion is interpreted in terms of Zola's characteristic crowd psychology. The collective thirst for miracles has no more intellectual foundation than the collective hunger for bread in *Germinal*, but it is an equally imperious need. The parallel is not a fanciful one, for the imagery of *Lourdes* links the two novels. The crowd are hungry for 'l'aliment du divin, le festin du merveilleux' (161). Their religious fervour is an unrecognised need of social change and material improvement: they yearn for 'l'égalité du bonheur', 'la folie sainte de l'universelle joie' (166). But the anarchic force of Zola's crowds is always terrifying and, whatever its goal, has an invariable end: horror. The dead man is dropped into the pool where the sick bathe in search of a cure, 'et le mort restait mort' (139).

Mass fervour, not Bernadette's visions, constitutes for Zola the true phenomenon of Lourdes. What people seek there is 'ce pain du mensonge, dont la pauvre humanité a besoin pour vivre heureuse' (167). This image, uniting the religious, humanitarian, socialist and anti-supernaturalist elements in his thought, indicates the road that he now sees lying open to a new 'religion': faith in a better future, but a future on this earth, shorn of the illusion of belief in a world to come. This had been Zola's faith all through the Rougon-Macquart years; *Lourdes* confirms it, raises it to a level of universal hope, as the necessary prelude to *Les Quatre Évangiles*. Zola reiterates his concept of a religion of life, based on Man's longing, not for heaven but for a limitlessly extended and healthy life on earth, of which the Christian doctrine of 'eternal life' is a stylisation, a façade designed to console but which can never do so – which is why God is the second prize in the happiness stakes, and Christianity a religion of suffering, not of joy. Zola thus explains Lourdes in his terms: as a collective frenzy of desperate individuals worshipping life under the symbolic name of 'God' or 'Christ' or 'Virgin'. It is a creation of the crowd.

When he arrives in Rome at the start of the second novel of the trilogy, Pierre still hopes to find within Catholicism the means to alleviate the suffering he has witnessed at Lourdes. He goes there to defend a book he has written on *La Rome nouvelle*, expounding his progressive view of the Church as the leader of a world-wide campaign for social justice. But his hopes founder as he is confronted on the one hand by the simple evangelism of the lower clergy, represented by the abbé Rose, and on the other by the implacable conservatism of the hierarchy, in the person of Cardinal Boccanera. His dream of an intellectually reformed papal Rome dead, Pierre turns his attention to Italian Rome, the capital of the new democracy, where he sees new values burgeoning: social equality, based on work, truth and justice. Zola has put behind him his disappointment with science; not the solution of all ills, it still represents man's best hope. In the light of its discoveries, 'non seulement le catholicisme en était balayé, tel qu'une poussière de ruines, mais toutes les conceptions religieuses, toutes les hypothèses du divin chancelaient, s'effondraient' (999). Pierre embraces a new religion of science which will combat the *inconnu*, not cultivate it as Christianity is fated to do.

At the start of *Paris*, he is less headily optimistic. Whereas the first two novels of the series had begun with a hopeful quest, the third opens with Pierre's regret at the lack of any possible reconciliation between the Church and the Parisian working class. The Church's social doctrines are expounded by Monseigneur Martha, the spokesman for the Pope's Ralliement policy, ostensibly designed to persuade French Catholics to abandon their instinctively conservative political stance and espouse modern democratic ideas, even embrace the Republican regime. But, listening to the bishop's sermon in the Madeleine, Pierre sees the 'esprit nouveau' programme as simply a way of achieving survival for the Church until such time as it can exert its reactionary influence again. He condemns the new spirit of mysticism as part of a campaign against science, and he rejects the view he had reached at the end of *Lourdes* – namely, that *mensonge* is necessary to happiness. Brutal truth-telling is preferable, as the first step to a terrestrial religion of health, joy, justice, which will work for the provision of real bread for the masses, not 'le pain de l'illusion' (1180). He dreams, like Zola's gradualist socialist heroes of the Rougon-Macquart novels, of a fertile harvest 'où pousserait le monde meilleur de demain' (1191).

A new, as yet tentative interest appears in Zola's work at this stage: the ideas of the utopian social thinker Fourier, to which Pierre is introduced by friends of his brother, the chemist Guillaume. The most ardent disciple of Fourier in the novel is Bache, who heralds him as 'le vrai Messie attendu des temps modernes' (1315). The image reveals, however, Zola's misgivings about Fourierism at this stage: namely, that it is another messianic cult, as dependent on mystical faith as traditional religion. What attracts him in Fourier, and in other figures like St-Simon, Comte and Proudhon, is their concern for justice, peace and equality. Here, in the concentration of his efforts on the improvement of man's lot on earth, is Pierre's final intellectual resting-point, and modern Paris, city of 'libre intelligence' (1559) is its symbol. The enemy is again Catholicism, whose latest attempt to annex the world is embodied in the building of the Sacré-Cœur, monument to the miraculous. But science will prevail: 'La science achèvera de balayer leur souveraineté ancienne, leur basilique croulera au vent de la vérité' (1560). Through Pierre's apparent hesitations, his migration from idea to idea, Zola dramatises the intellectual turmoil of the turn of the century. But his own supposed recognition of the need for a religious sense, for mystery and hope in the 'au-delà', which is sometimes seen, by those who do not look beyond the later Rougon-Macquart novels, as his definitive ideological position, was very short-lived. The only dream which he would contemplate, now as always, was the dream he would describe in *Fécondité* as 'le rêve que la science autorise' (VIII, 506).

* * *

Zola's continued adhesion to the strict limits of the material world represents an important stable factor in his otherwise notoriously fluctuating and often confused thought. 'No other great novelist that I can think of,' says Philip Walker, 'is more radically incoherent on the philosophical or religious level than Zola.'[11] Certainly, the various ideals fervently espoused by Zola, and on which he was intermittently willing to bestow the status of 'religion' – fertility, truth, justice, reason, love, life – are presented with an absence of logic and clarity that justifies Walker's description of them as 'a vast cacophony' (ibid., 88). His rejection of the miraculous and the supernatural, however, was consistent, resolute and rigorous. The reason for this is clear. While the depth of his interest in ideas for their own sake should not be underestimated, his most profound concern was for their utility as an intellectual underpinning of his own art. Even his championing of science, as Hemmings has argued (op. cit., 59), was motivated by the need for a 'rubber-stamping' of his novels. As a corollary to this, his denial of Christianity had, as its prime motive, the defence of Naturalism in its widest sense: literary theory, mode of cognisance, epistemology. The *Trois Villes* trilogy has never been clearly seen for what it is: the vehicle of this defence.

Zola's tactic is to isolate those aspects of Christianity which can be integrated into Naturalism, and thus to present Catholicism as a partial, unconscious and inferior form of Naturalism. Much of *Rome* is devoted to an exposure of alleged contradictions within Catholicism. Supposedly a profoundly spiritual creed, it seems to Pierre, during his visit to the Catacombs, to proclaim totally human values, inspired by a flesh-and-blood agent: the man Jesus, 'un homme [. . .] semant l'humanité rajeunie qui allait transformer le vieux monde' (655). When he goes to the Vatican, its paintings and sculptures appear to him to celebrate a religion of life, based on nature, sex and fertility. The role of the novel's sub-plot, involving the unhappily married Benedetta and her love for Dario, expresses in human form the lesson of Renaissance statuary: 'la toute-puissance de l'amour', 'l'éternité de la vie' (714), though it culminates in what, with some justification, Dominique Fernandez has called 'la scène la plus colossalement ridicule de tout le roman français' (512) – where Benedetta strips naked and makes love to the dying Dario in full view of her servant and Pierre, then dies herself in 'un flot de sang' (905). This act of love is confirmed as a religious act, a homage to 'le grand Pan', to nature and fecundity; here, under Pierre's very nose – literally! – is the true religion, the divine sexual act. The morality of Catholicism, Pierre tells himself, opposes nature and sex. Yet it is a schizophrenic religion, unaware of its own true nature. Set in a landscape which itself offers a hymn to nature, Rome exudes 'l'odeur même de la virilité' (679). Pierre sees the Pope in the midst of the natural splendours of the Vatican gardens, and Catholicism strikes him as a Southern European cult of nature, unlike the soul-centred cults of the North. The message of Rome is that Nature and Life 'règnent [. . .] et gouvernent le monde, souverainement' (686).

Rome, in short, affirms without knowing it what Naturalism consciously preaches. Zola's point is clear: his critique of Catholicism implies the superiority of Naturalism.

In *Lourdes* too, Zola propagates his religion of love and procreation, synonymous with his religion of life. The virgin mother of Christ is recuperated by Zola, not as Virgin, but as Mother; Marie may think she is worshipping the Virgin, but she is unconsciously worshipping 'la Mère unique' (377), symbol of the life-creating process which chastity opposes. Pierre's renunciation of Marie is 'suicide', acceptance of a life 'hors nature' (382). Bernadette's enforced retirement to a convent is used by Zola to denounce the very doctrine enshrined in the Virgin's alleged words to Bernadette: the Immaculate Conception, in which he sees the denial of the beauty of sexual reproduction. Here Catholicism becomes the anti-religion, the opponent of the religion of life of which Naturalism is the Gospel. He imagines poor, misled Bernadette saying: 'Va-t'en, va-t'en, Satan! Laisse-moi mourir stérile.' 'Et,' his imaginary narrative runs on, 'elle chassait le soleil de la salle, et elle chassait l'air libre entrant par la fenêtre, l'air embaumé d'une odeur de fleurs' (ibid.). Her actions reverse the entry, through windows, of these same life-affirming natural elements in *La Faute de l'abbé Mouret* and *Le Docteur Pascal*.

Zola saw a role for Bernadette in the elaboration of his own religion. He presents her, not as a Catholic saint, but as the patron of a 'religion nouvelle' (80). She is a 'sainte humaine' by dint, not of her visions, but of her historically attested suffering in the years following them, when she was a prisoner of the Church. Bernadette's story is told in a parallel narrative, composed of episodes at the end of each of the book's parts, justified internally by Pierre's need to 'faire une enquête' (43). Like Zola, he has no doubts as to Bernadette's sincerity: 'Elle ne mentait pas, elle avait eu sa vision' (80). To give movement and contrast to his narrative, Zola sometimes has Pierre sway towards face-value acceptance of Bernadette. Seeing no way of making sense of her story by simple 'physiological' analysis, he is almost prepared to accept her as 'une élue de l'inconnu', 'une messagère de l'Au-delà' (94). But to Zola, this 'au-delà' would also mean 'au-delà des limites du Roman', and Zola, just like Bernadette, has to 'défendre la réalite de sa vision' (161).

To this end he absorbs Bernadette into his own fictional archetypes: into the type to which Angélique belongs, derived initially from his reading of Letourneau's pages on Saint Theresa. Typology is a vital element of Realist characterisation, the bridge between fiction and the real. By typifying Bernadette, Zola naturalises her into his own familiar world. Pierre embraces her as 'une sœur humaine', offers her 'un culte de fraternelle tendresse' (314). Like many of Zola's central consciousnesses, he is a surrogate novelist, representing the legend in natural terms, creating a paradigm of Naturalist narrative based on documentation, observation, reason, explanation. His purchase of a photograph of Bernadette, 'd'après nature', establishes her reality, and his account of her is based on Taine's method, the study of 'race', 'milieu' and 'moment'. He ascribes her susceptibility to the miraculous to local tradition, to peasant tales of apparitions, usually diabolic, to her known love of legend and Bible stories, and to the story of Mélanie, to whom the Virgin had appeared at La Salette.

Zola's strategy is most effective when he describes Pierre's visit to Bernadette's former home. The role of objects is important here: 'les objets vagues, inquiétants, qui emplissaient les coins, [. . .] de vieux tonneaux, des débris de cages à poule, des outils cassés, toutes les loques qu'on balaie' (302). Bernadette's humanity, as a human being in a world of objects, is stressed: 'le plafond enfumé, [. . .] cette saleté des vieux tonneaux, des outils hors d'usage' (307). Here is that part of her experience that the discourse of Realism can express, and can exploit to turn Bernadette into a Naturalist heroine, a lay saint, whose story illustrates, not the revelation of a supernatural order, but the common experience of despair and hope on which the new religion must be built. Bernadette is the apostle of this new religion. Pierre identifies her 'logis misérable' with the humble origins of Christianity: with Bethlehem (305). Bernadette's lowly humanity makes her home 'le lieu de rencontre, où naissent les religions nouvelles de la souffrance et de la pitié' (ibid.).

There are aesthetic as well as religious implications in this passage. Zola implies that the pomp of the Lourdes Basilica, the pomp of Rome itself, so different from the humble home of the Soubirous family, is a betrayal of the lowliness of primitive Christianity. Humble objects are not incompatible with true Christianity, but only with Catholicism's splendid and corrupt exterior. True religion must be based in the ordinary dimension which Realism reveals – in concrete reality shorn of the myth of supernature. Of this bedrock reality, Realism itself is the vehicle of revelation.

Realism's revelation comes to the eyes. The theme of physical sight runs through *Les Trois Villes*, and the entire trilogy illustrates the idea discussed in this present book's first chapter: the pre-eminence of the visible in the Realist and Naturalist aesthetic and its necessary clash with the invisible domain on which Christian belief depends. Throughout the trilogy, Zola shows that sight, on which Naturalist epistemology depends, is also at the heart of religious yearning. 'Ce besoin du divin,' he writes in *Paris*, 'n'est-ce pas simplement le besoin de voir Dieu?' (VII, 1560). The worthy abbé Rose, in *Rome*, is 'certain de ne pas mourir sans avoir vu Dieu sur la terre' (523). The cult of the Sacred Heart, which is the focus of Zola's satire in *Paris*, is founded on Saint Marie Alacoque's vision of the heart of Jesus beating in his open breast (1487). The visions of Bernadette represent the same phenomenon on a spectacular scale. Those who believe in these visions and in the miracles that they have generated give credence to a world that the eyes of the flesh cannot see. The needle emerging from Célestine Dubois' hand 'peuplait l'invisible, montrait à chaque malade son ange gardien derrière lui' (70). To see the invisible, blindness to the material world is a positive asset: père Massias, lost in his inner vision, stops seeing: '[Il] avait cessé de voir les malades autour du lui, il s'en allait en plein triomphe divin, dans l'aveuglement de sa foi' (350).

As for Marie, her moments of intense faith follow moments of 'seeing' the Virgin: she tells Pierre the Virgin has smiled and nodded to her. 'Avait-elle dormi,' Pierre wonders, 'les yeux ouverts?' (225). Even he longs at times to 'see', and the very eyes of those who have 'seen' fascinate him. He peers into Marie's eyes – 'grands ouverts, pleins encore de l'éclat des merveilles' (93). Even vicarious seeing, the possibility that others have seen, stirs belief. Eyes fall on eyes when the pilgrims watch Marie taking communion at the Grotto, 'avec ses yeux élargis': 'elle communia éperdument, le Ciel descendait visiblement en elle' (170). Seeing believers in the moment of their spiritual 'sight' reinforces the chain of belief from pilgrim to pilgrim, so that the crowd becomes 'ces milliers d'êtres dans une sorte de songe éveillé, en pleine vision de paradis' (204). The spectacle of Lourdes encourages the feeding of the eyes; as M. de Guersaint watches the candlelight procession, he exclaims: 'En vérité, je n'ai jamais rien vu de si extraordinaire' (210). Perfumes and natural sounds also combine to encourage belief in the invisible: in the darkness, the pilgrims can smell 'les roses invisibles' even if they cannot see them (212–3); the murmur of the mountain stream has 'une légère voix de cristal, qui semblait venir de l'invisible' (217). For poor Dr Chassaigne, the sight he longs for, obscurely mixed with his visual contemplation of the Virgin and the Grotto, is that of his dead loved ones: 'revoir dans une autre vie ses chères mortes' (230).

The ironic use of religious bric-à-brac discussed in the first chapter also plays an important part here: the idolatry of Lourdes, as Zola sees it, revolves on the large-scale commerce in rosaries and plaster Virgins (333). In the Roman Catacombs, a girl buys a paperweight bearing the sacred symbol of the Icthos (684). The magnificence of St Peter's is an invitation to the worship of concrete objects: believers kiss the bronze foot of the saint's statue (650). The great basilica is like 'une salle d'opéra' (650); it is empty of soul, a skeleton of 'un colosse monumental dont la vie se retirait' (651). It strikes Pierre as an icy museum, as 'un temple païen, élevé au dieu de la lumière et de la pompe' (652); above all as a feast for the eye, a visual spectacle out of keeping with the invisible domain it is supposed to represent. In the many Roman churches visited by Pierre, there is nothing that cannot be seen: 'Nulle part, pas plus qu'à Saint-Pierre, un coin d'ombre, un coin de mystère, ouvrant sur l'invisible' (653). Zola has developed here, on the massive scale of the Eternal City's ecclesiastical architecture, the de-symbolising techniques which he and other Realist novelists had applied to religious objects and artefacts. As in the Goncourts' *Madame Gervaisais*, which *Rome* often recalls, the Pope himself is transformed into an object in his statuesque 'raideur hiératique' (691); the image is stressed by the dressing-up of the statue of St Peter 'telle qu'un pape vivant' (700–1). Elsewhere the Pope is a wax idol (932). He is a necessary concrete and visible element, without which this allegedly spiritual creed cannot survive. The tourists thronging the great square, are 'bien contents d'avoir vu ça' (693). The Pope is 'Dieu dans un homme, Dieu sans cesse là, [. . .] Dieu visible!' (691), no less than a visible substitute for the invisible deity: 'les femmes [. . .] derrière lui, voyaient Dieu' (694). The idea that Christ himself was a visible front-man for an invisible (because non-existent) order is implied throughout these passages.

La Salette and Lourdes had raised 'seeing' to a new status. During her lifetime, seeing Bernadette herself was the next best thing to seeing the Virgin; the *voyante* had become the *vue*. Bernadette says of the Bishop who visits her: 'Il vient me faire voir.' 'Des princes de l'Église, de grands catholiques de combat voulurent la voir'; she expressed her 'horreur d'être en spectacle' (386). Now that Bernadette is dead, the Panorama at Lourdes offers compensation in the form of a visual narrative of her visions. The main focus of spectacle at Lourdes, however, is the statue of the Virgin in the Grotto. Pierre, hoping to regain his faith, stands before it, but it remains . . .

a statue: 'Et il n'éprouvait là que gêne et inquiétude, en face de ce décor, de cette statue dure et blafarde dans le faux jour des cierges' (124). As in *Mouret*, the statue sometimes 'semblait mouvante' (258); 'tous les yeux convergeaient [. . .] vers la tache blanche, mouvante de la Vierge de marbre' (259). Even Pierre imagines it moving: 'Il regardait la statue de la Vierge fixement, jusqu'au vertige, jusqu'à s'imaginer qu'elle bougeait' (275). The eyes of the statue and the eyes of those who behold it are linked in a further reinforcement of the theme of sight: 'le frère Isidore ne quittait pas des yeux la statue de la Vierge. [. . .] Ils la buvaient jusqu'à la mort. [. . .] Puis, rien ne bougea plus, les yeux demeuraient grands ouverts, obstinément fixés sur la statue blanche' (268). Even after Isidore's death, there is another reference to his eyes fixed on the statue, the dead watching the lifeless (271).

Naturalism, by revealing the visualising processes at the heart of Christianity, demystifies its creed. Catholicism is a religion of the seen, but its very falsity resides in its denial of this fact. Naturalism reveals our dependence on the seen, and is thus grounded in truth. For Zola, in the beginning is sight: each volume of the trilogy begins with an act of seeing. Marie, from the window of the white train, 'aperçut les fondations' (of Orléans, at dawn on the way to Lourdes) (23); *Paris* opens on a panoramic view of the city, with Pierre looking down from the steps of the Sacré-Cœur on this theatre of his own life and of the novel's totality. His first action on arriving in Rome is to have himself driven to a vantage point from which to see the entire city:

> Il voulait recevoir le coup en plein front, Rome entière vue d'un regard, la ville sainte ramassée, embrassée d'une seule étreinte. [. . .] Et Pierre, déjà, regardait de toute sa vue, de toute son âme, debout contre le parapet, dans son étroite soutane noire, les mains nues et serrées nerveusement, brûlantes de sa fièvre. Rome, Rome! la Ville des Césars, la Ville des papes, la Ville Éternelle qui deux fois a conquis le monde, la Ville prédestinée du rêve ardent qu'il faisait depuis des mois! elle était là enfin, il la voyait! (518–19)

In his survey of the different areas of the city, reminiscent of Hugo's 'Paris à vol d'oiseau', Pierre not only sees Rome, but also understands it, for sight transforms *inconnu* into *connu*. Knowing, in this context, has overtones – even sexual overtones – of possession:

> Un instant encore, Pierre resta debout contre le parapet. Depuis près d'une heure, il était là, ne parvenant pas à rassassier sa vue de la grandeur de Rome, qu'il aurait voulu posséder tout de suite, dans l'inconnu qu'elle lui cachait. Oh! la saisir, la savoir, connaître à l'instant le mot vrai qui'il venait lui demander! [. . .] Son cœur battait à ses tempes: quelle serait la réponse de Rome? (540).

The writer is caught here in his amorous rendezvous with his own material: 'il trouvait Rome telle qu'il la désirait'. The 'ardent' dream, the 'fever', relate the burning desire to see to what Armand Lanoux says about Zola's experience of 'brûler': to sexual excitement in the act of literary creation.[12]

Seeing, for Zola, was miracle enough. It was the satisfaction of a hunger no less intense than the spiritual yearning of the desperate pilgrims of Lourdes. Like them, he was, in his own words, 'affamé de choses vues'.[13] If religion is a creation of human longing, seeing is its mode of persuasion and alleviation, and religious 'vision' competes with Realism's doctrine of 'faire voir' as a means to truth. Zola had to demonstrate the illusory nature of the one to ensure the triumph of the other.

* * *

Religious, epistemological and artistic themes are brought together in *Paris* in the passages on the sculptor Jahan. Trying at first to sculpt a conventional angel, symmetrical and sexless, he revolts: what point is there in creating works of art which have lost all power to move and persuade? The redundancy of Christian art is a sure symbol of the redundancy of Christianity itself, Jahan concludes: 'Il faut bien aller à la foi nouvelle, et c'est la foi à la vie, au travail, à la fécondité, à tout ce qui besogne et enfante' (1308). So he turns to a new subject: a statue of Fécondité. Zola advertises here his own novel of that name, the first of the four planned volumes of his new cycle of novels, *Les Quatre Évangiles*.

Zola's reply to Huret's earnest enquiries about the health of Naturalism has never been given the attention it deserves. Less epigrammatically than Paul Alexis, he replied that there was life in the patient yet. He looked ahead towards 'une peinture de la vérité plus large, plus complexe, [. . .] une ouverture plus grande sur l'humanité, [. . .] une sorte de classicisme du naturalisme' (op. cit., 73). This is precisely what he provided in his last, unfinished cycle of novels. They are the result of a distillation of the principles and values which he had expressed in less concentrated form throughout the Rougon-Macquart years. They represent the systemisation and propagation of life-long enthusiasms, which he now embraced with a missionary fervour that bestowed on each of them the status of a doctrine, and on their combination that of a religion. This was the religion of life or, in his own phrase, 'la religion de l'humanité' (VIII, 849).[14] Its elements are fecundity, work, truth and justice. That Zola's untimely death prevented him from writing the fourth and last volume, *Justice,* scarcely reduces the impact of the three finished novels or obscures their collective sense, for, although each is centred on the ideal which its title conveys, they are mutually reflective of each other, their themes interwoven, so that none of the dreams on which they are built is long out of sight regardless of which of the three books one reads. Religion, ideal, dream – these are terms which could not readily have been applied to Zola's beliefs in earlier years. Now, stripped of supernatural associations, grounded in the human and the biologically possible, they were embraced by him: 'Le rêve restera toujours sans limites,' he writes, surveying the efforts of his fictional workers in *Travail* (958) – 'le rêve,' he makes clear in *Fécondité,* 'que la science autorise' (506).

Each of Zola's four Gospels has its evangelist. They are the four sons of Pierre Froment, called – in Zolian rather than New Testament order – Mathieu, Luc, Marc and Jean. *Fécondité* proclaims Zola's faith in his natalist theories, with every character and incident an illustration of the thesis that more life equals better life, that every advance in civilisation has followed the kind of population explosion which he now prescribes for France. The message of *Travail* is that work is ennobling, a natural passion corrupted by the social and ideological system. *Vérité,* in part Zola's reconstruction of the Dreyfus Affair, has as its central theme the heroic effort of secular education to found a future France on reason, science and the experimental method. The fragmentary notes for *Justice* indicates that it would have been a pacifist and anti-militarist novel.

Zola's doubts about science, such as they were, are now forgotten. The scientist's role in the building of a better future is shared, in *Vérité,* by the schoolteacher, whose scrupulous cartesianism will purify children's minds of superstition, so that the new generation will be capable of the happiness that comes from knowledge of the possible. In *Travail,* through the heroic figure of the sickly scientist Jordan, science is postulated as the foundation of all advancement and happiness, leading humanity 'à la vérité, à la justice, au bonheur final, à cette cité parfaite de l'avenir' (635). The identification of superstition as the enemy and the image of the perfect city, or new Jerusalem, as the goal of science indicate the location of the negative pole in the moral universe of *Les Quatre Évangiles*. It lies in Catholicism, which Zola attacks with a venom unparalleled in his earlier fiction, gathering momentum from book to book to the final, violent imprecations of *Vérité*.

Catholicism is a foil, used to highlight Zola's own beliefs. Fecundity derives its power as an ideal from its challenge to the cult of the Virgin, symbol of sexless womanhood and of impossible maternity. 'La vierge n'est que néant,' says Boutan, Zola's apostle of unrestricted procreation; 'la mère est l'éternité de la vie. Il lui faut un culte social, elle devrait être notre religion' (202). When France has learned to worship the Mother, he adds, not just the nation but all humanity will be saved.[15] For the perpetuation of one's own life in the form of one's children is a 'resurrection' in which Zola believes. 'Je vous assure que c'est la même femme,' says the unhappy widower Morange of his daughter Reine, comparing her with the mother who has died of an abortion; 'vous voyez bien que je ne rêve pas, que l'une a ressuscité l'autre' (270). Once again Zola naturalises a Christian concept, to integrate it into his own system of belief.

In *Travail* too he exploits traditional Christian images for the potency which their familiarity affords. He creates, in turn, a new Mass, a new prayer, a new temple, a new priest. For the first of these, he has Luc, saving the starving Josine, who will eventually become the mother of his children and later his wife, by breaking bread – 'ce pain de vie' – and feeding her with it by the roadside in a solemn 'communion' (564). The prayer is the *oraison* which the same couple intone to celebrate the religion of life and love. 'Il faut aimer les autres comme nous nous aimons,' (849) they murmur, in ironic echo of Christ's New Commandment, knowing that the 'divin amour' of which they speak is not the love of God, nor love for God, but human sexual love, divine in itself because creative of life. The temple is that of the new religion: it is the great hall at La Crêcherie, the experimental foundry built with Jordan's money and Luc's talent, and in which Luc, the new priest, 'le pasteur du peuple' (949), performs a service of marriage for two of his fellow workers. The factory's workrooms are 'larges et hautes comme des nefs d'anciennes cathédrales' (851); Zola had applied identical images to industrial buildings before, but never with so literal a religious meaning. The same is true of his use of the metaphor of hell, which reappears in the shape of L'Abîme, the old-fashioned factory which exemplifies the sordid drudgery of joyless work. It is suggestive of hell in its very name as well as through the imagery of fire and smoke which accompanies it, just as La Crêcherie conveys the idea of the crib. The novel tells of a new harrowing of hell, of its abolition by the founders of the new religion.

In *Vérité,* Zola makes similar ironic use of the Beatitudes. Rejecting 'Heureux sont les pauvres d'esprit' as a piece of anti-rationalist propaganda derived from 'le noir pessimisme de la Bible', he writes his own Beatitudes: 'Heureux ceux qui savent, heureux les intelligents, les hommes de volonté et d'action, parce que le royaume de la terre leur appartiendra!' (1131). And in the same novel the Catholic catechism is replaced by a new scientific one.

As well as being a device of contrast by which alternative beliefs are proposed, Catholicism is attacked for its inherent falsity and corruption. In his preparatory notes for *Travail,* Zola denounces 'l'exécrable cauchemar du catholicisme' (978). In the novel itself, Catholicism is held responsible for the joyless attitude to work which Zola seeks to change. The model of industrial organisation which Luc Froment adopts, after rejecting revolutionary socialism and state ownership, is a combination of paternalism and fraternal profit-sharing, based on the doctrines of Fourier. Zola's belated espousal of Fourierism, towards which he manifested a certain coolness in *Paris,* has been taken at face value by Hemmings, who describes the novel's opening section as 'the new Gospel according to Fourier' (op. cit., 297). What has not been noticed is Zola's radical distortion of Fourier's ideas, giving them an anti-Catholic slant which they did not originally possess.

Zola's knowledge of Fourier, almost certainly, came not from the works of Fourier himself but from the same popularising account of them which is read by Luc Froment. We are told its title – *Solidarité* – but not the name of the author. The latter was in fact Hippolyte Renaud, whose *Solidarité: vue synthétique sur la doctrine de Charles Fourier* was successful enough in its day to enjoy several reprints. Zola not only borrowed liberally from it but also, more importantly, changed several of its emphases. Renaud's book and the doctrine it expounds are never as explicitly anti-Catholic as *Travail.* Renaud presents Fourier as a believer in God; what Fourier rejects is not God, but mystery and the under-valuation of reason. His views are compatible with orthodox Catholic doctrines of grace and free will. Reason, according to Fourier, is God-given, and is not infallible: man has to learn to use it. Evil is not God's fault, but stems from man's misuse of reason. God is exonerated: a perfect world would have destroyed the joy and indeed the possibility of progress. Fourier presents work in early societies as 'pénible', 'la première douleur', but this was a result of Man's attitude, his 'inintelligence'.[16] Nowhere does Fourier blame Christianity for the pain of work, as Zola does. Likewise, Fourier and Renaud see the belief in life after death as an important source of comfort (41), contrary to Zola. As for education, Fourier defines its role as helping the child develop '[le] germe précieux que Dieu a déposé dans son organisme' (83), whereas Zola regards it as the means to independence of a supernatural benefactor. Fourier sees a key role for the Church in moral education (87) – again, he is totally opposed to Zola. Even when Zola adheres more closely to Fourier – for instance in the central notion of solidarity, or collective joy through collective endeavour – his interpretation is different. Fourier and Renaud believe that this solidarity is implicit in Christian teaching; Zola proclaims it as a new departure, stemming from Man's rejection of his supposed duty to God. Zola, in short, only uses those aspects of Fourierism that are useful to him. He creates his own system of values, not only contrary to Catholicism but contrary to Fourier as well. The summary he gives of Fourier's supposed ideas in *Travail* is a false one, its denunciation of 'la longue et désastreuse erreur du catholicisme' (656) an accretion and a distortion, for which Zola himself is responsible. Whereas the ideas he borrowed from theorists like Letourneau came with their ready-made anti-Catholicism, Zola had to write such bias into Fourier. The contrast shows how much his views had hardened.

Catholicism's representative in *Travail* is the abbé Marle, an intelligent priest, acutely aware of the declining state of the Church and of its role as buttress of a doomed class system. He lives 'dans la certitude que tout le vieil édifice serait emporté, le jour où la science et le libre examen feraient brèche' (610). This familiar Zolian motif of the breach, the cracking and eventual collapse of structures, is reiterated like a prophetic refrain throughout the book. In the end, the church, weakened by wind and rain and by the birds that nest in its stonework, falls in on the priest and kills him, and in a grisly parody of the mass, the dust eats his flesh and drinks his blood, so that his body, like that of Jesus after the crucifixion, cannot be found. The priest's wooden Christ also disintegrates, and with the loss both of its spokesman and of its totems, there is nothing of Christianity left. The last priest has said the last mass. Marle's fate completes Serge Mouret's, like a piece of unfinished business and *règlement de comptes*, bringing out more clearly still the meaning of that novel of thirty years earlier, and cementing the links that bind the Rougon-Macquart novels to the later cycles. Birds are important symbols of nature in both books: in *Travail* they fly to the workers' table as they eat in the open air, unafraid and confident in the presence of fellow creatures of flesh, celebrating a new post-Christian alliance between 'les hommes, les bêtes et les choses' (938). The final phrase makes crystal clear the conscious reference to *La Faute de l'abbé Mouret*.

Vérité is an even fiercer indictment of the corrupting power of Catholicism over both individuals and nations. It is Zola's version of the Dreyfus Affair, the story of Simon, a Jewish schoolteacher, accused and found guilty of the rape and murder of a young boy. The nature of the crime leads Marc Froment, however, to suspect a different culprit: 'Enfin, le viol et l'assassinat étaient comme signés, un sadisme cruel et sournois, un mélange d'ignominie et de religiosité, qui décelaient le froc' (1089). Zola, as prejudiced here as any religious bigot, reiterates the association of Catholicism with sadism, first made when discussing Barbey many years previously.

The case escalates into a battle between *simonistes* and *anti-simonistes*: in the negative camp, ranged against 'le sale juif', the social and political establishment; on the side of Zola's angels, progressives like Marc, devoted to truth in all things. His main target is the Church, opposed as always to justice, and interested solely in the maintenance of order through the imposition of false dogmas. It is 'l'ennemie, la faiseuse d'ignorance et de mort' (1120), a source of error and death 'depuis dix-huit siècles' (1372). Behind its encouragement of superstition, embodied in the 'répugnant fétichisme' (1327) of the Sacred Heart, Zola identifies more sinister forces: the Church's bid for political control, its alliance with militarism. What is at stake in the efforts of secular education is nothing less than the image which France will project to the world: either 'la France de Voltaire et de Diderot, la France de la Révolution et des trois Républiques', or reactionary Catholic France. France, concludes Marc, must destroy the Church or be destroyed by it. No country, warns Zola, has ever emerged unscathed from clerical domination, which is winning the present battle through its control of the minds of children, hence the centrality of education in the great ideological debate.

Even more strongly than before, Zola stresses in his last novel cycle the neurotic aspects of religious experience. In *Fécondité*, the girl Lucie is terrified of menstruation and revolted by every manifestation of life – ant-hills, bees, birds in their nests; but she takes refuge in dreams of angels. In *Vérité*, it is the priest who becomes neurotic, sexually depraved, unworthy of parents' trust if left alone with their daughters in the confessional. 'Il suffit d'un détraqué,' says Marc, 'et la confession n'est plus qu'une ordure' (1239). Even when they are not rapists or child-murderers, priests are agents of marital and national disharmony. Zola's old 'impregnation' theory, his view of the indelible mark of a woman's first lover, resurfaces, with Jesus himself in the key role as the haunting obstacle between husband and wife (1197), while the conflict between devout mothers rearing their children within the faith and rationalist but helpless fathers divides the nation intellectually and spiritually. 'Il ne fallait pas,' argues Zola, 'que l'Église et la femme fussent contre l'homme, mais que l'homme et la femme fussent contre l'Église.' For, he concludes, in a curious anticipation of Louis Aragon, 'seule, la femme libérée peut libérer l'homme' (1249).

The emancipation of woman from the Church is dramatised in *Vérité* by the four generations of women: Mme Duparque, Mme Berthereau, Geneviève, Louise, each representing one degree less of dependence. The death of Mme Duparque is the end of an epoch; from it, in another inverted religious symbol, a new life arises: 'l'éternelle vie renaissait de cette mort' (1402). As a precursor of women's liberation, however, Zola was severely handicapped by his slavery to all the sexual stereotypes of his age. He sees the role of women, if only the Church will let them get on with it, as being 'les épouses et les mères de demain' (1106) – no more, no less. His thinking, in *Fécondité*, if not exactly muddled, produces the awkward paradox of anti-contraception and anti-abortion views that are at least as intransigent as those of the religion he rejects. He is no more convincing, in *Travail*, as a political economist, for he has no clear view of how to transplant Fourier's romantic *phalanstères*, from the 'îles heureuses' where Jordan's sister originally imagines them (635), into a modern industrialised notion. The interest of *Les Quatre Évangiles* lies not only in what they propose, but also in what they oppose, and the ending of *Vérité* again makes Zola's target abundantly clear. It celebrates the triumph of truth and the death of

Catholicism, 'détruit par la science' (1413). The novel, like the others in the series, outstrips the date of its composition and its final chapters follow an ageing Marc well into the twentieth century. In this glorious period, unscarred by war or religious strife, churches stand empty: 'personne n'y entrerait plus . . .'. The Sacred Heart had turned out to be the 'incarnation nouvelle et dernière de Jésus' (ibid.). Only statues remain: '[la] grande statue de saint Antoine de Padoue dorée et peinturlurlée, debout parmi les fleurs artificielles et les cierges' (1465). The town church itself is destroyed by, of all things, a thunderbolt, hitting the bell-tower, killing père Théodose and the abbé Cognasse. This scene, right out of Barbey d'Aurevilly like so much in Zola's anti-Catholic satire, is narrated with delicious irony, but ends on the solemnest of natural explanations, for which Barbey, religious ideology apart, would surely never have forgiven him: 'Dieu voulait-il donc la fin de sa religion? Ou bien était-ce, plus raisonnablement, qu'il n'y avait pas de main divine conduisant la foudre, force naturelle qui sera la source du bonheur, lorsque l'homme l'aura domestiquée?' (1466).

* * *

Zola's three novel cycles are often regarded as being separate initiatives, with the two later series arising from a distinctly different creative impulse from that which produced the Rougon-Macquart books. The mythical and epic qualities of *Les Quatre Évangiles* have also been regarded as separating them from the *Trois Villes* cycle.[17] But in the context of Zola's religious outlook, the three series are intimately interconnected. *Les Trois Villes* function as a commentary on the philosophical bases of the *Rougon-Macquart*, while *Les Quatre Évangiles* present an intensification of the *Rougon-Macquart*'s main themes, an underlining of its moral values: the beauty of life-perpetuating fecundity, the nobility of work, the pre-eminence of truth and justice. The amplification of these *Rougon-Macquart* leitmotivs turns them into myths, but this is no departure from Naturalism as Zola had always understood it. Observable reality remains his starting-point, from which imagination lifts him into spheres that are only apparently beyond Realism.

Although all of Zola's fiction reveals his basic rejection of Christianity, he had moved, like Maupassant, to an increasingly fierce expression of his anti-Catholic stance in his last years. Having chronicled in the *Rougon-Macquart* the collapse of the Second Empire

– the denunciation of which had given that great cycle its polemical motive and unity – this naturally militant writer needed another target on which to unleash his energies, and the Catholicism which had been a partner of the hated regime, and which continued to exert its influence after its demise, was a natural target. Zola's clash with Catholics as the champion of Dreyfus was no doubt a further intensifying factor. But this final phase simply helps to underline the challenge to Catholicism which Realism and Naturalism embodied, and to identify Zola, more than any other single writer, as the opponent against which the Catholic novelist had to define himself and his art. For Zola as for the Catholic novelist, the primordial nature of religious beliefs, preceding social and political ones, was clear: 'Avant la question sociale, avant la question politique, il y a la question religieuse, qui barre tout' (1250). And his own conclusion on 'la question religieuse' is couched in his unfailingly combative style: 'Jamais nous ne ferons un pas en avant, si nous ne commençons par abattre l'Église, la corruptrice, l'empoisonneuse, l'assassine' (1250).

4

Huysmans and the Art of Conversion

One of the greatest challenges to Naturalism came from within its own ranks. If Joris-Karl Huysmans was not included among the Realist or Naturalist novelists discussed in the first chapter, it is because his work is so unique as to require separate discussion. Defender of Zola, contributor to *Les Soirées de Médan*, and writer of four novels that seemed to confirm his place as one of the leading exponents of Naturalism, Huysmans, via what is usually referred to as his 'decadent' period, crossed the great divide of late nineteenth-century French fiction to write his Catholic trilogy *En Route*, *La Cathédrale* and *L'Oblat*. Huysmans' literary odyssey was inseparable from his personal conversion to Catholicism, and his novels, especially the later ones, have been primarily regarded as source material for the biographer. It is as novels, as Naturalist and Catholic novels coexisting within the work of a single author, that they are important for this present study. The questions they raise exemplify its central concerns. What did being a Naturalist, in Huysmans' case, entail? What changes in his writing resulted from – or perhaps resulted in – his conversion to Catholicism? In approaching these questions, the critical themes identified in the previous chapters – the novelist's notion of totality, his presentation of the material and immaterial planes of reality, the role of concrete objects in this presentation – serve as guiding threads through Huysmans' tortuous evolution.

Huysmans' literary relationship with Zola has always been the yardstick of his Naturalism. Robert Baldick's remark that, compared to that of the Goncourts, the influence of Zola on Huysmans was 'negligible', limited to 'the latter's use, or abuse, of the card-index system in the preparation of his works',[1] has recently led Ruth Antosh to interpret Baldick as implying that 'Huysmans was never really a Naturalist at all'.[2] However, the majority of writers, including Cogny, Laver and Baldick himself, in his biography of Huysmans, see the influence of Naturalism's documentary method extending right through his work, up to and including the 'scenes of monastic life' in his Catholic novels.[3] Although Huysmans' general affiliation to Naturalism, at least in the early years of his career, scarcely needs re-establishing, the actual nature of his literary contribution to it, which has been studied rather less thoroughly than its biographical context, is an essential preliminary for the understanding of what was to come later.

Initially, Huysmans' place in the Médan circle was assured by his defence of *L'Assommoir* in 1876. Adverse reaction to the Rougon-Macquart novels was growing, and *L'Assommoir*, with its presentation of the sordid face of working-class life and its use of coarse Parisian *argot*, had brought protests from many corners of the literary and political worlds. Huysmans began his article 'Emile Zola et *L'Assommoir*' by assuring his readers that the then little known Zola was not to be confused with his character Mes Bottes, but was a man of exemplary personal decency, whose aim as a writer was not to delight in the ugly, but merely to describe the world truthfully. His solidarity with Zola is expressed in a device borrowed from Zola himself: his use of the collective 'nous'. 'Nous ne préférons pas,' he writes, 'le vice à la vertu, la corruption à la pudeur'.[4] The content as well as the style of the article shows that Huysmans was well acquainted with Zola's critical writings. His insistence on the depiction of the contemporary scene and his predilection for the unexceptional, his mistrust of over-imaginative embellishment and intricacy of plot, echo the arguments that Zola had been expounding for a decade.

The article is an important manifesto of Naturalism, and Huysmans' early novels show how faithfully he tried to practise what he and Zola preached. This is evident, firstly, in his choice of subject. His first novel, *Marthe*, is the story of a prostitute; the second, *Les Sœurs Vatard* (dedicated to Zola by 'son fervent admirateur et dévoué ami'), that of two sisters who work in a bookbindery; *En Ménage* chronicles a banal marital separation and reconciliation; *A vau-l'eau* the directionless life of an office clerk. 'La composition de l'œuvre,' Zola had written of the ideal Naturalist novel, 'ne consiste plus que dans le choix des scènes' (XI, 97). Of scenes, Huysmans' slices of life provide an abundance. In *Marthe*, the action moves from variety theatre to factory and to brothel; in *Les Sœurs Vatard*, the girls' workplace and the street are the main settings; in the other two novels, shabby flats and dingy restaurants provide the milieux of the action. The opportunity for documentary-type reporting is never missed: mention of Marthe's previous employment as a maker of artificial pearls is the signal for a two-page description of how such articles are manufactured, the plot suspended in the meantime; and in *Les Sœurs Vatard* the portrayal of life in a bindery is based directly on observation and memory of the establishment that Huysmans' mother and step-father used to run. 'Je fais ce que je vois,' says Huysmans in a preface to *Marthe*, 'ce que je sens, et ce que j'ai vécu, en l'écrivant du mieux que je puis' (II, 9).

Concerned to capture the coarse texture of 'low life', Huysmans shows Marthe first in a cheap theatre, singing to a rough audience more interested in her breasts than her vocal chords, and the language matches the décor. The actor Ginginet, whose slangy speech and shabby appearance identify him as a first cousin to the characters of *L'Assommoir*, reclines 'sur le velours pisseux de la banquette' (II, 11). In *Les Sœurs Vatard*, two women stage the obligatory fight on the floor of their workplace, in memory of Zola's Gervaise and Virginie. The attempt to write like Zola, and specifically like the Zola of *L'Assommoir*, but without the capacity to sustain the vigour of such writing over more than a brief space, is very evident in *Marthe*. The subtly contrived roughness of Zola's style is echoed in the passage when Marthe's new lover, the writer Léo, bumps into a crowd of working girls: 'une nouvelle râtelée d'artisanes en godailles, secouant leurs jupes, riant d'un rire stupide, hurlant à pleins poumons – Chahut! Chahut!' (II, 94). The semi-colloquial collective noun 'râtelée' is characteristic of Zola, the tone of whose writing is suggested in another scene, when old men in a drunken orgy 'avaient déboutonné leur gilet et se trémoussaient' (II, 105). Unbuttoned clothing is a recurring image of the uncouth and the slovenly. In the opening pages of *En Ménage*, the painter Cyprien appears on the scene, 'tout en rattachant sa culotte qui s'était déboutonnée' (IV, 5). Flaubert warned Huysmans against his somewhat self-conscious attempts at crude style (III, 336). He no doubt saw the potential originality of the new writer's style struggling to assert itself even within the limits of banal observation. In *En Ménage*, for example, there is a passage in which the central character eats a slice of bread and jam; the jam, running down the crust, is described in close and leisurely detail; simply to create the feel of an everyday world. This is typical Naturalist writing, certainly, but at the same time, it is purer and less rhetorical than the style of Zola, behind whose material descriptions there are abstract forces at play: scientific theories to underpin, class differences to uncover. Of such abstract intention, Huysmans was totally innocent. The paradox of the literary relationship between Huysmans and Zola was that the pupil was a purer Naturalist than the master.

The importance of objects in Huysmans' descriptive writing is apparent in the preceding quotations, and the visual manner of their presentation again confirms his affinities with Naturalism. 'C'est une des visions les plus colorées que je connaisse,' said Zola of his young colleague. 'La vie entre en lui par les yeux; il traduit tout en images, il est le poète excessif de la sensation' (XIV, 581–2). *Les Sœurs Vatard* opens with the sun's rays streaming into the bindery. The light falls on the neck of a jug, on the handle of a bucket, as in a Dutch interior painting. After the still life, animation: the working day begins. The rapidity of the narrative eye creates dynamic movement out of successively observed objects: 'La presse haleta et mugit plus fort, les massiquots grincèrent, les couteaux de bois firent entendre leur sifflement doux sur le papier' (III, 8). Compared to Balzac's description of Séchard's printing press at the start of *Illusions perdues*, Huysmans' scene is like a motion picture alongside a still photograph. Objects are assigned a semi-narrative function. In *Marthe* things rather than events chronicle the declining fortunes of the heroine and her lover when her theatre closes and his newspaper stops buying his copy. Objects and other sensory phenomena, like smells, are strung together by chains of demonstrative adjectives: 'Ces flaques d'eau sur le parquet, cet arome fade de lessive, cette buée de linge qui mouillait ses cuivres et ternissait ses glaces, désespérait [Léo]' (II, 62). They are the substance of regretful memories: 'Qu'étaient devenues les robes traînantes, les jupes falbalassées, les corsets de soie noire, tout ce factice qu'il adorait?' (II, 63). The verbs here are mere syntactical supports; it is the nouns that carry the action and convey the passage of time. Objects become the prime record of life: hairpins left in saucers, cast-off slippers, a petticoat hanging on a chair, an abandoned dish of soapy water – 'tout ce tohu-bohu d'objets' (II, 85) – tell us as much of Marthe's life style as a succession of narrated actions. The same 'ce' acts as narrative device in the account of Léo's life after Marthe has left him:

> Cette halle où des gens en gala viennent, à plusieurs, manger des viandes insipides et roses, ce brouhaha de bonnes en gris qui naviguent entre des tables de marbre, ces malheureuses topettes

> de vin, ces assiettes en pâte à pipe, cette gloutonnerie d'imbéciles qui dépensent deux francs en nourriture et huit francs en boissons de luxe, cette épouvantable tristesse qu'évoque une vieille femme en noir. . . (II, 85–6)

> Ces riens, ce linge en miettes qu'on ne raccommode pas, ces boutons arrachés, ces bas de pantalon. . . (II, 87)

In Balzac, the use of the demonstrative 'ce' points outwards to the real world, drawing attention to phenomena which the fictional world shares and by which it is thus authenticated; in Zola, 'ce' becomes a device of rapid description, the sketching of a scene before the action starts; in Huysmans, it replaces action and becomes his characteristic device, linking description to narration in what might be termed 'objective narrative'.

Like other Realist authors Huysmans also describes religious objects with ironic effect. Désirée and Céline Vatard return home along the rue de Sèvres, with its churches, chapels, convents and religious statuary shops. Their eyes fall on coloured statues of Jesus, Mary and of an infant redeemer 'sous un globe de verre' (III, 23); then on 'des Immaculées creuses en stéarine et en biscuit, des saint Joseph mal moulés et mal vernis, des crèches enluminées, des ânes pelucheux, toute une Judée de carton-pâte, tout un Nazareth de bois peint, toute une religion en toc . . .' (III, 27). Religion plays no part in the novel, but already Huysmans' interest is plain in its artefacts, as is his despair at their crassness; later, the revelation of a different kind of Christian art would radically change his attitude to religion. For the moment, the world which excites his artistic ambition is elsewhere. These *magasins de bondieuserie* alternate with wine-shops and cafés '[qui] regorgaient de monde', 'béaient sur le trottoir'. Here, next to the motionless religious symbols is the bustling life of ordinary folk which the Naturalist Huysmans had set out to record. Christianity was no more relevant to that aim than it was to the lives of the workers who hurry past the churches in this scene, while the rich arrive in their carriages to pay homage to their establishment deity.

A new note could soon be heard in Huysmans' writing, though expressed through derivative character types. His characters, like the Goncourts' and Zola's, include artists, through whom his own aesthetic preferences are expressed and explored. *Les Sœurs Vatard* introduces the painter Cyprien Tibaille, who believes that an artist 'ne devait rendre que ce qu'il pouvait fréquenter et voir' (III, 159). Here is the argument for contemporaneity, for an art based on 'le vu et le vécu'. Cyprien reappears in *En Ménage*, but this time as one of two central male figures, the other being the writer André. Through their dialogues, an important change in Huysmans' attitude begins to appear. André is apparently a Naturalist novelist, or so his declared intention of doing research for his next novel in a slaughter-house would suggest; but he is less committed to Naturalism than Cyprien. In this double self-portrait, André represents elements within Huysmans' deeper self, while Cyprien reflects that more external self which Huysmans was showing signs of wishing to discard. Cyprien makes another long speech on his taste for modernity, describing the industrial scene and the poor and down-trodden who inhabit it as the setting and subject to which he devotes his art. The city, the street, the poor quarters of Paris, the hospitals, the shops – these are the elements of his ideal landscape. He prefers the working-girl to the Venus de Milo and, echoing Zola's Claude Lantier, the Gare du Nord and the Hippodrome to Notre-Dame and St-Étienne-du-Mont (IV, 126).[5] While Cyprien lectures, André merely listens: there is perhaps in the former an element of Zola's dominant personality, his notorious assumption of leadership over fellow Naturalists.

Huysmans' disillusionment with the Naturalist prescription is confirmed in *A vau-l'eau*. At first glance another study in banality, it is turned into a minor masterpiece by humour and gentle self-mockery. But it clearly poses the problem of where Huysmans could turn next for subject matter. Its sheer plotlessness and lack of event suggest that Realism has been pushed to its logical extreme and has paid the price for its mistrust of imagination. The main and almost sole character Folantin, who is a kind of talentless Huysmans, punctuates his lonely life by visits to brothels, public baths (where he delights in producing splendid underwater noises) and restaurants. Although his predicament is given substance by references to the then fashionable philosophy of Schopenhauer, Folantin's existential despair rests mainly on the palate-destroying certainty of tonight's unspeakable food. The novel ends with him sinking into quiet resignation: rather than seek joy and meaning in life, one might just as well cross one's arms, go to sleep, smoke a cigar, or call on the local whore, for nothing good can be expected of life for those without money. In one of the most famous catch-phrases of Naturalism, Folantin sums up his philosophy: 'Seul le pire arrive' (V, 85).

There are indications in the course of the story, however, that new directions were suggesting themselves to Huysmans as well as to Folantin. The news of the death of a cousin, who also happened to be a nun, leads Folantin's thoughts to the notion of religion and of the monastic life. He vaguely regrets his lost faith, but admits he could never swallow the dogmas of the Church, palatable only to more simple-minded folk. As for living in a monastery, that, for the moment, would be to 'payer cher l'improbable bonheur d'une vie future' (V, 79).

However, the appeal of the monk's cell, or something like it, can be seen in the yearning of all his early fictional heroes for seclusion within four book-lined walls. To André in *En Ménage*, the resumption of the bachelor life in his little study brings joys that compensate in large measure for his wife's desertion. Marthe's lover Léo adds aesthetic fantasies to coenobitic ones in his desire for a room like those painted by Rembrandt. The glimmer in Huysmans' eye at the thought of 'something else' beyond the banal everyday world, and which was soon to burst into the vision of the mauve-tinted multi-sensory experience of des Esseintes' dream-house, shone albeit dimly from the very start of his writing career.

For the moment Huysmans was clearly a member of the Naturalist establishment. Even when, after *A Rebours* and *Là-Bas*, this ceased to be the case, he still called himself a Naturalist. When labels ranging from 'Catholic' to 'anarchist' were being liberally applied to him and his work, he protested: 'Je suis naturaliste – c'est-à-dire travaillant sur documents et écrivant le moins mal que je puis!'[6] His attitude to Zola had gone sour long before this, however, and his continued public lip-service to Zola until well into the 1890s contrasts with what Huysmans was saying behind Zola's back to correspondents like Destrées and Prins. To them, he mocks the 'imbecility' of *Le Rêve*, the 'coarseness' of *L'Argent*;[7] his dismissal of Zola's 'folly' in coming to the defence of Dreyfus is expressed in unpleasant anti-semitic language (P, 313); and Zola's premature death inspired merely the comment that Providence had been kind to kill Zola before his books stopped selling (P, 368). For these things, Huysmans has rightly been taxed with hypocrisy, but such judgements are too superficial.[8] Huysmans needed Zola as the sounding-board of his own achievement. When the publication of *Là-Bas* was imminent, he saw Zola's anticipated reaction as the measure of its revolutionary importance: 'C'est la brouille avec Zola et les naturalistes' (P, 206). Zola was the implied anti-reader of all he wrote, his hostility a proof of his own historical status. No biographer of either writer has yet plumbed the oedipal depths of their relationship, about which a great deal more needs to be discovered.[9]

Before leaving the subject, there is a further angle to their *literary* relationship which might be explored: namely, Zola's debt to Huysmans. Huysmans was no doubt a comforting ally for Zola in the early days – a writer who could help to establish Naturalism, but who, being short of creativity where plots were concerned and good at small-scale sketches of daily life, was unlikely to be a serious rival to the master. Furthermore, his professional knowledge as a civil servant was useful: he provided Zola with documentary information on building contracts and architectural details of houses in the Saint-Roch district when the latter was writing *Pot-Bouille*. Typical of Zola, and ironical given the destiny of his colleague, was the fact that Huysmans' description of the courtyard at 24 rue Saint-Roch – 'l'odeur n'est pas celle de l'encens ou de la sacristie, mais c'est une odeur de moisissure et de vieillesse' – should be translated in the text of *Pot-Bouille* as 'une odeur discrète de prêtre'.[10] It seems likely that even the title of this novel was suggested by Huysmans, who had used the unusual noun 'la pot-bouille' in *En Ménage* (IV, 324). One might also speculate on what *Nana* owes to the music-hall scene at the beginning of *Marthe*, or Zola's descriptions of railway engines to Huysmans' passion for them, indulged in *Les Sœurs Vatard* long before *La Bête humaine* was written. These questions lie outside the scope of this present chapter, as does the possibility of another minor debt: it might be thought the incorrigible Jésus-Christ, in *La Terre*, was Realism's first *pétomane* – but this earth-shaking breakthrough, so to speak, was actually achieved by the husband of la mère Teston in *Les Sœurs Vatard*.

* * *

The radical departure from Naturalism which is represented by *A Rebours* is even clearer to us today than it was to Émile Zola. The book becomes a seminal text for the symbolist generation, lighting the way to thrillingly new imaginative possibilities. In it, Huysmans created one of the most celebrated of fictional characters, duc Jean des Esseintes. Last of the noble family Floressas des Esseintes, aimless and disenchanted, without beliefs or ambitions, des Esseintes sees the world as the habitat of idiots; he is easily hurt; hypersensitive and near-impotent. He sells his ancestral home, the chateau de Lourps, and, dreaming of a hermit's life in some 'thébaïde raffinée' (VII, 10), buys a house at Fontenay-les-Roses. The book is devoted to the description of these new material surroundings and to the flights of fancy that they inspire or reflect. The Naturalist superstructure looks at first glance intact: des Esseintes' meditations on books and paintings might seem the structural equivalent of the pearl-making scene in *Marthe*. But these apparently peripheral matters are in fact the novel's entire substance. *A Rebours* rejects Naturalism through its concentration on such 'interior' subject-matter and in its choice of protagonist. Des Esseintes is not only a nobleman; he is a nobleman who despises the modern. He is a dunce at science and modern languages, and good only at Latin and theology! There are other, specific, gestures of mockery or defiance towards Zolian Naturalism. Des Esseintes' family is an aristocratic parody of the Rougons and Macquarts, fallen into genetic decline through over-active lymph glands. Des Esseintes is terrified of his own heredity, and for good cause: like Maxime, son of Aristide Rougon, he represents the weakly and feminised end-result of chromosomatic chaos. And like an Angélique or Clotilde Rougon (though neither had yet been created), he yearns for 'l'inconnu', 'l'idéal', 'les brumes de l'au-delà de l'art' (VII, 161–3): consciously Zolian terms which, far from having Zola's ironic sense, indicate the positive direction of the text, its exploration of a world of pure imagination.

Of this imagination, those Naturalist work-horses, objects, become the symbolic handmaiden, important not in themselves but in what they suggest. The mirrors and exquisitely coloured tapestries which wall des Esseintes' bedroom are artful reflections of his ultra-aestheticised soul. Delicacy and barbarism combine in the décor as they do in the man. A cricket is kept in a cage hanging from the ceiling, precious stones are encrusted into the shell of a luckless tortoise. In a last attempt to share his exotic pleasures with others, des Esseintes gives a dinner party of spectacular ostentation, the food served on black-lined plates by naked negresses as funereal music plays to celebrate the host's defunct virility. But tiring of human company, des Esseintes shuts himself in a world of total artifice, the antithesis of nature and of respect for the factual. Instead of embarking on a real sea-journey, a specially printed copy of Poe's *Narrative of A. Gordon Pym* makes an imagined one permanently available, helped by chemicals to simulate the tang of the briny and dangling ropes to give the feel of rigging. On a rare excursion beyond his doorstep, a visit to an English tavern in the rue d'Amsterdam exhausts des Esseintes' stillborn urge to venture across the Channel.

Sexual fantasies figure largely in these flights of imagination. In des Esseintes' nightmares, fear of venereal disease transforms plants into syphilitic phalluses, mouths of flowers into avid vulvas. He remembers, or invents, love affairs with an American circus *artiste* called Miss Urania, as well as with a woman ventriloquist and hermaphrodite clowns in Prussian army boots. He sucks 'woman-flavoured' sweets, and recalls how he corrupted a sixteen-year-old boy by taking him to a brothel. Transposed to the artistic plane, these fantasies are stimulated and satisfied by the paintings in the private gallery into which des Esseintes has turned his house.[11] Gustave Moreau's *Salome dancing before Herod* and *The Apparition* both hang there, and are the subject of two celebrated descriptions. In the first, Salome, her 'lubrique danse' transformed from the motionlessness of paint into rhythmic movement by the same process of animated description that was observed in the earlier novels, becomes for des Esseintes a goddess of lust, a symbol of indescribable temptation and danger. In the description of *The Apparition,* representing Salomé's horrific vision of the Baptist's severed head, the juxtaposition of her near-naked body and the gruesome spectacle reflects the inseparability, within des Esseintes, of eroticism and sadism. The same tastes are revealed in his admiration for Jan Luyken's engravings of scenes of torture and religious martyrdom, which adorn des Esseintes' blood-red bedroom, and in Bresdin's paintings of demons and phantoms in *La Comédie de la Mort*, which Huysmans also describes before turning to another of his idols, Odilon Redon, in whose work 'les mirages d'hallucination et les effets de peur' (VII, 96) remind him of Poe.

Painting is one means of reflecting des Esseintes' inner world, and literature, to which painting leads back here by analogy, is another. Through the diffuse accounts of des Esseintes' meditations on the authors and texts devoured by his voracious reading, Huysmans can be seen taking stock of his own preferences, and in his analyses of both ancient and modern literature fascinating parallels with his own evolution begin to appear. Des Esseintes' reading of Roman literature is discussed first. Rejecting as solemn and mechanical the 'great' Latin authors from Virgil to Cicero, whose lack of inventiveness he sees as equalled only by the 'great' authors of seventeenth-century France, des Esseintes prefers later Latin writing, which he divides into two types. The first, exemplified by Petronius, is '[le] roman réaliste'. The *Satyricon* is described, using the familiar critical terminology of Realism, as 'une tranche découpée dans le vif de la vie romaine' (VII, 47). It is close in spirit, des Esseintes reflects, to the few modern novels he can abide reading (no doubt they include Huysmans' own). The second type is Roman Christian literature. Christianity, writes Huysmans, brought new ideas and new words into the Latin language which the earliest Christian writers, Tertullian and his successors, had been unable to exploit for literary purposes, but from which Commodian of Gaza had drawn the inspiration for his 'vers tendus, sentant le fauve, pleins de termes de language usuel, de mots aux sens primitifs détournés' (VII, 52). Putting aside Commodian of Gaza, the interesting point here is that Huysmans equates the novelty of Christian ideas with potential novelty of style and literary renewal, with the provision of an alternative mode to the earlier realism. For a writer emerging from his own realist phase and seeking 'du nouveau', this was an association that was soon going to have enormously important consequences.

When, later in the book, des Esseintes surveys his library of modern authors, a similar division into two broad currents is identified: 'ordinary' profane literature and 'special', little-known Catholic writing. In exploring the latter, he has discovered, under 'un gigantesque amas d'insipidités' (VII, 219), a few works of great interest. He has read Lacordaire, de Falloux, Montalembert, Veuillot. All of these strike him as energetic stylists, though Veuillot is also typical of them in his 'pitiable' imaginative qualities. Eugénie de Guérin is naïve and trivial. Ozanam, Lamennais, de Maistre, are all discussed, but are not to des Esseintes' taste; de Maistre above all is dogmatic and pompous. From Catholic philosophers and polemicists, he moves on to imaginative writers: to Ernest Hello – 'une sorte de Duranty catholique, mais plus dogmatique et plus aigu' (VII, 234); to Léon Bloy, who had not yet written the novels that will be discussed in the next chapter, and who appeared to Huysmans '[un] pamphlétaire enragé' (VII, 238); and finally to Barbey d'Aurevilly. In *A Rebours*, if all roads do not (yet!) lead to Rome, they certainly lead to, or from, Barbey d'Aurevilly.

Huysmans' changing literary tastes, for example the attraction of Baudelaire, or that of Poe, whose haunting 'étrangeté' he now began to prize more than the 'art valide' of Balzac (VII, 271), were making possible a literary kinship with the old enemy of the Realists.

He had once written to Zola to congratulate him in one of his attacks on 'le pauvre matamore de Barbey',[12] but from the time of *A Rebours* he displays a totally different attitude. A letter to Destrées admits his admiration for a writer who on a personal level is still, he insists, 'à mes antipodes' (D, 34). Not long afterwards, the two had become 'personal friends' (P, 36), the forty years' difference in their ages notwithstanding. Later, Huysmans was to approve of an article by Destrées which 'told the truth' about Zola and Barbey by presenting the latter as the greater artist (D, 165–6). Barbey's work, like Baudelaire's and Poe's, was instrumental in showing to Huysmans the possibilities of escape, through imagination, from the strictures of banal observation of the real. All of the tastes unveiled by Huysmans in *A Rebours* could find some satisfaction in the reading of Barbey, especially eroticism or sadism. Huysmans' long appreciation of Barbey includes, on this aspect, an assessment which, on the face of it, resembles Zola's. Barbey, he says, represents the combination of mysticism with sadism – 'ce bâtard du catholicisme' (VII, 241). He worships Satan and manifests '[une] érotomanie diabolique' very reminiscent of Sade. The Christian God in whom he claims to believe, in *Un prêtre marié*, is an unmerciful and savage god. Huysmans' interpretation of Barbey at this stage was in other words no more enlightened than Zola's, but, whereas Zola saw Barbey's supposed erotic diabolism as damnable, the admirer of Gustave Moreau was bound to see it in a different light, as new and exciting rather than reactionary or ridiculous. Disinclined to criticise Barbey from Zola's humanist standpoint, Huysmans was not yet judging him from a Catholic angle either. Of all modern writers, says des Esseintes, only Barbey has the flavour of the Latin decadence. Barbey thus draws together the full range of Huysmans' literary enthusiasms, old and new.

However imperfectly Huysmans may have judged Barbey or other Catholic writers, his interest in the literary potential of 'Catholic' ideas as an alternative to realism is clear. Whether the discourse of Catholicism could be adapted to the needs of the novelist was another matter. This is a problem which he tackles in a few profoundly perceptive lines:

> Incapable de s'attaquer à la vie contemporaine, de rendre visible et palpable l'aspect le plus simple des êtres et des choses, inapte à expliquer les ruses compliquées d'une cervelle indifférente à l'état de grâce, cette langue excellait cependant aux sujets abstraits;

> utile dans la discussion d'une controverse, dans la démonstration d'une théorie, dans l'incertitude d'un commentaire, elle avait, plus que toute autre aussi, l'autorité nécessaire pour affirmer, sans discussion, la valeur d'une doctrine. (VII, 220–1)

Here speaks the Realist in Huysmans, the writer still committed to the evocation of the visible and the everyday, to the creation of multi-faceted characters, to the exploration of the problematic rather than the affirmation of the received truth, and finding Christianity's abstract dogmas alien to him. The abstraction of Christian thought is one of the greatest difficulties experienced by des Esseintes in his spasmodic attempts to regain the lost faith of his Jesuit childhood. He is lost in the subtleties of theological speculation: was the Christ on the cross one person or three? His head swims in a sea of paradoxes, which collapse under the pressure of his need for the visible and the concrete. He takes refuge in Moreau's processions of prelates and patriarchs, religion reverting to spectacle as, to a sceptical Realist, it must inevitably do. Huysmans, however, was no longer quite a sceptical Realist. He was aware of a dimension beyond the physical: the problem was to find a way of describing it. His mode of writing was that on which the rise of the novel had depended: the depiction of an observed reality. But how could he depict the unobservable reality in which he was increasingly tempted to believe? The search for a bridge between vision and discourse, which was to lead him, in *Là-Bas*, to the notion of 'un naturalisme spiritualiste', is already under way in *A Rebours*. There was a second problem: having crossed the Rubicon, in what territory did Huysmans now find himself? According to Barbey, the author of *A Rebours*, unless he were to kill himself, would soon end up at the foot of the cross'.[13] But Huysmans still had his season in hell to serve. Having given rein to his imaginative instincts, des Esseintes discovers that he cannot halt the process. From his perverse depths arise monstrous and sacrilegious images. As well as visions of God, he sees Satan, black masses, witches' sabbaths. These lurid images, inspired by Moreau and Bresdin, by Sade and by Barbey, gripped Huysmans' imagination, and in *Là-Bas* they were to be given the free and full exposure that was required, in the end, to exorcise them.

* * *

Là-Bas begins with a justly famous discussion on Naturalism between the writer Durtal and a doctor friend whose name – des Hermies – is appropriate for one so steeped in the hermetic or occult sciences. His role is to initiate discussion and provoke reaction. Thus his attack on what he calls 'les immondices' of Naturalism is the more extreme, Durtal's the more nuanced. The former echoes the Huysmans of the letters to Destrées and Prins, the latter the Huysmans of the public statements on Zola. Borrowing the vocabulary of Barbey's hoary anti-Realist polemic, he reproaches Naturalism for having incarnated 'materialism' in literature and glorified 'democracy' in art. He deplores its narrow intellectual perspective, its thematic monotony, its restriction of the novel's compass. Even if one adopts the sensory limits of Naturalism, what, he challenges Durtal, has Naturalism *seen*? What insight has it achieved into the mystery of human life? Its only explanation of human passion is to refer to notions of appetite and instinct: sexual desire and madness are its sole areas of psychological exploration. In other words, Naturalism reflects the lowest common denominator of popular interest; it is a bourgeois aesthetic.

Durtal shares some of these misgivings, but puts the case for Naturalism's achievements. It has exposed the absurd fantasies and puerile idealism of the Romantics; it has completed the half-baked linguistic revolution begun by the Romantics themselves; it has created visually real characters and placed them in their social setting; and it has not always pursued crassness of subject as unremittingly as des Hermies says. This speech is a compound of Zola's pronouncements on Romanticism and parts of Huysmans' article on *L'Assommoir*; also, in describing Naturalist characters as 'des êtres visibles et palpables' (XI, 7), it repeats the phrase in which, in *A Rebours*, Huysmans had identified what was lacking in Christian discourse: the capacity to record visual and tangible experience.

Privately, Durtal concedes the potential sterility of Naturalism, but sees no alternative to it; Huysmans is still inclined to accept Zola's view that it is the logical and historically inevitable final destination of the novel genre. Naturalism is not to be rejected but developed, its area of concern to be extended to the world of the spirit. Here he elaborates the theory for which he was already groping in *A Rebours*: the need to combine the great qualities of Naturalism – documentary truthfulness, precision of detail, vigour of style – with an exploration of the soul which will respect its mysteries and not dismiss them as the product of deranged senses.

'Il faudrait, en un mot,' says Durtal, 'suivre la grande voie si profondément creusée par Zola, mais il serait nécessaire aussi de tracer en l'air un chemin parallèle, une autre route, d'atteindre les en deçà et les après, de faire, en un mot, un naturalisme spiritualiste' (XI, 11).

But where, in literature, can a model be found for this extended Naturalism? Despairing of finding a literary mentor (other, perhaps, than Dostoyevsky whom he rejects on political grounds), Durtal seeks one in painting, and sees in the art of the Italian, German and above all Flemish primitives of the late Middle Ages the combination of solid reality and the expression of celestial joy for which he has been searching: a transformation of matter by the opening of a window to a world beyond it. Now, as Durtal reflects on the work of these painters, there enters Huysmans' world the image that will soon come to dominate it: the image of the crucified Christ, as painted by Mathias Grünewald. For the rediscovery of this little known fifteenth-century artist, Huysmans has been given widespread credit. Certainly, though Verhaeren wrote about Grünewald before Huysmans did, it was the latter who publicised him the more effectively. The painting Durtal describes in *Là-Bas* is not Grünewald's master work, the Issenheim altar-piece (which Huysmans was to discuss in his later book *Trois Primitifs*); it is the Crucifixion which Huysmans had seen in the museum in Kassell, and which is now in the Staatliche Kunsthalle in Karlsruhe. It portrays Christ's Passion in uncompromising detail. His body twists under its own weight, his feet are grotesquely swollen from the nail hammered crudely through them, his face curls into a grimace of near dementia. Grünewald's Christ, says Durtal, is not the beautified Christ of Renaissance art; he is not a rich man's Christ or a Galileean Adonis. He is a Christ ravaged by tetanos, a primitive Christ from the first centuries of the Church, a common and ugly Christ – ugly because he assumes the collective horror of men's sin. The cruelty of this painting makes of Grünewald, in Huysmans' eyes, 'le plus forcené des réalistes'. But its sublimity lifts him at the same time to a different realm. 'A regarder ce Rédempteur de vadrouille, ce Dieu de morgue,' writes Huysmans, 'cela changeait. [. . .] Cette charogne éployée était celle d'un Dieu, et, sans auréole, sans nimbe, dans le simple accoutrement de cette couronne ébouriffée, semée de grains rouges par des points de sang, Jésus apparaissait, dans sa céleste Superessence [. . .]' (XI, 18–19). Grünewald reveals himself now as 'le plus forcené des idéalistes' (XI, 19). He has joined the invisible to the tangible by allying Christ's divinity to the horrors of his mortified flesh.

Durtal is deeply moved by Grünewald's picture. But it is important to emphasise that the image of Christ's passion does not yet stir him to belief, although it confirms and stimulates further his awareness of a supernatural world. His own life provides evidence of that world's existence: too many strange things happen to be ascribed to chance; and 'chance', as a theory of life, is even harder to swallow than Christianity. Why not accept Christianity, then, on the basis of Augustine's *Credo quia absurdum*? On the very verge of doing so, Durtal retraces his steps, returns to the domain of art and literature from which his meditations had sprung. He has obtained from Grünewald what, artistically, he has needed: a 'prototype' (XI, 25). There is no need to go further, no need to leap into Christian belief. A sense of mystery, of supernature, has provided him with a liberating mechanism for his art, an avenue to new subjects. He can set his camp at that point, not as a Christian but as an explorer of the invisible world in which Christians believe. In a word – Huysmans' word – he can be a 'spiritualiste' (XI, 26).[15]

Durtal's researches into mediaeval satanism, in preparation for a book on Gilles de Rais, give Huysmans the fictional pretext for this widening of his subject matter. The Middle Ages attract Durtal, mainly because he detests the modern age, but the two time-planes are structurally and thematically interrelated in *Là-Bas*, the chapters on Gilles alternating with the narrative of Durtal's parallel explorations of occult practices in contemporary France. Huysmans thus skilfully combines the reporter's role with that of the initiate into the world of the spirit. His interest in Gilles is explained to some extent by his identification with the latter's love of refinement in both intellectual and physical matters. He is a scholar and an epicurean: a fifteenth-century des Esseintes! (XI, 77). And he also represents the combination of mysticism and sadism which Huysmans could not resist. In the days when he had been the companion of Joan of Arc, Gilles had witnessed the effects of God's intervention into her life and into history; later, after Joan's death, his encounters with magicians and occultists led him to embrace the worship of Satan, as both insurance against ill fortune and help in the pursuit of the 'philosopher's stone'. Durtal is astonished by the nature of the evidence which led men, in the Middle Ages, to believe in the devil: not just second-hand accounts of visions, but evidence of visible wounds inflicted by evil forces. Seeing these led Gilles to believe; he was obviously, under the impact of 'le fait matériel, visible et tangible' (XI, 133), a Naturalist *avant la lettre*! Huysmans himself no longer stopped at these physical surfaces, but regarded them as mere external signs.

Durtal's investigations into satanism are undertaken with the help of des Hermies, who, in deliberate antithesis to Zola's doctors, scorns the claims of medical science, preferring the wisdom of astrologers, kabbalists and demonologists. Durtal's other informants include Carhaix, bell-ringer at Saint-Sulpice and expert on campanological symbolism, and the astrologer Gévingey. The latter knows canon Docre, said to be one of the arch-priests of occultism in modern-day France, the other being Dr Johannès. These two are 'les Gilles de Rais modernes' (XI, 228). Docre is the more sinister of the pair, able to poison his enemies at a distance or drive them to suicide by hypnosis, while Johannès has the mission of saving France from the satanists and preparing the coming of the Holy Ghost. Uninformed readers of *Là-Bas* might well wonder how much of this farrago is intended seriously, and whether Huysmans is not writing a satirical novel, but Baldick's book, which identifies the real-life equivalents of these characters and describes Huysmans' fascination with them, uncovers the astonishing truth of the flourishing state of occult practice in the France of a hundred years ago.

None of this has much to do with what normally passes for Christianity, although Durtal and his friends all broadly concur with Barbey d'Aurevilly's view – and Balzac's – of the compatibility of most forms of occult belief with each other and with Catholicism. 'L'enfer,' in Barbey's celebrated aphorism, 'c'est le ciel en creux' (*Les Diaboliques*, II, 155). Huysmans' passage through his occult period is comparable in many ways to Barbey's journey to Catholicism via the fantastic, and in literary terms, *A Rebours* and *Là-Bas* occupy a place in Huysmans' career which is analogous to the one filled in Barbey's by *Une vieille maîtresse* and *L'Ensorcelée*. One important difference was that Barbey's fantastical material was derived from literary sources; Huysmans, exemplary Naturalist that he was, had to do his field courses!

Practical explorations, including attending a black mass, are part of Durtal's programme too, and his sexual involvement with the satanic initiate Hyacinthe de Chantelouve has research as at least one of its aims! Her letters introduce Durtal to the phenomena of the incubus and succubus, those night-demons that prey upon the sexually tempted. Patristic writing, inevitably, is quoted by Durtal's indefatigable companions as evidence of the existence of such creatures. Saint Augustine mentions them, as do Saint Bonaventure, Denis le Chartreux and Pope Innocent VIII. Carhaix recalls Saint Thomas's anguished meditation on whether the child born of an incubus' copulation with a woman has, as its father, the demon itself, or the unwitting donor of the sperm, the poor wretch whose nocturnal emission supplied the semen for the otherwise sterile incubus. Reading *Là-Bas* persuades one that there is very little that is not mentioned in the writings of some father of the Church or other. Gévingey is critical of the modern Church for its suppression of so much of this material, for it underpins the supernaturalism on which revealed religion depends. To the Catholic novelist, be he Barbey, Huysmans or Georges Bernanos, the supernatural, whatever its precise nature, was a major source of literary persuasion, and demonology a field well worth turning over once more. Durtal's provisional comment on succubism is that of the ascetic man of letters: 'au fond, c'est plus littéraire et plus propre' (XI, 234). On learning that Mme de Chantelouve has incubus-type relations with the spirits of Byron, Baudelaire and Nerval, he comments: 'Décidément, rien n'arrive comme on le prévoit' (XI, 251): which represents an advance on Folantin's 'Seul le pire arrive!' Beneath the too often neglected black humour of Huysmans' novel of the occult, the expression of personal anxieties can be obscurely perceived. The invading succubus can be interpreted as a fear of predatory woman on the part of a neurotic bachelor, happy to live in the reclusion of study or cell, and to limit his contacts with the female sex to ever-present maternal housekeepers and regular trips to the brothel.

At the end of the book, Durtal has still not found faith. He tells des Hermies that one thing is certain: of all religions, Catholicism satisfies him most. 'Eh bien, crois!' retorts his friend. 'Je ne peux pas,' answers Durtal; 'il y a là-dedans un tas de dogmes qui me découragent et me révoltent' (XII, 221). He envies the faith of Carhaix, but cannot emulate it. In other words, on the religious plane, the novel stops at the same point, exactly, as it does on the aesthetic one: the necessary awareness of a world beyond matter is postulated, but this is not finally translated into an affirmation of Christianity, because Durtal – and Huysmans – have not yet made that leap of faith.

* * *

A leap of some sort was being contemplated by Huysmans in the wake of *Là-Bas*. To several correspondents at this time he confided his desire to write a book that would be the spiritual antithesis of his novel of the occult. 'Je veux faire une sorte de Là-Haut,' he told Prins, 'un livre blanc, l'à rebours de *Là-Bas*' (P, 219). One of the sources of this wish, he revealed, was his meetings with fervent Christians in Lyon, where he had gone to gather information for his previous novel: 'Ils vaudraient un livre blanc, ceux-là!' (P, 216). He feared, however, that if he described such people directly, he would be accused of inventing, as in *Là-Bas*, 'des créatures préternaturelles' (ibid.): such was the influence that Naturalism and 'toute la séquelle zoliste' had on public acceptance of what was plausible in literature. In any event, the book would depend more on the inner state of its author than on external models. To create his 'white book', wrote Huysmans to the priest who would soon be his confessor, 'il faudrait que je me blanchisse moi-même'; 'avez-vous du chlore pour mon âme?'[16]

It was believed for many years that Huysmans' white book had been destroyed, as he had requested, after his death. However, the manuscript was later discovered, and published in 1965 under the name *Là-Haut, ou Notre-Dame de la Salette*.[17] It turns out to be an early draft of *En Route*, with some sections that were incorporated into *La Cathédrale*, but it includes otherwise unpublished passages which paint a fascinating last portrait of Durtal as a still hesitant believer. Persuaded by the abbé Gévresin to accompany him to La Salette, Durtal is unconvinced by the tale of the Virgin's apparition there to 'deux galopins sur un mont!' (185). Huysmans seems here to return, as to a secure haven, to the robust language of Naturalism. 'Tu crois à la Vierge, toi, à cette gonzesse?' (146) his mistress Florence challenges Durtal. Such a formulation is an effective obstacle to the confession of faith which might otherwise be on Durtal's lips. It also gives a tantalising glimpse of the book, provisionally entitled 'La Bataille charnelle' (12), that Huysmans was never to complete, and in which the polarity of mistress and Virgin might have formed the basis of his definitive investigation of his own most intense conflict. A fragment of this survives at the start of *Là-Haut*, when Durtal ponders the sexual attraction of Christ for nuns, which makes their receiving of his body in the mass a source of satisfaction that is inaccessible to men, forcing the latter to turn instead to the person of the Virgin. This passage offers so clear an echo of Serge Mouret's inextricably mixed sexual and spiritual yearnings as to make Huysmans' wish to have his manuscript destroyed very understandable. It is significant that the same passage's final version, in the text of *En Route* (XIII, II, 178), forms part of a demonic temptation of Durtal; the devil, to Huysmans, was in part his own past self, speaking through his own former writing.

The question of how writing related to faith, on the knife edge on which Huysmans now stood perched, is a vital one to raise at this stage. His incorrigibly literary ambition, the drive to provoke and impress by the creation of an original and successful book, is evident in the letters in which he anticipates his 'livre blanc'. 'C'est une voie inexplorée dans l'art, comme était le satanisme,' he assured Prins, 'Je vais tenter le divin. [. . .] Ça ne serait pas mal de foutre à la gueule de ce siècle de muffles [*sic*] un livre comme cela, un vrai livre du Moyen Age' (P, 219). In other words, Huysmans gives the impression at this stage of seeking moral regeneration as a means to a literary end. But signs of another urge, a rival to the priority of writing, are also increasingly evident. He expressed to Prins his nervousness on the eve of departing for the Trappist monastery at Igny, an anxiety counterbalanced, he added, by his absolute need to go there – 'beaucoup plus, du reste, pour mon âme que pour l'art' (P, 240). He was now seeking religious renewal, and assigning second place in his life to art.

In the Catholic trilogy, the gap between Huysmans and his main character, always a narrow one, finally almost disappears. Durtal's experiences in the Trappist monastery of Notre-Dame-de-l'Atre and with the Dominicans at Le Val des Saints, in *En Route* and *L'Oblat* respectively, are faithful reflections of those of Huysmans at Igny and Ligugé; only the period he spends in Chartres, described in *La Cathédrale*, has no precise equivalent in Huysmans' life. He was as true as ever to his understanding of Naturalism's mission of recording the *vu* and *vécu*; what had changed was his realisation of what it was possible to see, and what living could entail. The transformation in Durtal is announced at the start of the second chapter of *En Route*. He suddenly discovers that after years of incredulity, he has come to believe in the Catholic faith. How has this come about? His first answer – and it is a vital one, often overlooked in accounts of Huysmans' beliefs – is that the change in him is due to God's will; only after recognising this does he look for psychological factors. Among the latter, he finds the influence of the memory of his Christian boyhood, working hand in hand with a hereditary inclination towards faith. Secondly, he identifies within himself that disgust with life which had brought both Folantin and des Esseintes to the brink of seeking refuge in religion. Unlike Folantin, who had preferred Schopenhauer to the Bible, Durtal's reading of Ecclesiastes, Job and Jeremiah have led him to see his horror of the world in religious terms, and to realise that to reject it does not imply a rejection of God, but rather an accusation of Man.

Thirdly, there is Durtal's passion for the art of the Church, for its architecture, its statues and paintings, its music. Here is the most problematic aspect of Huysmans' Catholicism. His passion for art was, like Durtal's, so intimately linked with his religious experiences that the pejorative label 'aesthetic Catholic' has long been attached to him.[18] Such views of Huysmans are ill founded, and they stand in the way, not only of an understanding of his faith and his view of art, but of a true evaluation of his art itself.

Huysmans' acute awareness of the gulf between aesthetic and spiritual response is expressed as early as *Là-Bas*. To bridge this gulf would be a radical step, one that frightens Durtal: 'Si je suis logique,' he tells himself, 'j'aboutis au catholicisme du Moyen-Age, au naturalisme mystique; ah non, par exemple, et si pourtant!' (XI, 20). In *En Route* the bridge has been built, but what is it made of? 'Il est bien certain,' the abbé Gévresin tells Durtal, 'que l'art a été le principal véhicule dont le Sauveur s'est servi pour vous faire absorber la foi' (XIII, I, 124), and Durtal himself is anxious: 'Il s'usait en disputes, en arrivant à douter de la sincérité de sa conversion, se disant en fin de compte, je ne suis emballé à l'église que par l'art; je n'y vais que pour voir ou pour entendre et non pour prier; je ne cherche pas le Seigneur, mais mon plaisir' (XIII, I, 58). His analysis of the process which leads from art to faith is, however, an intricate one; it consists, not of one direct bound, but of a series of steps. The architecture of Saint-Séverin or the plainsong of Saint-Sulpice drew him to Christian art in general, which, he admits, 'l'avait à son tour dirigé vers Dieu' (ibid.). But his careful formulation here is important: works of art have led him *towards*, not *to*, God. The way in which he describes the process finds an interesting echo in the account which the art historian Otto von Simson gives of the relationship between aesthetic and religious response in the writings of Suger, abbot of Saint-Denis: 'Every word of Suger's interpretation seeks to battle down that very sense of detachment which is characteristic of purely aesthetic observation, and to lead visitors to the new sanctuary on to the religious experience that art had revealed to Suger himself.'[19] In the mediaeval mind's admiration of architectural beauty, von Simson states, 'religious emotions overshadowed the observer's aesthetic reaction' *(xviii)*. So it was with Huysmans: his aesthetic exaltation was merely the prelude, the vehicle to an essentially different order of things. Too often he has been seen with modern eyes, his profoundly mediaeval spirit overlooked.

Between *Là-Bas* and *En Route*, Huysmans' study of medieval mysticism had become more serious. Far from confusing aesthetic and spiritual categories, he now saw beyond the beauty of works of art and discovered a new element linking them to God, an element which provided him at last with the proof of Catholicism. What this element is, and what type of art is capable of revealing it, is made clear in an important passage in the first chapter of *En Route*, where Durtal is listening to the choir of Saint-Sulpice. He reflects that he is less moved by 'la musique humaine dans les églises' (XIII, I, 8) – the precise example he gives is an eighteenth-century motet – than by plainsong, 'cette mélodie plane et nue, tout à la fois aérienne et tombale' (XIII, I, 9). Many great composers, he says, from Vittoria and Palestrina to Handel, Bach and Haydn, have tried to translate the biblical texts into a musical idiom, often inspired by genuine mystical effusion, but their works retain a certain pomp and pride compared to the humility and sobriety of Gregorian chant. In more recent 'church' music, including that of Berlioz and Franck, the artist is too clearly visible, worshipping at the altar of his own talent, omitting God. To listen to such music is to be aware of the men who composed it, their vanity and their sins. Liturgical chant on the other hand, created by anonymous composers in their obscure cloisters, has an extraterrestrial quality. It projects no reflection of its human origin; it is free of all trace not only of sin but of artistry. Here, says Durtal, is the true idiom of the Church, a musical Gospel, as accessible as the Gospel itself to sophisticated and simple tastes alike. Here too, he says, is 'la vraie preuve du catholicisme'; it lies in '*cet* art qu'il avait fondé, *cet* art que nul n'a surpassé encore!' The demonstratives, italicised here, are important. Huysmans is not talking about art in general, but about the particular art which he has just described: a selfless, anonymous art uncorrupted by personal pride or ambition, and whose sole aim was encapsulated in 'une touffe de pensées unique: révérer, adorer, servir le Dispensateur, en lui montrant, réverbéré dans l'âme de sa créature, ainsi qu'en un fidèle miroir, le prêt encore immaculé de ses dons' (XIII, I, 10). He lists its exemplars: in painting and sculpture the primitives, in literature mystic writers, in music plainsong, in architecture the

Romanesque and the Gothic. By 'cet art', Huysmans means the art of what he calls 'cet admirable Moyen-Age', in which 'le concept divin et la forme céleste furent devinés, entr'aperçus, pour la première et peut-être la dernière fois par l'homme' (XIII, I, 11). To call Huysmans an aesthetic Catholic is totally misleading, for the crux of his adoration of mediaeval art lies in its very anti-aestheticism, its promulgation of art not for art's sake or for Man's sake, but for God's sake. Only this pure art can be called religious art, and the proof of God to which it leads resides not in itself but in the example of the artist's God-inspired faith.

Mediaeval art, too, is the sole repository of true Catholicism, the only remaining access, in this age of lukewarm religion, to 'la zone brûlante' of faith (XIII, I, 70). This view is constant throughout the trilogy. In *La Cathédrale*, Renaissance art is seen as representing the end of the great era of belief, the 'flight' of the Holy Spirit (XIV, I, 204). An age of wholly human art had begun, a self-consciously aesthetic age of 'great' artists, celebrating worldly values rather than spiritual ones. Whether consciously or not, Huysmans replies here to Zola's observations, in the novel published two years before *La Cathédrale*, on the pagan art of Renaissance Rome. In essence he agrees with Zola, but this does not shake in the slightest his belief in the truth of Catholicism. For art is the work of Man, not of God; God's inspiration may underlie and be reflected in it, but when Man has turned elsewhere for inspiration, the result is, in two senses of the phrase, no reflection on God.

Given the importance of religious artefacts in Realism's sceptical presentation of Catholicism, this is an interesting aspect of Huysmans' relationship with Realism, especially when it comes to the *objets de culte* which had provided Flaubert, the Goncourts, Maupassant and Zola with such a rich source of irony. The early Huysmans had followed their example, and the Catholic Huysmans, though believing now in the unseen order that such objects were supposed to represent, reiterated the same view of their crassness. In *La Cathédrale* he describes the room in which Gévresin's auxiliary, the abbé Plomb, lives as being full of gaudy madonnas, Magdalenes weeping globules of silver paint, saint Josephs which look neither like saints nor carpenters – all of them stamped 'articles de Munich' (XIV, I, 205). The art of La Salette presents the same ugliness of modern devotional art on a public scale, with its obligatory bronze statue in a 'Mohican' bonnet (XIV, I, 21). Huysmans further illustrates his uncomplimentary view of modern Catholic art in

Les Foules de Lourdes, written after the trilogy, but which it is useful to discuss at this point. What first struck him when he went to Lourdes was its sheer aesthetic horror. The cathedral looked as if it had been designed by a maker of wine-bottle corks, with a roof like a piece of Savoy cake. The Basilica was more like a hippodrome or casino than a church, filled with pretentious copies of Italian paintings to make it look more expensive. Even the sacred objects of the mass were vulgarly sumptuous. His description of Lourdes could have been written by Zola, down to the ironical details: the use of electric lights to illuminate the head of the Virgin on the Esplanade, or the ungainly brass taps distributing health-restoring waters. In what had clearly become his tactic, Huysmans turns his other cheek to Zola, agreeing with his superficial observations the better to refute him on fundamentals. Zola was right to regard Lourdes as an incongruous visual spectacle, an illustration of Man's need to see in order to believe. 'Nous ne voulons voir à Lourdes,' writes Huysmans, 'que du palpable et du visible!' (XVIII, 156); 'le peuple [. . .] ne peut être touché que par du visible et du palpable' (XVIII, 316). It disturbs him that an extra-material faith should depend, for so many of its adherents, on the evidence of their senses. But unlike Zola, he regards this as a weakness of human nature and not of the Catholic religion. To him, the evidence of the eyes is second to what goes on within souls. The statue of the Virgin in the grotto, to which Zola attached such importance, is ultimately 'inutile' – and, according to Bernadette, a poor likeness in any case! The true miracle of Lourdes is the unseen miracle, the spiritual sustenance obtained by those who leave Lourdes without their prayers for physical cure having been answered. Basically, Huysmans' attitude is that, since miracles can happen anywhere and at any time, the truth or untruth of any particular miracle at Lourdes makes no radical difference to his faith. This allows him to adopt an independent stance, expressing his misgivings on the difficult question of 'cured' pilgrims who have a subsequent relapse, but accepting miraculous interpretations when this seems warranted, and above all refuting Zola's detailed observations at every possible turn. On Zola's interpretation of the phenomenon of Lourdes as stemming from 'le souffle guérisseur des foules', he argues that this is a mere synonym for a well attested source of miraculous change: prayer! (XVIII, 320)

For Huysmans, the material world no longer represented the totality of the universe, but was symbolic of the spiritual dimension on which Christian belief rests. Though men succeeded in producing ugliness out of even the most supposedly sacred of objects, humble objects could be effective and moving symbols of spiritual truths. The example he gives in *Les Foules de Lourdes* is the candle:

> Le cierge se compose de trois parties: de la cire qui est la chair très blanche de Jésus, de la mèche insérée dans cette cire qui est son âme très pure cachée sous l'enveloppe de son corps, du feu qui est l'emblème de sa divinité.
>
> Le cierge est donc la figure du Christ. . . (XVIII, 42)

Thus objects, those witnesses, in Realist novels, to the material nature of life on earth, are converted by Huysmans into symbols of the divine. He reverses the process which he saw beginning in the eighteenth century – 'une époque de bedon et de bidet [qui], dès qu'il voulait toucher au culte, [. . .] fit d'un bénitier une cuvette' (XIV, II, 149). Thus, in *La Cathédrale*, the altar cloth becomes the symbol of Christ's shroud, the chalice becomes the tomb from which he springs resurrected. On a larger scale, the fluid forms of Gothic architecture show 'le suprême effort de la matière cherchant à s'alléger' (XIV, I, 216). Even natural phenomena, flora and fauna, which Zola and Maupassant had placed in a world alien to religion, contribute to the symbolic process, inspiring the artist and architect; the opening sequence of *La Cathédrale* is a description of Chartres as a mighty forest in stone, with the echo of Baudelaire's 'forêt de symbôles' more than faintly discernable.

* * *

Christian belief had totally transformed Huysman's view of the world. But what had it done to his art? Richard Griffiths has shown that his preoccupation with religious art was matched by a declining interest in other, contemporary works of art.[20] More important is the effect of conversion on Huysmans' own art as a novelist. Viewed as novels rather than as autobiography, at least two of the books that compose the Catholic trilogy have, following the exciting originality of *A Rebours*, the whimsicality of *A vau-l'eau* or even the solid competence of the early Naturalist works, a distinctly anti-climactic quality. *La Cathédrale* is essentially a discursive essay, in dialogue form, on the history and symbolism of Chartres, *L'Oblat* a meditation on the Benedictines' renovation of the liturgy. They are given the thinnest of fictional disguises by the presence in them of Durtal and that of his housekeeper Madame Bavoil, who occasionally interrupts Durtal's thoughts to remind him of the necessity of taking food and drink – the only contact which the texts have with the everyday world. There is no plot, no narrative impetus, and little character development apart from Durtal's intermittent anxieties. *L'Oblat* is given a semblance of a historical setting by references to the Dreyfus Affair and the anti-monastic measures of the Republican government, but these matters are not organically linked to Durtal's personal drama. It is ironic, but not insignificant, that Catholic critics who barely hide their unease at the delicate relationship between faith and fiction should so often praise Huysmans' last two novels, the least fictive of any that he wrote, above the others. Ernest Seillière found *L'Oblat* the most 'sympathique' of Huysmans' works.[21]

The seeds of the change in Huysmans' later works lie in his changed attitude to the writing of novels. Durtal's meditation on mediaeval art at the start of *En Route* contains ominous implications for the modern artist in general and for the would-be Christian writer in particular. Using the classic Realist metaphor of the mirror ('le miroir', in Stendhal's words, 'que l'on promène sur une grand'route'), he reminds us that art reflects its age, and in the modern world the artist's mirror cannot but be turned away from God. Modern art cannot be religious art, which only a religious age can produce. One essential feature of religious art is its selfless anonymity – a notion which Huysmans develops in *La Cathédrale*, for the art of Chartres, 'l'art le plus surhumain, le plus exalté qui fût jamais' (XIV, I, 337), is the epitome of anonymity, Who were its artists? 'Nul ne le sait. Humblement, anonymement, ils travaillèrent' (XIV, I, 340). But we know, from their work, something of their souls: 'Et quelles âmes ils avaient, ces artistes! Car nous le savons, ils ne besognaient que lorsqu'ils étaient en état de grâce' (ibid.). And knowing their souls, we know something of God, for the superhuman effort of the building of Chartres can only have been undertaken 'sous la conduite de l'Esprit-Saint' (XIV, I, 341).

The modern artist and the Christian literary artist are at a disadvantage unknown to the creators of Chartres. Religious art is an art inspired by sacred texts; the musical and visual art forms admired by Durtal are essentially transpositions of Scripture into new media. They were the means by which, as Gévresin reminds him in *La Cathédrale*, the illiterate masses could be offered instruction in their faith: stained glass and statuary were the great narrative forms of the Middle Ages. Chartres is, once again, the shining example of this. It is a great book in stone and glass. 'Toutes ses figures sont des mots; tous ses groupes sont des phrases' (XIV, I, 156). It is 'une traduction de l'Ancien et du Nouveau Testament' (XIV, I, 312). Its statuary is a history of the prophets, and also a narration not only of the Gospel, with Christ's earthly life recounted in the two hundred statues ranged between the old and new towers, but of the acrocryphal gospels too: the narratives of St Joachim and St Anne, the Gospel of the Nativity or the Protogospel of James. For the writer, such transposition of biblical narrative into new media is not possible; the Bible tells these stories so sublimely that there is nothing left to transpose.

The problem defined here by Huysmans relates primarily to subject matter. By religious art, he means, among other things, art which directly treats a religious subject: the depiction of the holy personages. Obviously, a novelist would not normally attempt such a subject in any case. Moving to the level of style, what equivalents can the novelist find in religious art which might serve as a guide? Durtal had discovered two possibilities: the realism of Grünewald, the symbolism of Chartres. In *La Cathédrale*, he explains why the first of these is a difficult option. In the fifteenth-century book of prayers of Gaston Phoebus, Durtal sees the verbal equivalent of the super-realism of the pre-Renaissance painter: especially a dramatisation of the mass, in which Christ's body is described as being literally torn and chewed by the teeth of the communiant. Modern Catholic taste could not accept such writing, he says. Its milk-and-water sensibilities are an obstacle to the Catholic novelist, and have caused Catholicism, which used to be in the vanguard of artistic change, to disengage itself from the major literary movements of modern times, Romanticism and Naturalism. The novel, 'cette forme, si souple et si large de l'art moderne' (XIV, II, 59), has developed without Catholic involvement, left to the enemy camp, despite the fact that the Catholic writer was especially well placed, by his awareness of the theological explanation of life, to lead the novel's exploration of the human condition. Huysmans reiterates here the arguments of Barbey d'Aurevilly; and like Barbey, what he was really expressing was the difficulty of reconciling his new-found Christianity with the sexuality he had so insistently reflected through all his previous writing. Sexual explicitness, he goes on to say, is censured by Catholic literary critics although it is a feature of mediaeval religious statuary. He quotes, as a slogan for the Catholic novelist, the words of Gregory the Great: 'Dites la vérité, mieux vaut le scandale que le mensonge' (XIV, II, 63). But in fact, whether for the external danger of censorship or because of inner scruples, Huysmans drops the sexual theme from his repertoire after the passage in *En Route* in which Durtal, in a demonic attack, is assailed by visions of the temptress Florence – and his last two novels are the poorer, because less personal and more abstract, for the absence of this major theme.

As for the second option: symbolism, Huysmans exploits it only intermittently. The countless pages on symbolism in *La Cathédrale* are chiefly for the purposes of discussion and elucidation, and seldom invite a symbolic reading of Huysmans' text. Certain 'symbolic' moments occur: in the opening pages, Durtal walks up the nave of the great church and sits at its intersection with the transept, facing the choir. With the help of Gévresin's later identification of the nave as the symbol of earth and of the choir as the symbol of heaven (XIV, I, 212), Durtal can be located as at the crossroads of his destiny. However, Huysmans' exploitation of the symbolic meanings of his faith is meagre compared, say, to the narrative use to which Barbey puts the doctrine of substitution. Likewise, the long discussions of mystical writers sit on the surface of the text, unconnected with the story of Durtal. In general, Huysmans seems uninterested, in the trilogy, in developing his technique as a novelist. The dialogues within Durtal are presented for the most part in the simplest possible fashion, with none of the interior monologue or indirect free style of the earlier novels, but in straightforward direct-speech alternation of inner voices: 'Mais, fit-il. . .' (XIII, I, 33).

All of this suggests that Huysmans now regarded his own writing, and perhaps literature in general, as of a secondary order. Because the novelist was restricted to portraying the human and profane, the novel's claims to be regarded as the vehicle of a total vision of reality were untenable. The novel was the great modern genre; its 'scènes de la vie réelle, its depiction of 'le jeu des passions', had made it 'une étude de psychologie, une école d'analyse' (XIV, II, 59–60). But totality was beyond it, and was achieved only in the collective work of anonymous architects, sculptors and glaziers; it was achieved, in a word, in Chartres. Gévresin tells Durtal;

> Tout est dans cet édifice, [. . .] les Écritures, la théologie, l'histoire du genre humain résumée en ses grandes lignes; grâce à la science

du symbolisme, on a pu faire d'un monceau de pierres un macrocosme.

Qui, je le répète, tout tient dans ce vaisseau, même notre vie matérielle et morale, nos vertus et nos vices. [. . .] Notre-Dame de Chartres est le répertoire le plus colossal qui soit du ciel et de la terre, de Dieu et de l'homme. (XIV, I, 156)

The contemplation of such a total art, initially a stimulus to Huysmans, was eventually a barrier. The sense of a short phrase in *Là-Bas* now becomes clear: the ideal represented by Grünewald, says Durtal, is ultimately 'hors de portée' (XI, 20) for the writer. His last novels bear every mark of being designed to fill a secondary, and literally subservient role, filling a merely useful place in the chain that leads from art to faith. Unable to attain in themselves the status of religious art as he defines it, they become, progressively, descriptions of those works that *can* reach that status, and which can therefore lead men to God. The same humility marks his increasingly simple and unadorned style, which Durtal, contemplating a book on Saint Lydwine of Schiedam, sees as necessary for such a subject. His narrative, in *La Cathédrale*, of the life of Marie-Marguerite des Anges exemplifies this: its bald, matter-of-fact statements reach precisely the same level of banality which des Esseintes had found intolerable in Eugénie de Guérin! Now, simple faith, simple events, seem to need neither comment nor embellishment; the narrator merely records, like the purest of Naturalists, but shorn of a Naturalist's scepticism. His observations are edifying and uncritical: in his portrait, in *En Route*, of brother Siméon, who looks after the monastery's pigs, Huysmans identifies as innocence and purity what most readers would see as unbelievable ignorance of the world.

Huysmans' example might appear to confirm the suspicion that religion and the novel are incompatible bedfellows: he himself clearly thought so at the end of his life. But one need not take him at his word. While denying the possibility of Catholic novels, Huysmans wrote at least one novel which occupies an important place in the history of the genre: *En Route*. This can be read, on the documentary level, as a Naturalist *enquête* into life in a monastery, as a description of the daily ritual of a Trappist's life. But it also generates new forms of drama, creating suspense and conflict out of both Durtal's struggles and the ceremony of the Church. Before his lapse into the final asceticism of style and technique which characterises the rest of the trilogy, Huysmans makes his last contribution to the techniques of Catholic fiction. The presentation of the movement of grace within a fictional character, inclining his decision but without inhibiting his free will, was to prove technically difficult for a writer like Mauriac, but Huysmans achieves it when he describes Durtal's hesitation before deciding to enter the monastery:

> Alors Durtal éprouva, dans ce moment, une chose étrange; ce fut, ainsi que plusieurs fois à Saint-Séverin, une sorte de touche caressante, de poussée douce; il sentit une volonté s'insinuer dans la sienne, et il recula, inquiet de se voir ainsi géminé, de ne plus se trouver seul dans ses propres aîtres; puis il fut inexplicablement rassuré, s'abandonna, et dès qu'il eut prononcé ce 'oui', un immense allègement lui vint. . . (XIII, I, 248)

There are also interesting dramatic sequences in *En Route*, like the account of Durtal's 'long night of the soul', when he is assailed by the mocking voice of Satan and tortured by demonically inspired sexual hallucinations. The writing rises to a much higher level of intensity and metaphorical density: Durtal undergoes a kind of crucifixion, is aware of a total separation of body and soul. Suddenly comes the sensation of the devil leaving him, whether because of his inner resistance or because of the sound of the *Salve, Regina* sung by the monks. Here Huysmans introduces a new kind of fictional scene into the French novel, one which anticipates the encounter between the priest and the devil in Bernanos' first novel.

The climactic passage which follows Durtal's night of trial is probably the most expressive of the change in him and in Huysmans of any in the entire trilogy. The sacrament of communion after his ordeal fills Durtal with the joy of the unshakeable convert. As he goes out into the grounds of the monastery, 'le jour entra à flots chez Durtal. . .

> Des fenêtres de ses sens qui plongeaient jusqu'alors sur il ne savait quel puisard, sur quel enclos humide et noyé d'ombre, il contempla subitement, dans une trouée de lumière, la fuite à perte de vue du ciel.

> Sa vision de la nature se modifia; [. . .] les arbres bruissaient, tremblants, dans un souffle de prières, s'inclinaient devant le Christ qui ne tordait plus ses bras douloureux dans le miroir de l'étang, mais qui étreignait ces eaux, les éployait contre lui, en les bénissant. (XIII, II, 212–3)

In Durtal's eyes as in Huysmans' fiction, the material world is here transformed by grace. The ugliness of the dank well of the tenement ('puisard') is illuminated by the light streaming through the windows of his soul: the language of *Pot-Bouille* gives way to that of Saint Theresa. The pond, hitherto reflecting a distorted and troubled image of the giant cross which dominates the monastery – a symbol of Durtal's imperfect vision of Christ – is now smooth. Nature, harmonious and joyful, is united to Christ. The water image is expanded a few pages later, in contrasting images of river and pond. The river is a symbol of life's course, of movement and of the temporal dimension of terrestrial life, while the pond represents stasis and timeless contemplation, eternal reflection of God's immutable glory. The presence of a pond in the grounds of a monastery, where monks repeat their unchanging acts of adoration, is appropriate, reflects Durtal, but 'une rivière n'aurait, là, aucun sens' (XIII, II, 222–3). Durtal, though his experiences were to fill two more volumes, had through conversion turned the crucial bend in the river of his own life, and so had Huysmans. The turbulent and unpredictable flow of life, which it is for the novelist to chart, now interested him less than passive contemplation of God. Like Durtal, Huysmans had found his still waters.

5

Léon Bloy's Symbolist Imagination

Huysmans' reputation as an 'aesthetic' Catholic owes much to the image created by Léon Bloy in the satirical sections of his novel *La Femme pauvre*. There, in the guise of the artist Folantin, painter of canvasses such as 'La Messe noire' and 'Les Trappistes en prière' – titles in which literary equivalents are instantly recognisable – Huysmans is derided as one of those privileged mortals who have discovered God lurking in a stained-glass window.[1] Despite these public shows of scorn for his former friend, which arose from personal resentments that need not concern us here,[2] the two most important Catholic novelists of the century's closing decades had many ideas in common. They included the conviction that Christian art, from the Renaissance onwards, was in a state of decadence. According to Bloy, Raphael and his contemporaries, the ancestors of 'notre bondieuserie sulpicienne' (FP, 80), had done as much harm to the Catholic cause as Luther. Their art, he writes in his other novel *Le Désespéré*, is inferior to 'les extracorporelles Transfixions des Primitifs' (D, 180). The thousand years of 'patient ecstasy' – the Middle Ages, an epoch venerated by him as by Huysmans – had been replaced by a falsely religious and profoundly profane art represented by paintings of Galathea's well rounded buttocks (D, 178). As for religious bric-à-brac – saints dressed in tartan or made of liquorice (D, 180) – he mocked it no less cruelly than Huysmans. Of modern works, only those that retained vestiges of the Middle Ages' symbolic expressiveness escaped his scorn. He included among them the statues at La Salette, execrated by Huysmans but praised by Bloy (X, 19) – though to understand this, one has to remember his particular devotion to La Salette, as well as his particular antagonism to Huysmans! Another modern work, Henri de Groux's painting 'Le Christ aux outrages', struck him as thoroughly unmodern, suggesting an '*anachronique* inspiration religieuse'. He admired in it what Huysmans had admired in Grünewald: a portrait of a tortured Redeemer, 'un Seigneur Dieu ruisselant de sang' (XI, 17), far removed from the cosmetic Christs of middle-class salons.

Such exceptions apart, Bloy argues that there is a radical separation, in modern times, of Christian from artist. 'Il ne saurait y avoir,' he concludes, 'un Art chrétien' (FP, 159). He means, in part, what Huysmans meant in denying the possibility of a modern religious art: that our irreligious age is condemned to create an art in its own image. But he takes his analysis to a deeper theological level than would have been to Huysmans' taste. If the artist were able to enjoy the direct contemplation of Eden that would be necessary for him to reflect the glory of God, this would be a denial of original sin, to which the artist is prey like any other man. Being an artist is certainly inferior to being a saint, and Bloy, who had dreamed for himself the destiny of a saint or miracle worker, lamented his inferior status as 'un homme de lettres'.[3] He had done all that his inevitably imperfect vision of God allowed him to do, he protests through the mouth of Marchenoir in *La Femme pauvre*: 'Il ne me reste que l'expédient de mettre au service de la Vérité *ce qui m'a été donné par le MENSONGE*' (FP, 161). Art is second best, and is dangerously idolatrous. When Christ comes again, warns Bloy, we shall be too busy looking at representations of him to see his light.

This might suggest that we can expect no more from Bloy, as from the later Huysmans, than works of humility and piety, unlikely to appeal or succeed as novels. What saves his work is that, despite these misgivings, he saw art as a means of revolt, and literature as the only form of sublimity accessible in a 'reasonable' world. There were no more Crusades to join, no stirring adventures left to experience: 'Il ne reste plus que l'Art [. . .], l'unique refuge pour quelques âmes altissimes condamnées à traîner leur souffrante carcasse dans les charogneux carrefours du monde' (D, 54). Revolt – against a father who wished on his son a steady job as a railway clerk, against a literary establishment that would not own him, and even against a God who would not end Man's long vigil by inaugurating his ultimate reign on earth – is what gives Bloy's writing the passion that lifts it out of the ordinary. The term he used for this passion, productive of that 'art passionnel' which alone could 'donner un semblant de palpitation à des cœurs humains pendus à l'étal de triperie du Démon' (FP, 160), was 'enthusiasm'. Enthusiasm, which in Bloy's system creates beauty, is itself created by love, and love is the product of suffering. All these interlinked terms, recurring throughout his work, have a meaning particular to Bloy and integral to his Catholic beliefs. 'L'enthousiasme,' he writes, 'est un Dieu dans le cœur' (II, 23). When he accuses most modern literature of lacking enthusiasm, he means that it is without spiritual fervour, which is another way of saying that Bloy, who regarded conclusions as existing in order to be jumped to, saw it as tainted by the all-pervading atheism of contemporary culture: 'Athée, fille d'athées, mère d'athées, [. . .] cette littérature est devenue quelque chose comme le vomissement définitif de la pensée et du langage' (ibid.). A writer without enthusiasm, he argues, 'n'a même pas le droit d'exister' (II, 27).

So much of Bloy, already, is revealed in these last words, which come from that aptly entitled volume of essays, *Propos d'un entrepreneur de démolitions*. Bloy's aim, here and everywhere, is to denounce, demolish and ultimately eradicate godless literature, an enterprise which was related to his apocalyptic visions of the extermination of the godless world for which he impatiently waited. His is the voice of an absolutist. A former 'communard' socialist converted to Catholicism under the influence of Barbey d'Aurevilly, Bloy brought with him the 'besoin d'absolu' (II, 17) that had marked his earlier political convictions, and which made of him an outspoken Catholic polemicist whom many have compared to Veuillot.[4] More properly, because his polemical violence was allied to a spiritualism of a sort totally alien to the latter, Bloy belongs to that three-man angry brigade of Catholic writers which is completed by Barbey and Bernanos.

Bloy sweeps together, into one compound image of inseparable parts, the categories of writer, believer and sufferer. He was all three, and the three combined, in his idealised self-portrait, to form the one, the 'un contre mille', as he described himself in his essay *Léon Bloy devant les cochons*. Another essay, *Belluaires et porchers*, employs the same imagery, dividing humanity into two categories, those who fight the beast, and those who nourish it. The former represent the militant spirit of Christianity, but in modern times they are exhausted, outfought by sheer weight of numbers. Artists are made in the same image; like the beast-fighter, like the primitive Christian, they are 'enfants de la Douleur [. . .] conclamés sur un pavois d'immondices' (II, 173), so that once again, the suffering artist, the believer and the Christian warrior coalesce, each a metaphorical figure of the other two. As for the swineherds who oppose them, they speak the language of beasts in order to control them. In literature, they are currently triumphant.

To translate Bloy's teeming metonymy into plain language is not easy. What is clear is that to him all the various manifestations of a given culture – its religion, its thought, its art, its language and its literature – were inseparably linked, and all indicative of each other. His duty, he said, was to expose these links and, by revealing the literary symptoms of 'la Débâcle sublime' (II, 245), draw attention to the whole corrupt edifice of modern times. If one aspect of the contemporary 'débâcle' was its lack of what he called 'order' – an obsessively recurring complaint on his part – this was as much the concern and responsibility of writers as of politicians and statesmen: 'L'ordre essentiel ne sera pas ressuscité par les Naturalistes et les Parnassiens' (I, 28). That a nation's literature was a sure thermometer of its spiritual health was a fact that had not gone unnoticed, even by the Almighty: for why had the Virgin chosen to reveal herself so often in contemporary France if not to warn against the values espoused by its thinkers and writers? (X, 17). Like Barbey, Bloy saw literature as the battleground of a holy war, but to him the combatants were not just flesh-and-blood novelists and poets, but supernatural forces acting in and through them.

Anti-Christian literary movements were not just symptoms of cultural decline to Bloy. They were actually alternative religions, and the most significant of them, 'la religion des jeunes et tépides crétins, fils des bourgeois glorieux qui ont adoré la morale et percé tous nos tunnels' (II, 56) was that of which Flaubert, Goncourt and Zola formed 'la Trinité divine' (ibid.). These three were his principal targets. Though he was not without a grudging admiration for Flaubert ('ce grand diable ingénieux'), his scorn for the Goncourts ('espèce de veau romancier à deux têtes et à une seule langue') and his ferocious hatred of Zola, 'le Triton de la fosse d'aisances naturaliste' (II, 54), were, like all else in Bloy, undiluted. His celebrated scatological style or 'lavatorial' language is nowhere better illustrated than in his attacks on these writers. Just as a doctor, he writes, might smell the faeces of a patient to help diagnose his disease, so can one detect the infection of the Goncourts by sniffing their disciple François Poictevin: such is the legacy of 'cette école de romanciers qui mettent leur tête au-dessous de leurs testicules pour contempler la nature' (II, 56–7). In the same vein, the seeing 'eye' of the Realist novelist is imagined by Bloy as being located in the bottom of a chamber pot, providing a glimpse of the human heart by quite another channel from that exploited by the traditional moralist! 'Les oculistes ont changé tout ça,' he laments; 'l'œil de la conscience est allé rejoindre l'*Œil de la Foi*' (II, 156).

Bloy's own eye was often blinded by hatred where Émile Zola was concerned, especially after the latter declined to lend money to the self-styled 'mendiant ingrat'. Like Huysmans, he greeted Zola's death as '[un] heureux événement', a timely obstacle to the completion of the *Quatre Évangiles* (XII, 118), and the supposed decline of Zola's literary standing, in the year of Huret's *Enquête*, was gleefully heralded by him in *Les Funérailles du naturalisme*. Literary criticism gives way to personal vilification in much of his writing on Zola. In the essay *Je m'accuse* (a parody of Zola's pro-Dreyfus pamphlet), he pretends to apologise for any good things he might have said about the writer whom, after *Lourdes*, he dubs 'le crétin des Pyrénées'. The 'merdeux romans' which Zola sells by the kilo project a vision of human life which, he mocks, consists of no more than 'gagner de l'argent, bien manger, bien dormir, bien faire l'amour et bien faire caca' (IV, 214). This abuse spills over into a broader attack on values and attitudes associated with Zola, including his scientific optimism. Faith in science, scoffs Bloy, is a worthy product of a brain like Zola's, but when will science invent a ray to pierce the darkness of human hearts? (VIII, 29). Science, even medical science, Bloy dismisses as having usurped the role of knowledge, of 'la divine SCIENCE' (VIII, 136). He regards inoculation techniques with suspicion, and Jenner and Pasteur as poisoners. Cannot scientists see that their celebrated Microbe, on which they blame all ills, is no more than the material disguise in which Satan causes evil to appear to their gullible eyes? (XIII, 30–1). Belief in rational and scientific ideas could clearly not be expected from a man who swore that his mother's body, exhumed for reburial several years after her death, was perfectly preserved, while that of his father, buried the same year, was decomposed (ibid.). As Bloy's wife, the angelic Jeanne Molbech, said to Rémy de Gourmont: 'Vous êtes pour l'évolution et Léon Bloy est pour le miracle' (XI, 67).

* * *

Like Barbey, whom Bloy's ideas and language so often echo, Bloy's attacks on novelists were all the more urgent because of his sense of the genre's paramount importance. More clearly than any other Catholic novelist he saw the parallel between the novel's rise and religion's fall. 'Le roman,' he wrote, 'est monté à l'empire du monde, dans le temps que la virginale foi des peuples en descendait' (XV, 72). This, to Bloy, was a gulf that had to be bridged. More sharply than either Barbey or Huysmans, he sensed that the novel was an art form in which every aspect of knowledge and experience could be accommodated in a potentially conclusive way, and that its role in the clash of competing world-visions was a central one. He speaks of 'la portée énorme de cette chose absolument moderne qui s'appelle le Roman', and describes it as '[une] forme littéraire vraiment babélique et définitive, dans laquelle toutes les autres tiennent et qui atteste avec puissance un étrange besoin nouveau d'unité, de simplification, de centralisation à tout prix, dût-on en crever'.[5] In the extraordinary expansion and versatility of the novel he saw the decline of other, more traditional, modes of exploring and explaining man's condition.

One of these modes was history, now stultified by the documentary method and by suffocating factualism, so that its true purpose as a revealer of God's hand in the affairs of men was utterly circumvented. The novelist, because he has the capacity to dream and to imagine, is a kind of refractory historian, able to free our minds of obsession with 'la petite bête'. But, argues Bloy, the novelist has duplicated the historian's error by a voluntary restriction of vision, a closing of 'les yeux de son âme' (VI, 322). He wrongly sees his role as the study of 'le possible humain', rather than 'le possible de Dieu, qui est le véritable réel de l'homme' (I, 85). He has wandered into a world which ought to be alien to him, like a 'un superbe ruminant qui s'avancerait dans un pâturage étranger, de toute la longueur d'une corde fixée dans la prairie de son maître' (ibid.). The guide-rope on which he imprudently relies is the much vaunted documentary method of the Realist and Naturalist, 'le Document seul, dans la parfaite sécheresse, la lettre morte des faits, le renseignement infinitésimal, l'investigation corpusculaire' (I, 174).

The novel's true ally, Bloy argued, is theology. As early as 1876, he anticipated the notion of experimentation which Zola was not to formulate fully until three years later. Rather than be the handmaiden of science, verifying its theories in the imaginary test-tubes of the *Rougon-Macquart*, the novel, said Bloy, should strive to confirm experimentally, to illustrate exemplarily, the truths enshrined in Catholicism (XV, 73). Bloy thus advanced by a further stage the theory of the Catholic novel, tentatively explored by Barbey before him. Not only must Catholic writers seize their share of the novel in the interests of Catholic expression; the novel, in order to fulfil itself as a genre, must accept its responsibility to reveal God's truth. Bloy might have parodied Zola further: 'Le roman sera catholique ou ne sera pas'.

He does not let his theory rest there, and his refinement of it has escaped the attention of critics who protest that the 'Catholic' novel cannot exist because no man can represent a monolithic body of belief. A novel, Bloy accepts, is the product of an individual imagination, of 'une conception géniale et unipersonnelle de la vie humaine' (II, 80). But this individual idea derives its coherence from its relationship to a collective corpus, however subjective might be its form of expression. 'Il faut nécessairement,' writes Bloy, 'qu'il y ait en lui [the novel] ce qu'on appelle une idée, c'est-à-dire une pomme métaphysique cueillie sur l'arbre de la science du bien et du mal et déposée, pour y mûrir, sur la paille d'un style quelconque' (ibid.). The individuality of the Catholic artist, in the form of his particular style, is enshrined here, and so is the doctrinal context in which he must work. Can there have been, could there be, a better definition of the Catholic novel?

It is also a definition which, asserting the individual writer's role within Catholicism, leads Bloy straight to the moral problem encountered by every Catholic novelist from Barbey to Green. The objection that novels themselves are dangerous because they depict sinful acts, and that a Catholic thus reads and, *a fortiori*, writes a novel at his peril, has been raised against the Catholic novel along every inch of its history. On this matter, Bloy spoke what for him was a most atypical common sense. For him the source of the problem did not reside between the writer and his material, for the novel must, and indeed can only, depict the fallen world of human passions, nor between the novel and the reader, for 'le roman n'est qu'une cause seconde du mal qu'il fait, ensuite il ne fait pas le *même mal* à tout le monde' (XV, 72). The problem lay between the Catholic writer and Catholic opinion, which lagged light years behind literary development. Bloy's scorn for the artistic tastes of the Catholic bourgeoisie is a further attitude shared with Huysmans. Both men were at least as ready to blame their fellow Catholics as they were to blame atheists and agnostics for the conditions that had severed the traditional links between the Church and the arts. Middle-class Catholic society, writes Bloy, treats beauty as if it were by definition obscene (IX, 85). Hence the fate of Barbey, 'un catholique, un indubitable chrétien romain par la tête et par le cœur' and the author of *Un prêtre marié* – *l'unique* roman chrétien qui puisse être lu par des êtres appartenant à l'espèce humaine' (II, 252–3) – who had seen his work not only dragged through the civil courts but also censured by the Archbishop of Paris. Bloy's many expressions of praise for Barbey, in *La Méduse Astruc*, in the articles of *Le Pal*, in *Un brelan d'excommuniés*, and even as the hero of a satirical short story called 'Barbey d'Aurevilly, espion prussien' (the only thing of which Barbey had not been accused!), represent his homage to the writer whom he was the first to recognise as the pioneer of a new genre.

* * *

The Catholic novelist, then, is he who undertakes the perilous task of plucking the metaphysical apple from the tree of knowledge and eating it in his own individual way. Bloy's way was via symbolism. Mediaeval art attracted him because of its 'représentation symbolique des réalités surnaturelles dont toute chose terrestre n'était [. . .] que l'énigmatique miroir' (II, 135). '*Toute* chose terrestre': symbols were not just emblems in art as they were, primarily, for Huysmans. They come down from stained glass and stone to exist in the world around us, as the very language of the apparently – only apparently – material universe in which we live. All that happens and all that exists are symbols of some great truth, the medium of some great message. The totality which Naturalism, following empirical science, tries to capture, is not total at all, because it stops at the boundaries of the seen. 'Nous parlons de l'Invisible,' insists Bloy: 'Je dis que tout ce que nous voyons, tout ce qui s'accomplit extérieurement, n'est qu'une apparence – un reflet énigmatique, *per speculum* – de tout ce qui s'accomplit, substantiellement, dans l'Invisible' (XI, 175).

The first field to which he applies his method of symbolic interpretation is history. The inspiration for this endeavour came from his reading of what he called the greatest history book: the Bible (I, 176). Under the influence of the abbé Tardif de Moidrey, confessor (of Barbey as well as Bloy) at Notre-Dame-des-Victoires, Bloy became the most devoted reader of the Scriptures of any of the Catholic novelists, although his reading was often, to say the least, idiosyncratic.[6] The Bible was for him the model of what all historical writing should be, the chronicle of God's dealings with men, but as well as chronicling the past, the historian had to interpret it symbolically. History was 'une révélation surérogatoire ajoutée à l'autre Révélation' (I, 309). Unlike Bossuet, who believed that everything is made clear by God in history, Bloy believed that everything was unclear, that truth's imperviousness to rational exploration was itself a revelation of the shortcomings of man's reason. Truth is hidden in enigmas which only a blend of intuition and faith can decipher. This conviction informs all his historical writings, which range from Joan of Arc to Napoleon and from Byzantium to the Third Republic.

A full discussion of Bloy's historical imagination is beyond the scope of this chapter, but a glimpse of it offers a valuable foresight of the philosophical assumptions underlying his novels. He shows us Saint Joan, her life marked by 'le surnaturel intégral': the saviour of her nation, virgin of Orléans and figure of the Holy Virgin. He hails Columbus, and indeed campaigns for his canonisation, as the greatest Christian of all time, the man who had revealed the totality of God's created world and rescued half the globe from the darkness of Satan's power. Columbus' mission was a consciously and intentionally evangelical one, utterly falsified by modern historians' failure to see it in its supernatural perspective. Leaping three centuries to Marie-Antoinette, Bloy draws the same conclusion from her life: that it conveys a spiritual meaning to the world, for the death of the 'chevalière de la mort' redeemed the sins of the French royal family. Atonement was the hidden meaning, too, of the destiny of the so-called 'Louis XVII', the Prussian clockmaker Naundorff whose claim to be recognised as the lost dauphin of France was fervently espoused by Bloy. He is the Son who metonymically as well as mystically confers on Louis XVI the role of Father; the absence of both deprives the nation of its spiritual substance, and the Revolution becomes a re-enactment of the Crucifixion. As for Napoleon, Bloy's 1900 version (in *Le Fils de Louis XVI*) has him as an anti-king, a Lucifer and betrayer of the Trinity, while twelve years later, in *L'Âme de Napoléon*, he has become 'la Face de Dieu dans les ténèbres', the figure of the One whose coming is imminent (V, 271).

A number of important themes can be rescued from this frenetic rewriting of history. One is the role Bloy assigns to France. 'C'est *surtout* pour la France,' he states, 'que Jésus a sué le sang' (V, 94). France, the eldest daughter of the Church, the mother of other nations, symbolised by the 'gallus' or gallic cock which he identifies as the bird that crew three times for Peter, has a mystical role in history which equals in importance that of the Jews. Her history is 'quelque chose comme le Nouveau Testament continué' (V, 95), a fifth Gospel, carrying its own supernatural message.

A second important theme is that of identity. What all Bloy's historical figures have in common is mystery. Napoleon, for example, is unknown and unknowable, more than the sum total of his recorded deeds and words. What counts is the symbolic meaning of his life. This, says Bloy, is true of all of us: 'Il n'y a pas un être humain capable de dire ce qu'il est, avec certitude. Nul ne sait ce qu'il est venu faire en ce monde, à quoi correspondent ses actes, ses sentiments, ses pensées; qui sont ses proches parmi les hommes, ni quel est son *nom* véritable, son impérissable Nom dans le registre de la Lumière' (V, 273). Other themes come pouring out of these lines: the correspondences between individuals, the bonds which tie them to others, without their knowing, in a mysterious solidarity which the Church explains in the doctrine of the Communion of saints; and the theme of Names. 'J'ignore le *nom* de mon âme,' laments Bloy (IX, 238). Some names guide us to the mysterious identity of their owner. Christopher Columbus is both Christ-bearer and Dove, 'la Colombe portant le Christ', the image of the Holy Ghost (I, 93). The mystery of names and of identity, says Bloy, has been sensed by writers since the time of Sophocles, but its literary potential has been grasped more than its mystical significance. The symbolic meaning of an individual's life is taken for granted in fiction and ignored in life; the writer must persuade us to read our lives as we read his books, to see that 'chaque homme est sur terre pour signifier quelque chose qu'il ignore' (V, 277). To grasp this is to encounter a totality far greater than that envisaged even in Balzac's system of typology: the totality of God's purpose, at large in his creation.

Yet more notions arise from the above, or are implicit in Bloy's system of thought, where ideas run into and overlap with each other to form a continuous and seamless tapestry in which people and things remote in space and time are obscurely linked. Modern concepts of time are overthrown in this system. Christ's words 'Before Abraham was, I am' cannot be grasped, says Bloy, by 'les âmes cyclistes du vingtième siècle' (VIII, 80). The connections between concepts are fluid. Symbols merge with other symbols. Like names, they convey as much meaning as their referent, become consubstantial with it, as the bread and wine of the mass with the body and blood of Christ. 'Notre misère inénarrable,' says Bloy, 'est de prendre sans cesse pour des figures ou des symboles inanimés les énonciations les plus claires et les plus vivantes de l'Écriture. Nous croyons mais non pas *substantiellement*' (X, 23). He offers a clue here to the meaning of his own most frequently recurring symbol: Money and its concomitant, the Poor Man. For money, whether exemplified by Bloy as silver or as gold, is both substance and symbol. Its material and spiritual identities sometimes coalesce, and at others are opposed. The gold that Columbus brought back from the New World was intended for the building of the City of God, described in *Revelations* as being made of gold; here gold symbolises God's purpose. But Columbus' Spanish paymasters, in exploiting this gold for material ends, reconverted it into base matter (I, 120). Likewise, silver, in its biblical, metaphorical sense – the Word of God – was deposited with the Jews, and rejected by them when they crucified Christ, which is why Jews are, in Bloy's estimation, unavoidably rich, forever associated with money in its material form (I, 305). In an intricate development of this symbolism, Money becomes the Bread which it alone can buy, and thus we eat Money; but Bread is also synonymous with God, and it is God's wish that we eat him, partake of his substance in the mass. Bread, Money and God are thus the same (VIII, 32). Therefore, says Bloy, pursuing the same chain of ideas in another text, when we 'eat' God, we eat Money, in its embodiment as spiritual wealth, giving a new sense to the old cliché: 'manger de l'argent'. While the Christian eats money, the Jew crucifies it (IX, 31).

The contiguous notions of poverty and wealth share similarly complex interrelationships. The poor represent grace (I, 88), or, alternatively, God (I, 306). They share the lot of the earthly Jesus, the Poor Man of Nazareth. The rich man is spiritually poor; he is fit only for extermination, the fate Bloy wished on all his enemies. Yet Bloy also argues that poverty is an abject state, from which money in its material form can save, that poverty is sinful and that it is our duty to be rich (VIII, 26). The only way to find coherence in Bloy is to admit that he passes from material to symbolic plane in mid thought, and to translate him as follows: that poverty is a condition of physical misery and spiritual abandonment; that the gift of money which alleviates it is an act of charity by which the giver does God's will; and that while the poor man waits for betterment, he has the supreme comfort of following in the footsteps of Christ. This idea, or series of ideas, is central to Bloy's novel *La Femme pauvre*.

As befits a writer, Bloy gives extended consideration to the sign system on which his own art depends: to language, both as symbol in itself and as vehicle for the expression of other symbols. He embraces the history of language as confidently as any other aspect of history. The original 'langue morte de l'homme', he affirms, the universal language lost in the chaos of Babel, was replaced by the language of the prophets, and became through their mouths 'la Parole vivante de Dieu' – a process which symbolised the Resurrection, and which was symbolised in its turn by the return of the Dove, or Holy Ghost, to Noah (I, 50). He also accords a special role to Latin, which existed through centuries of blood and war in order to produce the liturgical text of the *Stabat Mater*, and whose grammatical system developed its imperative voice for the express purpose of creating the CRUCIFIGE! which transformed and saved the world (II, 307). Latin is God's chosen language, the medium by which faith in him is propagated. A startling parallel between it and another 'carrier of God' leaps to Bloy's mind: 'Sait-on que le latin est la langue immaculée, *conçue sans péché*, [. . .] et que c'est en elle que furent inscrits les symboles qui ne peuvent pas mourir?' (II, 308). Bloy is surely the only French novelist who ever wrote a full chapter of one of his novels in Latin (*La Femme pauvre*, Chapter XXV).

Language is thus as charged with meaning as every other phenomenon is. As Bloy said of the title of Rémy de Gourmont's *Le Latin mystique*, 'Comme si tout n'était pas mystique!' (II, 308). French too is charged with meaning, but is used every day by people impervious to the fact. Bloy's *Exégèse des lieux communs*, his reply to Flaubert's *Dictionnaire des Idées reçues*, analyses the unconscious religious sense of the platitudes of middle-class speech. To Bloy, God is present in our very mouths, but we do not notice him.

* * *

Bloy took the same symbolical system with him when he turned from the interpretation of the external world to the interpretation of his own life. In truth, there was a great deal in his life that required interpretation![7] How could he explain rationally the series of apparent coincidences which punctuated his existence? There was first the death of his father, occurring suddenly and mysteriously just after Bloy entered into a relationship with the former prostitute Anne-Marie Roulé. This combination of events, if that is what it was, was sufficient for Bloy to regard himself, even though his father was unaware of the liaison, as being guilty of patricide. Then there was the visit to La Salette with Tardif de Moidrey and Bloy's premature return to Paris, against Tardif's wishes, to find awaiting him on arrival there . . . the news of the death of Tardif, whom he had left hale and healthy a day or two before. Was this the result of Bloy's failure to grasp the Virgin's message? Then, two months to the day after he had become the godfather of Henri de Groux's child, there occurred the sudden death of Bloy's own young son in apparent mystical substitution. Appallingly bad luck? Chance? 'Qu'il faut être sot pour croire au hasard!' exclaimed Bloy (XI, 72). Marchenoir goes further: 'A ses yeux, le mot *Hasard* était un intolérable blasphème. . . – *Rien n'arrive sans Son ordre ou Sa permission*, disait-il aux blasphémateurs' (D, 136). The idea of chance, concludes Marchenoir, constitutes a philosophy, a way of looking at the universe which is at odds with Christianity; it is a 'rival de mon Christ' (ibid.). Everything that happens to us carries a message that we must decipher, for we are essentially dual creatures with a supernatural identity obscured by our earthly one.[8]

The personal myth which Bloy created out of his desperate search for transcendent significance intertwined with his myth of history. As Albert Béguin says, 'Le destin personnel de Bloy et le destin de la Création [. . .] sont la même chose.'[9] In his poverty, Bloy became another incarnation of the Poor Man, lack of money 'la forme de [sa] captivité' (XI, 70). Like his heroes from the past, like Columbus, or Joan, like Marie Antoinette or Naundorff, he was also the Victim, both of men and of God. God's cruelty lay in his failure to reveal himself, his delay in allowing the longed for Second Coming. But there was a consolation for Bloy in the conviction that this event would happen in his own lifetime and that he, Léon Bloy, would be at its centre. This certainty had been vouchsafed to him through the visions of Anne-Marie, to whom it was revealed that the reign of the Holy Ghost was imminent, that it would manifest itself through her, and that Bloy would be the reincarnation of Elijah, himself a figure of the Holy Ghost. The visionary and her 'Joseph', as she called him, anticipated that all this would come about on the Feast of St Joseph, 1879. Forty years later, with Anne-Marie long since dead, Bloy was still awaiting the coming of the 'Quelqu'un' who would appear as the lowest of vagabonds (IX, 234).

Anne-Marie's 'secret' merged in Bloy's imagination with other 'secrets', for Bloy was addicted to enigmas of all types. France's spiritual identity, for example, was the 'secret' of Jesus Christ (V, 95). But the greatest secret was the one which the Virgin had confided in the peasant children Mélanie and Maximin at La Salette in 1846 – by strange uncoincidence the year of Bloy's birth. She had instructed the children not to divulge the details of her message until she told them to do so, but in the absence of further communication from on high, Mélanie's secret was eventually revealed with the imprimatur of her confessor, the Bishop of Lecce, Monseigneur Zola (oh! mystical symbolism of names!). It consisted of an expression of heaven's wrath on the mediocrity of the priesthood and the political corruption of France, and of a warning of the violent coming of the Holy Ghost, to wreak the destruction necessary for the subsequent installation of a new reign on earth. All this would be heralded by a series of disasters which would fall especially heavily on France and Italy. The Virgin promised that she was trying to stay the angry hand of her son, and shed tears for the holocaust that was to come. Although these predictions, like those which are often read into the Book of Revelations or into the prophecies of Nostradamus, are susceptible, especially with hindsight, to infinite interpretation, they alarmed Napoleon III and the French Church enough for them to try to suppress or delay the publication of the Virgin's message.[10]

Bloy, whose apocalyptic imagination was much more profoundly stirred by these pronouncements than by the sweeter message of Lourdes, wrote two books about La Salette, *Le Symbolisme de l'Apparition* and *Celle qui pleure*, as well as an introduction to Mélanie's own account of her life. Mélanie's secret, made all the more significant for Bloy by Anne-Marie's secret – the promise of *his* role in the providential plan – combined with his inimitable readings of the Bible and the influence, in all probability, of occult texts, to produce his own private theology. The fullest expression of this comes in *Le Salut par les Juifs*. In this text, Bloy dissociates himself from the form which anti-semitism took in the writings of Edouard Drumont, which he saw, not so much as wrong or repulsive, but as an *incomplete* account of the identity of the Jew. The Christian's hatred of the Jew, says Bloy, is justified, and is symbolised in Jesus' anger against the fig-tree. The drama of Good Friday is a dialogue between Christ and the Jew. All the pairs of good and bad brothers in the Bible prefigure this: Abel and Cain, the prodigal son and his reliable brother, Isaac and Ishmael, Jacob and Esau, Moses and Pharaoh, David and Saul, the good and bad thieves on Calvary. There is a conflict within the Trinity, between the Word (Christ) and the Spirit (the Jew), between Love and Wisdom. This was paralleled on earth: while the Christian embraced the Poor Man, the Jew took the Money. Until Money resumes its original form – the Holy Spirit –

and the Jews recognise the divinity of Christ, the Redemption is unfinished; Christ still hangs on the Cross. The Cross is also a symbol of the Holy Spirit, which the Jews gave to Christ by nailing him to it, signifying their rejection of both. The two must be separated, Jesus must descend from the Cross. The coming of the Paraclete will achieve this, and will introduce, after the reign of the Father and that of the Son, the Third Reign, that of the Holy Spirit – whom Bloy identifies, in a startling finale to this passage, as being indistinguishable from Lucifer.

Bloy certainly seems here to herald a post-Christian age, and to come closer to one of nineteenth-century France's most celebrated heresies, the Vintrasian cult, than to Christianity. This cult, the founder of which, Pierre Vintras, proclaimed himself (before Anne-Marie gave the part to Bloy) as the incarnation of Elijah, held that the Second Coming would be that of the Holy Ghost, not of Christ, as Bloy also appears to do. Vintras' heretical beliefs are discussed in Chapter XX of Huysmans' *Là-Bas* by Durtal, des Hermies and Carhaix, and Bloy's quarrel with Huysmans seems to have originated partly from this fact, for many initiates saw Carhaix as a caricature of Bloy himself.[11] Raymond Barbeau goes further than Huysmans, accusing Bloy of being not just a heretical Catholic but a secret satanist, a conscious follower of Lucifer.[12] So the question arises, and is more easily asked than answered: was Léon Bloy, Catholic writer, really a *Catholic* at all? Griffiths' argument that Bloy's thinking is not so much heretical as 'untidy' and 'contradictory'[13] does not really convince. Bloy, very consistently, attributes to Marchenoir the same view of the 'rédemption *inaccomplie*' as that which he expressed on his own behalf (D, 148). To the same Marchenoir, Christ speaks of the atrocious hardness of the cross to which he remains pinned, and of his agonising wait for Elijah to set him free – when, he promises, echoing the Virgin at La Salette, he will descend in a blaze of fire on his miserable flock and their wretched pastors: 'Toute la terre apprendra, pour en agoniser d'épouvante, que ce Signe [the Cross] était mon Amour lui-même, c'est-à-dire l'ESPRIT SAINT, caché sous un travestissement inimaginable' (D, 279–80).

Though scattered widely throughout his work, and rarely brought into focus, Bloy's references to the reign of the Paraclete are consistent and coherent. There are, on the face of it, grounds for querying the object of his belief. In the end, he is his own best defender. When, long before Barbeau's book, he was attacked on similar grounds by a certain 'Calamus' in the Lyon periodical

L'Université catholique, his protestation of his horror of 'cette vieille hérésie, bien antérieure au misérable Vintras' (XI, 134) seems genuine, and when further pressed he responded with biblical quotation to underpin the orthodox sources of what he had written (XII, 222–3). His description of Marchenoir's beliefs in *Le Désespéré* is followed by the same careful reference to orthodoxy: 'Doctrine qui ne le séparait pas du catholicisme, puisque l'Église romaine a tout permis de ce qui n'altère pas le canonique Symbole de Nicée' (D, 60). Although the notorious passage in *Le Salut par les juifs* remains one of the most problematic and disturbing in Bloy's work, the accusation of conscious and intentional heresy seems ill founded. Led on by his own galloping symbolism, Bloy was striving to realise a total vision of the final integration of all things in God's providential scheme. The return of the Jews from their self-imposed spiritual exile was a vital part of this, for which the return to grace of the fallen angel Lucifer functions as both parallel and image. Ernest Seillière commented that Bloy only rarely foresees the reign of the Holy Spirit.[14] Developing this, one can observe that he tends to do so when in his aggressive mood, attacking the society which failed to recognise his distinction, and on which he invokes heaven's rage. But there is also a tender Léon Bloy, who, through the mouth of his Poor Woman Clotilde, longs for the presence of 'le doux Christ' (FP, 51).

* * *

Bloy's two novels, published ten years apart in 1887 and 1897 respectively, illustrate the importance to him of the novel genre. They are the most concentrated and most readable expression of his ideas and beliefs, forming, when taken together, a kind of summa of his thought and of the personal experiences from which it in large measure sprang. They are both an extension of his polemical and historical writing and a recasting of them in a new, narrative form. This dual identity explains their hybrid nature, the coexistence within them of elements which the modern novel had for the most part discarded – authorial declaration, direct satire, apocalyptic warning – and more acceptably fictive elements of narrative structure, scene and characterisation. But all these elements unite well to produce Bloy's important contribution to the Catholic novel.

Whereas Huysmans' novels chronicle the search for faith, those of Bloy express the anguished vigil which faith entails. Or entailed for *him* – because, like Huysmans, Bloy draws his material from his own life. The difference between them is that, while Huysmans followed the narrative-descriptive formula of his early novels to record in barely transposed form the events of his later life, Bloy interprets his life, seeks the meaning within and behind it. His novels are based on the same search for symbolical sense which informs his non-fictional writing. Marchenoir, the central figure of *Le Désespéré*, is embarked on a parallel search for the underlying meaning of history. While Balzac's or Flaubert's young writers want to be the Walter Scott of their generation, Marchenoir's ambition is to be like the egyptologist Champollion, but 'le Champollion des événements historiques envisagés comme les hiéroglyphes divines d'une révélation par les symboles, corroboration de l'autre Révélation' (131). He takes as his starting-point the notion of Suffering: 'Toute chose terrestre est ordonnée par la Douleur' (137). This becomes his Cogito. Suffering is the great constant, the essence of Man's condition; in history and in individual lives a constant re-enactment of Christ's suffering is taking place. To Marchenoir, the revelation of his own life's meaning has come in a dream in which the sacrificial nature of his suffering becomes clear to him, and with it a sense of the revelation of his identity, its inseparability from 'la Face épouvantable de son Christ' (58).

His Christian name Marie-Joseph underlines this identity, as names in Bloy so often do. But his father has inflicted on him the given name Caïn, to match that of his brother Abel, which suggests that he is also a figure of the bad brother, the outcast, the Jew, the Holy Spirit, all of which, we have seen, are associated by Bloy with Adam's erring son. Marchenoir represents both exemplary suffering and exile: he remarks that the most significant literature of the nineteenth century is the literature of exile and desperation (50). The prostitute with whom he lives is called Véronique, which suggests her responsibility for caring for Marchenoir/Christ as Saint Veronica did in wiping Christ's face; the imprint of that face on Veronica's cloth might also point to Véronique's role as guardian of Marchenoir's true image. But in always addressing him as Joseph (as Anne-Marie did Bloy) she also identifies her own alternative image as that of Mary, as well as that of the Magdalene to which her former profession befits her. Thus the two poles of her identity are fixed. Bloy's historical essays accustom the reader to such switches and layers of meaning, and justify the recognition of them in his novels.

The form which Marchenoir's suffering takes is lack of literary success, engineered by enemies who fear the sharpness of his pen, and his resultant poverty. To the turpitude of the literary fraternity, Bloy adds the corruption and mediocrity of the Church: these are the twin targets of his polemic. The Church, and Bloy's fellow Catholics, are attacked through straightforward authorial digression, the discourse of the essays simply spilling over into the novel. For his satire on contemporary writers, however, Bloy exploits more fully the potential of the novel: he invents a rich gallery of portraits, and places them in fully realised surroundings. For prospective publishers of *Le Désespéré*, they were indeed too rich and fully realised, and above all too easily identifiable for publishers' legal comfort. Dulaurier and his friend Des Bois (two branches of the same tree?) are obviously Paul Bourget and the society doctor Albert Robin, while in the long and impressive sequence of the Beauvivier dinner, where Marchenoir is trapped into reading his work for the entertainment of the mocking guests, caricatural versions of Catulle Mendès (Beauvivier), Maupassant, Daudet, Bonnetain, Richepin and others are much in evidence.[15] Bloy tried later to defuse these scenes, insisting in the preface to a subsequent edition that he was not aiming at individuals, but creating a broader social satire in which the lampooned writers represented types (22). He was perhaps right to prefer other aspects of the novel to this one, but the polemical chapters nevertheless should not be regarded as incidental or superfluous. Some of Bloy's main themes are elaborated in them. Dulaurier, for example, is the enemy of 'le Pauvre'; from his work, much acclaimed by the Academy, 'le dolent Famélique, le sale et grand Pauvre, ami du Seigneur' (33) is missing. His response to Marchenoir's plea for money – 'Je suis plus pauvre que vous' (40) – is, in Bloy's beatitudinal paradox, ironically and profoundly true. Dulaurier reveals the emptiness of a work written just for success and money, with no point to convey. He is 'un évangéliste du Rien' (33); 'ses grâces [sont] faites de rien du tout, comme sa science' (39). These Bernanosian images are followed by others: his coldness, his 'imagination glacée' is expressed in images of Norway, the North Cape, 'neige psychologique' (37), the antithesis of Enthusiasm and of the Fire which is the positive symbol of God's love and of Man's duty to emulate it.

Love, for Marchenoir, is an ambivalent quality. The opening of his heart to the love of God has also stimulated his sensual awakening, and at the age of twenty-eight, he has discovered both God and Woman. The conflict of the two passions is at the centre of his moral struggles. Bloy comments that the generation of Zola will see no psychological or literary interest in this kind of conflict, that of 'un catholique ballotté par d'impures vagues au-dessus d'absurdes abîmes' (67); but 'Qu'importe!': he is not writing for the public of his time. He narrates Marchenoir's personal life, and that of the two women and a child, now dead, involved in it. The first woman was a prostitute with whom he lived for two years, and who had died of tuberculosis in a poor-house. The second was also a prostitute, who had died giving birth to their child; Marchenoir had raised the boy to the age of five, but he had then died of hunger, after being missing from home for three days. 'Comment et pourquoi? Questions sans réponse, mystère insoluble que rien ne peut éclaircir' (76). As for Véronique, alias 'la Ventouse', she has become converted, 'son amour [. . .] transfiguré, tansporté dans l'infini' (81). Bloy makes no attempt to explain this conversion in psychological terms. It happened 'par miracle', a transformation from sexual 'machine' into 'une fille très pure et un encensoir toujours fumant devant Dieu' (81). She and Marchenoir do not have sexual relations, for he regards love for woman as a 'defiguration' (106), a 'distant symbole' (162) of the love of God. Véronique, when her charms become more than Marchenoir can resist, and determined to keep his soul pure, makes herself physically repugnant by having her hair cut off and all her teeth pulled out. Bloy comments that this action will be unintelligible to a modern reader, an act of supreme spiritual heroism in a supremely unheroic and unspiritual age. It is typical of Véronique's simplicity, which Bloy praises in terms that suggest a conscious opposition to Flaubert's portraits of simple hearted folk:

> Jamais il ne s'était vu un cœur plus simple. Le langage moderne a déshonoré, autant qu'il a pu, la simplicité. C'est au point qu'on ne sait même plus ce que c'est. On se répresente vaguement une espèce de corridor ou de tunnel entre la stupidité et l'idiotie (102).

The ending of the novel, with Véronique eventually driven mad by her realisation of the threat she poses, even disfigured, to Marchenoir's soul, and Marchenoir fatally injured in a street accident, is a purely formal one, a means of closure for a plot that has nowhere else to go, but it also sums up the destiny and unrelieved suffering of Marchenoir. The final sentence suggests, however, that Marchenoir is saved despite the non-arrival of the priest who has been summoned. His friend Leverdier, the embodiment of Christian charity, arrives by his bedside 'à onze ans du soir', at the eleventh hour precisely.

The plot of Bloy's first novel is a spare one, and is often suspended in favour of chapters which read more like essays. The importance of the novel form, and what it can provide which straight polemical writing cannot, is suggested, however, by Bloy's use of dream sequences, and of the device of the substitution of voices, when a voice from on high seems to speak in or through Marchenoir. His impassioned speech on the shortcomings of the Church is heard by Véronique as if pronounced by the mouth of 'un autre', and Leverdier agrees: 'Mais ta voix, encore plus que tes paroles, était inouïe. C'était à supposer que tu voyais, je ne sais quoi. . .' (224). In this way, the flesh-and-blood characters of fiction become the vehicle of messages from beyond. For the most part, though, Bloy's discourse is as abstract in this novel as it is in his non-fiction. The nature of the material world as simply the husk of meaning relegates it to a secondary role, and Bloy's language reflects this; even his scatology is metaphorical. In one solitary sequence, the usefulness of scenic description to convey mood and atmosphere seems to strike him. It occurs when Marchenoir is returning to Paris after a brief stay at the Grande Chartreuse. Both the countryside seen from the train, 'une contrée polaire en harmonie avec la désolation de son âme' (153), and the interior of the train, with its harsh light falling on a mentally handicapped boy who makes Marchenoir think of his own dead child, are used to conjure up the sensations, as distinct from the thoughts, of the character. Bloy's second novel, though it did not appear until ten years later, would contain much more of this concrete discourse.

* * *

In terms of composition and structure, *La Femme pauvre* represents a marked advance on *Le Désespéré*. The two parts into which it is divided are indicators of its movement and meaning: the central figure Clotilde is first 'l'épave des ténèbres', then 'l'épave de la lumière', even though in material terms her life might seem to take a downward rather than the upward curve which these titles suggest. Each stage in her life is given a fully dramatised form, with its particular spatial setting and significant male figure. A parallel is suggested with *Madame Bovary*, in which the heroine's fate involves a spatial movement – from home to Tostes, then to Yonville and to

Rouen – and an affective one: from her father to her husband Charles, then to Léon, to Rodolphe and back to a changed Léon. Clotilde's destiny takes her from the sordid home dominated by her mother's 'protector' Chapuis, to the artist's studio of Gacougnol, to the Jardin des Plantes where the guiding male spirit is Marchenoir, and to the home she shares with her husband Léopold – each move and each man representing, in a reversal of Emma Bovary's career, an upward step towards the realisation of her identity.

At the beginning of the novel, Clotilde's material life could scarcely be worse. She has no clothes and sleeps on a filthy mattress. The door of the house where she lives with her mother and Chapuis is 'la plus fâcheuse entrée de l'enfer' (29). Chapuis himself is an artisan, a 'balancier-ajusteur': that is, on the material plane he works with clocks or pendulums, and on the symbolical one plays a role in the spiritual balance of the world, as one of those rogues, says the narrator, who are required 'pour l'équilibre des Séraphins' (28) – 'Sans Barabbas, point de Rédemption' (ibid.). Clotilde, though her physical grace makes her angelic in comparison to her mother, has no sense of a religious vocation, the abject condition of her life blinding her to any possibility of elevation; the action which exemplifies this is her sexual 'fall' with the first man who comes along. The condition of womanhood, at this stage of Clotilde's life, means dependence on the male. If she spends time dreaming in churches, we are told, it is because there is no man in her life. Later, when she meets Gacougnol and Marchenoir, the thought of an amorous relationship with either of them crosses her mind, and she will marry Léopold – but her vocation will only be realised after the death of all three. It is predicted by a mysterious old missionary who tells her that her life's meaning will be revealed to her at a moment when she will be consumed in flames. The plot of the novel and the unravelling of the prediction are, as in *Un prêtre marié*, one and the same thing.

Gacougnol, to whom Chapuis has virtually sold Clotilde as a nude model, reveals an unconscious association with the missionary, repeating his very words: 'Pourquoi pleurez-vous?' (58). In dressing her (by buying her clothes) rather than undressing her for the purposes of art or pleasure, the kindly Gacougnol is restoring her lost purity. The money he gives her not only alleviates her material poverty, but represents, like all acts of true charity, the love which symbolises grace. Such notions are foreign to Gacougnol, for the true sense of his actions escapes him. In his own eyes he is simply an artist, using Clotilde's head as a model for his painting of Saint Philomena being devoured by lions – which leads to the novel's next turning point: the visit to the Jardin des Plantes in order to sketch wild animals. It is here that Clotilde meets Marchenoir, whose words Gacougnol had already quoted to her: 'Plus une femme est sainte, et plus elle est femme' (66). This man, more than the literal-minded painter, promises to enlighten for Clotilde the meaning of her sex.

Marchenoir had already died at the end of the previous novel. Bloy had to reassure his anxious friend de Groux that this was no literal resurrection, only a literary one, and that the two novels are concurrent in their date.[16] The Marchenoir of *La Femme pauvre,* however, is not quite the same character as in his earlier incarnation. His freedom from the central role makes him less tortured, more objectively authoritative in his guidance of Clotilde. His role in respect of Clotilde is like that of Tardif de Moidrey to Bloy: he is a revealer of secrets and of the need to decode them. He talks to her of God's totality, the alphabet of Creation in which even animals have their part to play, for their suffering contributes to the total sum of pain on which atonement depends. These things had been taught to him by 'l'Ami des Bêtes', whom he had encountered at La Salette, and who, in words that seemed like those of another voice speaking through him, had revealed his 'Secret sublime' (94). This was that, despite all the suffering of Christ and the saints, and that of the animals represented by the ox and the ass in the stable at Bethlehem, the act of Redemption remains incomplete. 'La grand'messe du Consolateur n'a pas commencé' (84).

Clotilde's role in God's plan is clarified further by the appearance of a new character, Léopold. Two aspects of his experience mark him as fit to be Clotilde's soul mate. He is associated with the Christian Middle Ages by his art as an illuminator, and he has experienced great suffering through an involuntarily incestuous relationship with a woman who turned out to be his sister. As if to clear the way for this new phase in her life to begin, Bloy jettisons his other characters. First, Clotilde has a dream in which she sees Gacougnol stabbed to death, Marchenoir departing under a burden of sorrow, and Léopold consumed by flames. She wakes to find her curtains on fire: for even Bloy recognises the utility of rational explanations in novels. But the first two parts of the dream are not long in being realised: Gacougnol is murdered by Chapuis, and Marchenoir, after delivering a chapter-long speech, or prose poem, on redemptive suffering, also dies, presumably in the same way as in the first novel. Clotilde's resultant suffering, material and moral, means that, like Marchenoir in *Le Désespéré*, 'elle se ressemble davantage' (174).

Léopold fills the gap left by these deaths. Violently seized by God, he confesses his past, both to Clotilde and, sacramentally, to a priest. The final phase of the book sees Clotilde and Léopold married, and living a life of extreme poverty. Their suffering is the external sign of their selection by God for his providential purpose, confirmed by the demonic attacks that are unleashed on them. The house in which they live is haunted, and despite an attempt at exorcism, their child dies. These events, incredible though they seem, are directly inspired by the real-life events, including the death of their son André, which, according to Bloy's *Journal*, overtook him and his wife Jeanne Molbech. This section of the novel represents Bloy's anguished search for the meaning of their tragedy. It is of Jeanne and himself that he is writing when he describes Clotilde and Léopold as exiles from the Eden of their former happiness.

Moving to another house, the couple have a brief respite, then the attacks recommence. The house, like the first, is infested by foul smells, and the hostility of their neighbours, M. and Mme Poulot, add to their horror, for in this pair Clotilde recognises the reincarnated images of her mother and Chapuis. The possession of Mme Poulot by Satan is shown in her demonic laugh, 'une espèce de convulsion sardonique' (236); she is joined by another neighbour, Mme Grand, in an 'œuvre démoniaque' (230) directed against the young couple. Bloy's novel has lurched now into the territory which Barbey had colonised – the fantastic, but imbued with Christian meaning. The answer to occult evil is Christian miracle: and it comes. Léopold's prayer that God punish their tormenters is answered: Mme Grand is found dead, half-eaten by her own dog; the Poulots, stricken by financial disaster, leave the district.

The rising tide of miracle carries the book to its end. Clotilde asks God for a final sign of grace: to enter his house forever. She at once undergoes the final initiation, the most sublime suffering, as, in fulfilment of the missionary's prophecy, she feels consumed by fire. At this same moment, Léopold is being physically burned to death, in the historically real fire at the Opéra-Comique on May 25th 1887, into which he has run in an attempt to save others. His blazing body, standing in the flames, 'les bras croisés' (266), confirms his final assumption of his redemptive and christic role, and this is also the moment of what Bloy called, in his *Journal*, '[le] délire d'amour divin dans l'âme de Clotilde' (XI, 216). The historical, the fictive and the personal are thus united in the one symbolic fire of God's love.

* * *

As well as by the devices of its impressively articulated plot, the novel's meaning is conveyed at other levels, and above all in its language. Bloy's view of language as a corrupt and vestigial parody of Man's paradisiac or pre-Babelic means of expression informs the speech of the characters of *La Femme pauvre*. The way they speak identifies their role in the spiritual conflict in which they are at best semi-conscious participants. The novel opens with Chapuis' words as he passes in front of the open door of a chapel in the rue de Sèvres: 'Ça pue le bon Dieu ici!' (25). It is known that, to help him capture the coarseness of Chapuis' speech, Bloy consulted the same source-book on popular Parisian usage as Zola when the latter was writing *L'Assommoir*. This was *Le Sublime*, by Denis Poulot[17] – which Bloy acknowledges by giving the author's name to his demonic couple, who speak in the same idiom as Chapuis. So, incidentally, does the heroine of one of Bloy's pieces in his *Exégèse des lieux communs*, the landlady who despises her church-going guest as a 'sale calotin', and who rejoices in the name of . . . Madame Zola! (VIII, 44). The setting of *La Femme pauvre* in the working-class world of *L'Assommoir* and *Germinal*, and the ironical bestowing of religious significance on its everyday speech, shows the Catholic novelist once more exploiting Naturalist stereotypes for his own expressive purposes.

Clotilde's mother's language also identifies her, but in a different way. Her use of religious terms is conscious and hypocritical, and brutally parodies the central themes of the novel: 'Hélas! mon doux Jésus [. . .] Vous êtes témoin, bonne Sainte Vierge, qu'il n'y a plus rien dans la maison. . . [. . .] Ah! mon aimable Sauveur, quand me retirerez-vous de ce monde où j'ai déjà tant souffert?' (30). Gacougnol, on the other hand, is innocent in his use of religious language, for he is impervious to the deeper meaning of his own words. When he says of his relationship with Clotilde: 'Je suis Dieu pour elle, en ce moment, Dieu le Père!' (66), or refers to himself as 'le bonhomme providentiel' (69), and to the coach in which he takes Clotilde to buy clothing as 'le char du prophète Élie' (66), he does not know what truths he is voicing. Nor does Clotilde, from whose mouth, says the narrator, flows a language like that of the great mystics, the pure expression of '[les] humbles choses de la nature qu'elle avait pu voir' (70). She is described as 'la Poétesse de l'Humilité', and speaks with an inspired simplicity reminiscent of the discourse of a woman writer in whom, through Barbey, Bloy had come to be interested: who else but Eugénie de Guérin?[18]

The spoken word is the vehicle of God's message in a different way in the superb Chapter XXIII. Here, Clotilde and Léopold go to church, their thoughts distracted by deepening financial worries: the monthly rent is due to be paid, and they are penniless. The text of the sermon seems to promise comfort: it is the parable of the two debtors (Matthew XVIII). But the inexperienced young priest who delivers it, warned by his superiors to say nothing to upset the well-heeled majority of the congregation, turns this potentially revolutionary text into sheer banality, and literally sends Clotilde to sleep. As she sleeps, the voice of the priest penetrates her consciousness, his words transformed into other words which denounce those who, in persecuting the poor, persecute Christ. This scene, like the similar one in *Le Désespéré* in which another voice speaks through Marchenoir, is the miraculous antithesis of Realist discourse. It is Bloy's equivalent of revelatory visions or divine messages, such as those at La Salette. He has found here the technical device by which to relate human agency to divine intention, and his example would not be forgotten when Bernanos came to write the 'countess scene' in his *Journal d'un curé de campagne*.

* * *

The voice we hear most often in *La Femme pauvre* is the narrator's, speaking for Bloy himself. His constant presence, his comments and interventions, in this novel as in *Le Désespéré*, might irritate readers to whom the Flaubertian ideal of an invisible narrator is sacrosanct. In this novel, however, it is absolutely necessary as a way of expressing meaning. The belief that the generation of meaning in fiction is a function of its purely fictive elements, the action and dialogue of characters, and that it should be relative to them, would leave little place for a novelist like Bloy. For him, meaning is not relative but absolute, and furthermore, it lies beyond the understanding of characters whose limited human condition leaves them grappling with the enigma of their own lives. The technical problem which any novelist has to face – the need to convey to the reader information which the characters do not possess – is encountered in an especially acute form in Bloy, to whom the vital information is 'secret'. In the opening scene in Chapuis' house, from where is a religious meaning going to come if not from the narrator? When Clotilde's destiny needs to be explained, at a time when she herself is as yet unable to explain it, what recourse does Bloy have but to intervene, to reveal the heavenly mystery behind 'son *apparente* vie terrestre' (48)? But Bloy is also concerned, where it is appropriate, to inflect his ideas through the consciousness of his characters. After her encounter with Marchenoir opens her mind, at least partially, to the total pattern of which she is a fragment, Clotilde's own reflections supplement those of the narrator. This gives to the novel's controlling voice a variety impossible in *Le Désespéré*, in which narrator and protagonist are indistinguishable. It is through Clotilde's thoughts that the nature of the world is discussed as a place 'rempli de compagnons invisibles', peopled by angels and demons (102). This division of the theme-carrying role between narrator and character is one of the most effective of Bloy's techniques in *La Femme pauvre*.

What Bloy described to his prospective publisher Quantin as the main theme of the book[19] is expressed in this dual way, once through the semi-comprehending Clotilde, once in its full symbolical elaboration by the narrator. The theme is that of the secret and mystical nature of the female condition. This was the 'secret' divulged by Bloy to Quantin: 'Pour parler net, entre nous, la Femme dépend de sa vulve, comme l'homme de son cerveau' (ibid.). The novel provides the exegesis of Bloy's dubious commonplace! First of all, scenically: Clotilde, surrounded by the paintings in Gacougnol's studio, remembers a lithograph she had once seen, depicting the interior of a brothel, in which a group of brigands are drinking with the girls. The artist had left out one of the four walls of the room, and put in its place a shining vision of Christ, as he had appeared to the Magdalene in the garden of the Resurrection, holding out his hands in pardon to the youngest of the girls, who has left the group and kneels before him (51). This pious image, of the sort that Bloy himself would have rejected for its naïvety, impresses the uneducated Clotilde. It is the image of her destiny, the ascent from imminent prostitution to her final severance from all men in the love of Christ. Much later, the narrator addresses the same idea, after carefully warning the reader who dislikes digressions to skip this section (and the rest of the book while he is about it!). He explains that the female body represents paradise, both the paradise of pleasure sought by eternities of Don Juans and paradise in a religious sense. Since the incarnation of Christ, the womb has been the tabernacle of the living God. Woman must venerate her body; to give it to a man in loveless union, and worst of all to sell it, are a profanation of her whole essence. This is why, he goes on, rejoining and developing Balzac, there are two essential modes of womanhood: beatitude and voluptuousness. Between them lies the irredeemable mediocrity of the respectable woman, the bourgeois wife, unaware of the mystical meaning of her sex and the choice it imposes on her. The two extremes of woman's destiny, Bloy argues, are not irreconcilable opposites, 'une sainte peut tomber dans la boue et une prostituée monter dans la lumière (110). This, indeed, is the movement from darkness to light which his book's structure expresses.

The combination of showing and telling works well in *La Femme pauvre*, although the interventions and digressions which it permits ran counter to the increasingly frequent reliance of the mainstream novelists on scenic presentation, with little or no overt authorial control. Scenic technique is the logical development of Realism's stress on the visible, and Bloy's allocation to it of a merely partial role underlines again the technical implications of the Catholic novelist's insistence on the primacy of the invisible. Clotilde's favourite lithograph, the brothel with its missing wall, portrays the world we see, the working-class world of Paris, the artist's studio, the literary salon – but the missing wall provides the necessary opening on to another world, from which the sense of the whole derives. The lithograph is not only a symbolic representation of Clotilde's destiny; it is a model and a paradigm of Bloy's Catholic novel.

6

Belief and Narrative Form in the Novels of François Mauriac

'De Bloy à Huysmans, et à Claudel, le *Magnificat* n'a cessé de retentir dans les lettres françaises,'[1] wrote Mauriac, the first of the twentieth century Catholic novelists to be discussed in this book. Such is the distorting effect of centuries' beginnings and ends that his comment on the rise of a new Catholic literature might be mistaken for an elegiac description of a lost age. The apparent chronological gulf between him and the nineteenth century is one probable reason why Mauriac has not often been studied in the perspective of the Catholic novel tradition.[2] Yet he was born in the year of *Germinal* and *Bel-Ami*, at a time when, though Flaubert had just died, Edmond de Goncourt and Barbey were still living. When Huysmans died, Mauriac was in his twenties, and well into his thirties at the time of Bloy's death, and a close friend of Bloy's god-children, Jacques and Raïssa Maritain. If situating Mauriac's work in the context of the nineteenth-century opposition of Catholic and Realist offers a new and fruitful way of looking at it, the temporal leap required to do so is more illusory than real. The gap is narrowed further by the fact that almost all Mauriac's novels are set in the period between the turn of the century and the First World War, and reflect the same middle-class Catholic world accused of mediocrity by Bloy and Huysmans, and of racial bigotry by Zola.

On the literary plane, it would be wrong to see the problems which Realism posed for the Catholic writer as having disappeared with the nineteenth century. Realism remained the basic narrative mode, the canonical genre description, from which experiment and innovation had to begin. The new perspectives embodied in the work of Proust represented a development rather than a denial of Realism, conferring on its materiality a new role as the starting-point of deeper explorations of consciousness, but – and this is the crucial point – these explorations were of a world within rather than a world beyond. As for Realist discourse, Léon Bloy, in his final text *Dans les ténèbres*, saw the guarantee of its continuing influence in the inheritance by writers like Henri Barbusse of the stylistic legacy of *L'Assommoir*.[3] This was one of Bloy's better prophecies, for the post-war left-wing current in which Barbusse was an important figure, and the socialist realism into which it merged, did indeed look to Zola and Naturalism for its literary inspiration.[4] The twentieth century's literature of *engagement* took its lead to a large extent from *Germinal*, and in order to convince, whether on a political, philosophical or simply humanitarian plane, it found in Zola's doctrine of 'la soumission au réel' the necessary base on which to build.

Few writers have been so acutely aware as Mauriac of the double-edged sword of tradition. One of the main themes of his important essay *Le Roman* is the need for French novelists to look beyond the Balzacian model, with its alleged over-clarification of life, and to be aware of the example of Dostoyevsky, in whose work the illogicality and mystery of experience is predominant. Though he was ostensibly writing of literary issues, Mauriac was taking his lead from de Vogüé's book *Le Roman russe*, which had revealed Tolstoy and Dostoyevsky, not just as great novelists, but as explorers of a spiritual domain beyond the self-imposed limits of their French contemporaries. In his most important discussion of the Realists, in his *Mémoires intérieurs*, it is both the literary and religious aspects of Realism, and their interrelationship, which concern him. In a passage entitled, after Paul Alexis, 'Naturalisme pas mort', Mauriac uses Bloy's image of the novelist as a straying cow to argue that 'presque tous, en France, nous n'avons cessé de ruminer dans le pâturage naturaliste'.[5] The history of modern French literature, he writes, is that of a series of attempts to escape from 'ce morne enclos où les descendants de Balzac, de Flaubert, de Zola, broutent la même herbe depuis cent ans'; but most novelists cling to a Realist prescription which affords a superficial vision of the human condition. Foreign writers, meanwhile, work 'presque toujours dans le sens antinaturaliste' (MI, 243). The home-grown tradition of not looking beyond appearances, which Mauriac identifies in the Goncourts 'qui voient tout et ne comprennent rien' (MI, 97), is particularly manifest, he argues, in Zola. His dislike of Zola . . .

> . . . n'a pas tenu à ce qu'il montrait, mais à ce qu'il ne montrait pas. Ce qu'il écrivait m'eût moins rebuté si l'invisible n'avait pas été non seulement absent mais nié. Je n'ai jamais eu besoin que cet

invisible y fût affirmé pour respirer à l'aise dans un univers romanesque. Qu'il demeure possible me suffit; qu'aucune porte ne soit condamnée. (MI, 244)

He reacted similarly to Maupassant's exclusively materialist world: 'un monde bouché, hermétiquement clos', in which 'Dieu est mort', and Man with him, before Nietzsche said so (BN IV, 243). The same absence of a transcendental dimension marked Flaubert's work: his pursuit of stylistic perfection stemmed, says Mauriac, from an unconscious yearning for an absolute only to be found in a God in whom he did not believe (MI, 145). Thus Mauriac, identifying the challenge to Christian belief in the Goncourts' optics, in Zola's and Maupassant's metaphysics, and in Flaubert's aesthetics, reworks the same critical themes, and reiterates essentially the same analysis of the mainstream novel's religious standpoint, as Barbey d'Aurevilly a century before him. His own attempt to escape the confines of Realism is motivated by religious as well as literary impulses. The two are indeed inseparable. As Mauriac says, 'Si le surnaturel existe, c'est tout de même un appauvrissement effroyable, du point de vue de l'art, que d'écrire comme s'il n'existait pas' (BN V, 119). His ambitions at the start of his literary career closely resembled those of the nineteenth-century Catholic novelist. 'Ne redoute pas de peindre les passions,' he instructed himself in his *Journal d'un homme de trente ans*, 'mais victorieuses ou vaincues. Ne les montre que dans leurs rapports avec la Grâce.'[6]

This prescription, however, proved easier to write than to swallow, and it led Mauriac straight into what is always called, following the title of Charles du Bos' book, 'the problem of the Catholic novelist'.[7] This 'problem' is discussed by du Bos and others as if it had not existed before Mauriac. It is in fact his inheritance from the nineteenth century, the double inheritance of the moral problems with which Barbey d'Aurevilly had struggled and the literary and technical problems of depicting the spiritual within the novel's realist compass. Mauriac's work brings into sharp focus many of the issues already discussed in the preceding chapters of this book. He is a twentieth-century novelist coming to terms with the options plotted by those of the nineteenth.

Mauriac's early view of the apologetic role of art was soon replaced by the perception of an insoluble conflict between the independence of the writer and the expectations of fellow Catholics. There was nothing new in this dilemma, as Barbey's correspondence with Trebutien shows; and like Barbey Mauriac sought refuge in a compromise which works better at the theoretical level than in practice: namely, the notion that true representation can never be anti-Christian. But Mauriac saw more clearly than Barbey that this formula simply avoids the issue of the manner of representation. To Jacques Maritain's advice that the solution lay in the artist's maintaining his personal purity and remaining aloof from his creation, he replied in *Dieu et Mammon* that such a view of the writer's relationship with his work reflected '[les] vieilles conceptions du naturalisme'.[8] The novelist, contrary to Zola's formula, is not a 'physiologist', observing and recording a pre-existing reality; he is the creator of his own fictional world, for which he is solely responsible.

These tensions were acute enough for Mauriac to contemplate the abandonment of novel-writing. There was never, in truth, the remotest possibility of his doing so. Barbey, faced with a similar option, had said it all: 'Voulez-vous tuer le Roman? [. . .] Faut-il casser mon moi?' The writer, says Mauriac, 'ne peut pas ne pas écrire. Il obéit à une exigence profonde, impérieuse' (P II, 819). To follow this inner necessity, he refused the prescriptive label 'Catholic novelist' and declared that his two faiths were separate and independent: 'Je suis romancier et je suis catholique.'[9] But this proposed cleavage between art and faith, for a writer whose imaginative world as well as his real one was so permeated by Catholicism, was not only unnecessary but impossible. Perhaps in the end it was a public stance, an offer, like Solomon's, to cut the baby in half so that it might survive intact. To go on writing meant, for Mauriac, to go on writing 'Catholic novels' as this present book defines the term – not of the proselytising sort which his critics saw the label as implying, but novels which depend for their quality and interest on the relationship, and often on the tension, between Christian belief and narrative form.

* * *

Mauriac's reluctance to be seen as a Catholic novelist is part of a complex network of emotions resulting from his having been born into the Catholic faith rather than freely opting for it. He often wished he could shake off the bonds of faith, not definitively, but in order to experience reconversion: 'perdre la foi pour la retrouver, comme c'était mon vœu secret' (P II, 785). His novels translate this wish into characters on the rebound from faith, like Claude and Xavier, in *La Chair et le sang* and *L'Agneau* respectively, who are refugees from the seminary. By a more radical imaginative leap, he places himself in the consciousness of those who live outside religion: Daniel Trasis in *Le Fleuve de feu*, Louis in *Le Nœud de vipères*, whom he brings to conversion, and especially Thérèse Desqueyroux, who remains unreconciled through three novels and two short stories. On the other hand, his fear of having inherited the mere birthright of his class, 'un ensemble de rites dépourvus de toute signification autre que sociale' (P II, 402), turned him into a determined critic of superficial, 'socialite' religion, contrasting true Christianity with the bigotry of family or class. But he was equally capable, in the pendulum swings so characteristic of him, of a more sentimental recognition, in *Le Mystère Frontenac* and *Un adolescent d'autrefois*, that even those Catholics whose beliefs are contaminated by prejudice possess basic truths.

Being born into the faith had other consequences, making his concept of reality different from that of the novelists discussed in earlier chapters. Barbey and Huysmans had arrived at the Catholic novel via other traditions: Barbey from the fantastic, Huysmans from Realism. But Mauriac had no need of the fantastic to alert him to the existence of the immaterial world shunned by Realism. From the outset, 'l'habitude prise très tôt de parler à quelqu'un qui est là et qu'on ne voit pas, et qui nous voit' (MI, 243) meant that fairy-tales had little impact on his imagination. 'Je n'ai jamais été bon public pour le merveilleux' (BN II, 27), he wrote. The invisible was not magical, but an integral part of the real. It did not need to break the laws of physical nature to convince him of its existence – 'Je n'ai rien vu de mes yeux,' he insisted; 'je n'ai rien entendu'[10] – for it was felt as a living reality from within. Mauriac's faith was a fundamentally affective one, inseparable from the emotional climate of childhood and the company of an adored mother from whose teaching and example his beliefs had sprung. It was developed in the same sense by a Marist education designed, he said later, to promote Catholic sensibility rather than Catholic intelligence.[11] He stressed many times his indifference to rational argument or historical proof; and if he was attracted to the modernist theology of Laberthonnière and Tyrrel, and especially to the notion of interior revelation, it was because these seemed to concur with his own experience of a tangible inner presence. It would be wrong to overestimate his first-hand knowledge of such writings, to which his attention was drawn by his friend André Lacaze, but his awareness of their existence increased his confidence in the validity of his experience. 'Le peu que j'en ai lu,' he wrote to Lacaze after receiving from him a volume of Laberthonnière's essays, 'm'a déjà séduit, d'autant qu'instinctivement j'avais été choqué par cette conception de la religion qui la fait consister en un ensemble de dogmes imposés à l'homme et lui venant de l'extérieur. J'ai toujours pensé que la vérité religieuse était en nous et procédait de notre nature même.'[12] But the narrator's comment in the early novel *Préséances* about a character who has these same modernist leanings shows Mauriac's misgivings: 'Ce goût des marques sensibles de la Grâce témoignait d'un tempérament sensuel, porté aux excès' (P I, 406). In his fear that the reliance on the tangible contact of Christ was the sign of a reprehensible sensuality lay the influence of another, more profoundly embedded set of theological attitudes.

This was Jansenism, the seventeenth-century heresy nurtured by Saint-Cyran and other 'solitaries' at Port-Royal-des-champs, and which was associated in different ways with Mauriac's most cherished writers, Racine and Pascal. With the heresy itself, the doctrine according to which the gift of grace is the privilege of a selected élite, predestined to be saved independently of any act of their will, Mauriac expressed a consistent lack of sympathy. But he was prone to anxieties which brought him to the brink of the theological pessimism inherent in this theory of grace. One was the view of sexual love as the greatest obstacle to the love of God, irredeemable even within marriage – a notion rooted in Mauriac's own sexuality and given support by Pascal's view of 'holy wedlock' as 'la plus périlleuse et la plus basse des conditions du christianisme' (P I, 278). Another was a sense of the inevitability of sin, except in the privileged moments of Christ's presence: moments which, in another recurring term, were 'intermittent'. The Proustian theme of 'les intermittences du cœur' was applied by Mauriac to the realm of spiritual experience, especially to his own, which moved from hot to cold 'avec la régularité d'un balancier' (OC VII, ii). The sense of a divine presence ebbed and flowed; its absence brought a terrifying feeling of abandonment, a divine silence worse than any threat, says Mauriac in *Commencements d'une vie* (OC IV, 152). But there was also the reverse sensation: the return of Christ experienced as inhibition, as an obstacle to freedom. In these latter moments, the temptation was to say to Christ: 'J'avais, hier, besoin de vous; ce matin, vous m'importunez; demain, peut-être, si je ne me sens trop las de vos créatures.'[13] Mauriac wrote these last words in the midst of the much discussed 'crisis' to which his brooding anxieties eventually led him, and when the feeling of dependence on the arbitrary intervention of God created a total vacuum of certainty:

> Qui peut se vanter de connaître les rapports réels d'un homme avec Dieu? [. . .] Quelle est notre foi? Est-elle plus ou mieux qu'une espérance ou qu'une terreur? [. . .] Nous n'avons pas choisi Dieu. *Il* nous a choisis; et quand nous croyons jouer avec Lui, c'est *Lui* peut-être qui joue avec nous (ibid.).

Intermittence, alternating sensations of abandonment and oppression, the need for reassurance that the flow of grace has not been permanently withdrawn – these experiences and attitudes, replicating the patterns of dependence on the mother figure, give to Mauriac's religious outlook an anxious, vulnerable and passive character, marked by a lack of confidence in the efficacy of individual will. The individual seemed handicapped by the weight of inherited sin – not only of original sin in its theological sense, but specific and recurring sins passed on by previous generations. 'Tu es le carrefour', he wrote in his wartime diary, 'où par tes quatre familles les tendances accumulées au long des générations se confondent. Pauvres plans de vie, que pouvez-vous contre une hérédité torrentielle?' (OC IV, 253). Heredity was, due mainly to Zola, a central theme in turn-of-the-century literature, but the truest literary exploration of it lay, for Mauriac, not in Naturalism's pursuit of 'organic lesions' but in the Jansenist imagination of Racine and especially in the figure of Phèdre who, he argued, represented 'un moment de sa race' (OC VIII, 105). His use of Taine's terminology here allows him all the more tellingly to refute nineteenth-century positivistic forms of determinism in favour of theological ones: what Racine's heroine has inherited is the wrath of a Jansenist God: 'Le Dieu de Saint-Cyran pèse effroyablement sur Phèdre' (ibid., 102). In her lineage stands Thérèse Desqueyroux, bowed like her under the weight of an obscure ancestry, and victim of 'une puissance forcenée en moi et hors de moi' (P II, 26) the true nature of which is cloaked from her by her lack of religious insight.

* * *

Before Thérèse, Mauriac's early characters embody the patterns of his own spiritual experience. Both Jean-Paul in *L'Enfant chargé de chaînes* and Jacques in *La Robe prétexte* oscillate between the anguish of God's remoteness and the irksomeness of his demands. Although Jean-Paul 'souhaitait ne pas voir et ne pas entendre' (P I, 41), God descends upon him 'comme sur une proie' (P I, 61), omnipotent and irresistible. He is nailed to the spot 'au seuil des pires infâmies' (ibid.) – invariably by an unsolicited memory of childhood or, in a scene in a Parisian night-club, by the vision of himself as an unsullied infant (P I, 52). Jacques feels the same 'implacable protection': 'je n'avais pas comme les autres hommes,' he complains, 'la liberté de pécher' (P I, 179). As he bends over the willing lips of the enticing Liette, 'quelque présence invisible' intervenes (P I, 178). The psychological inhibitions of Jean-Paul give way in Jacques' case to the interference of an external force, the most spectacular example of which is the death of his grandmother, obliging him to return home, and interpreted by him as a protective act of providence. Both young men accept these restrictions as necessary and, ultimately, good. Through them they are halted on the brink of abortive sexual initiations which arouse in them more fear than desire. At this early stage in Mauriac's career, the return to the fold, symbolised by the pull of the family and of the home environment of Bordeaux, drawing Jean-Paul and Jacques away from the temptations of Paris, is seen as a process of harmonisation rather than of imprisonment. However, moral choice is absent from the crucial moments of decision in the lives of both characters, for it is made redundant by the overriding intentions of God.

This image of God as a preventive force recurs in Mauriac's novels, up to at least the novels of the 1920s and 30s. Jean-Paul's inhibiting vision in the night-club is replicated almost exactly in the experience of Yves Frontenac, as is the sudden, providential death of a close relative in *Thérèse Desqueyroux*. But the novel in which the intervention of God most affects the technique and structure of the work is *Le Fleuve de feu*. Its denouement is entirely dependent on the presence of divine grace, nullifying not just the will but the logic of the characters. In its final pages, the hero Daniel pursues Gisèle, the object of his obsessive sexual drives, to the church in her home town. Here he is confronted by the spectacle of Gisèle seated at a harmonium, accompanying a group of girls singing canticles. The woman to whom he had made love a few days previously, and who is the mother of an illegitimate child as a result of an earlier affair with a young soldier, is now transformed: 'Elle dominait les enfants de Marie à genoux, pareille à la Vierge d'une Assomption' (P I, 578). Her hair lit by a spark of sunlight, she wavers for a moment, 'comme mal assurée de son support angélique', 'comme suspendue entre le ciel et la boue'. Daniel thinks that he can determine once and for all the outcome of this conflict: 'Qu'elle me voie, et elle sera précipitée. . .' Yet he also feels that there is a power here that he cannot overcome, a supernatural obstacle to his claiming his prey. He feels 'cette étrange terreur d'interrompre un miracle'. The narrator at this point takes up the thread: Gisèle, he says, would not in any case have seen Daniel, for her eyes are focused elsewhere. She is 'repliée sur soi, refermée, lente et comme alourdie d'un poids délicieux qui l'empêcha de s'élever encore, la retint à terre, abîmée, perdue, sauvée'. Daniel still hopes that his defeat may be temporary: '—Je ne réussirai pas, si près de la communion: elle sera encore sous l'influence de. . . . Il n'osa prononcer le Nom.' Again the narrator imposes his view on Daniel's: 'Mais de la nuit où elle s'était enfoncée, Gisèle de Plailly ne revint pas.' Daniel, not fully comprehending what is happening, but moved enough to dip his hand in the water of the baptismal font and cross himself, leaves, and the novel ends.

There has been no psychological change in Gisèle; indeed, the previous scene, in which she has broken free from her self-appointed protectress Lucile de Villeron, seems to leave her more exposed than ever to Daniel's approach. What saves her is not an effort of will, but the protection accorded her, seemingly independently of her desires, by an all-powerful God. This protection, offered and withdrawn in turn, is evident not just in the final scene, but at intervals throughout the novel. When Gisèle yields to Daniel, it is because 'Dieu était loin' (P I, 572); when Daniel is rebuffed, it is through an intervention from 'un ciel inconnu', manifested by a sudden darkening of the skies as the couple lie side by side (P I, 522). Gisèle, far from welcoming God's protection, resents it: 'Cette armure adamantine, qu'elle la trouvait pesante! Qu'elle eût voulu être abandonnée, sans armes, nue! (P I, 556). Not surprisingly, Catholic criticism of the novel was severe, the uncertainty of whether Gisèle is to be regarded as permanently saved seen as a weakness[14] – though this uncertainty is a necessary illustration of one of the book's central themes: 'Qui peut, avant la fin, se dire sauvé?' (P I, 573).

The Jansenist flavour of this last question is obvious, and of all Mauriac's novels, *Le Fleuve de feu* is the one which most fully corresponds to his own description of the way in which his work was influenced by Jansenism:

> Trop de critiques ont relevé dans l'œuvre du romancier des traces de cette hérésie pour qu'il puisse douter d'en avoir subi quelque atteinte. On peut dire, en gros, que beaucoup de ses personnages sont pris ou rejetés par une grâce dont aucun mouvement libre, chez la créature, ne complique le jeu souverain. Il y a une certaine manière de mettre l'accent sur la nature invinciblement corrompue, sur l'irrésistibilité de la concupiscence, sur la délectation victorieuse de la grâce, qui porte la marque de Port-Royal.[15]

Yet, in terms of Mauriac's theology, the presentation of grace in *Le Fleuve de feu* is not flawed. Gisèle's experience faithfully reflects his conception of the divine presence. When Mauriac says, as he often did after the publication of this novel, that divine grace cannot be depicted in novels, his statement should be treated with greater caution than has been shown by the dozens of critics who have quoted it as an axiomatic truth. What Mauriac really means is one of two things – and probably both: first, that the grace which he depicts extremely clearly in *Le Fleuve de feu* reveals his heretical leanings too overtly for comfort; second, that his particular concept of grace cannot be depicted in novels without doing structural damage to them. The latter point is obviously the more important of the two as far as literature is concerned. God's intervention into a world of fictional characters shatters its self-sufficient economy, frustrates the reader's expectation of a convincing psychological outcome. On a strictly literary level, it has the disadvantages of any extraneous element, like the unforeseen coincidences that resolve many a work of romance. On a philosophical level, in the modern climate of unbelief, it is less innocent than coincidence.

Technical problems also arise. The intervening deity has to find a place alongside another notoriously problematic presence, that of the narrator. When Flaubert, explaining his belief in the impersonality of art, describes the novelist's position within his work as analogous to that of God in creation – 'invisible et tout-puissant; qu'on le sente partout, mais qu'on ne le voie pas'[16] – he omits any reference to the role of the narrator, functioning somewhere between the novelist and the fictional characters in an infinitely redefinable relationship to both. Flaubert's narrators are more visibly interventionist than his theory ought to allow, and they comment in a variety of ways on the actions of the characters. The narrators of Mauriac's early novels extend this process, commenting in addition on the actions of God, who becomes, quite specifically, a character within the fiction. When Jean-Paul, feeling 'importuned' by God's presence, tries not to heed it, the narrator tells us: 'Le Consolateur s'éloigna de cette âme qui ne voulait pas de Miséricorde' (P I, 41). The narrator of the novel slips into the shoes of the biblical narrator, and what that, by implication, makes of the novelist who controls him, is obvious.

Mauriac expresses this very implication. The novelist, he states in *Le Roman*, is 'le singe de Dieu' (P II, 751). His relationship with his creatures is exactly parallel to that of God with his; it recreates 'ce débat de la Grâce, transposé sur le plan de la création artistique' (P II, 767). If the novelist directs the destiny of his characters with an inflexible logic, presents them as being controlled by a force other than that of their own will, he is adopting not merely the stance of God in general but, specifically, that of 'le Dieu de Jansénius' (ibid.). Mauriac's Jansenist conception of God makes Flaubert's old metaphor more dramatic; but it also goes beyond metaphor. The narrator's stance is itself an expression of man's dependence on a higher power. Formal features in Mauriac's novels are the direct reflection of his particular theology.

* * *

The novels that follow *Le Fleuve de feu* attempt an 'indirect' Christian apologetic. The phrase was Mauriac's own, used in an interview with Frédéric Lefèvre, in which he declared his intention to write in a less consciously Catholic vein, allowing the 'misère de l'homme sans Dieu' which his novels would thus reveal to make his Christian point for him.[17] The formula is obviously too simple, for in practice literary presentations of the significant absence of God, as opposed to the Realist's natural exclusion of a non-existing God, pose as many technical problems as the introduction of God does. Mauriac tries to solve these by allotting to his narrators the responsibility of clarifying the destiny of the characters. In *Le Désert de l'amour*, since neither Raymond Courrèges nor his father are able to see that only God can fill the gap in their lives caused by their mutual frustrated longing for the symbolically named Maria Cross, it is left to the narrator to make the point: 'Il faudrait qu'avant la mort du père et du fils se révèle à eux enfin Celui qui à leur insu appelle, attire, du plus profond de leur être, cette marée brûlante' (P I, 861). Likewise, in *Le Mal*, the need to make clear the religious significance of Fabien's first sexual experiences inspires another narratorial comment: 'Il ne pressentait pas cette puissance en nous de la chair, ce cri forcené du désir, cette tempête pendant que Dieu dort à la poupe' (P I, 649). These interventions are not always necessarily weaknesses in the novels. When, as in these two cases, they supply the reader with an angle of vision that is not obtainable via the characters, their artistic legitimacy can be defended. Often, however, they take the form of a moralising correction of a character's viewpoint, as other examples taken from *Le Mal* illustrate. Fabien, the central character, rejects his mother's puritanical strictures on sex, even within marriage, and formulates a less extreme view – which the narrator brutally refutes in mid-sentence: 'L'erreur de sa mère [thinks Fabien] était de ne pas savoir la chair aussi est sanctifiée [. .]. Il comprenait ces choses que sa mère ne comprenait pas. Il se glorifiait de ce qu'il n'avait point de peine à défendre son amour conte les pensées troubles de la veille; il s'en glorifiait, oubliant que, grâce aux caresses récentes de Fanny, dans sa chair un démon repu s'était assoupi' (P I, 695–6). And when Fabien reflects that in marrying Colombe he will discover a happy and pure love, the narrator again intervenes to ridicule his deluded hero: 'Qu'imaginait-il d'autre dans le mariage, cet imbécile? Quel était ce rêve d'une sensualité qui serait chaste?' (P I, 711).

That these moralising comments and abrupt switches from character's to narrator's angle were damaging to the quality of his writing, Mauriac well knew. Sartre's celebrated diagnosis of their source – Mauriac's instinctive adoption of a god-like stance (but God, alas, is not an artist!)[18] – had been anticipated by Mauriac himself in his equation of omnipotent novelist with Jansenist God. Whether the intervention be that of 'grace' or merely that of a narrator eager to label his characters, the literary result, Mauriac had admitted, was the same: to restrict the apparent liberty of his characters, on which depended the necessary illusion of life. But whereas Sartre sees the apparent independence of literary characters and the ethic of liberty as complementing and reinforcing each other, Mauriac was aware of deep divisions between the literary and moral planes. His anxieties on this score take us to the heart of the tangle of moral and literary issues which underlie his work, and into which Sartre's analysis does not probe deeply enough.

In *Le Romancier et ses personnages*, Mauriac expresses his misgivings at what fictional characters reveal of their creator. They can never express the whole man, never represent 'ce tissu vivant où s'entrecroisent des millions de fils, qu'est une destinée humaine' (P II, 847). They represent aspects of the novelist, moods or desires which in his life are absorbed into the totality of his personality, but which his novels isolate, magnify and distort. The example he gives is a banal one – a writer's controlled irritation with his family at the end of a tiring day swelling into a fictional account of total estrangement, as in *Le Nœud de vipères*. But it is easy to see others: his resentment at the limitations on personal freedom which family life can entail, exploding into the violent acts of the 'poisoner' Thérèse and the homicidal Gradère of *Les Anges noirs*. The novelist, says Mauriac – and he is speaking primarily of himself – is so absorbed in the creation of characters that he identifies himself with each of them: 'Il joue tous les personnages; il se transforme en démon ou en ange. Il va loin, dans l'imagination, dans la saintetè et dans l'infâmie' (P II, 860). His predilection, like the shepherd of the parable, is for the lost sheep. Rebellious characters make exciting literature, but what they do to their creator is another matter, laying bare as they do the divisions cloaked by the public persona. The art of the novelist, releasing suppressed instincts in the form of fictional beings, is a threat to his own sense of moral integrity. 'C'est la personnalité même du romancier,' he wrote, 'c'est son «moi», qui, à chaque instant, est en jeu. De même que le radiologue est menacé dans sa chair, le romancier l'est dans l'unité de sa personne' (ibid.). In his personal life, Mauriac comforted himself, he could reunite 'les puissances opposées de son être', find his own unity, through union with God (P II, 861), but his art exerted a pull in the opposite direction, towards fragmentation.[19]

The notion of moral and psychological unity is carried into the novels themselves, and is especially important in *Thérèse Desqueyroux*, where the seductive urging of Jean Azévédo that Thérèse should 'be herself' – that is, unleash the rebellious instincts within her – is countered by her obscure notion of a moral 'self', the self that we become 'dans la mesure où nous nous créons' (P II, 62). But the lack of conviction with which Thérèse, as a partial and limited character, as one strand of the novelist's self, can express this creates the need for a further voice, alongside that of the central character, to provide something nearer a moral overview. That voice, despite the technical difficulties involved in introducing it, can only be that of the narrator.

To tell Thérèse's story, Mauriac had two basic modes available to him: first and third person narration. The former, discarded by the Realists in favour of the theoretically more objective third person, had had a new lease of life among the generation of writers after 1900: Gide, Proust, Alain-Fournier, in whom self-exploration took priority over the broad social concerns of Naturalism. As a novelist whose inspiration came, like Proust's, from his own life and the memories of childhood, Mauriac's instinctive style was the first person. Several of his novels were originally drafted in this mode and then rewritten in third person form: they include *Le Baiser au lépreux*, *Le Mal*, *Thérèse Desqueyroux* and *Les Chemins de la mer*. Among the several reasons for this change of point of view, the most important was Mauriac's need for a controlling element, a commentator, able to intervene and clarify the Christian sense of his text. The structure of his novels is more often than not dependent on the conflict between the point of view of the character and the point of view of the narrator. And one of the narrator's most noticeable strategies is that of concealment, to prevent the character, left to his devices, from exploring areas that were too delicate or daring for the Christian novelist to contemplate with equanimity.

The two drafts of *Thérèse Desqueyroux*, the complete novel and its short, unfinished first version *Conscience, instinct divin*, are very instructive in this respect. The latter is Thérèse's own account, the start of her story of how she tried to kill her husband Pierre. Almost immediately, she identifies the sexual nature of her motive, namely her inability to bear any longer the advances of a man whom she admires and respects but whom desire turns into what she calls 'cette bête hideuse et soufflante' (P II, 6). Has she made the wrong choice of husband? No, for Thérèse is adamant that she prefers Pierre to any other man. It is when she explains why she married him that her rejection of him becomes explicable: it was in a misguided attempt to be closer to his sister, Raymonde. Here Mauriac introduces a theme which, as is well known, exerted a powerful attraction for him: the theme of homosexual love. In the numerous novels in which he skirts the edges of the subject, he never allows himself so overt a treatment as in the brief sketch of Thérèse's feelings for Raymonde, although even here, Thérèse is permitted only a few words of description of the sunlight playing on Raymonde's hair, her 'chère tête renversée', her 'cou gonflé', before the writer's unease stops her short: 'Je m'égare' (P II, 11). In the novel, although Thérèse still abominates her sexual 'duties' as the wife of Bernard, and has married him because of her friendship with his sister Anne, the sexual themes, and especially the homosexual theme, are much less in evidence. Bernard is made generally less admirable than Pierre, so that he is not rejected just because of his sex. Anne inspires affection in Thérèse, but this is based mainly on memories of carefree youth, and the differences in their education – Anne is the convent girl, Thérèse the product of the state *lycée* – create a significant mental gulf between them; later, Thérèse is not only jealous of Anne's happiness but also conspires with the family to end her relationship with Azévédo. And although Thérèse herself has no sexual interest in Azévédo, the possibility that another man might make her happy is specifically expressed (P II, 88). Above all, the switch to the third person creates a filter, allows the narrative to slip away from Thérèse's inner thoughts and emotions at crucial moments. The motive for her poisoning of Bernard becomes less narrowly sexual, becomes, in fact, a more richly suggestive product of subconscious resentment, combining with circumstance and with fate to lead her into unpremeditated action. To make the ultimate mystery of her act more plausible still. Thérèse herself, who in *Conscience, instinct divin* refers with casual ease to *Polyeucte*, Josephus, Saint John of the Cross and Descartes, is now a less well educated woman, too easily impressed by Azévédo's reading. Although she can connect events into a coherent narrative, analysing their significance is beyond her. It would be wrong to suggest that all of this comes about simply because of Mauriac's desire to cloak his taboo theme; no doubt, he saw the potentially wider resonances of his character and her situation, and these eventually turn Thérèse herself into a more interesting character than her prototype. But the wish to conceal, as a contributing factor to the differences between his two drafts, is nevertheless suggested by this comparison of the one with the other. The same impulse can be seen at work in *Le Fleuve de feu*, where Lucile's thoughts on the nature of her interest in her protégée Gisèle soon reach a well-defined boundary: 'Dieu seul,' says the narrator, 'savait si Lucile de Villeron, fouillant son cœur, [. . .] n'y aurait pu découvrir soudain un germe inconnu d'elle [. . .] Si Dieu seul le savait, du moins ne voulut-il pas qu'elle le trouvât jamais, ni que fût troublé dans ses profondeurs ce cœur délivré du mal' (P I, 566). And there the issue is dropped.[20]

The narrator, fortunately, pursues less negative strategies. In *Thérèse Desqueyroux* his role in establishing a Christian perspective of meaning is evident at many levels. Before the novel proper itself begins, his *avant-propos* predetermines at least one angle of reading, expressing the hope that Thérèse will not long remain alone on the Parisian pavement on which the last page will leave her. 'J'aurais voulu que la douleur, Thérèse, te livre à Dieu,' the narrator states; '[. . .] Mais plusieurs, qui pourtant croient à la chute et au rachat de nos âmes tourmentées, eussent crié au sacrilège' (P II, 17). The provocative nature of these lines – the attack on those critics who had found Gisèle's salvation in *Le Fleuve de feu* too daring a mixture of the holy and the profane – is clear; but so too is their controlling purpose. They switch to the beginning of the novel the message that, in *Le Désert de l'amour*, waits until the end and comes too late to affect our reading of the text.

The superficial Christianity of the other characters is a further clarifying device, exemplified not only in Bernard's routine accomplishment of his religious duties, but also in Azévédo's half-baked mysticism. Thérèse's alienation from both of these attitudes is channelled in the direction Mauriac wishes by her sense of affinity with the young priest in the Corpus Christi procession, who communes with an invisible companion as he walks along. He has found a solace which eludes Thérèse, but which she cannot understand. She remembers the priest when tempted by suicide, and the thought of the Being in whom he believes plays a central part in the most explicitly Christian passage in the book, where narratorial rhetoric and symbolism combine. The window of Thérèse's room is open: an invitation to another world. Outside, the cocks are crowing – an image which always in Mauriac evokes the challenge and choice associated with the denial of Peter. The countryside is bathed in moonlight: 'Comment renoncer à tant de lumière?' (P II, 84); the light which Thérèse regrets leaving behind her in death is, the text gently suggests, not just of a natural sort. Doubts suddenly attack Thérèse: she wonders what death is, is not sure that it entails the annihilation of her person: 'Thérèse n'est pas assurée du néant. Thérèse n'est pas absolument sûre qu'il n'y ait personne. Thérèse se hait de ressentir une telle terreur' (ibid.). This incantatory three-fold repetition of her name creates an uncanny, nightmarish effect, loosening the realistic fabric of the novel in preparation for the strange event which is now going to unfold. Thérèse, in her despair, issues a challenge to God:

> S'il existe cet Être (et elle revoit, en un bref instant, la Fête-Dieu accablante, l'homme solitaire écrasé sous une chape d'or, et cette

> chose qu'il porte des deux mains, et ces lèvres qui remuent, et cet air de douleur); puisqu'Il existe, qu'Il détourne la main criminelle avant que ce ne soit trop tard; —et si c'est sa volonté qu'une pauvre âme aveugle franchisse le passage, puisse-t-Il, du moins, accueillir avec amour ce monstre, sa créature. (P II, 84–5)

The switch in mid-sentence from 's'Il existe' to 'puisqu'Il existe', partially disguised by the long intervening parenthesis, is a change of point of view, from character to narrator, for we can scarcely believe that Thérèse sees *herself* as 'ce monstre, sa créature'. The intense emotional pitch of the scene perhaps sweeps the reader more willingly past Mauriac's sleight-of-hand than in other instances of this technique. Certainly, suspension of disbelief is needed for what follows. God is not merely invoked; he actually intervenes, and in the same strange way as in *La Robe prétexte*, apparently taking the life of one character to save that of another. For no sooner has Thérèse pronounced these words than the house is filled by the noise of shouts and running feet, halting her on the brink of suicide: her aunt Clara has been found dead, her life, like that of Jacques' grandmother in the earlier novel, sacrificed by divine or narratorial whim to preserve the central character. But Mauriac pretends to allow a more rational interpretation of this event. Thérèse, contemplating her aunt's dead body, prefers to believe in coincidence. If anyone were to suggest that providence has exerted its 'volonté particulière', adds the narrator, Thérèse would shrug her shoulders (P II, 85). But, as in similar circumstances in Barbey's novels, the reader is invited to infer differently. What Mauriac intends us to understand is suggested in a passage in his diary: 'Est-ce le hasard, ce vent qui me pousse? Où bien ma destinée obéit-elle à une volonté particulière?' (OC IV, 235). He believed in chance no more than did Huysmans or Bloy. Thérèse, however, remains unconscious of providential influences in her life, or else refuses to contemplate them. Much of the significance of her experience is expressed through the narrator's suggestions, not through her own mind, which is capable of seeing symptoms but not causes and meanings. When she tells herself that suffering is 'sa raison d'être au monde' (P II, 92), she is unaware of the redemptive promise hidden in this very fact, although Mauriac must convey this thought to the reader. His text is full of such necessary rhetorical prompting.

The most important example of the unconsciously Christian nature of Thérèse's experience is her instinctive yearning for confession and absolution. The origins of this lie in *Conscience, instinct divin,* which takes the form of a written confession to a priest by a Catholic Thérèse. Although Mauriac abandoned this project, both the idea and the form of confession persist in the novel, giving the opening sequence its shape and purpose. As Thérèse travels back from the law-court after the enquiry into her poisoning of Bernard she tries to prepare an account of herself to satisfy her husband. This journey into the depths of her character, taking its impetus from the parallel spatial journey, does nothing to lighten her burden of despair, for her proposed confession is a secular one, unable to provide the relief of its sacramental counterpart. The contrast is specifically pointed in the text, for Thérèse remembers Anne's description of Catholic confession, and this is the model on which she bases her imagined reunion with Bernard, from whom she expects forgiveness. But Bernard is not a priest; the absolution she craves cannot come from him, but only from God, through the mediation of the Church.

Implicitly the novel thus defends the institution of the Church, showing the futility of secular 'confession'. The full resonance of this theme is suggested by the title of its first draft, for the phrase 'Conscience, instinct divin' comes from Rousseau's *Profession de foi du vicaire savoyard* – and Mauriac, writing of Rousseau a year or two later, denounces his concept of 'conscience' as typical of the modern world's usurpation of God's judgement by arrogant self-assessment (OC VIII, 357). In *Le Roman,* he reveals the source of his view of Rousseau: namely, Maritain's *Trois Réformateurs,* from which he quotes the following very significant lines:

> [Rousseau] a appris à notre regard à se complaire en nous-mêmes et à se faire le complice de ce qu'il voit ainsi, et à découvrir le charme de ces secrètes meurtrissures de la sensibilité la plus individuelle, que les âges moins impurs abandonnaient en tremblant au regard de Dieu. La littérature et la pensée modernes, ainsi blessées par lui, auront beaucoup de peine à retrouver la pureté et la rectitude qu'une intelligence tournée vers l'être connaissait autrefois. Il y a un secret des cœurs qui est fermé aux anges, ouvert seulement à la science sacerdotale du Christ. (P II, 757)

This critique of the heritage of Rousseau is applicable both to Thérèse, for whom 'sa conscience est son unique et suffisante lumière' (P II, 28), and, from a different angle, to Mauriac, anxious of the supposed dangers of delving too deeply into the intimate 'secrets' of his characters – and of his own heart. Hence the care with which the presentation of Thérèse's sombre and anarchic personality is accompanied by the orthodox moral promptings of the narrative voice.

At this point, however, the concordance of narrative function with divine perspective breaks down. Metaphorically and structurally, the narrator can occupy the position of a god on high, omniscient and interventionist, but his judgement of the characters can only reflect the novelist's preferences. Thérèse lacks one vital requirement, without which, in the eyes of the Church, absolution could scarcely be accorded to her: namely, the sense of sin. Her reconstruction of events does not lead to a recognition of guilt: she sees no pattern of criminal intent. Mauriac, as Michel Raimond argues, aids and abets her by switching from analysis to narrative, from *pourquoi* to *comment*, at vital moments.[21] This is because he wishes to allow Thérèse to say: 'Je ne connais pas mes crimes' (P II, 26) – although, in his essay on Rousseau, he charges the old reprobate with the wilful non-recognition of *his* (OC VIII, 367). As a Catholic moralist, Mauriac can identify and censure hypocrisy; as a novelist, he is wooed by his characters. It is not stretching imagination too far to see the act of wooing at work in the embryonic *Conscience, instinct divin*. Thérèse only ostensibly addresses the priest. What is really happening, as Mauriac writes these pages, is that he is letting the half-formed creature within him introduce herself to him, in the first person, 'comme je fais souvent,' he says elsewhere, 'pour faciliter le démarrage' (BN I, 43). The act of writing – 'Ecrivez, écrivez, pauvre enfant; ne redoutez pas de couvrir des pages. . . n'omettez rien' (P II, 4) – is Thérèse's form of confession, the story is the confessional, the 'priest' who hears it is the novelist, listening to the voice of his character before taking over the writing process and reformulating it in his 'objective' third-person style. But he is no more objective than Zola's surrogate novelist, the scientist. Thérèse, because he loves her as his creature, is certain of receiving his absolution, emerging as nobler than any of the practising Christians around her, and indeed, as the preface tells us, as a potential saint.

The Christian intentions of the novel, evident in its confessional form and through the narrator's voice, clash in the end with Mauriac's love of his renegade creature. Thérèse is the supreme example of the free character, resisting her creator's original schemes. This is no doubt why Mauriac argued that *Thérèse Desqueyroux* is not a Christian novel, even if it is a novel that only a Christian could have written (BN III, 182). His semantic caution need not prevent its being seen as a Christian and Catholic novel in precisely the same way as *Un prêtre marié*, for the salvation of the soul of its central character is its overriding concern. That the character in question has no concept of soul, but only of a humanistic 'conscience', does not alter this interpretation. It merely makes Thérèse more worthy of the novelist's compassion, and his refusal to condemn or convert her more honest. Unable to understand herself, seeing her action as merely an 'affreux devoir' (P II, 103), Thérèse remains mysterious to Mauriac too. She is the embodiment of the creative goal sketched in *Le Roman*: 'laisser à nos héros l'illogisme, l'indétermination, la complexité des êtres vivants' (P II, 765). In her he creates a character whose complexity defies both understanding and condemnation. No less a Catholic novel for all that, *Thérèse Desqueyroux* expresses Mauriac's Catholicism at crisis point.

* * *

The crisis was not long in coming to a head. It has been described many times, the most detailed account being Jean Lacouture's, and the different strands have been identified: Mauriac's clash with his critics; his accusation of Christianity as an impracticable religion, demanding all of man and underrating the impulses of the flesh; and a destabilising relationship – with 'another woman', affirms one critic, with the novelist Bernard Barbey, suggests another.[22] And because of all these factors, or perhaps as their cause, there was a particularly deep and long-lasting trough in his 'intermittent' sense of God's presence, a period of two years or more in which, says Mauriac, 'je fus comme fou'.[23] Throughout this period, Mauriac bitterly denounces his fragile and fluctuating religion, so dangerously dependent on 'cette délectation sensible' (OC VI, 323). Such self-reproach was probably the most fruitful way through the crisis, for when he emerged from it, with the help of the abbé Altermann, a new idea appeared in his writing: the importance of self-judgement. 'La présence de la Grâce dans un homme,' he wrote in his essay on Rousseau, 'se mesure à la netteté du regard dont il se juge [. . .] Le salut n'est plus loin lorsque nous commençons de nous voir tels que nous sommes' (OC VIII, 357). And again, in his book on René Bazin: 'Je suis persuadé [. . .] que la sainteté est, avant tout, la lucidité. «Il faut aller jusqu'à l'horreur quand on se connaît», écrivait Bossuet au maréchal de Bellefonds' (OC VIII, 482). So diametrically opposed is this formula to the pre-crisis shrinking from self-knowledge, seen in Mauriac's cloaking techniques, that it would seem that the refusal to accept himself, the repression of instincts to the point at which they burst from the subconscious in the form of terrifying fictional characters, was at the heart of his spiritual difficulty in the first place. This would explain the peculiar efficacity of the abbé Altermann in helping Mauriac, for one of Altermann's techniques, described by Charles du Bos, who had introduced Mauriac to the abbé, was precisely to lead the penitent towards a total view of his faith, in which recalcitrant strands could be seen in a more total context.[24]

Whether the crisis had any effect on Mauriac's novels is a question that is often asked, and to which his new-found emphasis on self-knowledge provides one answer. From Thérèse Desqueyroux, saved because 'she knows not what she does', to the characters of the 1930s novels, saved by their uncompromising awareness of their wretchedness, there is a radical leap. The change is already apparent in *Ce qui était perdu*, begun before the crisis and completed afterwards. Through the gradual clarity with which the odious central character Hervé Blénauge sees himself for what he is, the value of lucidity is illustrated. Hervé sets the psychological pattern for the protagonists of the following group of novels. The old miser Louis in *Le Nœud de vipères*, the 'poisoner' Thérèse in *La Fin de la nuit*, the murderer Gradère in *Les Anges noirs*, the self-righteous Brigitte Pian in *La Pharisienne*, all recognise their wretchedness. 'Le trait dominant de ma nature,' says Louis, 'c'est une lucidité affreuse' (P II, 388). For Thérèse also, understanding her actions is the starting-point for a new attempt to come to terms with herself. Gradère, impelled by the same urge, expresses his desire to 'atteindre la limite extrême de la sincérité' (P III, 216) in laying his heart bare for himself as well as for the priest.

As always in Mauriac, technical questions follow hard on thematic ones. The relationship of narrator to character is at once affected by this change of outlook. To express Hervé's hypocritical self-deception at the start of *Ce qui était perdu*, Mauriac has to rely on the narrator: 'Lui-même qui se croyait bon [. . .] tâchait de se dissimuler ce goût dévorant pour le malheur des autres' (P II, 279). But the change in Hervé is expressed from within his own consciousness and in his own words: '«Est-ce que je suis un être horrible? Mais non, simplement lucide, sincère . . . . Mais si: je suis horrible.» Tout d'un coup, il se voyait, tel qu'il était, et cherchait en lui une trace de sentiment noble comme s'il eût cherché un lambeau d'étoffe pour couvrir sa nudité' (P II, 346). Finally the character's and narrator's views are harmonised, inner realisation and external judgement concur: 'Son immense misère lui apparaissait, mais dans une lumière de miséricorde et de pardon' (P II, 347).

If characters are themselves capable of such judgement, it follows that the controlling and explanatory voice of the third-person narrator is no longer so necessary, and it is therefore no coincidence that Mauriac's next novel, *Le Nœud de vipères*, was the first since the less problematic period of *Préséances* to be written in first-person form. It represents a renewed attempt, and a successful one, to reconcile the vitality and apparent freedom of fictional characters with the expression of his Christian view, to 'leur souffler une âme ou, plutôt, les obliger à découvrir en eux leur âme, sans risque de les déformer ni les rendre moins vivants' (P II, 851).

The switch to first-person narrative, which Mauriac had been reluctant to adopt for the reasons suggested above, does not necessarily solve the technical problems inherent in a novel about religious experience, but it eases some of them. God's presence or absence, those two alternating determinants of the meaning of Mauriac's novels, are no longer absolute elements of a total fictional world. They become strands of belief within the character, true or illusory; the reader may reject the character, but has no reason for rejecting the book, at least from the outset. He may read it, initially, as a novel about delusion. But the important thing is that he will read it, and thus expose himself by its end to the suggestions and persuasions of the text. *Le Nœud de vipères* is one of Mauriac's most satisfying novels through the very fact that it embodies an understanding of these reading strategies.

Louis' writing of his text, and the gradual development of his character, are intimately interrelated. *Le Nœud de vipères* is a novel about conversion in a text which itself brings that conversion about through the process of its own writing. Commenting as he writes on the function of his text, Louis gradually realises in what self-discovery he is involved. His account begins, ostensibly, as a letter which he hopes his wife Isa will read after he is dead, but he senses other, deeper motives which he cannot yet define: 'Quelle est cette fièvre d'écrire qui me prend?' (P II, 387). He learns that he is not writing for Isa, but for himself: 'Vieil avocat, je mets en ordre mon dossier, je classe les pièces de ma vie, de ce procès perdu' (P II, 418). The legal metaphor, with its suggestion of clear judgement – the reverse of the way in which the over-simplifying mentality of lawyers is presented in *Thérèse Desqueyroux* – is important. For one of the functions of Louis' text is to act as a vehicle of lucid self-understanding. His reconstruction of his past, his narrative of the long estrangement from his wife following her insensitive wounding of his sexual pride, is his *mea culpa*. He refers several times to his letter-cum-diary as 'cette confession'. Like Thérèse, he strives to fulfil an unconscious need for confession and absolution which, in his irreligion, he tries to satisfy by opening his heart to Isa, as Thérèse had hoped to do to Bernard. Yet the confessional element in his retrospection already prepares the way for his final embracing, not of a human confident, but of God. Isa's death plays an important part in this: the letter meant for her, but never read by her, is transformed from a private means of communication from husband to wife into a document of supreme spiritual importance for its writer.

As he gains in lucidity, Louis begins to see that he has been maligned by those around him. After the stage of self-criticism comes that of self-respect, in which he recognises his capacity for nobility. He compares himself with the members of his family and finds his own qualities more in keeping than theirs with the religion they profess but which he claims to despise. This change of attitude is underlined by a switch in the application of the image which gives the book its title:

> Dans un soir d'humilité (says Louis] j'ai comparé mon cœur à un nœud de vipères. Non, non: le nœud de vipères est en dehors de moi; elles sont sorties de moi et elles s'enroulaient, cette nuit, elles formaient ce cercle hideux au bas du perron, et la terre porte encore leurs traces. (P II, 478)

But even this is merely a transitional stage in his development, for he realises that, if the members of his family have so completely failed to understand him, perhaps he is equally misled in condemning them in return. By the end of the book this process is complete. From self-knowledge to self-acceptance and to the acceptance and forgiveness of others: this is the pattern of Louis' development. Importantly, it is not presented as a sudden change, but as an awareness gathering momentum in the course of time, and made convincing by the subtle arrangement of time sequences in the text. Louis takes up his pen at a moment when his resentment has passed its peak. 'Vous avez eu la chance que je survive à ma haine,' he tells Isa on the first page of his letter (P II, 385). The change in him, more plausible because it has been in process for some time, allows him to recollect the different periods of his life, his early happiness as well as his later misery. But this psychological vantage point is not yet accompanied by a clear sight of where his evolution is taking him in religious terms: the full implication of this becomes clear only in his dying moments, and too late for him to commit it fully to paper.

The religious change in Louis has often been regarded as less convincing than the moral one. Susan Suleiman sees 'a last-minute conversion' at work here, a sudden transformation of the book 'into an edifying tale'.[25] This charge could be levelled at early Mauriac novels but not at this one, for, technically, he had learned his lesson. The reader is prepared from an early point in the book for Louis' religious conversion, not through an arbitrary *coup de grâce* but because of the awareness within Louis of a supernatural dimension. Here Mauriac makes a direct challenge to the Realist conception of the cosmos. As Louis, with Isa in Luchon, contemplates the Pyrenean night, 'j'eus soudain,' he says, 'la sensation aigüe, la certitude presque physique qu'il existait un autre monde, une réalité dont nous ne connaissions que l'ombre' (P II, 404). More tellingly still, when their daughter Marie dies, Louis, unlike the inconsolable Isa, has a sense of the child's continuing existence in a world beyond matter (P II, 448).

Le Nœud de vipères is the first and perhaps the sole novel in which Mauriac has the confidence to entrust the expression of his Christian viewpoint to the central character, free of the watchdog narrator. It is a sign of his sureness of the clarity of this underlying meaning that he issues two challenges to the reader, one at the end of each half of the novel. The first takes the form of a protest, in a document which Louis intends leaving for Isa, against the possible misinterpretation of any eventual death-bed recantation: this will not be a genuine conversion, he insists, but the result of weakness and fear. Martin Jarrett-Kerr sees this as a flaw in the novel, and accuses Mauriac of forgetting about this apparently problematic detail.[26] Mauriac, in fact, does no such thing: he makes Louis withdraw his protest in terms that draw attention once more to the central theme of the post-crisis period. Whereas the younger Louis had seen religious belief as incompatible with rational thought, the older man now admits that 'c'est lorsque je me sens le plus lucide que la tentation chrétienne me tourmente' (P II, 459). Theoretically, the reader is free to decide which Louis to believe, and to judge the end of the story accordingly; Mauriac's preference is clear.

The second challenge comes in the two letters which follow Louis' unfinished text, one from his son Hubert to Hubert's sister Geneviève, the other to Hubert from his own daughter Janine. These letters again pose the question of the sincerity and validity of Louis' conversion. The first letter, while allowing his humanity, ridicules his supposed religious change of heart. The second, though not ignoring his faults, argues that his Christian faith is genuine. The fact that Janine has not been allowed to read Louis' account is important, for hers is an independent testimony based on her observation of her grandfather during the last weeks of his life. The letters stand without authorial comment, for which there is no structural framework even if Mauriac wished to comment: they represent the only passage in his entire fictional work to float in a totally narrator-less space. It is hard to agree with John Flower that Mauriac is 'preaching' here,[27] but it is equally hard to accept Susan Suleiman's view that 'these letters emphasise the altogether relative status of the "right" interpretation' (op. cit., 230), for on the basis of what we know of the characters, we can only conclude that Hubert's prejudice blinds him to the possibility of change in his father and that Janine's view is the correct one. To argue, as Suleiman does, that 'in order to be convinced of Louis' conversion and of the power of divine grace that it manifests, one must (like Janine) believe in it already' (ibid.) seems to deny the novelist any power of persuasion and to overstate the degree of relativism possible even in a first–person narrative. As argued above, the reader has less reason for rejecting the philosophical assumptions of a first-person novel from the outset, but in the face of the novelist's rhetoric, however subtle or non-committal and couched in whatever technical framework, he cannot postpone the decision to accept or reject beyond the final act of closing the book, or else the activity of reading will have been a literally meaningless one. There is a habitable halfway house between Flower and Suleiman: it is to say that in terms of the fiction, Louis' conversion is a true one, and that, transposed to the real world, it might be true if. . . . No serious novelist, Catholic or otherwise, would expect more from his reader.

* * *

One more Mauriac novel is worth discussing here, if only because it illustrates the often underrated variety, within his little changing thematic and stylistic range, of Mauriac's narrative forms. In *Thérèse Desqueyroux* he had written a Catholic novel of revolt, in which the unreconciled characters and narrative tensions hark back to the tradition of Barbey d'Aurevilly. In *Le Nœud de vipères* he had produced the novel of conversion attempted with less success by Huysmans. And in our final novel *L'Agneau* he makes a rare approach to the allegorical fiction with which one would associate Léon Bloy.

Bloy's cryptogrammatic conception of the world was an extreme form of a temptation to which the Christian imagination is often prone. The reading of symbolic meaning into life's events is an extension of belief in the workings of grace and in the existence of a providential pattern. Mauriac, unlike Bloy, was disinclined to read history as if it were a second Book of Revelations. He was willing to leave the esoteric aspects of religion to his friend Lacaze, whose *alter ego* Donzac, in *Un adolescent d'aujourd'hui*, is adept at detecting the 'le point secret où la vérité de la vie, telle que nous l'expérimentons, rejoint la vérité révélée' (P IV, 685). But, as the novels discussed above have shown, Mauriac's decipherment of the traces of divine will in individual lives is a recurring element in his work. Xavier, the central character of *L'Agneau*, regards the apparently chance happenings of life as things which were meant to be, external signs of 'une volonté particulière de Dieu' (P IV, 467). He is convinced that he has been singled out by God for a special purpose, for a mission which will take the form of a sacrifice. He is conscious like Mauriac's earlier characters of God's vice-like grip, but unlike them he regards the unknown future to which God is taking him as his form of adventure, and when the nature of his task becomes clear to him – to intervene in the destinies of Jean and Michèle de Mirbel, to save not just their marriage but their souls – he accepts it willingly. He becomes what even his name indicates that he must become, their Saviour, eventually dying in circumstances that bring them to a deeper realisation of their responsibilities.

What prevents this transposition of the Passion from being a simple novel of edification is the psychological development of Xavier, his gradual growth into his christic role. At the outset he is motivated more by an insatiable curiosity into people's lives than by selfless love. He sees the satisfaction of the priestly vocation for which he believes himself destined as residing in the power to have privileged insight into the souls of others. As Philip Stratford argues,[28] this is also the privilege of the novelist, and the change in Xavier is another version, after the one embodied in Louis, of Mauriac's own evolution: this time, from an 'amateur d'âmes' to a novelist possessed of charity for his characters. When he arrives at the Mirbel home, Xavier is immature, inconsistent, imagines he loves the girl Dominique whom he meets there, and still fondly hopes that God's plan for him will entail his personal happiness: perhaps he was sent here for the express purpose of meeting Dominique?

The truth begins to be revealed through Xavier's concern for the orphaned boy Roland, whom the Mirbels have taken on trial adoption but whose life with them is wretched. When Xavier goes to fetch a ladder in order to release Roland from the room in which Mirbel has locked him, the allegory of the story becomes clear. As Xavier carries the ladder to the house, his feet torn by pine-needles, he re-enacts in his flesh the suffering of Christ carrying his cross to Calvary. He understands for the first time that the Christian way is no abstract notion, but a commitment to physical sacrifice. In a 'vision' that is rare in Mauriac's works, he sees Christ walking before him, and literally follows in his footsteps: '[Il] croyait voir bouger devant lui un dos maigre; il en discernait les vertèbres, les côtes soulevées par un halètement précipité, et le sillon violet des vieilles flagellations: l'esclave de tous les temps, l'esclave éternel' (P IV, 534). It is as if the Christ of Grünewald, the Naturalist Christ, has come down from the cross to transform into the language of the novelist the abstract concepts of faith.

The love Xavier has felt for Dominique now expands and transforms itself into a love for boy and for all humanity, a 'passion monstueuse, passion divine, oui! c'était cela! Passion d'un Dieu pour sa créature' (P IV, 547). This love then finds a new focus: Jean de Mirbel, for whom Xavier knows he must sacrifice himself in an act of vicarious substitution. The novel rejoins here the thematic and structural lineage of the nineteenth-century Catholic novel, the redemptive suffering of characters for each other on which Barbey and Bloy had based their novels. Xavier has to die for Mirbel, and die at the hands of Mirbel, to bring the latter, through guilt and remorse, to faith. He has also to die in a mysterious way, to make his death a problematic one for the other characters and for the reader. Does Xavier deliberately cycle into the headlights of Mirbel's car? Is he blinded by them? Does Mirbel kill him intentionally, or in anger, or by accident? Is Xavier a saint, as the local priest whose faith he has also restored believes? These questions are unanswered at the end of the book, and are transcended by Mirbel's final speech: 'Pourquoi le pleurons-nous, Michèle? Il possède enfin Celui qu'il a aimé' (P IV, 570). But Xavier's death, because he has been presented as a flesh-and-blood character, is sharply felt, and the price he pays in human terms is not minimised by the novelist. In this creation of living beings lies one of the principal ways in which Mauriac enriches the Catholic novel tradition.

* * *

L'Agneau might seem to give the lie to Mauriac's opinion, expressed in *Dieu et Mammon*, that the novel of sainthood can never be written (P II, 818). Yet to see it, like André Blanchet,[29] as the culminating point to which his work progresses, would be very misleading, and this is certainly not implied in this present chapter. The driving force in Mauriac's creative writing is not towards the novel of sainthood, but towards the expression of the conflicts and obsessions within himself: his anguished and half-veiled attitude to love and sex, his fluctuating view of the family and of bourgeois values, his conviction of the presence of Christ mingled with anxiety at its intermittent nature. These were artistic goals renewed with each successive novel, not a concerted effort to a fixed end. 'La fin?' said Mauriac, speaking of the poem *Le Sang d'Atys* which occupied him for years and reveals so much of the inner man; 'la fin? Rien n'est fini [. . .] Mon poème ne sera jamais fini [. . .] J'y travaille toujours.'[30]

This sense of the writer's task as endless, his goal of rendering his own ever fluctuating consciousness and myriad complexities an ultimately inaccessible one, underlies all Mauriac's work. The novelist's art, he says in *Le Romancier et ses personnages*, is 'une faillite' (P II, 848) because the dictates of clarity force him to isolate and immobilise emotions and passions which can only be understood within context and flux. Thérèse Desqueyroux expresses this frustration when she tries to concoct 'une histoire simple, fortement liée' for the sake of a husband who, like the traditional novelist 'classe tous les sentiments, les isole, ignore entre eux ce lacis de défilés' (P II, 27). This simplification of life is epitomised, Mauriac argues in *Le Roman*, in the Realist tradition, in its ossification of characters into types, in opposition to which he himself strove to 'mettre en lumière le plus individuel d'un cœur, le plus particulier, le plus distinct' (ibid., 762). The very reticence which Mauriac's puritan conscience caused him to feel in the face of 'delicate' subjects – homosexual and incestuous loves – serves his artistic purpose, for it contributes to the sense of the unplumbed mystery of character which his best work embodies. And if the impossibility of judging such mysterious beings conflicts with the moral norms of Christianity, the implication that only God can judge Maria Cross, Thérèse, Louis, Gradère or Xavier is never far below the surface. The final function of the indetermination of his characters is to leave room for the possibility of a reconciliation between them and God, which the reader may not see, but which is implied and predicted. It is in stressing this ever possible alleviation of the *misère de l'homme sans Dieu* that Mauriac makes his contribution to the Catholic novel.

7

Julien Green's Scale of Realities

Although Julien Green is still writing in the last quarter of the twentieth century, his encounter with the nineteenth-century Realists was an important factor in his career. Green recalls his reaction, as a recently converted Catholic, to the novels which he read at the rate of one a day in the closing months of the First World War, and which contributed to the awakening of a sexual awareness that was to interfere increasingly with the practice of his religion. In them, he says, he unconsciously sought reasons for no longer believing in the sinfulness of sexuality. Against the teachings of his puritanical mother, Zola, Maupassant and the Goncourts freed sex from moral stricture and proclaimed it 'la grande chose de la vie'.[1] He read their books as a source of information about sex, of which he was by today's standards almost unbelievably ignorant, and, more subversively as far as his religious faith was concerned, accepted them as an accurate reflection of the views and values of the modern world (V, 914). More broadly still, for a young man who had not yet begun to write, the notion that there was a yawning gap between religion and literature was an important preconditioning factor. Green was always to believe that literature, being about sex, was the province of the devil. What attracts Satan to the writer, he once wrote, is the potential for the expansion of his kingdom through the hallucinatory temptations of 'les pantelantes émotions sexuelles' which the novelist is obliged to describe (V, 1367). Green accepted that Catholics could be writers – reading Huysmans had encouraged his intermittent monastic instincts (V, 953), and Bloy showed that one could write about Catholicism 'sans fadeur' (V, 965); but novelists could never be saints, and writing novels was incompatible with a state of grace (IV, 829). Green shares with Mauriac the view that literature stems from the base instincts of the writer, and that fictional characters are the vehicles of his repressed sin. But Mauriac, even in his most tortured moments, never wrote as intensely as Green does of the feeling of Satan's presence in the act of writing (V, 1454), or of the transformation of the writing process into something obscurely akin to the sexual act (V, 1442). In this last detail, Green is oddly close to Zola.

To Green, Catholics risk climbing into the same moral boat as Realists as soon as they pick up a pen. But he sees their philosophical and aesthetic differences as dividing them into two distinct camps. The world depicted by Maupassant, he writes, had in Maupassant's eyes 'une réalité extraordinaire', but in his own no reality at all (IV, 1329). What he meant by 'reality' emerges from his description of one of the crucial moments which he identifies in his autobiography as decisive turning points in his life. He recalls a day when, as he looked through the window of his schoolroom at the brown brick building opposite, material reality struck him as inessential, secondary and even illusory. He was filled by 'la certitude qu'il existait un autre monde que celui que je voyais autour de moi, et que cet autre monde était le vrai.' This feeling produced great joy, which evaporated on his return to the 'prison' of 'ce qu'on appelle la réalité' (V, 697–8). To this experience, his memory constantly returns. In an attempt to express philosophically his sense of the fragility of the physical world, he says that matter is so relative to the individual's perception that its nature and very existence must be open to doubt. What cannot be doubted is the true reality beyond, and which is 'essentiellement invisible' (V, 976). Nor can we deny that at the heart of this true reality there is God, a presence as certain as that of light behind clouds (V, 694). On this conviction, Green constructed what he called 'une échelle des réalités' (V, 730). The highest and truest reality is that revealed by the Bible; what men call the 'real' world, by contrast, 'en était frappé d'une sorte d'irréalité' (ibid.). The only material objects to which he allows an assured existence are religious objects, of which the authenticity is guaranteed by the sacred function accorded to them. The priest's robes or the altar cross are not merely the signs of an undeniable order; they also partake of this order's truth. The communion host, above all, is the object most worthy of trust, 'la seule réalité dans un monde d'apparences', more real, writes Green, than his own hand as he writes or the paper on which he is writing (V, 976). Green thus reverses the values inherent in Realist epistemology.

If the spiritual and material levels of being represent the top and bottom rungs of Green's scale of reality, the middle rung is occupied by imagination, which outreaches the limits of base reality and fosters an extra-materialism that is favourable to religious belief, but without being synonymous with it. This view is illustrated by an anecdote showing Green's rejection of Naturalist theories of art. He describes his encounters with a drawing-master who never arrived for a lesson without a volume of Zola under his arm, and who was a fervent believer in the techniques of exact pictorial representation. Although the young pupil skilfully produced photographically detailed flower-pots and waste-paper baskets, his teacher had no idea of how much richer a source of inspiration lay in imagination than in the concrete models on which his method relied (V, 763–4). Like Barbey and Huysmans, Green sensed the alliance, against the common Realist adversary, of imagination and Christian supernaturalism. The two were not identical, but both were forms of what, borrowing the label which Zola's Doctor Pascal applies to the paintings of his niece Clotilde (Zola, VI, 1166), Green calls 'fantasmagorie'. Green's 'fantasmagorie' extends, like Clotilde's, from flights of fancy to movements of the heart towards God; he applies the term, in rapid succession, to the suggestive evocations of literature, to obsessive visions conjured up by the devil, and to the images inspired by the Bible (V, 722, 727, 730). All three are preferred by him to the allegedly banal object-painting of 'ce lourdaud de Zola' (V, 98).

On the eve of his own career as a novelist, Green reiterates his rejection of the Realist prescription of working from direct observation of 'reality'. As he sits in his Paris home in the company of his widower father and sisters, he writes in his diary: 'Un roman! Je n'aurais qu'à lever les yeux et regarder autour de moi, dans cette pièce, pour en trouver le sujet. Mais ce n'est pas encore celui-là que je veux écrire. Pour le moment, je veux faire des livres entièrement imaginés par moi' (IV, 5). As well as aesthetic preferences, however, there were more personal factors behind his unwillingness to exploit his immediate life as a source of writing. The most intimate elements of his personal life could not be revealed, and had to be denied a direct reflection in his novels. Green's 'secret', necessitating a distance between his life and his art, and not divulged until the publication of his autobiography decades later, was his homosexuality. While pursuing 'true reality' on the metaphysical level, he denied its expression on the psychological one. The unavoidable connection of the two explains the enigma of Green's career: the peculiar fact that his unshakeable belief in the existence of God goes unaffirmed, and religion is denied a central role in his novels, until a quarter of a century after he began writing. Sexual and religious experience were so inseparably intertwined for Green that the exclusion from his work of the one implied the omission of the other.

Homosexuality never eroded Green's beliefs. But its irresistibility led him into a life-style incompatible with Christian practice. Christ inhibited his sexual freedom; therefore he tried to ignore Christ's existence. 'Je ne pouvais faire,' he writes, 'qu'il oubliât la mienne' (V, 977–8). During the many years before his return to the Church in 1939 (V, 1402), he did not challenge the Bible's teaching on sex, and continued to believe that 'hormis le mariage, puisque l'Évangile le disait, le péché était dans le plaisir même, quel que fût le sexe du partenaire' (V, 1201). This was despite the fact that his powerlessness to resist his instincts made it impossible for him to regard his own 'sin' as an option freely chosen against the dictates of his faith (V, 1199). As he says, 'j'eus le sentiment qu'un monde de cristal venait de heurter un bloc de granit' (V, 1194). Christianity was the true religion, and homosexuality his true nature: the result was a moral *impasse*.

The late 1920s saw Green at his furthest remove from the Church, accusing it of overstressing sexual sin, and of failing to see that resistance to sexual desire is not only impossible but self-defeating, for desire feeds on frustration (IV, 53–4). He was very close, once more, to Mauriac, who in precisely the same period was arguing much the same point in his celebrated outburst: 'Le christianisme ne fait pas sa part à la chair' (Mauriac, OC VII, 229). Mauriac, his immediate crisis over, did his best to bring his friend Green back to the fold, which merely irritated the younger writer (IV, 161). Solicited in one direction by Gide and in the other by Mauriac, the thought of committing his art to any non-literary cause was repugnant to him. It was in this period that he rejected the notion of the Catholic novelist, in its limited sense as a proselytiser (IV, 42). But throughout his career, there remained in him and in his writing a sense of a suspension, rather than a rejection, of Christianity. Just as, in the passage quoted above from the *Journal*, he uses the phrases 'pas encore' and 'pour le moment' to dismiss *temporarily* from his novels what he calls 'models' (IV, 6) drawn from life, he seems always to envisage the probability of an eventual return to Christian practice. It is not just with hindsight that his novels of the 1920s and 30s can be read in the light of this pattern, for they contain clear evidence of their place in an overall drama of departure and return, of self-imposed exile and spiritual repatriation. Like Huysmans' 'decadent' novels, like Barbey's gothic fiction, it is plain where they are leading. In the words in which, in a dream recorded in the *Journal,* his former confessor père Crété describes Green, 'le vêtement qu'il porte ne cache pas aux yeux de Dieu l'habit qu'il devait porter' (IV, 12).

* * *

The temporary banishment from Green's work of the upper stratum of reality and his rejection of the lowest as illusory leaves the field open for a middle course: unbridled invention. His early novels, from *Mont-Cinère* to *Épaves,* are ostensibly pure works of imagination, unlike the thinly autobiographical novels with which most writers embark on their careers. However, through their common themes of flight and of the repression of the protagonist's liberty, instinct or identity, they translate at a deeper level the tensions within the author, expressing their force but without revealing their precise nature. *Le Voyageur sur la terre* embodies a paradigm of Green's aesthetic as well as spiritual odyssey, for it moves from a 'realistic' opening sequence – the young man Daniel O'Donovan's life with his aunt and uncle, in an environment in which his identity is stifled – to a narrative of escape that is less spatial than metaphysical. Daniel runs away to the university town of Fairfax, where he meets Paul, a youth who is his physical double, symbol of the difficulty of escape from the self. After exploring his consciousness through a series of dreams, he eventually commits suicide; his death is not just the only possible conclusion but indeed a form of grace. Dream sequences, and the gothic theme of the *doppelgänger*, reappear in *L'Autre sommeil*. The narrator dreams of two naked male figures sleeping on a bed, and discovers on closer inspection that 'J'étais l'un et j'étais l'autre' (I, 840). A whole range of suggestive images is embodied here: the creative impulse of the artist's self-replication, the divided self, autoeroticism, as well as the powerful but undefined attraction which the narrator feels for his male cousin.

The longer texts of this period record more substantially, but still indirectly, the tremors of frustrated passions. In *Mont-Cinère,* the object of the heroine's desires is the old family house, of which she craves possession. When her unexpectedly self-assertive husband makes it clear that she will never be mistress of the house on her own terms, she burns it down. This finale is reminiscent of the crumbling house of Usher[2] or of the blazing house at the end of *Jane Eyre* – both stories being much admired by Green, whose American parentage gave him more direct access than most French novelists to English and American literature. *Adrienne Mesurat* returns, in greater psychological depth, to the theme of the stifled individual life, finally exploding into the heroine's killing of her father, the obstacle to her freedom. In *Léviathan*, the contiguity of violence and sex is more closely broached through the character of Guéret, who brutally beats the girl Angèle in a frenzy of frustration, and who is betrayed to the police by another woman because she cannot have his love. Finally, in *Épaves*, the most ambitious novel of this first group in structural terms, several characters trapped under the same roof struggle to determine their identities.

It is not difficult to see that a psychoanalytical reading of all these early texts reveals the sexual, though not yet the homosexual, obsessions of the writer, from which comes their creative impetus. One facet of Green is visible in them. But what of the other, Green the believer in a divine order? Religion is seen primarily from the standpoint of the characters, who are either indifferent or, at most, retain a vestige of habitual Christian practice. It is presented, through the minor characters of *Adrienne Mesurat* for example, as a purely conventional form or, especially in *Mont-Cinère*, as excessively puritanical. In terms of the central characters' lives, it seems mainly an irrelevance. When Adrienne, in her instinctive flight from her father's home, boards a train and arrives haphazardly in Dreux, the absence of emotional relief is suggested not just through the indifference of the passers-by but by the physical ambiguity of the building which she takes to be the church but turns out to be the town hall. In *Léviathan*, Angèle, equally unhappy, looks at the crucifix which hangs above her bed and which matches her half-focused interest in its blind unresponsiveness: 'La tête de côté, les yeux clos, il avait l'air las de cette femme et du spectacle de son inquiétude' (I, 644). A little later, she enters a church, where her meditation on the unfulfilled childhood dreams of happiness merges with the feeling that religion is equally illusory: 'Vraiment, était-ce la peine d'aller passer un quart d'heure dans une église pour en sortir ainsi, le cœur plein de colère et de désespoir?' (I, 655). In *Épaves*, Éliane, whose selflessness in encouraging her sister to marry the man she herself loves stems from a half-forgotten impulse to Christian martyrdom, also enters a church in a very similar scene. She too is struck by the lack of solution to her problems that is offered there, and she quickly rejoins the life of the street outside, where 'elle préférait ces cris et ces appels à la paix dormeuse des chrétiens' (II, 76).

None of these examples, at first glance, would be out of place among the redundant churches, dead statues and empty religious ceremonies of the Realist novel, and passages like these contrast diametrically with Green's insistence, in his non-fictional writings, on the uniquely intense reality of *objets de culte*. He is like the Realists too, and especially like Maupassant, in his recourse to religious attitudes and behaviour as a source of metaphor, but applied in a wholly non-religious context. *Adrienne Mesurat* contains several examples of this. In her impeccable housekeeping for her unwitting taskmaster of a father, Adrienne is described as being like a nun who has lost her faith but plods on blindly in respect of the rule of her order (I, 299). Her realisation that she need not chain herself to this routine is felt as the absence of a *religious* obligation (I, 309). The austere Madame Grand in the same novel is also compared to a nun, confined to the stale air of her convent (I, 418–19). These devices of style convey very clearly Green's sense of inhibition within the faith. At the same time the frequency of such imagery in his novels shows the hold that religion had on his imagination, and in the central sequence of *Léviathan*, describing Guéret's flight from the scene of his violent acts, Green's Christian imagination shapes and informs the text in an unmistakable way.

Guéret has gone to Angèle's house after feverishly imagining her in bed, 'offrant sa gorge au crime et à l'amour' (I, 665). As he walks through the town, familiar objects transform themselves into nightmarish shapes; plane-trees and houses discard their apparent reality for the reality of dream. After the murder of the innocent bystander who has witnessed his beating of Angèle, Guéret takes refuge in a coal-merchant's yard, in which three pyramid-shaped heaps of coal suggest a pre-Christian universe, reinforced by further specific images of the abyss, of hell, of cosmic tragedy, of a city that is not of this earth (I, 692–3). These pagan and infernal resonances transform the small provincial town into a landscape of myth; even the river which flows through it, and on whose banks he commits his brutal acts, is called 'la Sommeillante', in which name the suggestion of the Lethe, river of hell, is conveyed. Guéret, indubitably, is in the pit of hell, a notion which images of verticality and frustrated ascent further underline. Twice he tries to climb walls – first, up to Angèle's window, secondly out of the coal yard. Each time, the upward climb presents difficulty and danger. But falling is easy: 'Il se laissa tomber à l'intérieur de la maison et roula sur le plancher' (I, 674); 'il s'était laissé glisser de la fenêtre pour tomber en boule au pied du mur' (I, 675); 'Se laisser glisser? Comment? Tout à coup, il poussa un cri et tomba' (I, 697). To equate arduous upward movement with vain moral struggle and precipitous fall with damnation is not to stretch Green's meaning into areas where it will not easily extend. There are other examples to support the interpretation: the opening section of *L'Autre sommeil*, in which the hero is held vertiginously over the parapet of the pont d'Iéna, his physical terror mingling with the sexual hallucinations caused by the nude statues along the river banks, the death-fall of Élisabeth in *Minuit* as she tries to follow her seducer Serge through her window, the plunge into water of Daniel O'Donovan. It is possible to relate this motif to the staircase scenes of Green's novels, which he himself has enumerated (IV, 236): Adrienne pushing her father to his death, Madame Grosgeorges in *Léviathan* alternately climbing and descending stairs in her moral and sexual anguish. Another instance, not listed by Green, comes to mind – that of Angèle's aunt, the demonic Madame Londe who has forced her niece into prostitution, and whose 'ascension' of stairs turns her into an image of the anti-christ, 'courbée en deux sous le faix de sa croix impie' (I, 741). Those readers who saw in Green's fiction of this period the reflection of a godless world were perhaps making no more than the superficial comment that was almost conventional in the 1920s whenever a novel by a known Catholic, or lapsed Catholic, was published, but a close reading of the texts adds substance to their perceptions.

Green disliked such 'Catholic' readings of his novels. 'Ce n'est pas dans cet esprit-là que j'ai écrit mon roman,' he says in response to Raïssa Maritain's view of *Léviathan* as 'un tableau de la nature sans la grâce' (IV, 30). Catholicism, because it rejected his sexual being, was a system within which he could not accommodate his life, and thus his work could not be circumscribed within it either. His short novel *Les Clefs de la mort* shows him moving away from psychological and moral reality altogether into a totally imaginative realm, where hallucinatory visions and voices determine action. This story represents an extreme form of fantasy in Green's early work, anticipating the middle phase of his career.

* * *

In the first of these middle novels, *Le Visionnaire*, Green's search for an imaginative myth, as an alternative to Catholicism, intensifies. The realism of the opening sequence stems from the spirit of its narrator, Marie-Thérèse: for her, the real is the visible, although she is aware that this view of life is an impoverishing one, and longs for the revelation of a more 'secret' order, of which sexual self-discovery is part. Like Green himself, she does not 'tell all' where sex is concerned; an important discrepancy between her account and that of her cousin Manuel which follows it is that in her version it is Manuel who tries to initiate sexual contact, while in his she sends him invitingly teasing smiles and glances. Her religion offers her no help in coping with her sexuality, and indeed seems to stem from her fear of it: her wish to be a nun is a desire for escape. As well as with sex, the girl is also preoccupied with death, but to her questions on the subject, her companion Sister Louise is silent: Christianity looks to an illusion beyond death, not at its grim reality.

Marie-Thérèse's narrative is merely the prelude to Manuel's, which elaborates a myth of sex and death which Catholicism denies her. For him these are matters of obsessive anxiety: he is dying of tuberculosis, sex is his means of contact with life. Reading Renan's Life of Jesus has eroded his belief in the Christian supernatural: Renan's Jesus is a human rather than divine figure, a man who sets an example to follow in purely earthly matters: 'qu'est-ce que le Fils de l'Homme aurait fait?' (II, 278). This does not prevent Manuel from having experiences which point in the reverse direction: the sense one night of a presence – 'Lui, peut-être?' (II, 291). But these fluctuations are swept aside as he suddenly *sees* – 'Je *voyais*' (II, 307) – the possibility of escape into an imaginative exploration of his experience, a way of exorcising his fears by writing an alternative narrative of his life. This is 'Ce qui aurait pu être', a tale within the tale, which shifts the book inexorably from reality to the fantasy which had become Green's preferred fictional mode. Already at the start of the book, Manuel had succeeded in persuading the literal-minded Marie-Thérèse of the existence of a castle called Nègreterre, which he has simply invented. He now imagines himself living there, in a world hopefully free of anxiety, a paradise where death cannot reach him: not, he insists, the paradise of the Christian, but 'un grand jardin ouvert à tous, où le méchant oublierait le mal et le juste son ennuyeuse vertu' (II, 324). In this wonderland Manuel, like Alice, turns flesh-and-blood creatures into imaginary characters. The viscountess and her brother Antoine, who dominate Nègreterre, are the distorted equivalents of Monsieur Ernest and his sister, who in Manuel's real life ran the bookshop in which he once worked.[3] The link is reinforced by the reference to both buildings, in the 'real' and imaginary narratives, as being built of volcanic stone (II, 207, 219).

Green is writing here an allegory of his own career as a writer, his rejection both of a traditional religious life-view and of subjects directly drawn from experience. '*Le Visionnaire*,' he writes in his *Journal*, 'c'était le roman du romancier, et la rêverie de Manuel explique assez bien la façon dont je m'y prends pour écrire mes livres' (IV, 393). What Manuel discovers is what Green's work always reveals: that dream narratives provide no escape from fear, but simply intense and terrifying images of its sources. Death haunts Nègreterre: Manuel is instructed to read to the dying count. Antoine is also death-obsessed, and so is the viscountess. The three inhabitants of the castle compose essentially one single figure (as do Manuel and Marie-Thérèse in the first two parts of the book): the individual at different stages in life, contemplating mortality. The viscountess is also sexually attracted to Manuel, but having seduced him she dies in his arms, linking death and sex as they are so often linked in Green.

Le Visionnaire shows Green reshuffling the interrelationships of fantasy and religion, explored before him by the nineteenth-century Catholic novelist, and deliberately breaking the alliance of the two which Barbey and Huysmans had forged in their different ways. Unlike them, Green denied Christianity its place at the centre of his myth-making. This denial, however, was a brief one, and had reached its extreme form in Manuel's text. From this period in the mid 1930s date the first signs of a reawakening of Green's faith, of which the intellectual basis had remained intact all along. An entry in his diary records another of the intermittent spiritual experiences which punctuated his life: a sense, while listening to music, of the proximity of another world, which he identifies as 'le monde de la vérité, ce royaume de Dieu qui m'intriguait tellement quand j'étais enfant'. He adds, as if to remind himself of the wholly provisional nature of his separation from both Catholic practice and Christian writing, that if ever he manages fully to grasp that truth, he will say so. He will say, perhaps, that death – the death so feared by Manuel – has in reality no substance, but is merely 'un cauchemar inventé par l'ignorance' (IV, 395–6). Although four years were to pass before his return to the Church, and several more before this return was reflected in his novels, this renewal of belief begins to inform his writing from *Minuit* onwards.

The latter is a companion novel to *Le Visionnaire*, its principal setting another dream castle populated by characters who represent the various potential forms of the main character's destiny. But, after the revolt of the previous novel, it allows a place for Christianity among possible interpretations of life's meaning. Its protagonist is another adolescent at the crossroads: Élisabeth, whose mother has committed suicide, and who escapes from the custody of her insensitive aunt, to live first with the family of the kindly Lerat and later as a member of a community in a former abbey called Fontfroide. This final phase, which occupies most of the book, relates to what precedes as Manuel's stay at Nègreterre does to his life with his aunt. The Fontfroide sequence, as Green said, is 'un long rêve' (IV, 395), an alternative narrative to the 'real' story, a 'what might have been' if Élisabeth had been rescued from her aunt not by Lerat but by Edme, the leader of the Fontfroide community. A final sequence written by Green, but omitted before publication, makes the irreality of Fontfroide finally clear: in it, Élisabeth wakes from her dream, having fallen asleep in a train. Green, as ever, preferred enigma.

As in *Le Visionnaire*, the 'real' section of the book introduces the options facing the central character, which the 'dream' section then freely explores. As Élisabeth wanders through the streets after fleeing from her aunt's house, the polarities of sexual and spiritual adventure are already apparent. Nude statues arouse her curiosity, but she is also strongly aware of a need for the unknown, the excitement of the unseen. That this need is not to be equated straightforwardly with religious yearning has been made clear in the previous sequence in her aunt's house. There Christianity is represented by a crucifix reflected in a dirty mirror, sullied and neglected by the world, unattractive to the girl. Yet its presence comments on the godless world in which she finds herself, and in which reappears the imagery of the central part of *Léviathan*. The room in which Élisabeth sleeps is cluttered with old furniture, boxes and a bath 'comme un sarcophage' (II, 427), piled up 'de manière à former une pyramide' (II, 428). This reminder of the pyramids of coal in the yard where Guéret had hidden suggests the same pagan world, in which Christianity is as much a lost civilisation as ancient Egypt.

At Fontfroide spiritual options are emphasised afresh, in conflict with those of the body. Its life-style reverses normal patterns. The inhabitants sleep by day and live by night, seeking in the unseen world of the dark the light of truth. The former abbey is an image of Green's alternative scale of being, in which dream is the true reality, night the true day, sleep the true state of waking, and eventually death the gate to true life. It houses the broad spectrum of his immaterialism, from fantasy to Christianity. The latter extreme is represented by Monsieur Agnel, but there are gradations of the same quality in Agnel's cousins, Bernard and Bertrande. The latter is one of three old women who replicate the three (Élisabeth's mother and aunts) in the 'real' narrative. They are counterbalanced, structurally, by the three men, Urbain, Agnel and Edme, who seem to represent, respectively, papal authority, simple discipleship and free-flowing spirituality. Edme is the proponent of the synthetic view which he hopes will bind Fontfroide together: the view that all the forms which the life of the spirit takes are compatible with each other. One form is imagination, living one's life in 'le Palais de Nulle-Part'; another is orthodox religion. He reminds them of the prophecy of the last nun to leave Fontfroide: that the house will survive as long as the trace of the cross which marks its façade. The cross, to Edme, symbolises any 'ferment de vie spirituelle' (II, 600): the precise form this may take is less vital than the crucial lesson – that the so-called real world is vanity and illusion, that even Fontfroide itself may or may not exist.

Fontfroide is no more literally real than Manuel's castle. It is a structure of the mind, of Edme's mind and of that of Élisabeth, who searches from room to room for a model of her destiny. The house's literary ancestry is interesting. Its gloomy corridors and mysteriously locked doors, the girl's belief that she can hear someone or something in the corner of her room, or trying to enter – all this has echoes of Radcliffe's *Mysteries of Udolpho*. The floorless room, through which she nearly falls, evokes another gothic tale, *Kidnapped* by Green's much admired Stevenson. These familiar images are given new meanings and associations. Agnel had told Élisabeth that Fontfroide was 'très vieille et très solide' (II, 498); to his Christian eyes, Christendom might look solid, but to others it is a crumbling edifice: the furniture of the collapsed room is heaped together to form another of Green's pyramids (II, 549). Like the house of Usher, like Zola's doomed churches, the fabric of the spirit can be flimsy and insubstantial. The nature of the danger is clear, for the room in question used to be that of Eva, image of potential 'fall'. Élisabeth will eventually, and literally, fall as she tries to escape with her seducer.

The Christian sense of this denouement depends on Agnel. He, more than Edme, is the significant figure in the context of Green's now rapidly changing religious outlook, for through him Christianity undergoes a reassessment. When Élisabeth arrives at Fontfroide, Agnel is her initial guide, but is rejected by her as unattractive and austere. He enumerates the virtues enshrined in the house as if they were allegorical figures out of *Pilgrim's Progress*: Ordre, Méthode, Ponctualité, Attention, Diligence – the source of which is no doubt those mysterious characters Pur and Impur who inhabited Green's childhood (V, 704). The puritanical ring of all this deters the spirited Élisabeth. Agnel is so immersed in his static and lapidary values that he dreams of seeing them carved in stone on the façade of Fontfroide. This exemplar of Christianity is a comic and slightly ridiculous figure, whom Élisabeth imagines with a halo round his head. Later, she sees him in even less appealing terms, as a sinister man, a hypocrite, a man of 'order', characterised by the gloomy black cloth of his garments. The 'Pascal lamb' associations of his name disintegrate into less sublime animal imagery. With his 'profil de chèvre' (II, 504), he appears 'comme un animal' (II, 506). So far, Agnel represents all that Green, in his period of estrangement from the Church, identified as rebarbative in Christianity, but his role in the novel's final pages places him in a quite different light. He has been shot dead, but as Élisabeth falls to her death she sees him walking across the sky, radiant with joy; with a smile of sublime goodness, he holds out his hands to her, and she feels herself lifted from the earth 'par une force irrésistible' (II, 617). The final victory over death, about which Edme had been merely equivocal, is achieved by the novel's most unambiguously Christian character, finally transformed into a saviour.

* * *

Having tested the boundaries of faith and fantasy Green, in his next novel, attempted his most spectacular reconciliation of them. *Varouna* is a startlingly original tale, stylistically remote from the rest of his work. Its three parts embrace three historical periods, the Dark Ages, the Renaissance and the early twentieth century, linked by a mysterious chain which the young Welsh boy Hoël finds washed up on the shore in the first section and which is thrown back into the sea by the Christian hermit Marcion, only to come into the possession, at several centuries' interval, of the protagonists of the book's other two parts. Hoël's story is a series of encounters with evil, stemming from the malificence of the chain. The most spectacular of these involves a mysterious horseman called Abaddon, identified as the exterminating angel of Revelations, on a satanic black horse and dressed in scarlet like the Beast of the same biblical text. In a sequence reminiscent of Balzac's *Jésus-Christ en Flandre*, Abaddon causes a storm to threaten the small boat on which he has set sail with Hoël and his companions; those who trust in him are drowned, but those who believe in God, as in the Balzac tale, are saved. Surviving the tempest but not the encroachment of evil, Hoël later kills a woman to obtain her treasure – which turns out to be the chain. He is hanged as a murderer, but the words of the *Pater Noster* come to his lips at the end, as the only source of hope in a destiny of violence and death. The next owner of the chain, the sixteenth-century noblewoman Hélène, is the object of her own father's incestuous desire. The third part centres on a writer, Jeanne, who is preparing a historical work on the same Hélène, having discovered the chain in a museum. Hélène appears to Jeanne in a dream, and attaches to the chain a cross, to exorcise its evil power. In the chain can be seen a symbol of original sin, against which the faith of individuals across the full sweep of the Christian era acts as a counterbalance. But the text also raises the question of identity, as the later characters ponder the possibility that they are the re-incarnations of previous human lives. This same theme is treated in the less successful *Si j'étais vous. . .*, in which the novelist's occupational desire to occupy the bodies and minds of other individuals is translated into a fantasy in which characters are transformed into each other at regular intervals. The plot is a basically comic one, but the humour with which some of the episodes are related jars with the seriousness of others. At least three of the characters embody Green's religious preoccupations, and while religion is not the thematic centre of the book, the scene in which the transformations come to a halt because an innocent child refuses to be invaded by a corrupt theologian introduces a heavily moralising note.

Varouna and *Si j'étais vous. . .* were both published after Green's reconciliation with Catholicism, and in the former, Green told Jacques Maritain, he recognised 'une étude de pré-conversion'.[4] As literary works, they still belong to the fantastic phase of his writing. Very different are the novels that followed, for the reintegration of his faith into his life implied the recuperation of both as thematic material. The significance of this change was emphasised by Green in a comment on a critical study of *Moïra*, the first novel of this final phase of his career. This student of his work is wrong, he protests, in seeing *Moïra* as a novel as dependent on dream as its predecessors: for in it 'des garçons que j'ai connus m'ont servi de modèles' (IV, 1176). In substituting for the inspiration of dream, which had served him so richly for two decades, the inspiration of 'models', Green was turning the clock back to 1926, as a writer as well as as a Christian, and starting afresh. In deciding to draw the substance of his books from memory he was declaring his readiness at last to write of his own experience of the interrelationship of religion and sexuality.

Moïra translates into fiction the sexual self-discovery of the student years in Virginia. Characters, situations and events are common to the novel and to the third volume of Green's autobiography, *Terre lointaine*, in which he directly records this crucial period of his life. Reading the two texts side by side reveals the true-life origins of the students with whom the novel's central character, Joseph Day, shares his lodgings on his arrival at the university.[5] Joseph himself is not a self-portrait of Green, but rather a caricature of the Christian. His tendency to regard everyone whose path he crosses as material for salvation, his puritanical rejection of 'erotic' literary works, the extreme providentialism which inclines him to deny all liberty and self-orientation – these are unattractive qualities in Joseph which make the novel, on one level, a critique of religious fanaticism.

Joseph is a bigotedly pious young man who is forced by circumstance to face his repressed sexuality. He feels discomfort in the presence of any sexual thought or innuendo, and prefers not to think of the act by which his parents conceived him. When he hears his fellow student McAllister boasting of his exploits with women, he feels 'habité par le démon' (III, 44). The intensity of this reaction suggests that Joseph is no mere objective critic. So does his declared hatred of the sexual act, a blind force, signifying evil and madness. 'Nous sommes conçus,' he argues, 'dans des crises de démence' (III, 88). The conflict between sex and religion, so acute that he perceives these forces as 'deux royaumes [qui] s'expulsaient l'un l'autre du cœur de l'homme' (III, 155), is waged not only in the world around him, but most crucially between his own body and soul. Green excels at conveying the insuperable difficulty of the mind's thinking 'pure' thoughts from within its bodily base. Thus the anger of Joseph against his sexually promiscuous colleagues, which he thinks is grounded in Christ's example of taking a whip to the money-changers, stems from the violence of his unrecognised instincts. The body, not the soul, governs Joseph when, in a mock echo of Jesus' attack on the fig-tree, he vents his frustration on a sycamore. His father, too, had been a violent man, blinded in a fight over his wife, which suggests even more strongly the physiological rather than moral sources of Joseph's anger, as well as his blindness to the significance of his violence.

Sex, to Joseph, means the relationship between men and women, and thus woman is the focus of his inhibitions. He identifies his landlady Mrs Dare as a fallen creature because she smokes and wears rouge – a colour that portentously matches that of Joseph's hair, the 'chevelure de flamme' which draws many comments. He feels the urge to save her, even imagining her making a public confession like sinners in days gone by (and in the pages of *The Scarlet Letter*, of which Green seems to be thinking here). He is not wrong in suspecting a sexual undercurrent in Mrs Dare, but he is unaware that in this very fact lies her resemblance to him. As she tries to sleep, her thoughts playing on the fact that Joseph's bed is placed directly below hers, she prefigures his obsession with her adopted daughter Moïra. The bed is the objective link between the characters. The realisation that his room is normally Moïra's, and that she will reoccupy his bed during the vacation is enough to unleash in Joseph sexual fantasies about a girl he has not yet seen, and who is as yet an abstraction, an image of his sexual destiny. He spends the next night, as penance, on the floor of his room and not in the bed, re-enacting the scene in *Terre lointaine* in which the man whom Green calls 'Mark', on the only night he and Green shared the same room, slept on the floor. The Joseph who yields to temptation in bed and the Joseph who fights it on the floor represent the two individuals within him whose existence he describes to his friend David: 'C'est comme s'il y avait en moi deux personnes dont l'une souffrirait et l'autre regarderait souffrir' (III, 148). The bed represents the body of Moïra, just as to Mrs Dare it represents the body of Joseph. Metonymically the body of Joseph and the body of Moïra are one. She is less a character in her own right than the sexual element within him, and his eventual murder of her is in reality the Christian's attempt to free himself of the body.

All Joseph's sexual obsessions centre on the *woman* – Mrs Dare, Moïra, the scarlet prostitute of *Revelations*, and even Catholicism, the 'whore of Babylon' as his fierce Protestantism sees it. This is because of his unawareness of the existence of homosexuality. Moïra, however, because she is an inner state rather than an external object, represents all sexuality, even those forms of it of which Joseph is naïvely ignorant. Sexual attraction between men is the novel's true theme, deliberately cloaked by Green through the device of Joseph's sexual stereotyping.[6] It emerges first through the character of Simon, one of the students with whom Joseph lives in Mrs Dare's rooming-house. Simon tests Joseph by asking him what he thinks of the beauty of Greek male statues, and Joseph's unresponsiveness is a factor in Simon's eventual suicide. Jacques Petit argues (III, 1586) that Joseph's obsession with Moïra is an escape from the idea of death which this suicide introduces, but it is just as clearly an escape from the idea of sex with Simon, or with the 'Simon-type', that is, the male – for Simon's death has the precise function of removing him as a character so that he can become an abstract figure, a 'fâcheux augure' (III, 154) of Joseph's development.

The contrary, Christian, element in the novel is introduced through the character of the 'providential' David Laird, who is studying to be a Protestant minister and who helps and advises Joseph, albeit in a possessive and domineering way. But the most important male character, after Joseph, is Bruce Praileau. 'L'histoire de Joseph et de Praileau,' writes Green in his diary, '[est le] vrai sujet du livre' (IV, 1142). At first Joseph identifies Praileau as his enemy and picks a fight with him because Praileau has made a joke about his hair. It is the strength rather than the supposed cause of this emotional reaction to Praileau that is the more important at this stage. Its true nature is never acknowledged by Joseph, who sees his later affection for Praileau as just an example of the Christian love he feels for all men. What Green is expressing here is the memory of how he fell in love with 'Mark' in all innocence before he was even aware of what was happening. Like this relationship, that between Joseph and Praileau has no physical consummation, remains undeclared, retains a nobility and a beauty that contrast with the vulgarity of the novel's female characters. Although the violence which Joseph perpetrates on Moïra in the book's somewhat conventional denouement is the violence to which all sexuality is prone, Green's presentation of the Joseph-Praileau friendship carries a plea of disculpation for the great love of his adolescence. Yet it is significant that Joseph decides in the end not to accept the help of Praileau to escape from justice, but to follow David's advice and give himself up. Praileau is not, as J.-P. J. Piriou argues, Joseph's 'guardian angel'.[7] He represents escape into a terrifying unknown, and Joseph's reliance on the duller but more orthodox support of David is important in the context of Green's development.

* * *

Because the universally symbolic sex-object in *Moïra* is female, Green had still not faced homosexuality directly as the unambivalent subject of a novel. In the words of Jean, the central character of his next published novel *Le Malfaiteur*, 'cela tient à une lâcheté particulière aux gens de lettres' (III, 292). 'Je ne sais si vous lisez beaucoup de romans,' he writes to his cousin Hedwige, '[. . .] mais si vous faites de ces lectures surestimées,il est temps que je vous instruise d'une des petites ruses littéraires les plus en vogue. Sachez donc que lorsqu'un écrivain entretient son lecteur d'une *personne* dont il est épris, d'une créature incomparablement belle et bonne, d'un être unique et délicieux, sachez, ma bonne Hedwige, qu'il s'agit d'un homme' (ibid.). *Le Malfaiteur*, and especially the section entitled 'La Confession de Jean', represent Green's 'coming out', his overt portrayal of the homosexual – and his partial defence of him as a victim of circumstance and prejudice. The dates of the composition and publication of the greatly varying versions of *Le Malfaiteur* show how difficult this act of self-revelation was for him. Written in the late 1930s, the novel was published in 1955, but without 'La Confession de Jean', which holds the key to its meaning, and which was not restored until the novel's inclusion in the Pléiade edition of 1973.[8]

Le Malfaiteur groups under one roof a collection of incompatible characters – the puritanical M. Vasseur, his wife and her hypocritical sister Mme Pauque, the seamstress Félicie, the Vasseurs' sadistic daughter Ulrique and her husband Raoul, and the two main characters, the two 'poor cousins' who are tolerated in the household, the innocent Hedwige and the writer Jean. It is when Ulrique, who delights in playing match-making games at the expense of others' feelings, invites to the house Gaston Delange, with whom Hedwige falls romantically but profoundly in love, that Jean decides to write to Hedwige to warn her of her danger – for Delange is one of Jean's numerous former sexual partners. Jean's letter, or 'confession', containing the story of his own seduction by his tutor M. Pâris, never reaches Hedwige, but is intercepted by Mme Pauque, and is used by her against him. Hedwige, meanwhile, ignorant of the very existence of homosexuality but vaguely informed by a friend that Delange is unable to love a woman, thinks he must be – in another term whose meaning is semi-clear to her – impotent. When she learns the truth – that he and Jean have been lovers, that Jean has been in trouble with the police for frequenting homosexual prostitutes – Hedwige commits suicide, as Jean has done shortly before. The only sympathetic characters in the book are thus both victims of impossible loves, and by associating the two, Green ensures that the reader's compassion for Hedwige extends also to Jean. In the end, both die because of society's anti-homosexual prejudice, embodied in Vasseur, Félicie, Mme Pauque and the police, and *Le Malfaiteur* is a moving protest against such prejudice.

In the 'confession', the themes of homosexuality and religion converge. M. Pâris, who shapes Jean's destiny, is his *alter ego* or older version. Respected by the priests in the seminary where he has been educated, Pâris has an impeccable moral reputation because no 'vilaines liaisons' (III, 282) – that is, with women – can be imputed to him. He is known to his pupils as 'le Curé', and the mystery is why he has not become one. He is a believer, and a man with a certain priestly vocation, which it hurts him deeply to have rejected. But Pâris 'le curé' is also 'Pâris de Troie', seducer and sower of discord. The mythological associations of his name are underlined when he introduces Jean to the world of Greek statuary, whose beauty troubles him. The young Catholic recoils before these 'demons', the artefacts of a pagan culture and the creations of men who did not even go to mass! Through Pâris' admiration for the Greeks, Jean learns the relativity of religious institutions. He learns too, as Green had learned from his reading of the Realists, that art and religion are two separate domains. When Pâris is dismissed for initiating him into what his family regards as 'un culte honteux' (290), an obstacle is created between Jean and religious practice, no matter how unchanged his fundamental belief remains. Although religion dominates his youth, he recognises like his tutor before him that to enter holy orders is impossible.

It is already clear that *Le Malfaiteur* is Green's psychological autobiography, that through its fictitious events he is relating the process of his separation from the Church. In the later stages of the 'confession', when Jean meets Pâris again and is led by him into the pursuit of physical pleasure wherever he can find it, Green gives a barely fictionalised version of the series of nightly 'rendezvous with the devil' (V, 1356) which he describes with total frankness in the final volume of his autobiography, *Jeunesse*. But Jean insists that he feels no shame. The pursuit of male beauty gives an ennobling aestheticism to what others might call his vice. He feels 'persécuté toute ma vie pour l'amour du beau' (III, 312). Thus his so-called 'confession' is not a Christian confession at all. No remorse motivates it, but rather the spirit of self-justification. It is as unrepentant as the confessions of Rousseau. The novel's title, as Green admits in his *Journal* (V, 29), is ironic. Neither the character nor the novelist sees Jean as a wrongdoer. Jean is actually writing a novel called 'Le Malfaiteur', so that the title of Green's novel, with an ambiguity that owes a lot to Gide, could refer either ironically to Jean or directly to the book he is writing. It could equally well refer to Pâris, or more subversively to Ulrique or to Mme Pauque or to 'l'armée des honnêtes gens' (III, 312) who condemn what for the individual concerned is a natural and irresistible urge.

The novel's truculent rejection of moral censure on Jean might appear to make it sit uneasily among the novels of Green's later period. It belongs in spirit to the 1920s and 1930s, but its unexpurgated publication was an essential part of his courageous self-revelation. False remorse would have been a worse stance, as Jean's 'condition' is not susceptible of 'cure' by any amount of conversions or reconversions. The book's Christian sense is embodied in Hedwige, through Green's characteristic device of a dream in which she is invited by a beggar to abandon her material possessions. This call from Christ and the call of the body create an opposition to which Green, even in the more serene last phase of his career, never claimed to have a solution.

* * *

The need to confront his most intimate self leads Green, in *Moïra* and *Le Malfaiteur*, to stress sexual themes more than religious ones. In *Chaque homme dans sa nuit* a balance is restored and a conflict created between forces of equal might. Wilfred Ingram, a menswear salesman in an unidentified American city, is divided between his irresistible need for women and his inalienable Catholicism, a split that attains schizophrenic proportions, with 'toujours une partie de lui-même qui essayait d'oublier l'autre' (III, 492). The crucifix over Wilfred's bed is shut out of sight when its presence importunes him – in vain, for this material symbol of his faith is the only object of significance in his room, beside which all else is as nothing.

Conversely, when he goes to mass on Sunday morning, Wilfred would like to forget the events of the previous night – again without success, for the hands that hold his missal retain a physical memory of their pleasure. The two halves of Wilfred's life mark each other, derive their very intensity from the conflict that exists between them.

All the novel's other characters are merely amplifications of this conflict, the women objects of desire, the men all doubles or alternative states of Wilfred. The technique of *dédoublement* is an aspect of Green's work from the start, but is particularly evident in this novel, which despite its length and its many characters and sub-plots remains a monodrama, a succession of subtly angled mirrors designed to reflect the central character. The shop in which he works has, literally, twenty mirrors, which project images of him to infinity, in metaphorical expression of the multi-faceted and fragmentary nature of his personality. An interesting entry in Green's *Journal*, as long ago as 1930, records how his companion Robert de Saint-Jean, during a visit to the Petit Palais, commented that the three executioners in Poussin's painting *Le Massacre des innocents* were in fact one single decomposed figure caught in three positions, as in a magic-lantern film (IV, 67). This may or not have been the source of Green's own technique, but it provides a close analogy with it. Wilfred's devout former schoolfriend Tommy, a Wilfred who has not tried to escape God through sex; Freddie, a sexual neophyte who relies on Wilfred for advice and support against his obsessive fear of venereal disease; the hired hand Ghéza and Wilfred's customer Joe Loveday, both about to marry yet both obscurely attracted to Wilfred; James Knight, Wilfred's austere but admirable relation; Wilfred's homosexual cousin Angus – all these figures represent Wilfred as he might have been in different circumstances. Through them Green amplifies his central character into a broadly ranging portrait of the male libertine, and, he says, into a composite portrait of himself: 'Tous mes personnages n'en formaient qu'un seul qui était tellement moi-même que je ne les reconnaissais pas' (III, 1635).

There are two further male characters who need separate discussion for, one in each of the novel's two parts, they both predict and determine the outcome of Wilfred's life. The first is his uncle Horace, to whose death-bed Wilfred is called in the opening chapters, and with whom he has two essential elements in common: Horace is a Catholic, exceptional in an otherwise Protestant family, and a sexual libertine. Uncle and nephew are linked through two obsessive Greenian images: a nude female statue adorning the hallway of the family house, and the bed. Wilfred associates Horace's death-bed with his beds of pleasure, and by implication sex with death. This inevitable twinning makes both men's thoughts turn to the question of their salvation. Wilfred consoles himself that unlike Protestants he has a chance to purify himself in purgatory, while Horace expresses his anguish at his distance from God. For the first time in his long career, Green thus deals with a specific Catholic theme, and the chapter in which he explores and develops it (Part I, Chapter 11) is worth close study as an example of narrative procedure in the Catholic novel.

Wilfred has entered his dying uncle's room, where Horace expresses his fear both of death and of the priest, because he no longer believes in God. Does Wilfred believe, he asks? Yes, Wilfred believes all that the Church teaches. But he feels inadequate, mouthing conventional words to a desperate man. He seeks to escape, but 'quelque chose le maintint sur place' (III, 462). He has a bottle in his pocket, which he carries to give him courage in his sexual exploits, but now he drinks to face up to the idea of death, personified as a woman, watching him. The alcohol serves another purpose: it blurs Wilfred's senses, so that all that follows is only dimly comprehensible to him. His uncle asks him to pray for him, and Wilfred finds himself obeying, but his alcoholic remoteness from actions makes them seem mechanical and unwilled, his hand moving automatically from brow to shoulders as he forms the sign of the cross, the words of the Credo coming unwilled from his mouth. But when he kisses the crucifix, he is awakened: 'quelque chose lui brûla le cœur' (III, 463). Until now, Green has stressed Wilfred's total passivity, but this last action triggers off an undefinable inner response. Horace's fear is now absorbed into his nephew, who assumes the uncle's torment in place of the priest he is replacing by the dying man's bedside. Wilfred weeps, 'à cause de vous et à cause de moi, les deux' (III, 464). Green's familiar theme of *dédoublement* here takes on a Christian sense, as Wilfred expiates the sins of this double and in doing so glimpses potential saintliness. 'Tout est bien,' he tells Horace, and the text goes on:

> Ces paroles sortirent de sa bouche comme si elles avaient été prononcées par un autre et avec une netteté qui le tira brusquement de sa torpeur. Il resta quelque temps à genoux, dégrisé,

> l'âme tranquille, et il lui sembla pendant l'espace d'une minute qu'il était absent du monde, mais aucune idée précise ne se formait dans son cerveau, sinon que le bonheur envahissait tout, un bonheur étrange qui effaçait la vie quotidienne, le temps et la terre. Et pourtant il savait qu'il se trouvait dans cette chambre, au pied du lit aux colonnes d'acajou, et que par la fenêtre en face de lui il voyait les troncs des bouleaux qui brillaient comme de l'argent dans le crépuscule (III, 464–5).

There are several important details here: the substitution for Wilfred's agency and even his voice of those of 'another'; the detachment from material reality; the notion of spiritual happiness as remote from the 'real' world with its mahogany bedposts and silver birches. Green conveys here the otherness of spiritual experience. Like Barbey, he allows the possibility of rational explanation: the effects of drink, of fatigue, of stress; but the text does not invite us to accept these suggestions. When, at the end of the scene, the real priest arrives and the surrogate priest Wilfred leaves, the reader knows that their efficacy as far as Horace's state of soul is concerned is in inverse relation to their social roles.

Looking back on this scene two chapters later, Wilfred remembers his uncle's last words: a plea for love. This plea is now answered within Wilfred. As he feels the encroachment of death around the house, Wilfred experiences a feeling of love – for whom or what, he cannot say. Again words spring unwilled to his lips, and to an unknown interlocutor: 'Je t'aime!' To Horace's need to be loved, corresponds Wilfred's capacity for infinite love. His love for his uncle, for mankind, potentially for everyone and everything – in a word his saintliness – combats and exorcises the sexual love which is its debased form. The kiss he had given his uncle, with the words: 'Puisse ce baiser en effacer beaucoup d'autres' (III, 465), is a saving gesture for both of them. God has spoken to Horace through Wilfred, and the old man has died in a state of grace. As in *Le Nœud de vipères*, which Green's novel often recalls, Horace's religious sincerity at the moment of death is doubted by his family, but neither it nor Wilfred's election as the agent of grace can be denied on the evidence of the text. But Wilfred's saintliness is short-lived, for in exchange for his spiritual strength, Horace bequeaths to him his own moral burden, symbolised by the gift of letters and photographs. Possessed by the irrational desire to find the girl pictured in one of the latter, Wilfred rushes to the nearest bar: his struggle goes on.

The other important character is Max, who eventually kills Wilfred, and who is another image of his contradictions, developed to their extreme. At first an apparently Christian influence in Wilfred's life, bringing him pious reading matter, Max emerges later as a tempter, urging Wilfred to forget Christian morality. His dual nature as religious believer and homosexual prostitute makes of him a kind of male Magdalene: the thought that he is the devil incarnate crosses Wilfred's mind and is maliciously encouraged by Max himself. Max is forever shifting, a protean figure, a compulsive liar, all things to all men, and the archetype of the human condition as defined by Wilfred, a creature in whom both God and Satan live: 'D'une certaine façon, tout le monde était le diable. Le jeune homme en était convaincu, mais il croyait aussi, sans pouvoir l'expliquer clairement, que Dieu était aussi dans tous les êtres' (III, 553–4). When Wilfred strikes Max, the latter is transformed into the sublime image of the victim of human violence: Christ. But when, turning to Max as to a substitute priest to whom he can confess, Wilfred finds him instead in a state of homicidal madness, the roles are switched. Max takes from his pocket, not the rosary which he usually keeps there, but a revolver, and shoots the man who has trusted him. As the dying Wilfred forgives his murderer, the 'imitation of Christ', the role assigned to Wilfred by one of the books Max has given him, is realised. But on another level, if Wilfred and Max are facets of the same personality, then the 'murder', like Joseph Day's killing of Moïra, becomes suicide, the destruction by Wilfred of his own being, which has fallen into irretrievable disarray.

Through his encounters with Horace and Max, Wilfred becomes aware of a supernatural dimension. 'Il faudrait liquider le surnaturel,' Max tells him, 'revenez sur terre' (III, 568); but this is Max at his most diabolic, and the devil's self-denial is his most dangerous tactic. The supernatural holds the key to life's meaning. Wilfred may divide his time between three material sites of action, identified by Max as 'le magasin, le bar et l'église' (ibid.), but all these places are less real than the extra-material forces that penetrate them. Wilfred 'regardait le magasin autour de lui en se demandant s'il existait ailleurs que dans son imagination' (III, 546). The shop is part of a shadow world, as Green suggests again in the passage where Wilfred wonders how Jesus would have reacted to Freddie's terror of disease: 'Bien entendu, le Christ serait allé vers Freddie et il lui aurait remis ses péchés; du même coup, il aurait écarté la maladie. Dans ce magasin, sous ses lampes électriques, avec tous ces vendeurs et tous ces clients? Oui' (III, 551). The lights, the customers are relegated to the fringe of reality, become surplus paraphernalia. The bar in which Wilfred meets a girl with a cross dangling prohibitively in her bosom is less important topographically than metaphysically; it is a place where he feels pursued by God. As for the church, the objects he sees there, in direct reversal of how Realist writers see them, are literally the containers of divine substance: the ringing of the bell in mass is '[un] bruit frénétique [qui] annonçait que l'hostie n'allait plus être qu'une apparence et que le Seigneur allait se trouver là' (III, 494).

All these glimpses of a spiritual order occur within Wilfred, as do the inner 'voices' which he hears throughout the book, the voices of God and the tempter, in alternation. The integration of religious experience into the psychological mechanisms of character is one of Green's most notable achievements in *Chaque homme dans sa nuit*, but at the same time it leaves open the possibility of delusion on Wilfred's part. Like Mauriac's characters in similar circumstances, he is well aware of this: 'Voilà que j'imagine toutes sortes de choses' (III, 492). The Catholic novelist uses again the psychological option of the fantasy novel. Are the voices real or imagined, replies from God or reflections of self? The narrative strategy is to open a gap between the connivance of narrator and reader on the one hand and the defective self-knowledge of Wilfred on the other. In the end, responsibility for knowing the truth of God's purpose is passed from the narrator to God himself. As Wilfred lies dying in the same hospital room in which Freddie had died earlier, the question is raised of the significance of these converging lives. The narrator's answer is that this must remain part of a mystery beyond the grasp of Man's reason. 'A dire les choses exactement, Dieu seul le savait' (III, 702). Here, for the first and only time in Green, the novelist's cloak of Nessus is dropped, his affirmation of a divine perspective directly expressed. And, one might add, God is made into an element of fiction, not without a tinge of edifying sentimentality.

* * *

L'Autre, Green's next study of the mutual contamination of sex and religious faith, is given a very different tone by the two characters who narrate its central sections.[9] Both, at the time of telling their stories, are atheists or at least serious doubters, so that, even more intensely than Mauriac, Green approaches religious issues through the conscience of characters who challenge the beliefs of the author. Entries in the *Journal* during the writing of the book show the great difficulty he had in thinking himself into the mind of an atheist (V, 465), but by doing so he avoids the pitfall of edification, and writes one of his most original and interesting novels.

The first narrator is Roger, a young French architect who, in pre-war Copenhagen, seduces a girl called Karin despite the opposition of her strong Lutheran morality. The second narrative is Karin's, written after the war during which, her sexuality having been unleashed by Roger, she has been the mistress of German officers. Now despised and ostracised as 'l'Allemande', she has rejected religious belief. In a reversal of the original situation, she is confronted again by Roger, now a converted Catholic, who comes to find her, full of remorse for his seduction of her and determined to convert her in turn. Karin's narrative, written with an extraordinary intensity of both erotic feeling and spiritual thirst, is the account of this reconversion.

Karin's intellectual doubts include some of the classic objections of Realism. The sexual element in a woman's love of Christ, the 'exhibitionism' of confession, the incommensurability of a Christ who died nineteen centuries ago with the specificity of today's world – these notions would have interested Zola. When she accuses God, if he exists, of cruelty towards his creatures, Karin echoes the protesting voice of Maupassant. In suspecting that her spiritual experience is based on self-delusion or even on madness, she follows the example of Realist writers in general. Her sense of what is real is the same as theirs and the obverse of Green's: it is bounded by the material world, the world of concrete objects. She relates how one night, trying in vain to pray, she switches on the light, and finds the spiritual order banished by the reinvasion of familiar things: 'Le réel, c'était cela: ces meubles stupides, ce chintz bariolé et cette ruine en sucre, le gâteau de la boulangère' (III, 979). In another scene, in which she associates her sexuality with objects, rejecting Roger's moralising in favour of the reassuringly real dressing-screen behind which she visualises them tearing off their clothes (III, 841), the physicality of her emotion is as strong as that of Zola's 'brutes humaines'. Karin herself, needless to say, is not conscious of such literary parallels and neither, in all probability, is Green, but these echoes are not coincidental. They reflect again the fact that the Realist corpus is the most substantial body of anti-Christian ideas in modern French literature and that the Catholic novelist, consciously or unconsciously, is bound to create his own world in opposition to it.

This, through Karin, is precisely what Green does. Her rediscovered belief embodies responses to many of these objections. Foremost among them is the realisation that the material world can be radically altered through the presence of Christ. Roger has described to her how, while watching two old women praying in church, his scorn for their gullibility suddenly gave way to the feeling of an invisible presence. Karin in turn longs for a physically present Christ, 'non pas du tout comme un fantôme, mais dans son corps, tel qu'il a paru en Judée', to whom she would react physically, kissing his feet and drying them with her hair (III, 923). Like Wilfred, she instinctively murmurs: 'Je t'aime', and the certainty of Christ's presence comes to her, in contrast to which the world is no more real than a bad dream.

To relate this sense of presence to a specifically Catholic belief, Green, in the final sequence of her narrative, shows Karin in church, asking a young girl to explain to her the meaning and function of the objects of the mass, especially what she calls 'ce petit disque blanc' (III, 984): the host. In the latter, the girl assures her, Christ is present. 'Vous ne le voyez pas,' says Karin, but she knows what the answer will be – that faith does not depend on seeing. On being told again by the girl that she believes in the central tenet of Catholic faith and practice – the real presence of Christ in the host – Karin says: 'Moi aussi, je le crois' (III, 985).

The case for belief, as presented in *L'Autre*, is thus based on a conception of reality that is directly opposed to Realist conceptions of the universe. Matter is not just matter; it can be penetrated by the spirit. In arriving at such a conclusion, however, Green, as entries in his *Journal* during the composition of the novel show, was conscious of the familiar Catholic novelist's bugbear: edification. 'Je ne veux pas,' he wrote, 'que le roman que j'écris en ce moment tourne au récit pieux' (V, 517). He even makes Karin herself object, slightly artificially, to her role in one of those 'affreux ouvrages qu'on appelle des romans chrétiens', in which the protagonist is caught in conversion like a fly in a spider's web (III, 955). This fear of entrapment is repeated even in her final declaration of belief, in the closing lines of her narrative. Breaking what she calls 'l'édifiant silence', she tells the young priest who has so sensitively guided her, 'Je suis tombée dans un piège' (III, 986). Green ensures here a necessary balance between the novel's ideology and the integrity of his heroine. Even in belief, Karin retains her sense of irony, realises the cost of her conversion in terms of freedom. The question even arises: is her final conversion final at all? Her character has been built on change; after her earlier statement of belief 'pour toujours' (III, 924) and desire to be baptised as a Catholic, she had accused herself of madness and written to the priest: 'Travaillez de votre côté à l'extension d'un royaume où je n'entrerai jamais pour la simple raison qu'il n'existe pas' (III, 927). What guarantee is there that Karin will not once again renounce the belief to which she has now returned?

The problem posed here is identical to that of *Le Nœud de vipères*, and Green's solution is the same as Mauriac's: the death of the central character in the moment of belief, achieving both the implied Christian meaning of the book and the illusion of the unpredictability and open-endedness of life. Karin, at this point in her narrative, stops writing and, in a brief epilogue, goes out, is accosted by two men, and falls to her death in the dock. The only certainty is that she has not given up this life willingly: 'elle remonta avec une seule pensée dans tout son être: vivre, puis de nouveau, exténuée, elle coula sans se débattre' (III, 990). Green's ultimate concern is for his character, not for his message, and he steers the novel safely away from becoming a mere exemplary fiction.

Chaque homme dans sa nuit and *L'Autre* are optimistic novels in that the central characters of both are spiritually saved even though both die. But in terms of the central problem of Green's life, the optimism has to be mitigated, for neither is shown to defeat the tyranny of sexual desire. In recent years, Green's *Journal* has suggested that he leans increasingly towards an ideal solution of the problem: a love for another human being that is not dependent on sexual expression. Possibly, he himself found that love, but it is a final sign of his consummate honesty that he does not impose such a solution on his young, tormented and divided characters. It is significant that in his most recent novel *Le Mauvais lieu* he does not directly seek a solution to the sexual problem through religion, but rather through depicting sex in ugly colours. In a series of characteristic doubling effects and mirror imges, this novel creates two central women characters – a frustrated widow and her sexually threatened young niece; two male predators and, despite the title, two 'mauvais lieux': a brothel called 'Le nid d'amour' and a school full of lesbian teachers and pupils. Christian elements are introduced only indirectly: religious images that hang neglected on walls, a silver cross dangling from the neck of a dead servant, a schoolmistress who prays for deliverance from sexual desire. Green has returned in this final text, reminiscent of both *Léviathan* and *Minuit*, to what might be called, in Mauriac's phrase, his 'indirect apology' for Catholicism.

8

The Bernanosian Synthesis

The coexistence in Georges Bernanos' novels of detailed external description and non-realistic forms of discourse has often been noted. Max Milner's observation that the 'metaphysical' landscape of his first novel is not 'dénué de réalisme'[1] is balanced by Philippe le Touzé's view of his last as 'à la fois réaliste et fantastique'.[2] Henri Debluë has shown the predominance of dream in the whole of the Bernanos corpus,[3] and J. C. Whitehouse the close link between natural and supernatural worlds in Bernanos' 'amalgame de spiritualité et de réalisme'.[4] Among novelists, François Mauriac, who often admitted the difficulty of reconciling the description of grace with that of fallen nature, commented generously on Bernanos' great gift: 'de rendre le surnaturel naturel, d'introduire à cette vie de la grâce qui est pour lui l'unique réalité'. Bernanos' art, Mauriac went on, 'se rattache au naturalisme car c'est en ne quittant pas un instant la nature d'un pas qu'il se heurte à chaque instant au surnaturel.'[5] As these comments suggest, Bernanos' work represents the union of the two currents explored in this present book. The expression of his Catholic vision of the world turned on his adaptation of the Realist modes which had come to represent the norm for practitioners of the novel. His novels often allude specifically to the struggle for the philosophical control of the genre and make conscious use of Balzacian and Zolian models as the starting-point for the transformation of the real. More sharply than Mauriac or Green, he was aware of his role in combatting the positivistic dominance of the novel. In this awareness, he rejoins Huysmans and Bloy and, above all, Barbey d'Aurevilly, his idol and literary mentor. Like Barbey he was conscious that Balzac's elevation of the genre to major status had turned it into a rich prize for both sides in a conflict which extended beyond literature.

A crucial text for the study of these issues is Bernanos' interview with Frédéric Lefèvre in 1926, in which he states that even his acknowledged 'master' Balzac does not satisfy him 'fully'. Balzac was more sensitive than any other novelist to the rhythms of human passion, but his canvas was limited to 'le réalisme humain', never extending to the more universal sphere of what Bernanos calls, coining a vital phrase, 'le réalisme catholique'. Balzac had seen the importance of Catholicism as a force for social order and, in literary terms, as a source of philosophical truth on which to build his hundred-odd fictions. But Balzac's Catholicism did not penetrate 'la matière même', nor did it inform his study of the inner recesses of conscience, 'la part de nous-mêmes dont le péché originel a détruit l'équilibre'. In other words, in neither of the domains which he had sought to encompass, the material universe and the psychological one, had Balzac, supreme analyst though he was, achieved 'ce suprême effort de synthèse' which would have afforded him the true totality of perception for which he strove.

Picking up Bernanos' allusion to the necessary 'synthesis' of a 'Catholic Realism', Lefèvre provocatively asks whether he does not risk obscuring his originality beneath the label 'Catholic novelist' – 'étiquette,' he adds, 'qui me demeure d'ailleurs incompréhensible: le roman catholique n'existe pas'. Bernanos' rejoinder: 'Vous avez parfaitement raison' is ironic. Catholicism, he explains, is not an option, not a particular optic on life which the writer can choose to adopt or reject. All art which seeks to enlighten the inner life of Man is bound to explore sin, and thus all literature which sets itself this aim is Catholic literature: all novels are Catholic novels. It is only in this tongue-in-cheek sense that Bernanos denies the existence of a *specifically* Catholic form of novel: the Catholic novel is not a subcategory of the novel, but is as synonymous with the genre itself as Zola had deemed Naturalism to be.

Lefèvre presses again: is not the Catholic novelist bound to be unexciting, clinging as he does to a classical conception of man? Bernanos answers that the classical 'honnête homme' is a mechanical animal, invented by Descartes and Malebranche, an automaton dependent on the functioning of springs and levers, a product of a rationalist age which had provided novelists with false models of character. Missing from the prescription is the notion of evil, which in turn devolves from the omission of the supernatural – 'les anges et les démons, qui ne subsistaient que dans les antithèses du père Hugo!' Hugo's poem *La Fin de Satan*, he says, was symptomatic of the nineteenth century's view of evil, denying its supernatural essence by making Satan first irrelevant, then non-existent. And shorn of the notion of evil, morality was reduced to mere 'hygiene'. Science usurped the territory once mapped by theology and reduced the inner life to a battle of conflicting instincts.

The novel, he goes on, is the first loser in this misappropriation of truth: 'Le romancier a tout à perdre en écartant de son œuvre le diable et Dieu: ce sont des personnages indispensables. Il est vrai que le naturalisme avait tourné la difficulté: il changeait l'homme en bête.' And Naturalism's heritage is plain: 'le roman moderne manque de Dieu, mais le diable lui manque aussi'. Developing what Mauriac had said about Proust just a year or two earlier, Bernanos adds that God is absent without trace from the work of the latter. Asked by Lefèvre if, in literary terms, this matters, he replies that it does. Proust is an observer; as Realism's heir he shares its ambition to record the whole of reality. Thus his indifference to good and evil is a flaw, for it causes him to omit what are not optional but essential elements of the real. Proust's world, like Balzac's, is less than total because of a moral blindness which stems from a metaphysical one.[6]

Bernanos developed these ideas to a lecture audience during this same period. The novelist, he argued, must enter the domain to which he was traditionally denied access by the supposed rules of the genre: the spiritual. 'Et sitôt le seuil franchi de ce monde invisible,' he said, 'j'y ai rencontré le diable et Dieu.' To omit these supernatural perspectives from his view of man is to restrict the novelist's role to that of a classifier, driven by mere curiosity, as far from the truth as 'un vieux naturaliste' is from recreating the dinosaur when he reassembles its skeleton. Although he uses 'naturaliste' here in its scientific sense, the analogy holds good for the literary meaning too. The literary Naturalist is the namer of parts, whose 'analysis' falls short of 'synthesis'. The latter is only complete when – and here Bernanos uses one of his most cherished images – 'le surnaturel [. . .] fait brèche dans sa fragile enceinte' (E, 1078–85).

* * *

The antithesis of the ideal Bernanosian writer is embodied in the figure of Ganse, in the posthumously published *Un mauvais rêve*. It is clear which particular novelist Bernanos has in mind as at least a partial model. Ganse is not Balzac, though he invites the comparison. His working routine leads his secretary, who at six in the morning finds him bearing all the physical signs of a night's literary labour, to exclaim: 'Je croyais voir Balzac, mon cœur . . .'.[7] Balzac has been his idol and example in the writing of his 'œuvre gigantesque', but his is a cruder talent, 'fait pour les grosses besognes' (879). He writes 'niaiseries', but his work derives its strength from one central organising idea or subject, and he has produced forty books at a steady five pages a day. He is a free-thinker, disdaining mysticism. If he has a religion, it is that of work: 'Le travail justifie tout' (938). He has been attacked by pious newspapers for his predilection for the vulgar: 'Je parle aux ventres, j'émeus les ventres . . . [. . .] Un ventre est un ventre' (915). All these details obviously point to Zola, although the traces are smudged by references in the text to Zola himself, mentioned as well as Balzac as one of Ganse's most admired forebears. It would be an overstatement to affirm that Ganse is Zola, but he is certainly the representative of the Realist tradition out of which, says his adopted nephew Philippe, it is hard for young writers to break. Realism is his aim: he seeks to create 'l'illusion que ces guignols existaient réellement' (894). His working method is to depict models from life and to expand them into types. When the novel opens, he is writing a book based on the life of his secretary. Such flat mimesis is supposedly redeemed by what Ganse sees as his penetrating 'look': 'il disait lui-même, après Balzac, qu'il «plombait les imbéciles»' (942). 'Seeing' is the basis of his art, which has no other end but itself and the prestige and money that it brings, and in relation to which human beings are mere 'guignols', 'marionnettes' or 'imbéciles'. A novelist with eyes but no vision, subordinating life to documents – in short, a Realist novelist, as seen from Bernanos' particular point of view – Ganse is Bernanos' negative, the bad writer at the heart of his bad dream.[8]

That Zola, more than Balzac, should bear the brunt of Bernanos' anti-Realist scorn is due in part to political reasons, for Bernanos never forgave Zola's support of Dreyfus. Zola 'le Vénitien' (E, 927), Zola 'le romancier génois' (E, 264) – the imprecision of the geographical epithet matters less than the scorn it conveys for this less than true Frenchman – had dealt 'un coup terrible [. . .] au moral français' (ibid.) with the publication of *J'accuse*. But no less subversive to the values for which Bernanos stood was the brand of realism in which Zola traded as a novelist. 'Il y a des gens bornés,' complained Bernanos to Jorge de Lima, 'qui n'admettent que les réalités de Zola.'[9] Zola is a frequent caricatural figure in his novels. Ganse shares, as well as Zola's working routine, his alleged sexual inhibitions: 'Il est chaste comme l'autre – comme Émile Zola' (878). The writer St-Marin, who appears in the final section of *Sous le soleil de Satan* and in whom most critics see the reflection of Anatole France, is bestowed with the same visceral panic at the thought of death as that which is often attributed to 'le père du naturalisme et des Rougon-Macquart' (289). Likewise, Arsène in *Monsieur Ouine* has an obscenely erectile nose with an olfactive capacity for which he is horrified to find himself compared to 'M. Émile Zola' (1394).

More seriously, Zolian echoes are used to underline important themes and aspects of character. Cénabre, the renegade priest of *L'Imposture*, comes from a family background of which the details are so reminiscent of *L'Assommoir* – his mother was a washerwoman like Gervaise, his father an alcoholic like Lantier – that they can only be conscious and deliberate. The point of the allusion is to refute, as an explanation of Cénabre's apostasy, the theories of heredity popularised in the *Rougon-Macquart*. 'Peut-être,' writes Bernanos, 'une autre hypothèse sera-t-elle mieux acceptée' (364): what has made Cénabre what he has become is not the allegedly irresistible force of his genetic inheritance but, on the contrary, his rejection of it, his free decision to turn his back on the God-given self. The same contrast is exploited in *Sous le soleil de Satan*, when the abbé Donissan meets Mouchette. Invested with miraculous knowledge of her crime, the priest tries to lead the girl into a spirit of self-charity, for as the inheritor of a burden of sin, accumulated through the previous generations of her family, the scales are loaded against her. The names of her ancestors pour inexplicably from Donissan's mouth, although until this moment he has never met Mouchette or heard of her family: 'C'étaient ceux des Malorthy, des Brissaut, des Paully, des Pichon, aïeux et aïeules [. . .]. (Ta tante Suzanne, ton oncle Henri, tes grand-mères Adèle et Malvina ou Cécile) . . .'. These names lead him back to 'le noyau du monstre même, la faute initiale, ignorée de tous, dans un cœur d'enfant' (206). Here Bernanos transposes into a Catholic context the 'scientific' genealogy of Zola's Naturalism, arriving at the 'faute initiale' of original sin by exploiting the idea of heredity, not as explicative cause, but as suggestive metaphor. The Catholic novelist thus repays the Realist by doing what the latter had often done to him: exploit for his own ends the adversary's cherished beliefs.[10]

Even without such precise examples, the challenge to Zola's beliefs and values is inherent in everything that Bernanos wrote, and above all in his insistence on the reality of the supernatural. If Man, he writes in *Les Grands cimetières sous la lune*, is capable of more good and more evil than moral philosophers give him credit for, it is because he is made in the image of God but vulnerable to the infiltration of the 'le plus grand des anges, tombé de la plus haute cime des Cieux' (E, 399). Man's enemy is no abstraction, to be understood 'à la façon cartésienne' (E, 400), but a supernatural being. Bernanos' resurrection of Satan, against the tidal wave of enlightened thinking which has transformed our culture in the last three centuries, is the most radical gesture of defiance of the modern age that one is likely to find in any twentieth-century writer. To do this within the genre which is the prime artistic product of that cultural transformation is an act of breathtaking boldness. Whatever one thinks of Bernanos' beliefs, his attempt to house them in novels challenges all the assumptions about the nature of novels that the twentieth century inherited from the nineteenth. The struggle for the soul of the novel here reaches its point of greatest intensity.

* * *

The three sections of *Sous le soleil de Satan* are each constructed on an act of diabolical invasion of the human sphere. In the prologue, Mouchette, her initially healthy spirit of revolt against her stultifying family background corrupted by satanic intervention, kills the wretched lover on whom has rested her hope of escape. In the middle section, the abbé Donissan undergoes several onslaughts from hell, notably when Satan appears before him in the guise of a horse-dealer. In the final section an older Donissan, still tormented by the devil, is tricked by him into attempting the resurrection of a dead child. Donissan's supernatural interpretation of these events, which Bernanos invites the reader to adopt, is ineffectually challenged in the prologue by the spoof medical terminology of the local doctor, who dismisses Mouchette's state of mind as 'hyperémotivité' and 'hyperésthésie' (98–9) resulting from the alcoholism of her parents, and in the last section by the 'cartesian' priest the curé de Luzarnes, a former chemistry teacher who prescribes better 'hygiene' as a remedy for Donissan's overworked faculties. As well as through the negative rhetoric of these obviously 'wrong' characters, Bernanos seeks to persuade by the gradual transformation of the novel's social and psychological base. The banal, even comic cameo of village society – a village with its womanising squire, medical officer and self-made industrialist, and marked by quarrels between church and secular authorities – undergoes total change when Mouchette confronts her lover, the aristocrat Cadignan. Her scorn for his fear of her father, his request for money in return for leaving her alone, his sexual approach to her, ignite a spark of violence in her. But over and above this psychological change, there is a sense of evil in the air. The door blows open, a stagnant odour fills the room – the wind, the nearby marsh, no doubt; but the uncanniness of the atmosphere in which Mouchette seizes Cadignan's shotgun and kills him is an active factor in the events. Likewise, when she visits her second lover, Doctor Gallet, strange noises are heard in the house, for which rational reasons are offered, but the hint of an unnatural presence is as strong as in any scene from gothic fiction.

The aim of this 'prologue' is to lay the foundations of the supernatural battle in which Donissan will find himself involved, and to this end Bernanos establishes Mouchette's enslavement to her 'abominable amant' (98) – not Cadignan or Gallet, but Satan. The association between her and hell is made explicit in the interlinked sentences she addresses to Gallet: 'Tu ne crains pas l'enfer et tu crains ta femme' and 'Tu as peur d'elle et tu n'as pas peur de moi' (108), and also in Bernanos' device, learned from Barbey, or interjecting words like 'diable' and 'satané' in both ironical and portentously literal senses, the effect coming from the ambiguity of tone in each instance. The 'satané député' (63), the 'diable d'homme' (66), the 'médecin du diable' (77) and the expletive/pathetic 'sacré pays de France' (69) are all subtle generators of meaning, as is the first allusion in the novel to the as yet unnamed young priest who has just arrived in the parish: '[ce] grand diable de vicaire' (82). Only with hindsight will the reader know that this priest is to be the novel's central character. The narrator who tells his story, however, possesses not only hindsight, but many other forms of 'sight' too, which determine the way in which Donissan is presented.

The pitch of the narrative voice represents the various levels of presentation, and implies different degrees of narratorial insight. Two levels are discernable in the opening pages, a 'higher' and 'lower' level. The first paragraph, which begins: 'Voici l'heure du soir qu'aima P.-J. Toulet . . . .', is pitched on the boundary of the fictive and the real: a fictive moment created in the text, a real person – the poet Toulet, who exists outside the text. Thus is suggested the narrator's total control of temporal register, of real time and fictional time. 'Voice l'heure . . .' is repeated three times, the third introducing a classic, 'Balzacian' history of Mouchette's family, articulated by the demonstrative adjectives that are characteristic of this mode of narration: 'un de *ces* Malorthy du Boulonnais . . .' (59), of whose lineage the narrator obviously knows all. Historian and timekeeper, he can observe simultaneous events: 'Dans le même temps, M. le marquis de Cadignan menait au même lieu la vie d'un roi sans royaume' (60). But as the narrator descends from the eagle's nook of these opening lines to begin his account, he disclaims omniscience: 'Entretemps, il [Cadignan] courait les filles; *on le disait, au moins*' (60 – my italics). The contrast could hardly be starker between the two narrative and epistemological levels: there is a vantage-point from which all seems clear and one from which our knowledge of men is relative and uncertain. The text switches from one to the other, but the coexistence of the two is constantly implied throughout the narration of the individual fictional acts.

The two levels subdivide into yet higher and lower branches of themselves. The Balzacian narrative voice is competent in the numerical and temporal registers: 'un soir . . .', 'huit jours plus tard . . . .', 'le lendemain . . . .' (62), 'c'était un matin du mois de juin . . . .' (67), 'la demoiselle atteignit seize ans' (61), 'Cadignan avait atteint son neuvième lustre . . .' (62); but there are areas into which it cannot intrude. The precision of the calendar and the clock is abandoned between Chapters III and IV of the prologue, the scene with Gallet following hard on that with Cadignan without any information being given of the interval of some months during which Mouchette has become more fully enmeshed by Satan. Such supernatural events lie outside Balzacian chronometry. So too, as the text specifically says, does knowledge of the future: 'literary psychologists' have the means to 'reconstituer le passé, mais non de prédire l'avenir' (83). But the sense of a providentially designed future, a divine plan of our destiny, is part of the Christian's idea of what constitutes reality. Therefore, Bernanos is implying, the full significance of his characters' lives, in which every choice has implications for all eternity, cannot be expressed without the creation of a narrative level loftier still than the so-called "omniscient" Balzacian level, which is not omniscient at all. So Bernanos intertwines with his narrative what one might call a kind of 'super-text', which informs us of Donissan's *later* status as 'le futur saint de Lumbres'. Through this super-text, making past, present and future equally accessible, catching life both in the moment of experience and in the perspective of providence, he can also inform us of other characters' destinies: those of minor figures like the père de Charras, 'futur abbé de la Trappe d'Aiguebelle' (143), or the servant woman who is to become Mère Marie des Anges (148). And of Donissan himself he can tell us that 'le saint de Lumbres, un jour, connaîtra la face de son ennemi' (147), that 'cet homme [. . .] regardera quarante ans le pécheur avec le regard de Jésus-Christ' (143). As well as predict, the super-text can also judge both Donissan's supernatural heroism and his fatal errors, and can even comment on the movements of God and of Satan – 'l'autre, qui s'est glissé entre Dieu et lui . . .' (147). Bernanos is not the first Catholic novelist to wish to predict and judge: the cases of Bloy and Mauriac have shown that this desire is a natural concomitant of Christian belief; but what often appears merely clumsy in Mauriac's casual references to his characters' futures or feverish asides on their conduct is made much more convincing, both technically and philosophically, by Bernanos. 'On a souvent reproché à Bernanos,' comments Debluë, 'ses interventions personnelles dans le récit' (op. cit., 80). But such reproaches miss the point: the voice of the super-text is not that of the 'person' Bernanos, who could never have laid claim to such cosmic understanding, but that of a narrative persona, not God and not Man, but viewing the world from the level of God, as the Catholic novelist's pursuit of a true angle of vision is bound to necessitate. Bernanos, in a technical *tour de force* which has not been previously analysed, has created a quite new narrative angle on a plane above that of the omniscient Balzacian narrator.

As for the lower level of narrative, it also divides. For the most part, it corresponds to the partial and uncertain knowledge of the characters. When Donissan and his superior, Menou-Segrais, discuss the reality or otherwise of the appearance of Satan, the super-text is silent: here is an issue on which the characters and reader have to decide, and the objective narrative style is the appropriate one. But its ultimate inadequacy is suggested in the curé de Luzarne's written report on the events of the final section, where so-called objectivity leads to distortion of truth. 'Je le vis, ou plutôt nous le vîmes . . . ' (247), writes Luzarnes. In this, and in his declared reasons for wishing to witness Donissan's attempted ressuscitation of the dead boy – 'par simple curiosité, pour voir' (250) – there can be recognised the spirit of Ganse and the caricature of the uncommitted Realist novelist, morally blind because he sees only with the eyes of the body.

These narrative levels, ultimately four in all – the super-text, the 'omniscient', the objective and (in the last part) the false – are more than technical devices; they effectively create a value structure, a hierarchy of truths and falsehood which controls the way in which Donissan's destiny is to be interpreted. His status as 'l'homme extraordinaire' is established by the heroic epithets of the super-text, and the extra-temporal significance of his saintliness by the discordance of its verb tenses. 'En quelques semaines,' runs the text, 'l'effort de cette volonté que rien *n'arrêtera* plus désormais *commença* d'affranchir jusqu'à l'intelligence' (135). The future 'n'arrêtera pas' grounds the sense in the real present of the reader, which is its natural grammatical concordance; the past historic 'commença' identifies the action in the context of a fictional past. Something is achieved here of Christ's sublime defiance, so admired by Bloy, of the chronology of orthodox narrative: 'Before Abraham was, I am.' Alternating with this is the less clairvoyant objective text, the presentation of the man Donissan in his earthly situation, to be interpreted by the reader or by the other characters. His story begins on Christmas Day, but the identification of this beginning with the birth of the Christ-child is not pressed on us by the super-text. It is suggested, for the reader to make of it what he will, through Menou-Segrais' words to the abbé Demange: 'Tout à l'heure, le monde commence' (125). Similarly, Donissan's closeness to the crucified Christ is suggested, not imposed, by the wound in his side, caused by his self-flagellation (132). Partial understanding is everywhere: Menou-Segrais 'ne démêlait qu'à demi' the inner struggles of his young colleague, for he is privy only to the 'signes physiques' which show on the surface (135). What external signs there are, soon disappear: 'Mais, de cette lutte intérieure, rien ne paraîtra plus au-dehors, jamais,' the intervening super-text informs us. 'Le visage est impassible, la haute taille ne se courbe plus, les longues mains ont à peine un tressaillement' (137). The language of the body, which Zola had regarded as a more reliable code than the scrutiny of a non-existent soul, vanishes from the novel, leaving, not the vacuum which Zola's theory implies, but a new dimension of verbal language, spoken through the mouth of the abbé: 'Les mots les plus communs, les plus déformés par l'usage reprennent peu à peu leur sens, éveillent un étrange écho. «Quand il prononçait le nom de Dieu presqu'à voix basse, mais avec un tel accent, disait vingt ans après un vieux métayer de Saint-Gilles, *l'estomac nous manquait . . .*' (137–8). This is more than a casual colloquialism: the old man did not need his stomach, or any bodily organ, to communicate with the priest, who 'entre dans les âmes par la brèche' (137).

Not that Donissan is superhuman. In conventional terms he is vulnerable, unimpressive; he stammers or speaks clumsily. He is grounded in earth like all men. He is of peasant stock, though his heavenly preoccupations make of him 'un paysan infidèle à la terre' (136). His duality is expressed in his 'pas rapide et un peu gauche', in his gait: 'son long corps penché en avant, les mains croisées derrière le dos' (136) – spiritual impetus, in both postures, inhibited by a physical brake. When 'il parcourait en tous sens l'immense plaine', the non-mimetic 'en tous sens' creates a mythical effect, but this multi-dimensional spiritual advance is anchored in the real by place-names: Brennes, the valley of the Canches. The landscape which Donissan inhabits has the same duality as he, its grainy realism permeated by symbol: clogging, inhibiting mud, cart-shafts pointing heavenwards (136).

In the novel's central sequence, Donissan's encounter with Satan, the mutability of this landscape into something other than itself effects the shift from nature to supernature, parallel to that from text to super-text in the modulations of narrative voice. Setting out on foot to visit a neighbouring parish, Donissan feels tired. He sits down 'sur la terre, au croisement des deux routes de Campreneux et de Vertou' (159): at a symbolic crossroads as well as a topographically exact one. From this point the familiar country, the well-worn track leading past the cemetery, is replaced by 'un champ inconnu dont la terre [. . .] luisait vaguement' (165). The very slope up which he climbs to obtain a better view of his surroundings disappears behind him. Time follows space into disorientation; Donissan finds himself in that time zone unknown to Balzac, 'une minute inexplicable' (166). At first, he takes comfort in the familiarity of objects, the hedgerows and barbed wire persuading him of the ordinariness of his adventure. But into this physical world there now enters the being which, the super-text has warned us a few pages earlier, we regard at our peril as a merely abstract notion. Donissan discovers he is not alone. By his side walks what seems at first to be an ordinary little man, jovial and good-humoured, an itinerant horse-dealer. But this creature is spatially unstable, like objects in a dream: 'tantôt à gauche, devant, derrière' (168). Although it is now pitch dark, he advances with confidence, pushing out of the priest's way 'le fil barbelé d'une clôture invisible'. He knows this place, he assures him, and does not need eyes to find his way through a darkness in which even 'le plus *malin*' could not see. He comforts Donissan, aids him like the good Samaritan when he stumbles through fatigue, then, his tenderness lurching in another direction, embraces him, kisses him on the lips, and reveals the identity that the priest has already guessed: 'Tu as reçu le baiser d'un ami; [. . .] je t'ai rempli de moi, à mon tour, tabernacle de Jésus-Christ, cher nigaud! [. . .] Mes délices sont d'être avec vous, petits hommes-dieux, singulières, singulières, singulières créatures! [. . .] moi, Lucifer . . . .' (174). Then comes the withdrawal. True to his nature as fount of untruth, Satan denies his own essence; he is, he pleads, just a poor dealer in Breton and Norman farmhorses. The text then lurches into total nightmare, as he assumes grotesque shapes, does somersaults, makes a pebble glow with heat and explode, in an exhibition as full of the conventional party-tricks of demonology as the satanic incarnations of Lewis' *Monk*.[11] Finally, he tells Donissan that he has been sent by God to try him, and to bestow on him the gift of miraculous insight into himself and others, which the ordinary vision of his 'yeux de boue' can never achieve. He turns into a double of Donissan, and the latter has his first experience of this supernatural faculty, seeing himself 'non seulement dans le présent, mais dans le passé, dans l'avenir . . .' (180): that is, as the super-text sees him, in an all-temporal clarity and totality. The novel functions here as a commentary on its own narrative levels, contrasting them with the limited sense-based epistemology of Realism, and finally confirming what Bernanos' super-text represents: an optic of saintliness, forged from the imagination of a writer to whom the experience of saintliness was a frustratingly inaccessible ideal.

The status of this whole scene is now questioned. As in the passage in *L'Ensorcelée* in which Thomas le Hardouey meets the satanic shepherds, and which is a possible source of Donissan's adventure, there are numerous opportunities for the reader to imagine that these events are happening only in a dream, that Donissan, having sat down at the start of the sequence, has fallen asleep. This rational option is offered again when Satan vanishes and the abbé finds himself being helped to his feet by a passing workman, who tells him that, together with the horse-dealer – 'un brave gars de Marelles, un marchand de bidets, retour de la foire d'Etaples' (185) – he has found him lying there. Reality comes flooding back, in a cascade of concrete detail: the man's name (Jean-Marie Boulainville), his job (quarryman at St-Pré), his family background (he is the brother of Germaine Duflos of Campagne). Is Donissan the dupe of his dreams? The last word on this will come from Menou-Segrais, who regards the devil's temptations as real, irrespective of whether they occur in waking or dreaming states. But several critics have overstated the reader's freedom to accept the rational explanation of this scene.[12] That Bernanos wants us to take it at face value, that we must indeed do so for what follows to be comprehensible, is underlined by the fact that Donissan *retains* his special sight, seeing first into the heart of the quarryman, and then into the third and final person he meets in the course of this 'inoubliable nuit': Mouchette. This providential meeting of priest and murderess, its inevitability implied in the parallel structure of their two stories, mimics the shape of God's plans for men. Mouchette, by now on the verge of madness because of the satanic undermining of her personality, needs Donissan, and he, to test the efficacy of his new gift, needs her. But the supernatural lucidity with which his eye pierces her darkness is 'dépouillée de toute pitié' (204), his revelation to her of his miraculous knowledge of her crime too brutal. Above all, in telling her that she is the victim of external forces, he robs her of her last vestige of personal identity, doing the job of Satan, who lies in wait for him, 'vautré dans sa proie' (ibid.). Mouchette flees, cuts her throat, and is carried, dying, by Donissan to the church – for which spectacular offence to modern sensibilities he is banished, after suitable psychiatric treatment, to a monastery.

The Donissan we meet in the final part is the old priest of Lumbres, with a legendary reputation for his saintly deeds, and knowing many things 'que la Sorbonne ne sait pas' (235), but no less than before the target of Satan. After the opening sequence of his meditation on his tormented life, 'le réel glisse et rejaillit, reprend son niveau' (239); he, and we, are brought back to the everyday by a string of concrete nouns: a door slamming, the chicken-roost in frenzy, a farm-dog rattling its chain, clogs echoing up the stairs, the creaking of a rusty lock. A similar catalogue of objects is evoked a few pages later, when Donissan, called to the room in which the dead child lies, compulsively empties his pockets as if trying to slough off the substance of this world before his attempted miracle: out come a tinder-box, a match, a horn-handled knife, letters, a red cotton handkerchief. Around him is a less tangible reality, a 'silence, comme une invisible buée' (265).

The eyes of the curé de Luzarnes, who accompanies Donissan to the house, are not good instruments for deciphering the invisible. For a moment, this 'modern' priest, committed to rational solutions for the ills of his parish and suspicious of 'miracle men' like Donissan who upset all his calculations, senses his own inadequacy. He listens to Donissan's account of the 'visions' he has had in the midst of banal reality, sitting on his straw chair in the sacristy. Disturbed out of his habitual complacency, not sure whether Donissan can or cannot bring the boy to life, but above all anxious, good liberal empiricist that he is, to *witness* the attempt, he encourages him to try. Some of this erosive curiosity affects Donissan too, and as in the encounter with Mouchette, his motives are contaminated by self-interest. The dead boy's eyes flicker open, and in them Donissan sees the presence of 'le maître de la mort, le voleur d'hommes, [. . .] le roi risible des mouches' (267). He raises the body aloft, challenges God to exert his superiority over Satan. The super-text appears to rebuke him: 'O le misérable vieux prêtre . . .' (268), but then reassures us, in terms that no-one can regard as those of a human narrator, that God will not refuse the saint's craving for a sign. According to Guy Gaucher, Donissan fails in this scene because he is calling on his own strength, not God's.[13] But neither half of this statement seems true. Donissan calls on God, offers his own peace of mind in exchange for the boy's life; and, as for his alleged failure, his written account in the next chapter suggests that in his heart he does not believe he has failed: he has seen the boy live again, even if others have not. The resurrection has been interrupted by the boy's mother, coming into the room and driven into grief-stricken madness by what she sees; but even this is the means to good, for she is later reconciled to God by a pilgrimage to Lumbres. The devil may have been tempting Donissan, and the woman may have gone mad; but the reverse is also true: the promise of eternal life has been kept, and the mother is saved. Apparent failure hides a true victory.

* * *

The final section also introduces the distinguished novelist St-Marin, whose career is founded on well-publicised scepticism and unpredictability. In this 'professeur de doute' (302) Bernanos sees the spirit of that commitment-sapping liberalism which plays into the devil's hands, making St-Marin a 'patriarche du néant' (287). Like the curé de Luzarnes, he is curious of Donissan's power, seeks to reduce it to material explanations. Seeing the old priest's habitat, he exclaims, as Zola might have done in the house of Bernadette, 'Je tiens mon saint!' (305). In fact, the supernatural truth of Donissan's life must always elude him; the peace he imagines the saint possessing is illusory, though perhaps obtainable in death. 'Tu voulais ma paix, viens la prendre!' (308) is the implied final message of Donissan as St-Marin comes across his dead body, still propped upright in the confessional.

What a trio gathers at Lumbres on the day of Donissan's death:

the socialist doctor Gambillet, the subversive writer St-Marin, the cartesian priest Luzarnes! A similar assembly, representing Bernanos' idea of the new alliance against traditional Catholicism, appears in his second novel, *L'Imposture*. Each of its members is a living contradiction: they include a 'voltairian' aristocrat, a modernist bishop, a Catholic journalist who writes for a Jewish editor. They all unwittingly represent mutually exclusive ideals, as in the gloriously satirical portrait of one of their number, Catani, whose 'convictions libérales' and 'confiance dans l'avenir' sit uncomfortably alongside his 'foi religieuse' and 'respect du passé', and whose determination to 'ne rien compromettre' is at once undermined by his perceived need for 'des formules d'union, de transaction, d'équilibre' (407). The mandarin of the group is the writer Guérou, fascinated by priests but dissecting religious experience, and the infiltration of its spirit into the Church itself is represented in the novel's central character, Cénabre, priest and writer. Of these two activities the latter takes precedence; the priestly gift of special insight is merely corrupted into a loveless analysis of his fellows. In the books which have made him famous, he writes of saintliness 'comme si la charité n'existait pas' (329). Worse, 'IL NE S'AIME MÊME PAS' (363), rejecting his family and childhood, so that, like the lame beggar he meets in the street one day and whom he drags around the city in pursuit of the secret of this alter ego, he has lost all substance as an integral human being. He has also lost his faith, but goes on practising his priestly duties because no other course is open to him and because his literary career demands it.

Cénabre reverses all that Donissan represents, and in *L'Imposture* and its companion novel *La Joie*, he in turn meets his reverse image in the form of two saintly characters: the abbé Chevance and the girl Chantal de la Clergerie. These two novels, taken together, are structured, like *Un prêtre marié*, on a chain of interlinked responsibilities, reflecting the notion of mystical substitution. Chevance dies an agonised death in place of Cénabre, with whom, like the prioress and the young novice in Bernanos' scenario *Dialogues des carmélites*, he has mystically 'exchanged' deaths. To Chantal, his *protégée*, Chevance bequeaths the mission of Barbey's Calixte: to atone for the renegade priest whose cold intellect has sapped his faith. She also shares Calixte's fragile health, being subject like her to cataleptic states which are indistinguishable from mystical trances. In one such state, she sees – 'de ses yeux de chair, qu'importe?' (685) – her suffering, in the shape of her own physical double. This vision then changes into that of Judas, identified as Cénabre, whose apostasy she has to redeem. She must also bear the burden of other troubled beings: literally, in the case of her grandmother, half-mad and embittered by hatred, whom Chantal physically carries back to the house when the old woman falls ill. 'Mais c'est toi qui me portes,' says Chantal, expressing the interdependence of saint and sinner. The theme is amplified by Fiodor, M. de Clergerie's Russian chauffeur and another of Bernanos' *possédés*. Both 'vampire' and 'demon' (618–19), drawn to saints by sheer demonic curiosity, he murders Chantal at the very moment at which Cénabre is regaining his faith.

The relating of this supernatural drama to flesh-and-blood reality is achieved through the dual nature of Chantal herself. She insists: 'Nous ne sommes pas de purs esprits' (588), but she is also of this world through her duties as housekeeper and her interest both in dress and motor cars. But the physical world around her often crumbles away as another dimension of reality returns. Familiar objects suddenly seem strange and remote. She fixes her eyes on a tree, on a bucket standing by a well, hears a door closing, and 'tout ce paysage paisible lui apparut transfiguré dans la lumière immobile' (604).

Cénabre's experience follows, at first, the opposite direction. In *L'Imposture*, the awareness of his lost faith includes that sense, already encountered in Green and highlighted in Zola's polemic, that sacred objects revert to pure materiality, the 'petit disque blanc' of the host included (448). 'L'une des marques des grandes convulsions de l'âme,' says the narrator, 'est de *se retrouver dans les choses*' (327). And Cénabre's reconversion, in the closing pages of *La Joie*, is marked by a reversal of this phenomenon: like Chantal, he becomes aware of another reality beyond the concrete: '[Des] images mystérieuses s'étaient merveilleusement substituées à la vision du réel' (710). He regains the sense of God's presence in an inner event 'aussi réel pourtant, aussi sûr qu'aucun de ceux qu'il avait vu de ses yeux' (716), and in the familiar objects around him, the flowered tapestry on the walls, the massive bed, he now sees, not obstacles to belief in a spiritual order but a physical world permeated by the spirit: 'une certitude', 'une évidence' (716). The concrete and spiritual domains have hitherto been presented by Bernanos as alternating ones, primarily because the discourse of the novel must start and finish with the evocation of a seen world. But to the Christian who believes in the incarnation of the spirit, the division must be illusory. Bernanos, in his best-known and probably best loved novel, *Journal d'un curé de campagne*, will seek a fictional form through which to express the ultimate synthesis of matter and spirit.

* * *

A shift in the way in which Bernanos perceives the relationship between everyday reality and the spiritual order is suggested by the subtly altered sense, at the start of the *Journal*, of an image already used in *Sous le soleil de Satan*. In the earlier novel, he writes of these 'deux réalités' as 'deux fluides d'inégale densité [qui] se superposent, sans se confondre, dans un équilibre mystérieux' (265). They are, in other words, two essentially separate worlds, though possessing a meaning the one for the other that is ultimately mysterious. In the *Journal*, a reference to 'deux liquides de densité différente' (1031) has a different sense, evoking two moral layers of good and evil, coexisting in the same physical universe, and with their 'centre de gravité [. . .] placé très bas' (ibid.): that is, both are at large in the lowly world around us. Grace and its satanic similacrum, the devil's power over men, do not invade the everyday from afar, but are an integral part of it. Whereas Satan, for Donissan, was an exteriorised being, the holy personages, for the curé d'Ambricourt in the *Journal*, are encountered within himself: 'Ma pauvre tête n'en pouvait plus. L'image de la Vierge-Enfant [. . .] s'y présentait sans cesse' (1197). His vision of the Virgin, in the midst of a period of great spiritual difficulty, arises from his 'rêveries' and from 'le déroulement de [ses] songes', but is transmuted into a form so tangible that he feels himself taking one of her hands in his. Even his miraculous ability to read into souls, as in the central episode with the countess, or to see the contents of a closed handbag – that of the countess' daughter, containing a letter announcing her intended flight from home and threat of suicide – is not accorded him in a spectacular encounter with the supernatural, but is an extension of his everyday faith and life's vocation.

The curé inhabits a village which Bernanos saw, in his mind's eyes, in the most realistic terms: 'Je voudrais aussi,' he wrote, 'que ce petit village fût un «condensé» de notre pays – le châtelain, l'adjoint, l'épicier, les gosses, je les vois tous.'[14] It is 'une paroisse comme les autres' (1031), its averageness manifest in its social structure, in the absence of any unusual incident, and in the evocation of the typical pursuits of the rural community: the eyes of a dead rabbit whose head protrudes from the count's game-bag

(1124) are like reality itself staring from the text. Typical too is the village's proneness to the modern ill of depressive drift, the 'ennui' which the curé identifies as a cancer. But if the medical term functions as metaphor here, it assumes, when the curé learns that he is dying of cancer, a literal sense that is at the same time inseparable from the symbolic. Bernanos' father had died of a liver cancer in which his son saw the mark of Satan's presence in the soul,[15] and the malignancy within the young priest's body represents the diabolically inspired 'ennui' of the world, which he personally assumes and helps to redeem. In the same way, his enforced diet of bread and wine, which is all his diseased body will allow him to swallow, stands for the union of physical and spiritual planes. His diet is a permanent mass, a constant communion with Christ, which for the Catholic Bernanos it would be as unthinkable to regard as mere metaphor as it would be to see the bread and wine of the eucharist as no more than symbols. The curé sums up the author's distaste for an over-abstract religious discourse, and indirectly suggests why Bernanos was drawn to the concreteness of the novel genre, when he writes: 'On ne saurait donner le nom de la foi à un signe abstrait, qui ne ressemble pas plus à la foi [. . .] que la constellation du Cygne à un cygne' (1126). And in his description of Christ he reveals the source of this faith in the real:

> A nous entendre on croirait trop souvent que nous prêchons le Dieu des spiritualistes, l'Être suprême, je ne sais quoi, rien qui ressemble, en tout cas, à ce Seigneur que nous avons appris à connaître comme un merveilleux ami vivant, qui souffre de nos peines, s'émeut de nos joies, partagera notre agonie, nous recevra dans ses bras, sur son cœur. (1050–1)

In the figure of the priest who is the central character of most of Bernanos' novels can be recognised the result of this determination to link heaven and earth in a flesh-and-blood reality. Unlike Huysmans, fascinated by the other-worldliness of the monastery, Bernanos relates his faith constantly to life in this world. He allows his curé a few words of mild satire on 'documentary' accounts of monastic retreat when he describes one of his colleagues' lectures on 'Ce que j'ai vu à Verchocq' (1033). Perhaps, in two senses, there is nothing to be seen at Verchocq, neither divine nor human truth to be encountered there. What interests Bernanos is how the invisible world of the spirit relates to the human and social aspects of everyday life. Central to this interest is his preoccupation with the secular role of the Church. The political observer in Bernanos unites with the novelist in the discussions between the curés of Ambricourt and Torcy and their friend Doctor Delbende, who has ceased to practise his faith because of his disappointment at the Church's neglect of the poor. To Bernanos, as conscious as any traditionalist French thinker of the 1930s of the new model of social organisation represented by Soviet Russia, the threat of revolution in western Europe was a terrifyingly real one. But like Léon Bloy, he saw poverty less in economic terms than in mystical ones. The poor man was the shadow of Christ, and to give him material wealth would be to rob him: to make him, as he says in *Les Grands cimetières sous la lune*, a 'faux riche'. 'Il s'agit de l'honorer,' he argues, 'ou plutôt de lui rendre l'honneur. [. . .] La Puissance de l'Argent s'oppose à la Puissance de Dieu' (E, 374, 380). The curé d'Ambricourt expresses this in its most sublime form: 'Problème insoluble: rétablir le Pauvre dans son droit, sans l'établir dans la Puissance' (1104).

The curé's diary is the perfect form for the blending of these transcendent problems with the 'mille petits soucis quotidiens' (1049) of his existence. It expresses the meeting in the priest's life of the spiritual and the concrete, and for Bernanos it is a synthetic form which allows the union of realist discourse and Christian meditation. Beginning as 'une conversation entre le bon Dieu et moi, un prolongement de la prière' (1048), it becomes a daily record of the apparently trivial events which form the curé's spiritual journey through near despair to the revelation of God's special purpose for him, and on to the paradoxical triumph of his redemptive death. The curé's initial hesitation about writing his diary reflects again Bernanos' concern with the writer and with the relationship between writing and faith. For Ganse and for Cénabre, writing is a form of self-glorification, a pursuit of worldly honours. Writing about oneself is particularly dangerous, the instinct towards self-love ever threatening to distort the writer's view, to inhibit the self-knowledge which is the basis of humility. The curé's determination to observe 'une rigueur inflexible' (1036), 'des habitudes d'entière franchise envers moi-même (1057), is counterpointed by the presence in the book of his negative image, the lapsed priest and self-indulgent writer Dufréty, whose letters to his former fellow seminarian reflect a grotesque vestige of his priestly nobility, 'dépouillé de tout caractère surnaturel' (1089). In seeing a 'supernatural' significance in Dufréty's destiny, the curé expresses the same notion as Bernanos in *La Grande peur des bien-pensants*: that the 'explication surnaturelle' of France's spiritual mediocrity is to be found in that of the Church, contaminated by the blinkered rationality of scientists and philosophers, and afraid to proclaim the truths it is supposed to defend (E, 205). Dufréty is the very type of what Bernanos calls the 'mediocre priest' (1089), his betrayal of God's truth evident in the self-indulgent and indeed mendacious account he gives of himself in his letters and, no doubt, in the autobiography which he is writing, grandiloquently entitled 'Mes Étapes'. One thinks of the *Mes Haines* of the still adolescent Zola, or even of the *Mein Kampf* of the megalomaniac Hitler!

The curé's diary, in total contrast to all that Dufréty writes, is a record of truth, of which the faithful daily jotting of apparently trivial events acts as a kind of guarantee, as does its simple and unadorned style. The very physicality of the diary, 'ces feuilles de papier blanc', and even the table on which it lies (1131) are a source of strength when prayer is impossible. Matter is harnessed to the needs of the inner life in reparation of the Realists' divorce of the two. Even the shoddy artefacts in the curé de Torcy's room, 'un assez vilain chromo [. . .] qui représente un Enfant Jésus bien joufflu, bien rose, ente l'âne et le bœuf' (1041), which he might have bought at Jacques Arnoux's or in the shops execrated by Zola or Huysmans, reflect a humility and simplicity which renders their aesthetic deficiencies utterly secondary.

In the celebrated 'countess scene', the presence of objects is an important factor, anchoring events in the real. Throughout the intense dialogue in which the curé fights for the countess's soul against 'l'ennemi', he is constantly aware of logs crackling in the fireplace, linen curtains hanging at the window, the sound of dishes and glasses being washed and dried in the kitchen. What Julien Green sees as hierarchical layers of reality here become concurrent and consubstantial. This is manifested not just through inanimate objects but in the person of the curé himself. His role in this scene is foreshadowed by the role imputed to an object, to the poker which the countess is holding when he arrives. This poker, says the curé, looking for an analogy through which to explain God's purpose, is an 'instrument', ready to do the countess' bidding (1146). As the curé leads the countess to see that her lack of love for her husband and daughter, following the trauma of her infant son's death, is the root cause of the family's tragic divisions, that lovelessness is the essence of hell itself, he is transformed into an 'instrument'. The words he pronounces are in themselves unimportant; other words could have been substituted for them. What matters is that through the person of the priest, 'une main mystérieuse venait d'ouvrir une brèche dans on ne sait quelle muraille invisible, et la paix rentrait de toutes parts' (1162). Like that of Mouchette, the countess' immediate reaction to the priest is violent. His revelation of her sin makes her fling into the fire the medallion containing her last precious relic of the dead child by love of whom she has been corrupted: a lock of his hair, and the curé, thrusting his arm into the flames to retrieve it, assumes quite literally the function of a poker in the hands of God. All borderlines vanish here between flesh and spirit, between the concrete and the sublime, and the theological problem of where providence meets free will in the moment of grace is resolved in total fusion of the two. In this scene Bernanos consummately achieves the synthesis for which he strives, the reconciliation of realism and Christian meaning.

* * *

The encounter between the curé and the countess is for both of them the summit of their itinerary. Here the curé's dark night of doubt ends in his election as an agent of God, and the countess, who dies within hours of their meeting, has met her end, the curé confidently asserts, 'avec Dieu, en paix' (1189). The priest's presence and example are not always so efficacious, however, as the final sequence of the novel, relating his death in Dufréty's flat, shows. Here, the bad priest and bad writer becomes the unworthy companion of the man who has fulfilled both vocations and reconciled the one with the other. No other priest is available to minister to the dying curé, and Dufréty finds himself pressed into service. Whether this has the effect of reawakening his sense of priestly responsibility, as is often said, is doubtful. Dufréty's letter to the curé de Torcy, which brings the novel to its close, still reeks of the false humility which had appalled the curé d'Ambricourt earlier, and Dufréty still lies about the supposed medical knowledge of his mistress, who is in fact a simple hospital auxiliary. John Flower seems right to assert that Dufréty 'remains uncomprehending to the end'.[16] Although Dufréty records the curé's last words, 'Tout est grâce', his own life manages to elude their meaning. Perhaps Dufréty belongs to that world for which, the curé says earlier, Jesus mysteriously refused to pray (1090). This problematic note in the novel's final lines suggests the darker side of Bernanos' vision, his doubt that the world would ever return to the ways of God. In a moving passage in the *Mémoires intérieurs*, Mauriac interprets the pessimism of his fellow novelist as follows: '«Le fils de l'homme est venu chercher et sauver ce qui était perdu. . .» Mais si ce qui était perdu devait le demeurer à jamais? Si la créature libre de se perdre l'emportait à la fin sur l'éternel amour?'[17] In Bernanos as in Mauriac, there is the recurring nightmare of the Pascalian 'misère de l'homme sans Dieu', and his last two novels express it sombrely.

The heroine of *Nouvelle histoire de Mouchette* is a peasant child, a representative of that social class for which Bernanos, in the *Journal*, expresses his concern. She lives in poverty with her alcoholic father, a mother who dies of exhaustion, and her new-born brother about whose future there can be no grounds for optimism; she is raped in sordid circumstances by the first man she trusts, and she commits suicide by drowning herself in a flooded sand-pit. Not only is there no human help in sight for Mouchette, but there is no spiritual comfort either. Religion plays no part in her life or in the community at large. The telling scene is that in which Mouchette, on the morning after the rape, and her mother having just died, walks through the village. It happens to be Sunday, an hour before mass – a mass to which nobody intends to go. The hour, nevertheless, does not feel like an ordinary hour, for a vague sense of preparation hangs in the air: 'Se préparer à quoi?' (1327). God's absence from the world is not a neutral omission, to be shrugged off and forgotten, as Zola predicted it would be, as the mark of inevitable cultural change; it leaves a hole in our midst, through which Mouchette, quite simply, falls. This is the significance of her story.

There is no priest in the book. It is the only Bernanos novel, not excluding even his detective story *Un crime*, without a priest character. Starting with Balthasar,[18] critics have often argued that the narrator, through the tone of profound compassion which he adopts towards Mouchette, replaces the priest. This has been developed into an optimistic reading of the novel's ending, again most typically expressed by Balthasar, who sees the novelist as 'co-operating' in God's plan for Mouchette by leading her to a redemptive death and to the negation of her misery through divine love. This reading has been persuasively challenged by Le Touzé and by Stefanson, who see the lonely death of the teenaged girl as, respectively, 'un désastre' and 'an irremediable tragedy'.[19] Their view seems unmistakably borne out by the text. The idea of death is sown in the girl's mind by the sinister Philomène who, as the village's 'layer-out' or 'ensevelliseuse des morts', literally lives on death, taking sustenance and satisfaction from the death of others. She leads Mouchette to see death as an attractive notion, as a romantic renewal of the 'secret' of her night with the poacher. There is a parallel between Philomène's attitude and the glorification of death by armchair war propagandists, which Bernanos denounces in *La Grande peur*. The 'désir terrible de vivre' (E, 57) of the soldier in the trenches stands for a positive value in that context, and so would Mouchette's survival in hers. Her death is rendered in atrocious detail: the water – 'l'eau insidieuse' – creeps up the nape of her neck, turns her onto her back. The sounds it makes in her ears, 'un joyeux murmure de fête' (1345), comparable to the 'sourd grondement de fête' made by motor cars going to the house of the dead countess in the *Journal* (1170), suggests the celebratory dancing of devils for which the act of self-destruction provides an occasion, like 'le glapissement des démons, la joie même de Satan, énorme et noire', which Bernanos describes elsewhere (E, 111). It is true that next to the sand-quarry stands a dilapidated sign, casting a cross-shaped shadow across the scene. Mouchette's place of death may, after all, be a redemptive Golgotha, but the suggestion persists that, through no fault of hers, it is the site of a tragic mockery of the crucifixion.

The starkest contrast to the grace-filled world of *Journal d'un curé de campagne* comes with *Monsieur Ouine*, which is its alternative, negative version. Both novels grew from the same inspiration, Bernanos having begun *Ouine* first and abandoned it to write other books, including the *Journal*. The setting is to all intents and purposes the same, a village, now called Fenouille, and in the range of characters one recognises again the social types which any novelist might include in his picture of rural society: the mayor, the doctor, the priest, the peasant family, the poacher, the teacher, the local squire and his wife, the widowed mother, her son and the governess. But into this apparently ordinary country setting, Bernanos introduces mystery, child murder, homosexuality, mob violence, insanity and suicide. The realistic picture gives way to a mythical image of evil, to, in Michel Estève's words, 'le mythe d'une paroisse totalement déchristianisée'.[20]

The characters are perceived through a series of dialogues. Most of the scenes in the novel, as in most of Bernanos' novels, are dialogues – between the adolescent Steeny and the governess, between Steeny and the *châtelaine* Jambe-de-Laine, Steeny and the crippled boy Guillaume, Steeny and the ex-teacher Ouine, between Ouine and the priest, the priest and the doctor and so on. Apart from one or two scenes of violent action – the scenes on the road, where Jambe-de-Laine apparently tries to run down Steeny with her horse and buggy, or in the churchyard when, after the funeral of the murdered farm-boy, the crazed mob attack Jambe-de-Laine – the novel is built on confrontation between two characters, with only rarely a third person present, like the midwife Mme Marchal who listens, in total incomprehension, to the crucial conversation between the curé de Fenouille and doctor Malépine. She reflects the reader's position, made difficult by the fact that the dialogues seldom appear to begin at the beginning, or continue to a clarifying end. The reader is an eavesdropper on conversations that have begun before he arrives, or else he finds the sound switched off in the middle. The deliberate denial to the reader of the sensory perceptions – *choses vues, choses entendues* – on which Realism has accustomed him to rely, is in itself an expressive function of the text. A different level of understanding is required, the text suggests, a faculty or means of understanding which we have lost, and without which our impoverished sense-based rationalism is always groping in the dark.

The limits of the physical senses are illustrated in a grimly comic form – the comic being a dimension of Bernanos, as of Bloy, which has not received much critical attention – through the obscenely erectile nose and exaggerated olfactory capacities of the mayor Arsène. Arsène sniffs the filth of the world, and endlessly washes himself in the hope of losing his obscure and painful sense of guilt. There is an echo here of Lady Macbeth and, through her, of Pilate, and of the New Testament symbolism of cleansing water. Another instinct in Arsène mimics the sacramental life of the Church: his yearning for confession. He leaves behind him, in his pyjama-clad flight from home, a manuscript which the doctor mocks: 'Le gaillard, comme Jean-Jacques Rousseau, a dû écrire ses *Confessions* à la chandelle' (1524). Like previous characters in Catholic novels, like Barbey's Ryno or Mauriac's Thérèse, confession 'à la Rousseau', outside the Church, has not released Arsène from his burden.

Two characters compete as commentators on the plight of which Arsène's condition is a symptom: the priest and the doctor. The value-roles are reversed between these two Realist stock-types: the spokesman for medical science is blind to truth, dismissing Arsène as a sexually obsessed man, for whose anxieties there are straightforward medical explanations. For the priest, the case raises other issues: Arsène's obsessions stem from a suppressed awareness of our fallen nature, of the impossibility of redemption in a world which denies the supernatural dimension of life. Because we do not believe in evil as a supernatural rather than psychological force, its victory – Satan's victory – over us is assured. The novel comments on the development of our outlook over the past two centuries, to which Bernanos refers in 'la boue d'un siècle ou deux' (1363) clinging to the walls of the house where Ouine lives. It draws an imaginary extension of the line which has led from the 'death of Satan' (celebrated by Hugo) to the 'death of God', proclaimed by Zola and Nietzsche, and continues, in the vision of the curé de Fenouille, into a nightmarish future characterised by the death of Man. The supernatural, denied by man, will burst into his world, he tells the doctor, and out of villages like Fenouille will come strange beasts. As he has warned the congregation at the funeral of the murdered boy: 'Satan aurait visité son peuple' (1488).

The modern world's attitude to the evil of which Arsène and the priest are variously aware is exemplified in Ouine, as is the form which that evil assumes. The two are in fact one: for Bernanos, evil resides within the world's attitude to it, is buried in the heart of an abstraction, is abstraction itself, fostered by the usurpation by reason of the instinctive love of the heart. Ouine represents rationalised non-commitment, spiritual apathy. 'Je n'ai jamais pu,' says one of the minor characters, 'obtenir de sa courtoisie une parole pour ou contre la religion, il semble ne s'intéresser qu'au problème moral' (1359). This 'moral problem' in which Ouine is said to be interested is an intellectualised morality, whereas morality's true foundation is in the spiritual, its true manifestation in action. Ouine, passionless and supine, is not against God or for him, neither encourages nor rejects belief. He is an observer, an academic analyst of the soul, the spirit of the 'liberal' consciousness that tolerates the best and the worst alike. The notion of good and evil, that worm eating away within the heart of that other worm, Man, irritates Ouine, and he suppresses it, preferring to ask questions of others rather than of himself: 'Honorez-vous Dieu, mon enfant?' he asks Steeny (1367). He stands for a society which, while aware of the notion of honouring God, behaves with utter indifference to Christ's teaching and example, for a world without beliefs or sense of purpose, unable to say Yes or No, or which says Yes and No simultaneously, like Monsieur Oui-Ne. Ouine, as Steeny's chosen master and guide, as a teacher – a former teacher of languages, speaking, perhaps, like evil, with many tongues – is a disseminator and propagandist of this insidious form of evil. He embodies it in his very person: 'Comme ces gelées vivantes, au fond de la mer, je flotte et j'absorbe' (1368). He is shapeless, viscous, inanimate, non-participating. But he tries to teach others to follow him: 'Vous apprendrez de moi à vous laisser remplir par l'heure qui passe,' he tells his young disciple (ibid.).

How far Ouine is a mere symbol or symptom of spiritual emptiness and how far he is an active agent of evil is one of the book's many enigmas. An earlier version of the novel, in which Ouine was identified as the murderer of the little boy, was altered by Bernanos, so that guilt is more universally spread. But strange things happen around Ouine: Florent the gardener dies soon after his arrival, his landlord Anthelme ages prematurely and also dies (aged forty-six, though described as an old man), and Jambe-de-Laine has gone mad, and she too dies – not of the wounds inflicted on her by the mob, but later, and apparently through her own volition. Ouine seems to have removed from these three the will to live, implanted in them a self-disgust and self-hatred that drives them to madness and to a simple withering away. He tells Steeny at the end that he had taught them to look at themselves; it is the cold look, like that of Cénabre on his miserable penitents, that has killed them.

Ouine, killer or not, is certainly a victim. As a child he has been corrupted by a homosexual approach by one of his teachers, and this has deprived him of his childhood, so that the purity of the child fascinates him and becomes the focus of his destructive instincts. There are three children in the novel, three young boys. There is Guillaume, the crippled boy, grandson of old Devandomme, whose physical suffering seems to expiate the sins of a family devoid of love because of the misplaced pride of the old man, obsessed with the supposedly aristocratic background of his family. Guillaume offers to suffer for Steeny too, dreams of himself crucified on behalf of his friend. There is the Malicorne boy, the murder victim, to whom the text refers with apparently casual but in fact deeply significant changes of title, transforming his social role into a redemptive one. 'Le petit valet' (1372) becomes 'le petit vacher' (1392), suggesting responsibility for a herd or flock – the image used at the start of the *Journal* to designate the spiritual leader needed by the village (1031). Later, he is referred to as 'le petit commis' (1456), defining his mission as having been sent – sent, quite literally, in Steeny's place, for Ouine sends him, implausibly, out into the night to tell Steeny's mother that Steeny will be spending the night in the château, and the boy is killed on the way. Steeny himself, the third boy, is the central figure in an existential drama: he is at the crossroads of his life, the moment of choice. He yearns to flee from an unhealthy home atmosphere in which his mother drifts passively through life, her 'douceur' a disguised indifference, in the company of the sexually ambivalent governess. At the other pole is Anthelme's château, dominated by the lodger Ouine, to whom Steeny is perilously drawn in search of a guide and master. Between the two houses is the road, 'vertigineuse amie' (1408), symbol of both escape and danger – the road which is the province of Jambe-de-Laine and her mad horse.

Jambe-de-Laine, like Arsène, bears the symptoms of the village's corrupt state; she too is on the verge of madness because of her acute sense of her fallen nature. At one moment denouncing Ouine as the killer, at the next seeking to protect him, she careers around the village looking for an escape from her moral and mental confusion. Like Ouine she is attracted to Steeny's youth and innocence; not for nothing does she habitually call him 'mon ange', for compared to her he is still in an unsullied, angelic state. Her giant horse on one side, Steeny on the other, Jambe-de-Laine is torn between two levels of being; 'ni ange ni bête', she is the epitome of the human condition as perceived by Pascal. The fragmentation of her personality is suggested by the multiplicity of names she bears: she is Ginette de Passamont, Mme de Néréis, châtelaine of Wambescourt, alias Jambe-de-Laine. She is the most striking example of several characters to whom Bernanos gives two or more names as a way of implying the fragility of their individual integrity. 'Dieu choisit parmi les médiocres des amis,' he writes elsewhere, 'leur donne tout [. . .] jusqu'à leur nom même';[21] and Menou-Segrais echoes: 'C'est Dieu qui nous nomme. Le nom que nous portons n'est qu'un nom d'emprunt' (133). The more 'noms d'emprunt' we assume, perhaps, the further we stray from God's intentions for us. The curé de Luzarnes is also called Sabiroux, Steeny's 'real' name is Philippe,[22] his governess is both Miss and Daisy. In the *Journal*, there is confusion in the curé's mind over the name of the drug-addicted doctor: Lavigne or Laville. And even Dufréty, when first mentioned, is called Dupréty. The only critic to mention this latter fact is Nettelbeck, who sees it as an error on the part of a novelist 'qui oubliait souvent le nom de ses personnages'.[23] Perhaps there is no error, but rather a deliberate blurring of names. It is significant that the nearest to God of all Bernanos' characters possesses no name, but is simply known by the sign of his vocation and of the community to which he gives his entire person: the curé d'Ambricourt.

* * *

One of the difficulties of interpreting the 'events' in *Monsieur Ouine* is that they may never actually happen at all. That the novel should be read as an extended dream-narrative has been argued, persuasively and fruitfully, by a number of critics. Steeny falls asleep on the first page: does he awake, or is what follows the account of a dream, in which, as for Alice by the river-bank, the familiar figures of childhood are transformed into nightmarish products of the subconscious: his mother and governess into Jambe-de-Laine, his missing father into Ouine? There are numerous references to dreams. 'Comme tout cela ressemble à un rêve!' thinks Steeny at one point (1366). 'On vous a dit des choses horribles, Steeny,' says Miss, 'ou bien vous les avez rêvées' (1444). 'C'est comme un rêve', says Arsène's wife (1504). The curé ends his conversation with the doctor 'comme s'il sortait d'un rêve' (1510). 'Ce qui m'arrive est extraordinaire' (1361) says Steeny; he might have exclaimed, like Alice, 'Curiouser and curiouser!' The world of dream offers Bernanos the ideal perspective in which to create his nightmare of a world given to evil, a way of combining the horror of evil with its imperviousness to rational comprehension. Once more, finding in the concrete world of the Realist a starting-point for the exploration of the supernatural, the Catholic novelist forsakes Realism for another flight into the fantastic. In his recourse to the fantastic, Bernanos, the greatest of the twentieth-century Catholic novelists, rejoins Barbey d'Aurevilly, with whom the tradition began. *Monsieur Ouine* often echoes Barbey's writings, especially *L'Ensorcelée*, from which comes the *motifs* of the mysterious murder and unidentified killer, and even the scene in the cemetery where Jambe-de-Laine suffers the fate of Barbey's witch-like female character, La Clotte: to be attacked by the mob, desperate for a scapegoat.[24]

The final sequence of *Monsieur Ouine*, in which Steeny sits by Ouine's bed, conversing with the dying man and apparently witnessing his death, only to be told by the doctor that Ouine has in fact been dead for the last two hours, has all the uncanniness of gothic fiction and of the ghost story. Through the doctor's mouth, Bernanos hints at the literary origins of the scene: 'Cela me rappelle le titre d'un roman lui jadis, *Les Morts qui parlent* ou quelque chose d'approchant' (1561). A novel exists with this precise title, written by the traditionalist critic and novelist best known for his *Roman russe*: Melchior de Vogüé. Bernanos probably knew it, but for reasons more to do with politics than literature, for the garrulous corpses of the title are parliamentary 'talkers', wasters of the nation's time and life-blood in the period of the Panama scandal. Apart from its title, this is not the source of the ending of *Ouine*; a much likelier one can be found in Poe's story *The facts in the case of Monsieur Valdemar*, the companion text of the *Mesmeric Revelation* from which Barbey probably drew inspiration for the sleep-walking sequences of *Un prêtre marié*. In this tale Valdemar (whose name, like Ouine's, is invariably preceded by the polite title, conferring an ironic dignity) is – like Ouine – dying of tuberculosis. He is the subject of an experiment, involving hypnosis *in articulo mortis*, which leaves his brain alive and his speech organs functioning, again like Ouine's, beyond the moment of physical death. The story ends in unmitigated horror, as Valdemar begs to be aroused from his sleep/death, only to dissolve into a putrefied mass on the bed; Ouine's death, his body dwindling into nothingness and leaving only the 'petite bête malfaisante' of his nose, is no less horrific (1562). Bernanos would almost certainly have read Poe's story in Baudelaire's translation, and he also knew Camille Mauclair, author of what is still one of the best books on Poe. Whether or not the parallels are conscious, they are at least very interesting; *Valdemar* exemplifies the gothic model, with its atmosphere of disorientating strangeness, which Bernanos transforms, as Barbey had done, into the expression of his Christian vision. For the denouement of *Ouine* seeks to create more than a conventional shiver. 'Je ne crains pas les fantômes,' Steeny tells Ouine (1547). What he witnesses by his master's death-bed is of another order, has a dimension of meaning more horrible than that of old wives' tales.

To Steeny is revealed the nature of evil itself. Evil is nothingness, it is the negation of God's created universe, and can only define itself in opposition to it, or rather *as* opposition to it. Ouine's spiritual emptiness only has meaning because of the plenitude of God's mercy. 'S'il n'y avait rien,' he tells Steeny, 'je serais quelque chose, bonne ou mauvaise. C'est moi qui ne suis rien' (1557). Because he is, in a spiritual sense, non-existent, Ouine cannot die. Death has no meaning for him. 'J'ignore,' he says, 'ce que vous entendez par ce mot' (ibid.). This is why the precise moment at which the bodily carcass, which he simply happens to inhabit, breathes its last breath is utterly insignificant. The blurring of the time of Ouine's death is Bernanos' way of expressing his never having lived. The midwife Mme Marchal hovers by his bedside, as if to answer a call that never comes, the call to deliver Ouine into his Christian birthright. To her, the best joke of all is that Ouine has been a teacher of 'langues *vivantes*' (1546).

Ouine is deprived of death, as of life, by choosing – through not choosing – to deny the Christian meaning of these phenomena. He complains that he 'misses' his death (1557), yet this cannot be, given his failure to comprehend even the word. What he misses is *seeing* his death. 'Que ne puis-je voir cette chose par vos yeux!' he says to Steeny. 'Je dis vos yeux, vos vrais yeux, [. . .] vos yeux si neufs, si frais' (1547). Seeing death is his frustrated ambition because seeing life, rather than participating in it, has been his passion. He has been the eye of the village. 'Jour et nuit,' says Jambe-de-Laine, 'M. Ouine est à sa fenêtre, observe tout' (1361). His delight, he confesses, was in watching the joys and sorrows of his fellow-men, deciphering their secrets. He was careful never to intervene, never to try to change them, content to indulge himself in 'ce passe-temps de Dieu' (1558): passive observation.

In these words, Monsieur Ouine gives the game away. The God of which he speaks cannot be the God of Bernanos or Mauriac, or of Barbey or Léon Bloy. The God of these writers is no bystander, but an intervening force in the lives of men. He is speaking, more plausibly, of the 'god' of Flaubert, present everywhere and visible nowhere, the deity of the Realist novelist, not all-powerful but merely all-seeing, the ideal of an 'objectivity' in which Bernanos recognises the betrayal of the Christian commitment on which Man's hopes have been founded for two thousand years. Ouine is not a writer, but he embodies what Bernanos saw as the contamination to which the writer was prone once he divorced his task from the assertion of God's truth. If Satan is, in the phrase of both Bloy and Bernanos, 'le singe de Dieu', the observing writer is the ape of Satan, destroying by cold analysis. When Ouine goes on his nightly sorties through the village, trying to perceive and possess the hidden dramas within humble houses, he walks in the footsteps of that pioneering Realist whom Barbey had first tried to oust from his monopoly of the art: Lesage's limping devil.

Concluding Note

The 'Bernanosian synthesis' brings this study to an appropriate close, for it is in Bernanos' novels that the notions explored in it reach their clearest illustration. Like all the six major Catholic novelists discussed in this book, Bernanos builds his work, quite consciously, on a *critique* of Realism, which he then readapts for the purpose of expressing his individual Christian's view of the world. This process of readaptation leads him to the creation, in *Journal d'un curé de campagne*, of the Catholic Realism first dreamed of by Huysmans, and in other novels, notably *Monsieur Ouine*, to the exploitation, essayed before him by Barbey and Bloy, of themes and techniques drawn from the fantastic tradition. In the intervening decades, Mauriac and Green had given the Catholic novel the psychological depths it may have lacked in the work of its earlier exponents, but it is Bernanos who completes the link between the twentieth-century Catholic novel and its nineteenth-century beginnings.

Bernanos' scorn for the 'gens bornés qui n'admettent que les réalités de Zola'[1] prefigures Robbe-Grillet's complaint that 'la seule conception romanesque qui ait cours aujourd'hui est, en fait, celle de Balzac',[2] except that Bernanos was not just, or even primarily, thinking of fictional technique. The Catholic novelist's response to Realism was not only, in historical terms, the first protest against the alleged limitations of Realism; from the outset, it couched that protest in terms that identified the struggle for the novel as crucial to the reflection which the modern world would give of its spiritual values. As this book has shown, however, his relationship with Realism was a two-edged one, not to be explained as a simple diametric opposition. Huysmans' Naturalist techniques are carried through to his Catholic novels; Bloy exploited Realist milieux for his effects; Green's attitude to Realism's use of 'models' was a complex and fluctuating one; and Bernanos wedded his religious vision to the creation of a physical world as convincing as any in the Realist corpus. Robbe-Grillet expressed his consternation that similar objections should be levied against his 'new' novel by Christians and 'materialists' alike, both groups remaining committed to a conception of novel-writing in which the artist's task is the recuperation and description of a total universe, including meanings held to exist beneath the surface of things. In truth, there is nothing surprising in this at all. The shared conviction that there is 'a world out there' awaiting the novelist's interpretation, and that the only important questions are what it consists of and how it can be described, does indeed unite Realist and Catholic novelist in relation to an allegedly more sophisticated theory of art which sees writing not as the record of the real, but as its creator and even its substance. The new novelist, like the surrealist, can choose to shift to a different aesthetic territory, but the Catholic novelist must share the same space as the Realist, accept his mimetic aims. His ambition is not an anti-realism but an alternative realism, exploiting Realist models of the world in order to construct his own persuasive model: one which, not circumscribed within the tangible and the visible, includes the spiritual dimension essential to his beliefs. This is why the history of the Catholic novel is polemically intertwined with that of Realism.

This book has been about similarities within difference, about the common ground of theme and technique that link to each other not only otherwise very different Catholic novelists, but, even more startlingly, Catholic and Realist. The novels that have been discussed span more than a century, which makes the existence of this common ground all the more astonishing. Even the differences in thematic emphasis or technical effect which have emerged arise from the shared concern to adapt the genre to the expression of a world-vision, sympathetic or inimical to Christianity as the case may be. Philosophical differences have directly led to thematic similarities. Notably, the role of physical objects and of the sense of sight by which they are perceived gives Realist and Catholic novelists a common theme, both groups debating from their contrary angles the reality of the unseen: a question crucial not just to their view of the world, but to their conception of the possibilities of the genre.

The same dual preoccupation: what is the world like? what can the novel do? governs the relationship of both sides with the rich field of fantastic literature. The inspiration of the fantastic, and especially the example of Poe, helped the Catholic novelists to break the shackles of a positivist and sense-bound conception of fiction, but created in turn the need to abandon the purely fantastic, reshape its dreams and extra-sensory intuitions into Christian meaning. A characteristic strategy links Barbey, via Huysmans and Bloy, to Green and Bernanos: the loosening of the reader's expectation of a fictional world perceptible to the senses, the suggestion of an unseen but no less real dimension, and finally the reintegration of this supernatural plane into the world of flesh-and-blood characters, whose moral and psychological dramas are intelligible in terms of the beliefs taught by the Church. The alternate exploitation and surpassing of the fantastic have been among the principal devices of the Catholic novelist.

Catholic Realism and a Catholic version of the fantastic: this book has established these as the two strands within a Catholic novel tradition which is itself sometimes denied meaningful existence by literary historians. It is in its twin movements towards and away from Realism that the Catholic novel proclaims and defines itself. To read, alternately and in a comparative light, the works of the great Realists and those of the principal Catholic novelists is to cross and recross the battle-lines of the religious debate on which our modern cultural identity has depended. Robbe-Grillet's point might suggest that we have come to the end of this debate. His throwing of both sides into one single camp, with the proponents of a new view of the novel in the other, perhaps indicates that we are indeed in a new period, no longer even in the post-Christian world defined by Zola, but in one where the argument itself is a thing of the past, where the very question of God has become redundant, and no longer a burning focus of concern for the writer. François Mauriac would not have agreed with this; he lived long enough to see the coming of the *nouveau roman* and to identify it as another symptom of the same religious war, its preoccupation with technique and with objects stemming from a devaluation of man. Most readers would see Mauriac's strictures as exaggerated, and accept Robbe-Grillet's plea that he is no less concerned with human values than any previous writer. The point is not which side we take, but that the argument goes on, in much the same terms as Barbey's with Zola. This book has sought to remain impartial, and to argue that the debate itself was the vital element, producing great literature on both sides. The pleasure and interest of reading both Realist and Catholic novelists can only be enhanced by our seeing them side by side in this broad context.

Notes and References

Unless otherwise stated, the place of publication of French books is Paris, and of books in English, London.

INTRODUCTION

1. 'Religion and Literature', *Selected Prose* (Harmondsworth: Penguin, 1958) 36.
2. R. Scholes and R. Kellogg, *The Nature of Narrative* (Oxford UP, 1966) 28.
3. *Theory of the Novel* (Merlin Press, 1978) 88, 71.
4. C. Jenkins, 'Realism and the Novel Form' in D. A. Williams (ed.), *The Monster and the Mirror: Studies in European Realism* (Oxford UP, 1978) 6.
5. J. Calvet, *Le Renouveau catholique dans la littérature contemporaine* (Lemerre, 1931) p. 23. See also G. May, *Le Dilemme du roman au dix-huitième siècle* (New Haven: Yale UP/PUF, 1963) 153.
6. Scholes and Kellogg, 226.
7. See M. Iknayan, *The Idea of the Novel in France: the critical reaction* (Geneva: Droz, 1961) 58, 86.
8. P. Citron (ed.), *Avant-propos de la Comédie Humaine*, 7 Vols (Seuil (L'Intégrale), 1965–6) I, 52. Subsequent quotations from this edition will show volume and page numbers.
9. Jenkins, 6.
10. Scholes and Kellogg, 231.
11. Preface to *Germinie Lacerteux*.
12. *Mimesis: The Representation of Reality in Western Literature*, translated by W. R. Trask (Princeton UP, 1974) 555.
13. A. Muller, *La Question du roman catholique* (Foulon, 1957) 1.
14. J. Vier, *Mauriac, romancier catholique?* (Tancrède, 1935); P. Colla, *L'Univers tragique de Barbey d'Aurevilly* (Brussels: La Renaissance du livre, 1965) Ch. 5.
15. Introduction to Mauriac, *Thérèse Desqueyroux* (London UP, 1964) 10.
16. *Crossroads: Essays on the Catholic Novelists* (York (South Carolina): French Literature Publishing Company, 1980) *vii*.
17. P. Bertault, *Balzac, l'homme et l'œuvre* (Boivin, 1946) 145.
18. B. Schilling, *The Hero as Failure: Balzac and the Rubempré Cycle* (Chicago UP, 1968) 39.
19. *Impressions*, 2e série (Mercure de France, 1927) 186.
20. *Le Pays*, May 25, 1854; reprinted in J. Petit (ed.), *Barbey d'Aurevilly, Le Dix-neuvième siècle* (Mercure de France, 1964) II, 92.

CHAPTER ONE

1. R. Ricatte (ed.), *E. and J. de Goncourt, Journal*, 27 Vols (ed. de l'Imprimerie Nationale de Monaco, Fasquelle-Flammarion, 1956) II, 112, and III, 163. References to this edition will be identified in the text by volume and page number.
2. J. Bruneau (ed.), *Flaubert, Correspondance*, 2 Vols (Gallimard, Bibliothèque de la Pléiade, 1973 and 1980) I, 340. Shown in the text as FC.
3. P. Borel (ed.), *Lettres inédites de Maupassant à Flaubert* (Éd. des Portiques des Champs-Elysées, 1929) 99.
4. According to J. de la Varende, 'la religion semble avoir été inconnue de Maupassant', in *Grands normands* (Rouen: Desfontaines, 1939) 220; cf. P. Cogny: 'Il n'a de la question que les très vagues notions qu'il pourrait avoir sur le bouddhisme ou la religion musulmane,' in *Maupassant, l'homme sans Dieu* (Brussels: La Renaissance du Livre, 1968) 39.
5. L. Forestier (ed.), *Maupassant, Contes et nouvelles*, 2 Vols (Gallimard, Bibliothèque de la Pléiade, 1974) I, 503. Shown in text as I, II.
6. A. Artinian (ed.), *Maupassant, Correspondance inédite* (Éd. Walper, 1951) 73.
7. 'Du Roman', in H. Mitterand (ed.), *Zola*, Œuvres complètes, 15 Vols (Cercle du livre précieux, 1962–9) X, 1395. Shown in text as I, etc.
8. *Une vie, Œuvres complètes* (Conard, 1925) 59. All subsequent page references are to this edition.
9. *Renée Mauperin* (Éd. définitive, Flammarion-Fasquelle, s.d. (1930) 65. Shown in text as RM.
10. *La Fille Élisa* (Union générale d'éditions, 1979) 122. Shown in text as FE.
11. *Émile Zola* (OUP, 1970) 105–6.
12. 'Zola's Mythology: that forbidden tree', *Forum for Modern Language Studies*, XIV (July 1978), 220.
13. *Bel-Ami, Œuvres complètes* (Conard, 1928) 445. All subsequent page references are to this edition.
14. *Soeur Philomène* (Éd. définitive, Flammarion-Fasquelle, s.d. (1936) 77. Shown in text as SP.
15. *Madame Bovary*, in A. Thibaudet and R. Dumesnil (eds), *Flaubert, Œuvres*, 2 Vols (Gallimard: Bibliothèque de la Pléiade, 1951–2) I, 323. References to this edition shown in text as I, II.
16. *Germinie Lacerteux* (Union générale d'éditions, 1978) 66. Shown in text as GL.
17. *Madame Gervaisais* (Gallimard (Folio), 1982) 97. Page numbers only given for the immediately following quotations; subsequently shown as MG.
18. *Fort comme la mort, Œuvres complètes* (Conard, 1929) 78.
19. *Manette Salomon* (Union générale d'éditions, 1979) 367. Shown in text as MS.
20. *L'Angélus, Œuvres complètes* (Conard, 1908–10).
21. *Charles Demailly* (Charpentier, 1876) 72.
22. *The Eighteenth-Century French Novel: Techniques of Illusion* (Manchester

UP/New York: Barnes & Noble, 1965) 265.
23. M. Regard (ed.), *Chateaubriand, Œuvres romanesques et voyages*, 2 Vols (Gallimard, Bibliothèque de la Pléiade, 1969) I, 19.
24. B. H. Bakker (ed.), *Zola, Correspondance*, (Montreal UP, 1979) I, 227.
25. R. Ricatte, *La Création romanesque chez les Goncourt* (Colin, 1954) 337.
26. *The Monster in the Mirror*, p. 15.

CHAPTER TWO

1. *Charles Demailly* (Charpentier, 1876) 146–7, 200; cf. Ricatte, op. cit., 123.
2. *Correspondance générale* (Les Belles Lettres, 1980–6) VI, 19. Shown in text as CG.
3. *Mémoranda*, in J. Petit (ed.), *Œuvres romanesques complètes*, 2 Vols (Gallimard, Bibliothèque de la Pléiade, 1964 and 1966) II, 933–4. References to this edition shown in text as I, II.
4. *Les Œuvres et les hommes* (Geneva: Slatkine, 1968) I, 175. Shown in text as OH.
5. *Le Pays*, June 1857; quoted in Ricatte, op. cit., 124 *n*.
6. First suggested by A. le Corbeiller, *Les Diaboliques de Barbey d'Aurevilly* (Malfère, 1939) 104.
7. *Thérèse Raquin, Œuvres complètes*, I, 614, for this and the next two quotations from this text.
8. Letter to Zola, in ibid., 680.
9. *Lettres à Mme de Bouglon* (Les Belles Lettres, 1978) 103.
10. *The Old Curiosity Shop* (Penguin) 319.
11. *Le Pays*, May 25th 1854. Quoted in J. Petit (ed.) *Barbey d'Aurevilly, Le Dix-neuvième siècle* (Mercure de France, 1964) II, 92.
12. Cf. P. Berthier: 'Le christianisme aurevillien restera toujours mêlé à une polyphonie dont il constituera une des voix maîtresses, mais sans l'épuiser', in *Barbey d'Aurevilly et l'imagination* (Geneva: Droz, 1978) 353.
13. Chateaubriand, *Œuvres romanesques et voyages* (Gallimard, Bibliothèque de la Pléiade, 1969) I, 164.
14. *Le Dix-neuvième siècle*, II, 311–13.
15. Ibid., 59.
16. *Barbey d'Aurevilly* (Laffont, 1945) 23.
17. Huysmans, *Œuvres complètes* (Geneva: Slatkine, 1972) VII, 222–3.
18. Trebutien (ed.) *Eugénie de Guérin, Journal et lettres* (Didier, 1863) 89. The following quotations from this edition are shown by page number only.
19. E.g. P. Colla, *L'Univers tragique de Barbey d'Aurevilly* (Brussels: La Renaissance du Livre, 1965) 109 and *passim*.
20. J.-P. Séguin (ed.), *Légendes traditionnelles de la Normandie* (St-Brieuc: Aubert, 1946).
21. Cf. P.-G. Castex, *Le Conte fantastique en France de Nodier à Maupassant* (Corti, 1951) 15. Unlike Balzac or Barbey, Castex sees the illuminist current of fantastic literature as profiting from the eighteenth-century

erosion of Christianity. A. Killen also sees an anti-Catholic current at work in the genre, *Le Roman terrifiant ou Roman noir de Walpole à Anne Radcliffe* (Champion, 1924). No previous study has been made of the Catholics' recuperation of fantastic techniques.

22. Barbey pressed Baudelaire to greater speed in translating Poe (CG IV, 62–3).
23. *Introduction à la littérature fantastique* (Seuil, 1970) 29, 47, etc.
24. 'Soyons Normands comme Scott et Burns furent Écossais' (CG IV, 232). In the novel Hermangarde is surprised 'de trouver vivantes, sur une côte écartée de la Normandie, de ces légendes semblables à celles que Walter Scott nous a rapportées de l'Écosse' (I, 414).
25. 'J'ai tâché de faire du Shakespeare dans un fossé du Cotentin' (CG III, 109).
26. *Une vieille maîtresse*, I, 241. For the remainder of this chapter, references to this and also to *L'Ensorcelée* and *Un prêtre marié*, which are all included in the first volume of this edition, will be shown in the text simply by page numbers.
27. See, for example, R. Griffiths, *The Reactionary Revolution* (Constable, 1966) 98–100.
28. See P. Leberruyer, *Au pays de Barbey d'Aurevilly* (Coutances, Éditions Bellée, s.d.) 40, and J. Petit, in I, 1423 *et seq*.
29. Néel's decision is similar to that of Jacques in *Le Chevalier des Touches*. and leaves the 'noble et pudique' Bernardine both 'veuve' and 'vierge' like Aimée de Spens in the earlier novel. For the biographical background to such flights from marriage, see M. Scott, 'Sexual ambivalence and Barbey d'Aurevilly's *Le Chevalier des Touches*', *Forum for Modern Language Studies*, XIX, No. 1 (January 1983), 42 *n*.
30. *The Novels and Stories of Barbey d'Aurevilly* (Geneva: Droz, 1967) 139.
31. *Barbey d'Aurevilly* (Éditions universitaires, 1957) 107.
32. Cf. J. Green, 'Byron', in *Barbey d'Aurevilly* (Minard, 1970) 13.
33. *Un prêtre marié* (Club français du livre, 1960) Preface, *x*. (Page numbers follow the other quotations in the text.)

CHAPTER THREE

1. Zola, *Œuvres complètes*, XII, 475–9, 506. Shown in text by volume and page number.
2. For a more detailed account of the various drafts of this review and their relationship to Zola's play *Madeleine* and subsequent novel, see M. Scott, 'Zola and Barbey d'Aurevilly: a case of impregnation?', in *Forum for Modern Language Studies*, XXI, No. 4 (October 1985), 291–302.
3. *Barbey d'Aurevilly, Œuvres romanesques*, I, 913.
4. Cf. J. Petit: 'leur commun romantisme, un goût commun de la recherche en matière de style', in *Barbey d'Aurevilly critique* (Les Belles Lettres, 1963) 535.
5. C. Letourneau, *La Physiologie des passions* (Germer Baillière, 1868) 3.
6. R. de Fourniels, *Floréal* (Maison de la Bonne Presse, 1902) 8. The original edition appeared in 1886.

7. For the intellectual background to Zola's later writings, see R. Ternois, *Zola et son temps* (Les Belles Lettres, 1961) *passim*, and D. Baguley, *Fécondité d'Émile Zola* (Toronto UP, 1973) Ch. 1.
8. H. Guillemin, *Présentation des Rougon-Macquart* (Gallimard, 1964) 322.
9. The three novels of the *Trois Villes* trilogy are all in Volume VII of the *Œuvres complètes*. Page numbers follow quotations in text.
10. J. Huret, *Enquête sur l'évolution littéraire* (Charpentier, 1891) 171. For Alexis' contribution, see pp. 188–90.
11. P. Walker, *Germinal and Zola's Philosophical and Religious Thought* (Amsterdam: Benjamins, 1984) 87.
12. A. Lanoux, *Bonjour, Monsieur Zola* (Grasset, 1978) 109.
13. *Zola, Correspondance*, III, 192.
14. The *Quatre Évangiles* appear in Volume VIII of the *Œuvres complètes*. Page numbers shown in text.
15. Guillemin's view of Zola's tolerance towards the cult of the Virgin scarcely stands up in the face of these passages. See *Zola, légende et vérité* (Éditions Utovie, 1982) 120 *n*.
16. H. Renaud, *Solidarité*, 6e édition (Librairie des Sciences sociales, 1877) 28.
17. For example, M. Tison-Braun, *La Crise de l'humanisme* (Nizet, 1958) I, 291, 299.

CHAPTER FOUR

1. 'Huysmans and the Goncourts', *French Studies*, VI (1952), 126.
2. *Reality and Illusion in the novels of J.-K. Huysmans* (Amsterdam: Rodopi, 1986) p. 9. Antosh overstates Baldick's view a second time: 'Baldick suggests that, contrary to prevailing critical opinion, Huysmans actually wrote only one truly naturalist work: *Les Sœurs Vatard'* (9). Baldick actually wrote that the latter was the 'last' of Huysmans' 'studies of working-class life' produced 'under his [Zola's] aegis': *The Life of J.-K. Huysmans* (Oxford: Clarendon Press, 1955) 45.
3. P. Cogny, *J.-K. Huysmans à la recherche de l'unité* (Nizet, 1953) 240; J. Laver, *The First Decadent: being the strange life of J.-K. Huysmans* (Faber & Faber, s.d. [1954]) 115, 169; Baldick, *Life*, 206.
4. *Œuvres complètes de J.-K. Huysmans* (Geneva: Slatkine, 1972 (reprint of Éditions de Paris, 1928–34) II, 161. All quotations from Huysmans' texts are taken from this edition; volume and page numbers shown in text.
5. For example, Cyprien's 'Ah! si tous, tant que nous sommes, nous n'étions pas gangrénés par le romantisme!' (IV, 129) closely echoes the same source as much of Huysmans' article on *L'Assommoir*, namely Zola's article on Flaubert, reprinted in *Les Romanciers naturalistes* (Zola, XI, 226).
6. *Lettres inédites à Jules Destrée* (Geneva: Droz, 1967) 32. Henceforth shown as D.
7. *Lettres inédites à Arij Prins* (Geneva: Droz, 1977) 145 (henceforth shown as P); D, 172.

8. See H. Suwala, 'Huysmans et Zola: ou l'amitié rompue', in *Huysmans: une esthétique de la décadence*, actes du colloque de Bâle, Mulhouse et Colmar (Champion, 1987) 98; P. Lambert in Huysmans, *Lettres inédites à Émile Zola* (Geneva: Droz, 1953) 108 *n*; L. Gillet in P, 369 *n*.
9. Especially as Baldick did not have access to Huysmans' letters to Prins, the most voluminous of all the now published correspondences (237 letters) and the most revealing on this subject.
10. *Lettres inédites à Émile Zola*, 76 *n*.
11. On works of art in Huysmans' writings see: H. Trudgian, *L'Esthétique de J.-K. Huysmans*, Éditions de Paris, 1934 (Slatkine Reprints, Geneva, 1970); C. Maingon, *L'Univers artistique de J.-K. Huysmans* (Nizet, 1977); and articles by various writers in *Huysmans: une esthétique de la décadence*.
12. *Lettres inédites à Émile Zola*, 9.
13. *Les Œuvres et les hommes*, XVIII, 271.
14. 'Grünewald et le culte des primitifs septentrionaux chez Huysmans', in *Une esthétique de la décadence*, 271–2.
15. 'Spiritualiste' and 'naturalisme spiritualiste' are difficult to translate into English. 'Spiritual' (preferred by Antosh) is too general, while 'spiritualist', as Laver points out (112 *n*), has misleading connotations. Baldick's freer 'mystical naturalism' (*Life*, 124) seems preferable.
16. Abbé Mugnier, *J.-K. Huysmans à la Trappe* (Le Divan, 1927) 11.
17. Edited by P. Cogny, Casterman. Page numbers shown in text.
18. See, for example, Bloy, *La Femme pauvre, Œuvres* (Mercure de France, 1972) VII, 198.
19. *The Gothic Cathedral* (New York: Bollingen, 1965) xix.
20. 'Huysmans et le problème de l'artiste chrétien', in *Esthétique de la décadence*.
21. *J.-K. Huysmans* (Grasset, 1931) 267.

CHAPTER FIVE

1. J. Bollery and J. Petit (eds), *Œuvres de Léon Bloy*, 15 Vols (Mercure de France, 1963–75) IV, 198. Throughout this chapter, references to this edition will be followed in the text by volume and page numbers, with the exception of the two novels, *Le Désespéré* and *La Femme pauvre*, which are in volumes III and VII respectively, and will be shown simply as D and FP.
2. The most direct view of the relationship is offered in D. Habrekorn (ed.), *Bloy, Villiers, Huysmans, Lettres: correspondance à trois* (Vanves: Éditions Thot, 1980).
3. Letter quoted in A. Béguin, *Léon Bloy: mystique de la douleur* (Éditions Labergerie, 1948) 9.
4. Cf. Huysmans' ironical comment on perceptions of himself and Bloy: 'Vous êtes un sous-Veuillot et moi un sous-Zola', in *Lettres*, 24.
5. Quoted in J. Bollery, *Léon Bloy: essai de biographie*, 3 Vols (Albin Michel, 1947–54) I, 273.
6. See B. Sarrazin, *La Bible en éclats: l'imagination scriptuaire de Léon Bloy*

(Desclée de Brouwer, 1977).

7. As well as Bollery's standard biography of Bloy, see J. Steinmann's *Léon Bloy*, (Éditions du Cerf, 1956).
8. See the letter to 'Maria X', quoted in Bollery, I, 94.
9. Op. cit., 11.
10. The authorised text of Mélanie's announcement appears in Volume X of Bloy's *Œuvres*. An extract is given in Griffiths, op. cit., 363–9.
11. See J. Lowrie, *The Violent Mystique* (Geneva: Droz, 1974) 110 *et seq*.
12. R. Barbeau, *Un prophète luciférien: Léon Bloy* (Aubier, 1957).
13. Op. cit., 142.
14. E. Seillière, *Léon Bloy: psychologie d'un mystique* (Éditions de la Nouvelle Revue Critique, 1936) 87.
15. See P. J. H. Pijls, *La Satire littéraire dans l'œuvre de Léon Bloy* (Leiden UP, 1959).
16. Quoted in J. Bollery, *Genèse et composition de «La Femme pauvre» de Léon Bloy* (Minard, 1969) 17.
17. Cf. Bollery, *Genèse* . . . , 13.
18. For Bloy's view of 'cette âme pure et paisible', 'la pauvre Eugénie', see XV, 99–101.
19. Bollery, *Genèse* . . . , 5.

CHAPTER SIX

1. *Le Nouveau Bloc-Notes 1958–60* (Flammarion, 1961) 389. Quotations from the *Bloc-Notes* will be shown in the text as BN I, II, etc.
2. The chapter on Mauriac in J.-L. Prévost, *Le Roman catholique a cent ans* (Fayard, 1958) does not specifically relate him to earlier writers. Griffiths' *The Reactionary Revolution* mentions Mauriac's first novel in a survey of the immediate impact of the Catholic Revival (281).
3. Bloy, *Œuvres complètes*, IX, 323.
4. Cf. J. E. Flower, *Literature and the Left in France* (Methuen, 1983) 80–2.
5. *Mémoires intérieurs* (Flammarion, 1959) 241. Shown as MI in text.
6. *Œuvres complètes* (Grasset/Fayard, 1950–6) IV, 263. References to this edition shown as OC in text.
7. *François Mauriac et le problème du romancier catholique* (Corrêa, 1933).
8. J. Petit (ed.), *Œuvres romanesques et théâtrales* (Gallimard, Bibliothèque de la Pléiade, 1978–85) II, 815–6. References to this edition shown in the text as P.
9. Interview with F. Lefèvre, in *Une heure avec* . . . (Gallimard, 1924) 217.
10. *Ce que je crois* (Grasset, 1962) 57.
11. P II, 787. 'Ce défaut,' agrees a publicist of Marist teaching, 'était général vers 1900. Le romantisme avait passé par là' (P. J. Hoffer, *Pédagogie Marianiste* (Centre de documentation scolaire, 1946) 415).
12. Caroline Mauriac (ed.), *Lettres d'une vie* (Grasset, 1981) 14.
13. *Hommage à André Gide* (Éditions du Capitole, 1928) 135.
14. Cf. G. Hourdin, *Mauriac, romancier chrétien* (Temps présent, 1946) 45; E. Jaloux, 'François Mauriac, romancier' in Mauriac, *Le Romancier et ses personnages* (Corrêa, 1933) 25.

15. 'L'Orgueil de Pascal', *La Vie intellectuelle*, April 1931. This article, with its uniquely clear self-assessment of Mauriac's Jansenism, seems to have escaped the attention of other writers on this subject.
16. *Correspondance*, II, 691.
17. F. Lefèvre, op. cit., 220.
18. *Situations* (Gallimard, 1947) I.
19. For an analysis of the implications of these tensions for Mauriac's political writings, see M. Scott, *Mauriac: the Politics of a Novelist* (Edinburgh: Scottish Academic Press, 1980) 41–55.
20. For further evidence of Mauriac's continuing tendency to avoid such subjects, to the detriment of his work, see his *postface* to *Galigaï*, OC XII, 165.
21. *La Crise du roman* (Corti, 1966) 460.
22. C. B. Thornton-Smith, critical edition of *Destins* (Methuen, 1983) 8; J. Monférier, *François Mauriac: du «Nœud de vipères» à «La Pharisienne»* (Champion, 1985) 23.
23. *Ce que je crois*, 162.
24. 'Dresser le bilan de ce que je crois, lier les intuitions tenues par moi comme indubitables en faisceau; alors – mais alors seulement – y aura-t-il lieu de voir si le total se rapproche ou non de la notion thomiste de *fides*': Du Bos, *Journal*, 9 Vols (Corrêa/La Colombe, 1947–56) III, 318.
25. *Authoritarian Fictions* (New York: Colombia UP, 1983) 89–90. See also H. Peyre, *The Contemporary French Novel* (New York: OUP, 1955) 114.
26. *Mauriac* (Cambridge, Bowes and Bowes, 1954) 12–13.
27. *Intention and Achievement: the novels of François Mauriac* (Oxford: Clarendon Press, 1969) 29.
28. *Faith and Fiction: creative process in Greene and Mauriac* (Notre Dame UP, 1967) 285.
29. *Le Prêtre dans le roman d'aujourd'hui* (Desclée de Brouwer, 1955) 82.
30. Claude Mauriac, *Conversations avec André Gide* (Albin Michel, 1951) 156.

CHAPTER SEVEN

1. J. Petit (ed.), *Green, Œuvres complètes* (Gallimard, Bibliothèque de la Pléiade, 1972–7) V, 193. References to this edition shown in text by volume and page numbers. A. H. Newbury's account of Green's reading during this period makes no reference to the Realist novelists: *Julien Green: Religion and Sensuality* (Amsterdam: Rodopi, 1986) 22–4.
2. Cf. A. Mor, *Julien Green, témoin de l'invisible* (Plon, 1973) 116.
3. Cf. A. Fongaro, *L'Existence dans les romans de Julien Green* (Rome: Signorelli, 1954) 135.
4. Green/Maritain, *Une grande amitié: Correspondance 1926–72* (Plon, 1979) 81.
5. The parallels are listed in A. Tamuly, *Julien Green à la recherche du réel* (Sherbrooke (Canada): Naaman, 1976) 45.
6. Newbury accepts Joseph's desire for Moïra at face value and sees the

'scarlet prostitute' as a metaphor for her (op. cit., 53) – rather than as a metaphor *like* her, as suggested here.

7. *Sexualité, religion et art chez Julien Green* (Nizet, 1976) 59.
8. Pre-1973 readings of the novel are thus weakened through no fault of their own; for example, P. C. Hoy: '*Le Malfaiteur* n'est pas le roman de l'homosexuel ni même un roman sur l'homosexualité', in B. T. Fitch (ed.), *Configuration critique de Julien Green* (Minard, 1966) 63.
9. Critics of the alleged thematic monotony of Green's later novels have not given credit to his variations of approach, for example: N. Kostis, *The Exorcism of Sex and Death in Julien Green's novels* (The Hague: Mouton, 1979) 109; J. W. Dunaway, *The Metamorphoses of the self* (Kentucky UP, 1978) 99.

CHAPTER EIGHT

1. *Georges Bernanos* (Desclée de Brouwer, 1967) 89.
2. *Le Mystère du réel dans les romans de Georges Bernanos* (Nizet, 1979) 168.
3. *Les Romans de Georges Bernanos, ou le défi du rêve* (Neuchâtel: La Baconnière, 1965).
4. *Le Réalisme dans les romans de Georges Bernanos* (Minard, 1969) 6.
5. Article in *Gringoire*, April 24th, 1936.
6. The full text of the interview, first published in F. Lefèvre, *Une heure avec . . .* (Gallimard, 1927), is reprinted in M. Estèrve (ed.), *Bernanos, Essais et écrits de combat* (Gallimard, Bibliothèque de la Pléiade, 1971) 1039–47. References to this edition shown in the text as E.
7. *Un mauvais rêve* in A. Beguin (ed.) *Œuvres romanesques; Dialogues des Carmélites* (Gallimard, Bibliothèque de la Pléiade, 1961) 894. All references to Bernanos' novels will be to this edition, with page numbers only shown in the text.
8. One aspect of Ganse contains an element of self-portraiture: the hard labour of his writing. The Balzacian model is applied to Bernanos himself in a letter to Robert Vallery-Radot: 'Je souffre d'une crise de reins. Raison: l'abus du café au cours de décembre. Vous voyez que lorsque je m'avise de jouer les Balzac . . . ', in J.-L. Bernanos (ed.), *Lettres retrouvées* (Plon, 1983) 179. His potential kinship with any writer is shown by his comment to the same correspondent: 'Ah! si des hommes comme Maupassant eussent eu une âme, je les aimerais bien!' (ibid., 123).
9. *Combat pour la liberté* in A. Béguin and J. Murray (eds), *Correspondance inédite*, (Plon, 1971) II, 523. Shown below as *Correspondance*, II.
10. Bernanos' use of Zola's genealogy motif has gone unnoticed; cf. P.-R. Lelercq: 'La technique de l'arbre généalogique chère à Zola n'est pas ici de mise', in *Introduction à Monsieur Ouine de Bernanos* (Minard, 1978) 139.
11. H. U. von Balthasar's comment that 'Bernanos [fait] trop de place encore à la mythologie romantique, et cette mythologie menace de tout gâter', and his view that such writing 'ne sera jamais une voie ouverte à des chrétiens' (*Le Chrétien Bernanos* (Seuil, 1954) 332) show

how Bernanos' art has often been unappreciated, even by his most respected critics, when doctrinal criteria are allowed to outweigh literary ones.

12. For example, Whitehouse, 14; Milner, 95.
13. *Le Thème de la mort dans les romans de Georges Bernanos* (Minard, 1967) 70–1.
14. *Correspondance*, II, 48.
15. *Combat pour la vérité* in *Correspondance inédite* (Plon, 1971) I, 288.
16. J. E. Flower, *Bernanos: Journal d'un curé de campagne* (Arnold, 1970) 31.
17. *Mémoires intérieurs* (Flammarion, 1959) 206.
18. Le Touzé, 333; B. Stefanson (ed.) in *Nouvelle histoire de Mouchette* (Methuen, 1982) 34.
19. *Bernanos* (Gallimard, 1965) 81.
20. *Correspondance*, II, 48.
21. The nickname is given to Steeny because of his mother's memory of her favourite 'English' novel (1355). The reference seems to be to *The Fortunes of Nigel*, in which Buckingham is given the nickname Steenie by the King because of his supposed likeness to portraits of Saint Stephen (*The Waverley Novels* (Edinburgh: Constable, 1904) XXVI, 179). Scott was read by Bernanos at the age of fifteen: *Correspondance*, II, 170.
22. C. Nettelbeck, *Les Personnages de Bernanos romancier* (Minard, 1970) 181.
23. There are two important articles on the relationship between Barbey and Bernanos: H. Hofer: 'Bernanos aurevillien, Barbey bernanosien', in *Barbey d'Aurevilly*, VI, and P. Gille, 'De Barbey d'Aurevilly à Bernanos', in *Études bernanosiennes*, XIV.

CONCLUDING NOTE

1. *Correspondance*, II, 523.
2. *Pour un nouveau roman* (Gallimard/NRF, 1970) 17.

Select Bibliography

NOVELS AND OTHER PRIMARY TEXTS

Barbey d'Aurevilly: *Une vieille maîtresse* (1851), *L'Ensorcelée* (1855), *Un prêtre marié* (1865), *Les Diaboliques* (1874), *Une histoire sans nom* (1882).

Flaubert: *Madame Bovary* (1856), *L'Éducation sentimentale* (1869), *La Tentation de St.-Antoine* (1874), *Trois contes* (1877), *Bouvard et Pécuchet* (1881).

Goncourt: *Charles Demailly* (1859), *Sœur Philomène* (1861), *Renée Mauperin* (1864), *Germinie Lacerteux* (1865), *Manette Salomon* (1867), *Madame Gervaisais* (1868), *La Fille Élisa* (1877), *Journal*.

Zola: *La Confession de Claude* (1865), *Thérèse Raquin* (1867), *Madeleine Férat* (1868), *Les Rougon-Macquart* (20 vols, 1871–93), *Les Trois Villes* (3 vols, 1894–8), *Les Quatre Évangiles* (3 vols, 1899–1903).

Huysmans: *Marthe* (1876), *Les Sœurs Vatard* (1879), *En Ménage* (1881), *A vau-l'eau* (1882), *A Rebours* (1884), *Là-Bas* (1891), *En Route* (1895), *La Cathédrale* (1898), *L'Oblat* (1903).

Maupassant: *Boule-de-suif* (1880) and other short stories, *Une vie* (1883), *Bel-Ami* (1885), *Fort comme la mort* (1889).

Bloy: *Le Désespéré* (1887), *La Femme pauvre* (1897).

Mauriac: *L'Enfant chargé de chaînes* (1913), *La Robe prétexte* (1914), *Le Fleuve de feu* (1923), *Le Désert de l'amour* (1925), *Thérèse Desqueyroux* (1927), *Ce qui était perdu* (1931), *Le Nœud de vipères* (1932), *L'Agneau* (1954).

Green: *Mont-Cinère* (1926), *Adrienne Mesurat* (1927), *Léviathan* (1929), *Le Voyageur sur la terre* (1930), *L'Autre sommeil* (1931), *Épaves* (1932), *Le Visionnaire* (1934), *Minuit* (1936), *Varouna* (1940), *Si j'étais vous* (1947), *Moïra* (1950), *Le Malfaiteur* (1955), *Chaque homme dans sa nuit* (1960), *L'Autre* (1971), *Le Mauvais lieu* (1977).

Bernanos: *Sous le soleil de Satan* (1926), *L'Imposture* (1927), *La Joie* (1928), *Journal d'un curé de campagne* (1936), *Nouvelle histoire de Mouchette* (1937), *Monsieur Ouine* (1943), *Un mauvais rêve* (post., 1950).

CRITICAL AND BACKGROUND READING

Space does not permit a full list of the books and articles read in the preparation of this book. This bibliography is strictly limited to the most relevant critical and background works. Details of other books and of articles are given in the notes. The place of publication, unless shown, is Paris for French books and London for books in English.

General

E. Auerbach, *Mimesis: the Representation of Reality in Western Literature*, tr. W. R. Trask, Princeton UP, 1974.

P. Bertault, *Balzac et la religion*, Geneva: Slatkine, 1980.

A. Blanchet, *Le Prêtre dans le roman français*, Desclée de Brouwer, 1955.
F. Brunetière, *Le Roman naturaliste*, Calmann-Lévy, 1896.
J. Calvet, *Le Renouveau catholique dans la littérature contemporaine*, Lanore, 1931.
P.-G. Castex, *Le Conte fantastique en France de Nodier à Maupassant*, Corti, 1951.
D. G. Charlton, *Secular Religions in France 1815–70*, Oxford UP, 1963.
A. Dansette, *Histoire religieuse de la France contemporaine*, Flammarion, 1965.
R. Griffiths, *The Reactionary Revolution*, Constable, 1966.
F. W. J. Hemmings (ed.), *The Age of Realism*, Harmondsworth: Penguin, 1974.
J. Huret, *Enquête sur l'évolution littéraire*, Champion, 1891.
M. Iknayan, *The Idea of the Novel in France: the critical reaction 1815–48*, Geneva: Droz, 1961.
A. Killen, *Le Roman terrifiant ou Roman noir de Walpole à Anne Radcliffe*, Champion, 1924.
H. Levin, *The Gates of Horn*, Oxford UP, 1966.
J. O. Lowrie, *The Violent Mystique: themes of retribution and expiation in Balzac, Barbey d'Aurevilly, Bloy and Huysmans*, Geneva: Droz, 1974.
G. Lukàcs, *Theory of the Novel*, tr. A. Bostock, Merlin Press, 1978.
G. May, *Le Dilemme du roman au XVIIIe siècle*, Yale U.P./Presses Universitaires françaises, 1963.
M. Milner, *Le Diable dans la littérature française de Cazotte à Baudelaire*, 2 vols, Corti, 1960.
C. Moeller, *Littérature et christianisme*, vol. I, Tournai: Castermann, 1953.
A. Muller, *La Question du roman catholique*, Foulon, 1957.
V. Mylne, *The Eighteenth-Century French novel: techniques of illusion*, Manchester UP/New York: Barnes & Noble, 1965.
C. C. O'Brien, *Maria Cross: imaginative patterns in a group of Catholic writers*, Burns & Oates, 1963.
J.-L. Prévost, *Le Roman catholique a cent ans*, Fayard, 1958.
R. Scholes & R. Kellogg, *The Nature of Narrative*, Oxford UP, 1966.
N. A. Scott (ed.), *The Climate of Faith in Modern Literature*, New York: Seaburg, 1964.
A. Sonnenfeld, *Crossroads: essays on the Catholic novelists*, York, South Carolina: French Literature Publishing Company, 1980.
S. Suleiman, *Authoritarian Fictions*, New York: Colombia UP, 1983.
T. Todorov, *Introduction à la littérature fantastique*, Seuil, 1970.
A. Viatte, *Le Catholicisme chez les romantiques*, Boccard, 1922.
I. Watt, *The Rise of the Novel*, Harmondsworth: Penguin, 1974.
B. Weinberg, *French Realism: the critical reaction 1830–70*, New York, MLA/Oxford UP, 1937.
D. A. Williams (ed.), *The Monster in the Mirror, studies in European realism*, Oxford UP, 1978.

Realist and Naturalist novelists

D. Baguley, *«Fécondité» d'Émile Zola*, Toronto UP, 1973.
V. Brombert, *The Novels of Flaubert*, Princeton UP, 1966.

E. Caramaschi, *Réalisme et impressionnisme dans l'œuvre des frères Goncourt*, Pisa: Goliardica, 1971.
P. Cogny, *Maupassant, l'homme sans Dieu*, Brussels: La Renaissance du livre, 1968.
J. Culler, *Flaubert: the uses of uncertainty*, Elek, 1974.
J. R. Dugan, *Illusion and Reality: a study of descriptive techniques in the work of Guy de Maupassant*, The Hague: Mouton, 1973.
H. Guillemin, *Présentation des Rougon-Macquart*, Gallimard, 1964.
F. W. J. Hemmings, *Émile Zola*, Oxford UP, 1970.
J. C. Lapp, *Zola before the Rougon-Macquart*, Toronto UP, 1964.
A. de Lattre, *Le Réalisme selon Zola: archéologie d'une intelligence*, Presses Universitaires Françaises, 1975.
R. Ricatte, *La Création romanesque chez les Goncourt*, Colin, 1954.
R. Ripoll, *Réalité et mythe chez Zola*, Champion, 1981.
E. D. Sullivan, *Maupassant the novelist*, Princeton UP, 1954.
R. Ternois, *Zola et son temps*, Les Belles Lettres, 1961.
A. Vial, *Guy de Maupassant et l'art du roman*, Nizet, 1954.
P. Walker, *Germinal and Zola's Philosophical and Religious Thought*, Amsterdam: Benjamins, 1984.

Catholic Novelists

Barbey d'Aurevilly:

P. Berthier, *Barbey d'Aurevilly et l'imagination*, Geneva: Droz, 1978.
R. Bésus, *Barbey d'Aurevilly*, Éditions universitaires, 1957.
J. Canu, *Barbey d'Aurevilly*, Laffont, 1965.
P. Colla, *L'Univers tragique de Barbey d'Aurevilly*, Brussels: La Renaissance du livre, 1965.
A. le Corbeiller, *Les Diaboliques de Barbey d'Aurevilly*, Malfère, 1939.
P. Klossowski, Preface to *Un prêtre marié*, Club français du livre, 1960.
J. Petit, *Barbey d'Aurevilly critique*, Les Belles Lettres, 1963.
B. G. Rogers, *The Novels and stories of Barbey d'Aurevilly*, Geneva, Droz, 1967.
P. J. Yarrow, *La Pensée politique et religieuse de Barbey d'Aurevilly*, Geneva: Droz, 1961.

Huysmans:

R. B. Antosh, *Reality and Illusion in the Novels of J.-K. Huysmans*, Amsterdam: Rodopi, 1986.
H. Bachelin, *Huysmans: du naturalisme littéraire au naturalisme mystique*, Perrin, 1963.
H. Brandreth, *Huysmans*, New York: Hillary, 1963.
R. Baldick, *The Life of J.-K. Huysmans*, Oxford: Clarendon, 1955.
P. Cogny, *J.-K. Huysmans à la recherche de l'unité*, Nizet, 1953.
J. Laver, *The First Decadent: being the strange life of J.-K. Huysmans*, Faber & Faber, s.d. [1954].
L. Maingon, *L'Univers artistique de J.-K. Huysmans*, Nizet, 1977.
E. Seillière, *J.-K. Huysmans*, Grasset, 1931.
H. Trudgian, *L'Esthétique de J.-K. Huysmans*, Geneva: Slatkine, 1970.
(Various): *Cahier de La Tour St.-Jacques*, special Huysmans number, 1963.

—— *Huysmans: une esthétique de la décadence*, actes du colloque de Bâle, Mulhouse et Colmar 1984; Champion, 1987.

Bloy:
R. Barbeau, *Un prophète luciférien: Léon Bloy*, Aubier, 1957.
A. Béguin, *Léon Bloy: une mystique de la douleur*, Éditions Labergerie, 1948.
J. Bollery, *Léon Bloy, essai de biographie*, Albin Michel, 3 vols 1947–9.
—— *Genèse et composition de «La Femme pauvre» de Léon Bloy*, Minard, 1969.
G. Dotoli, *Situation des études bloyennes*, Nizet, 1970.
S. Fumet, *Léon Bloy, captif de l'absolu*, Plon, 1967.
J. Petit, *Léon Bloy*, Desclée de Brouwer, 1966.
B. Sarrazin, *La Bible en éclats: l'imagination scriptuaire de Léon Bloy*, Desclée de Brouwer, 1977.
J. Steinmann, *Léon Bloy*, Éditions du Cerf, 1956.

Mauriac:
C. du Bos, *François Mauriac et le problème du romancier catholique*, Corrêa, 1933.
J. E. Flower, *Intention and Achievement: the novels of François Mauriac*, Oxford: Clarendon, 1969.
A. J. Joubert, *François Mauriac et «Thérèse Desqueyroux»*, Nizet, 1982.
J. Lacouture, *François Mauriac*, Seuil, 1980.
J. Monférier, *François Mauriac: du «Nœud de vipères» à «La Pharisienne»*, Champion, 1985.
M. Scott: *Mauriac: the Politics of a Novelist*, Edinburgh: Scottish Academic Press, 1980.
P. Stratford, *Faith and Fiction: creative process in Greene and Mauriac*, Notre Dame UP, 1967.

Green:
J. W. Dunaway, *The Metamorphoses of the self*, Kentucky UP, 1978.
M. Eigeldinger, *Julien Green et la tentation de l'irréel*, Éditions des Portes de France, 1947.
B. Fitch (ed.), *Configuration critique de Julien Green*, Minard, 1966.
A. Fongaro, *L'Existence dans les romans de Julien Green*, Rome: Signorelli, 1954.
N. Kostis, *The Exorcism of Sex and Death in Julien Green's novels*, The Hague: Mouton, 1973.
A. Mor, *Julien Green, témoin de l'invisible*, Plon, 1973.
A. H. Newbury, *Julien Green: Religion and Sensuality*, Amsterdam: Rodopi, 1986.
J. Petit, *Julien Green, l'homme qui venait d'ailleurs*, Desclée de Brouwer, 1969.
—— *Julien Green*, Desclée de Brouwer, 1972.
J.-P. J. Piriou, *Sexualité, religion et art chez Julien Green*, Nizet, 1976.
R. de St.-Jean, *Julien Green par lui-même*, Seuil, 1967.
J. Sémoulé, *Julien Green, ou l'obsession du mal*, Éditions du Centurion, 1964.
A. Tamuly, *Julien Green à la recherche du réel*, Sherbrooke, Canada: Naaman, 1976.

Bernanos:
H. U. von Balthasar, *Le Chrétien Bernanos*, Seuil, 1954.
H. Debluë, *Les Romans de Georges Bernanos, ou le défi du rêve*, Neuchâtel: La Baconnière, 1965.
M. Estève, *Bernanos*, Gallimard, 1965.
J. E. Flower, *Bernanos: Le Journal d'un curé de campagne*, Arnold, 1970.
G. Gaucher, *Le Thème de la mort dans les romans de Georges Bernanos*, Minard, 1967.
P. Gille, *Bernanos et l'angoisse*, Nancy, Presses Universitaires, 1984.
P.-R. Leclercq, *Introduction à «Monsieur Ouine» de Bernanos*, Minard, 1978.
P. le Touzé, *Le Mystère du réel dans les romans de Georges Bernanos*, Nizet, 1979.
M. Milner, *Georges Bernanos*, Desclée de Brouwer, 1967.
C. Nettelbeck, *Les Personnages de Bernanos romancier*, Minard, 1970.
J. C. Whitehouse, *Le Réalisme dans les romans de Georges Bernanos*, Minard, 1969.

Index